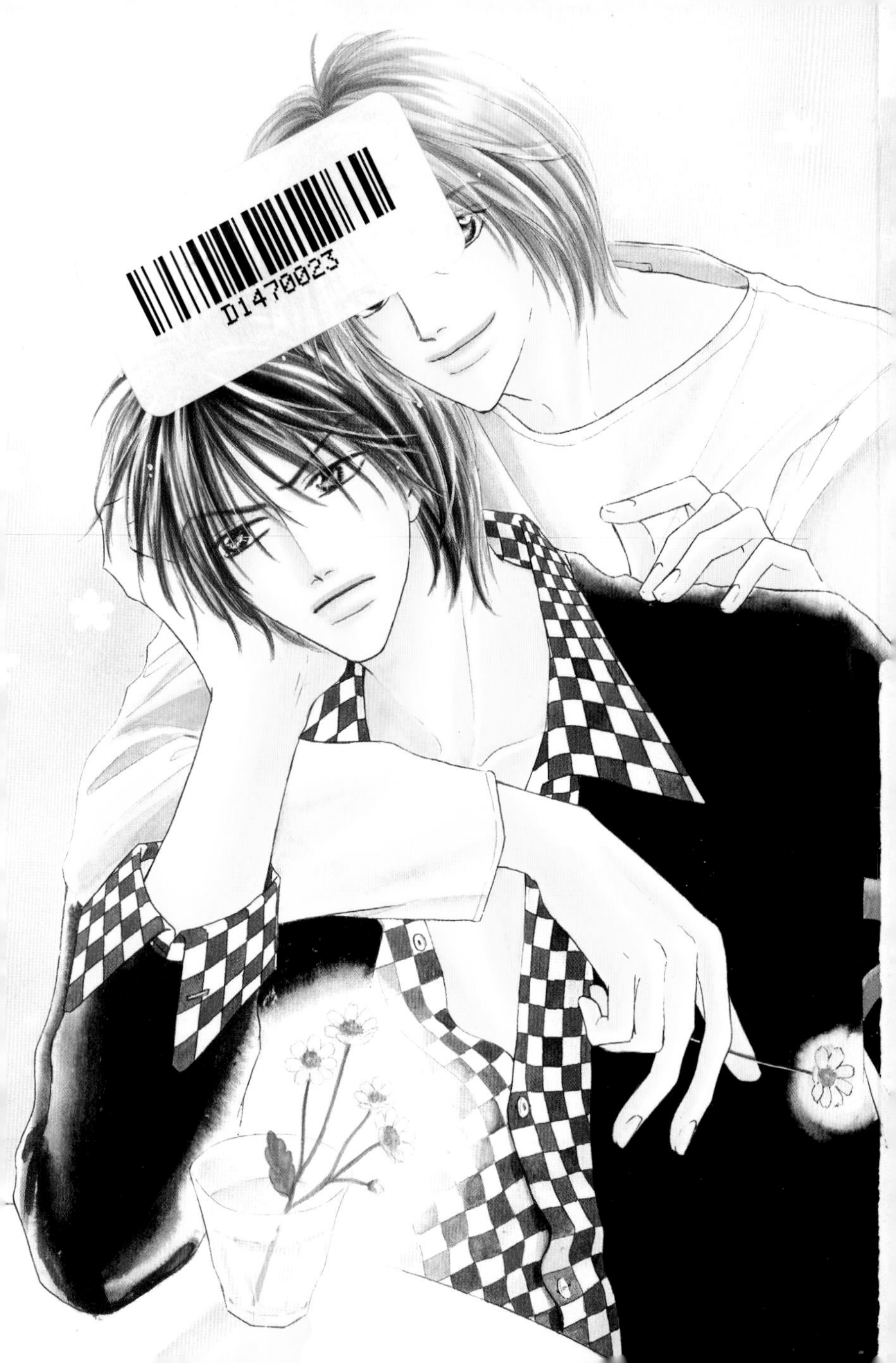

Translation / Ken Wakita
Editing / Daryl Kuxhouse
Lettering / Tawnie Wilson
Graphic Design / W. Johns

801 Media, Inc.
www.801media.com
contact@801media.com

ISBN-10: 1-934129-00-3
ISBN-13: 978-1-934129-00-5
First edition printed April 2007

10 9 8 7 6 5 4 3 2 1

Printed in China

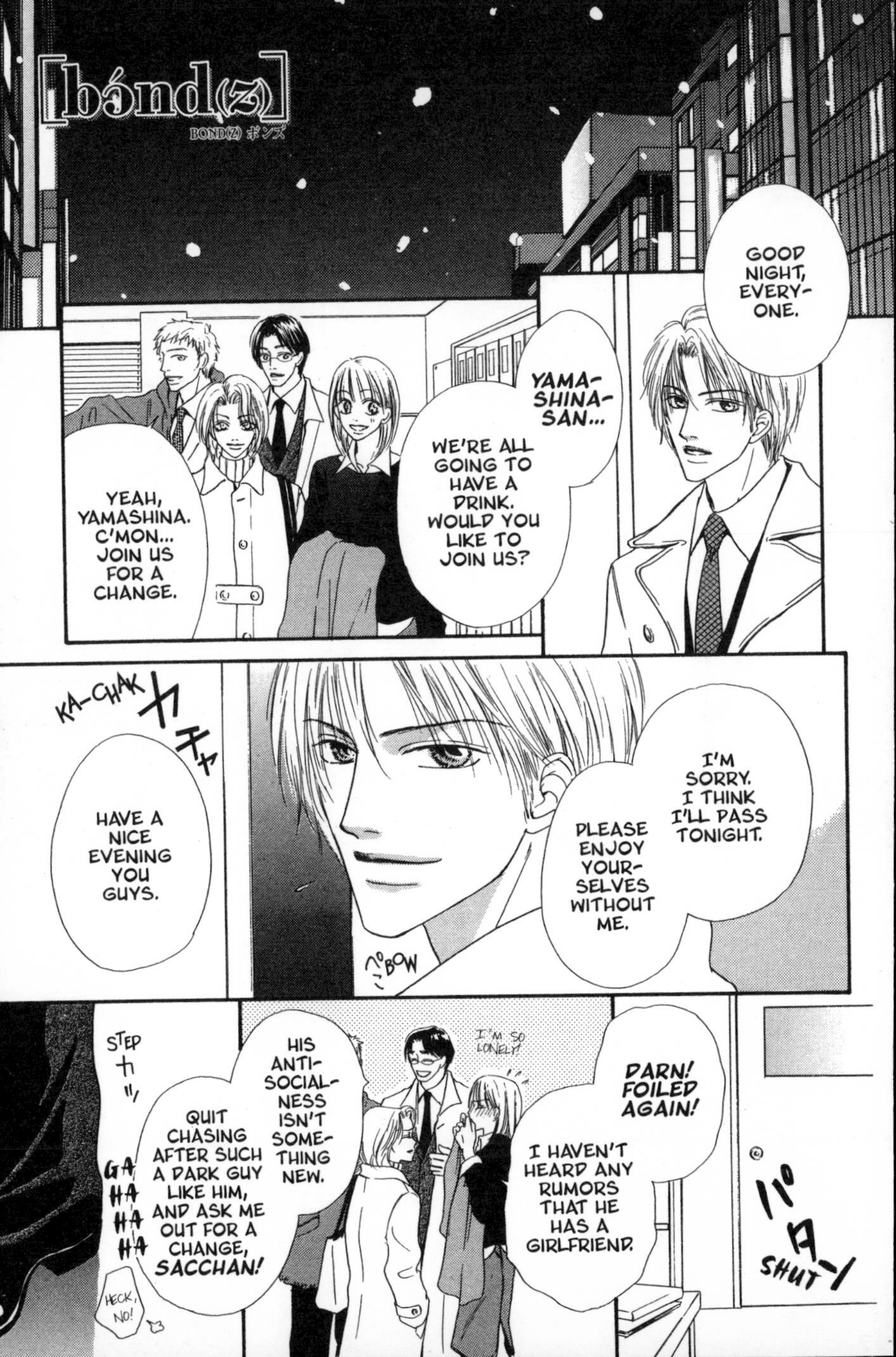
[bónd(z)]
BOND(Z) ボンズ
GOOD NIGHT, EVERY-ONE.
YAMA-SHINA-SAN...
WE'RE ALL GOING TO HAVE A DRINK. WOULD YOU LIKE TO JOIN US?
YEAH, YAMASHINA. C'MON... JOIN US FOR A CHANGE.
I'M SORRY. I THINK I'LL PASS TONIGHT.
PLEASE ENJOY YOUR-SELVES WITHOUT ME.
BOW
KA-CHAK
カチャ
HAVE A NICE EVENING YOU GUYS.
パタン
SHUT
DARN! FOILED AGAIN!
I HAVEN'T HEARD ANY RUMORS THAT HE HAS A GIRLFRIEND.
I'M SO LONELY!
HIS ANTI-SOCIAL-NESS ISN'T SOME-THING NEW.
QUIT CHASING AFTER SUCH A DARK GUY LIKE HIM, AND ASK ME OUT FOR A CHANGE, SACCHAN!
HECK, NO!
STEP
GA HA HA HA

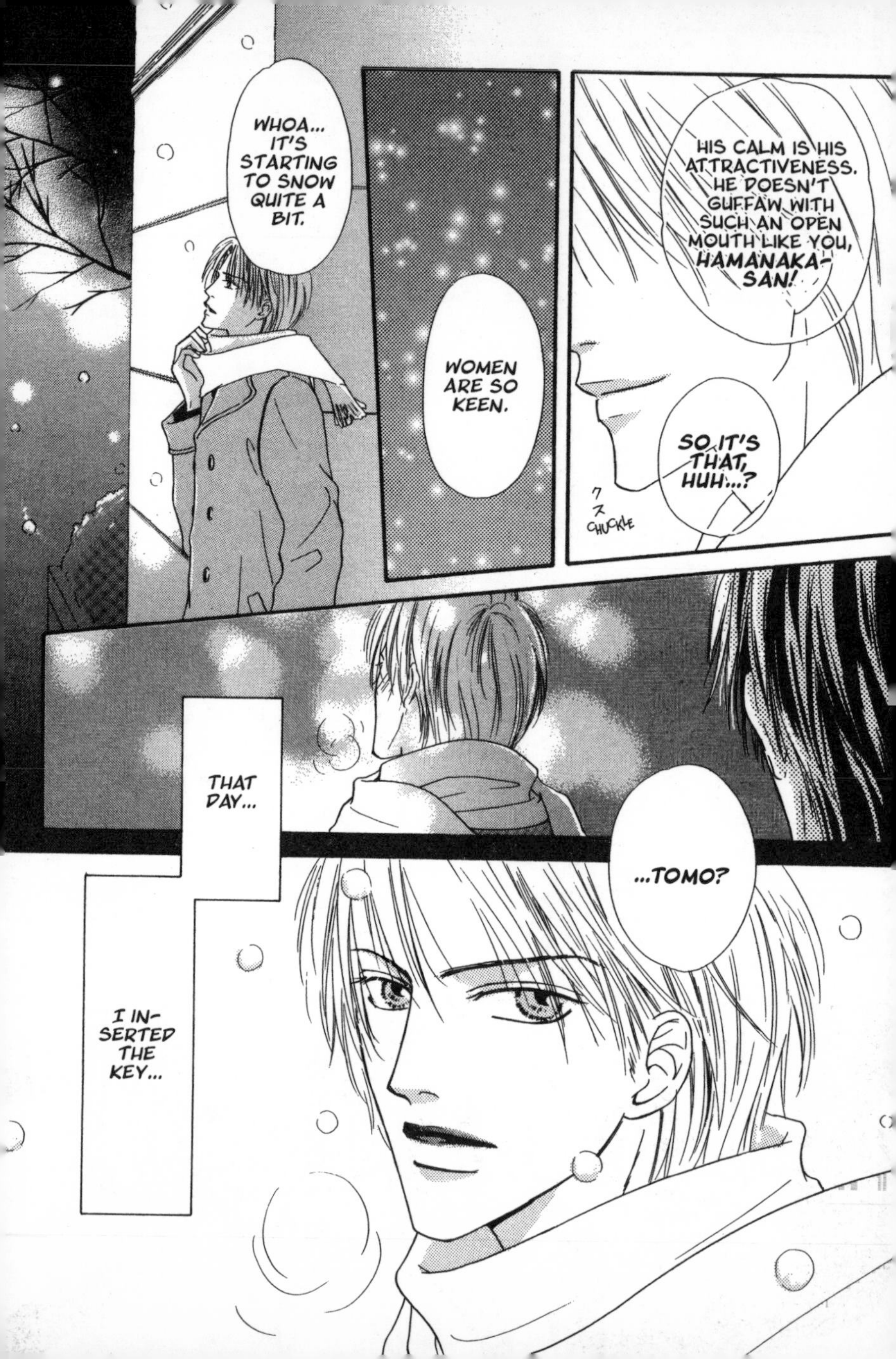
HIS CALM IS HIS ATTRACTIVENESS. HE DOESN'T GUFFAW WITH SUCH AN OPEN MOUTH LIKE YOU, HAMANAKA-SAN!
SO IT'S THAT, HUH...?
クス
CHUCKLE
WOMEN ARE SO KEEN.
WHOA... IT'S STARTING TO SNOW QUITE A BIT.
THAT DAY...
...TOMO?
I IN-SERTED THE KEY...

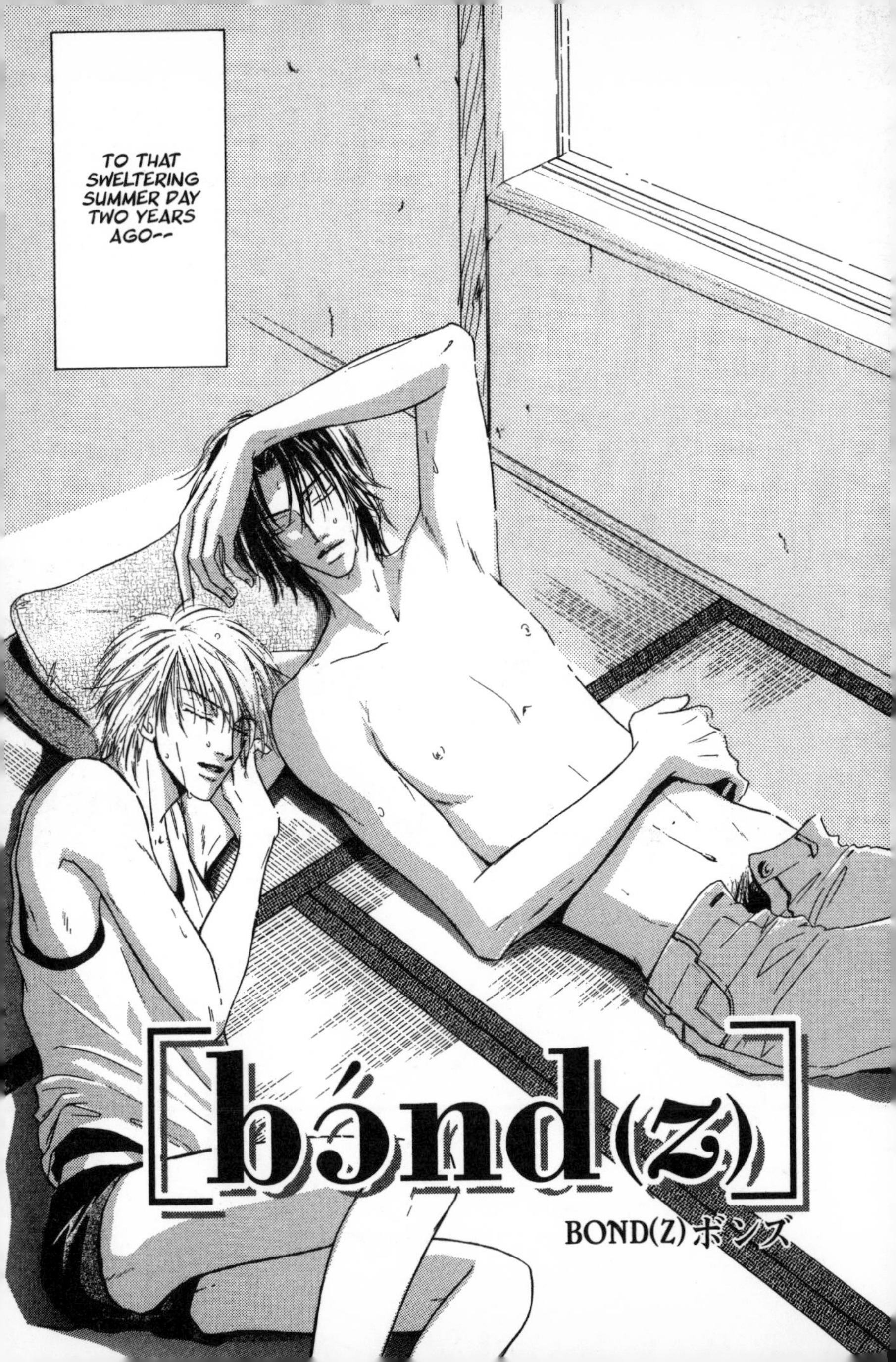

TO THAT SWELTERING SUMMER DAY TWO YEARS AGO--
[bɔ́nd(z)]
BOND(Z) ボンズ

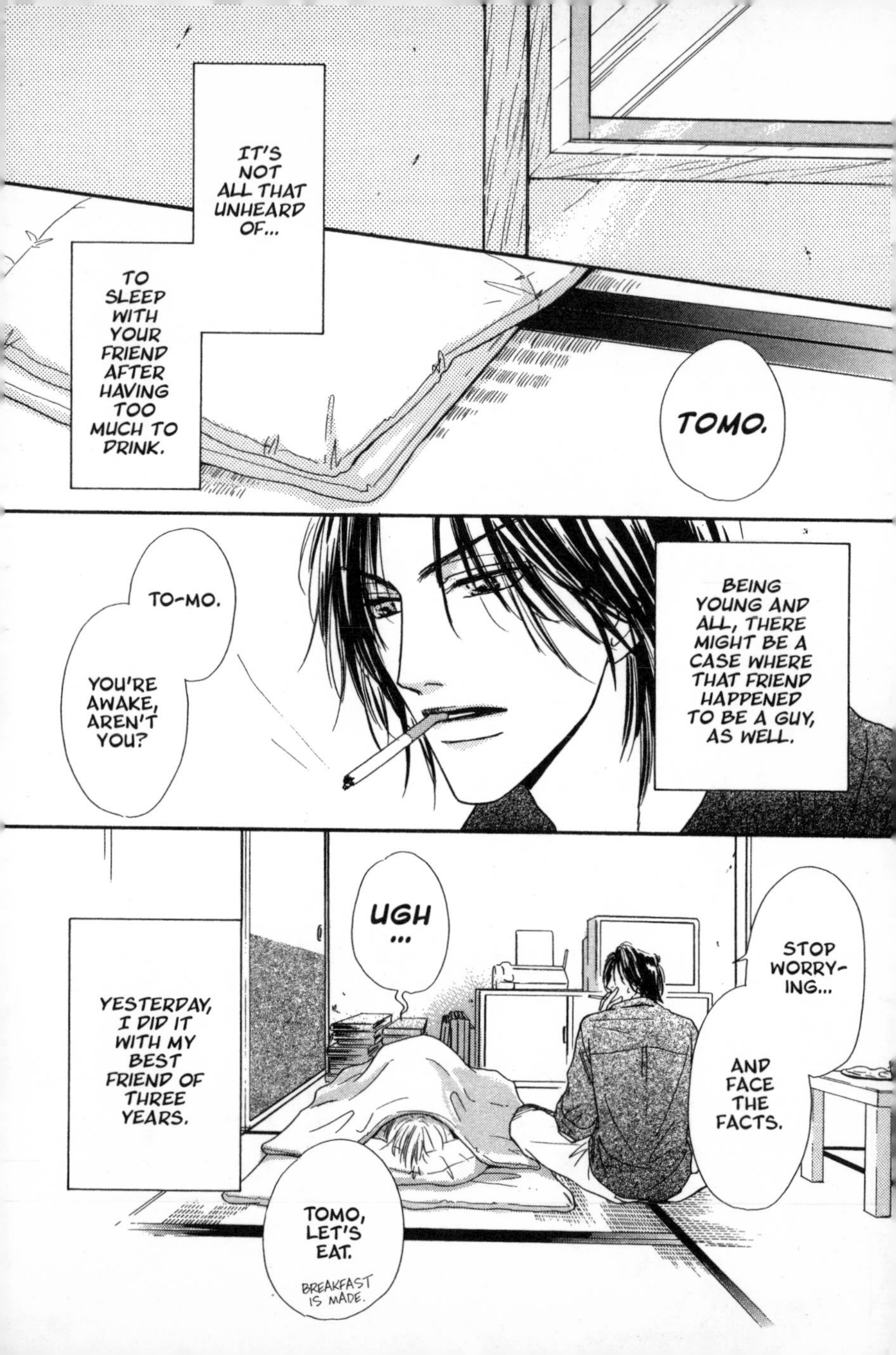
TOMO.
IT'S NOT ALL THAT UNHEARD OF...
TO SLEEP WITH YOUR FRIEND AFTER HAVING TOO MUCH TO DRINK.
BEING YOUNG AND ALL, THERE MIGHT BE A CASE WHERE THAT FRIEND HAPPENED TO BE A GUY, AS WELL.
TO-MO.
YOU'RE AWAKE, AREN'T YOU?
STOP WORRYING...
AND FACE THE FACTS.
UGH...
YESTERDAY, I DID IT WITH MY BEST FRIEND OF THREE YEARS.
TOMO, LET'S EAT.
BREAKFAST IS MADE.

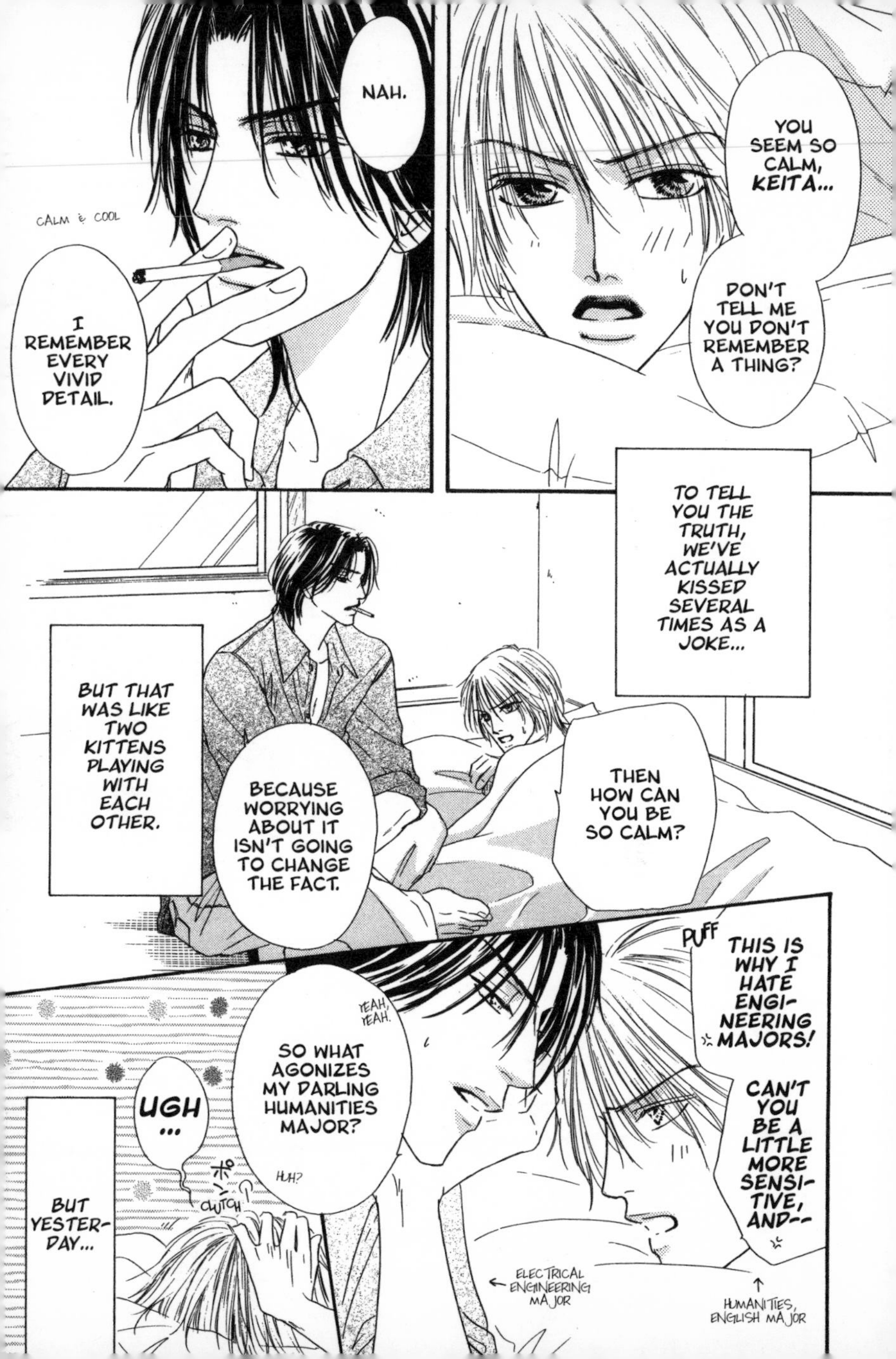
YOU SEEM SO CALM, KEITA...
DON'T TELL ME YOU DON'T REMEMBER A THING?
NAH.
CALM & COOL
I REMEMBER EVERY VIVID DETAIL.
TO TELL YOU THE TRUTH, WE'VE ACTUALLY KISSED SEVERAL TIMES AS A JOKE...
THEN HOW CAN YOU BE SO CALM?
BECAUSE WORRYING ABOUT IT ISN'T GOING TO CHANGE THE FACT.
BUT THAT WAS LIKE TWO KITTENS PLAYING WITH EACH OTHER.
PUFF
THIS IS WHY I HATE ENGI-NEERING MAJORS!
CAN'T YOU BE A LITTLE MORE SENSI-TIVE, AND--
HUMANITIES, ENGLISH MAJOR
YEAH, YEAH.
SO WHAT AGONIZES MY DARLING HUMANITIES MAJOR?
ELECTRICAL ENGINEERING MAJOR
HUH?
UGH...
CLUTCH
BUT YESTER-DAY...

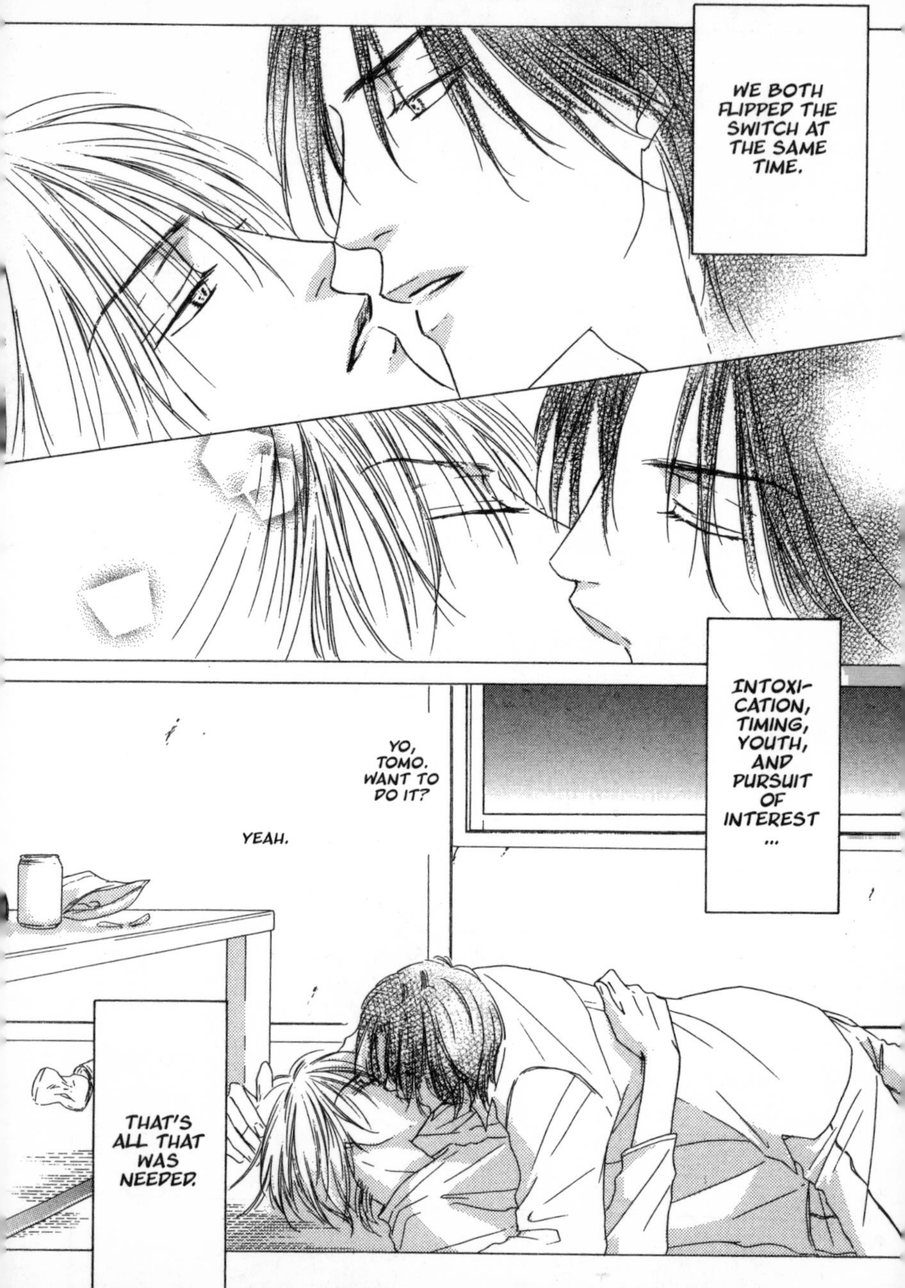
WE BOTH FLIPPED THE SWITCH AT THE SAME TIME.
INTOXICATION, TIMING, YOUTH, AND PURSUIT OF INTEREST ...
YO, TOMO. WANT TO DO IT?
YEAH.
THAT'S ALL THAT WAS NEEDED.

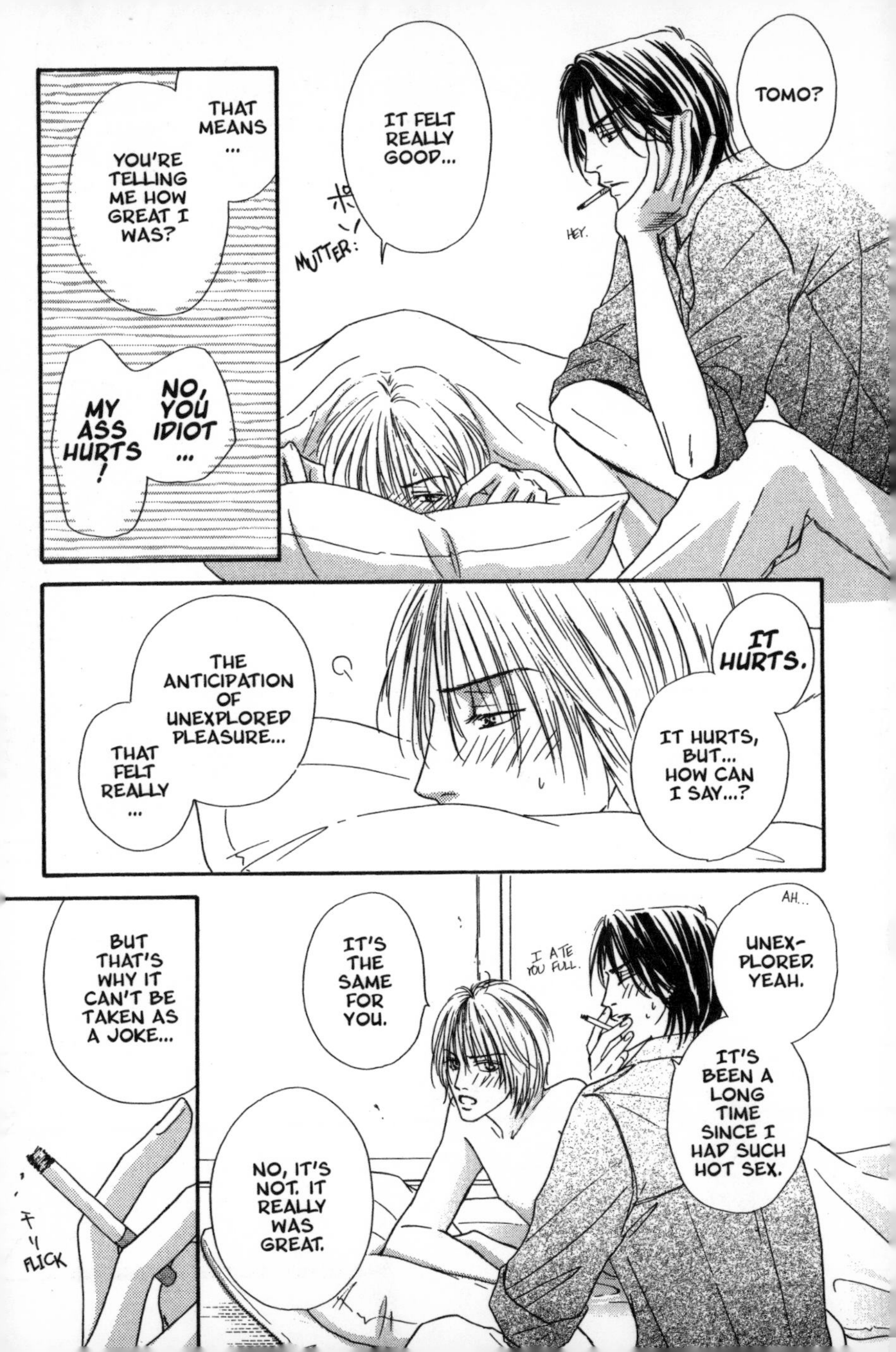
TOMO?
HEY.
IT FELT REALLY GOOD...
MUTTER
THAT MEANS...
YOU'RE TELLING ME HOW GREAT I WAS?
NO, YOU IDIOT...
MY ASS HURTS!
IT HURTS.
IT HURTS, BUT... HOW CAN I SAY...?
THE ANTICIPATION OF UNEXPLORED PLEASURE...
THAT FELT REALLY...
AH...
UNEXPLORED. YEAH.
IT'S BEEN A LONG TIME SINCE I HAD SUCH HOT SEX.
I ATE YOU FULL.
IT'S THE SAME FOR YOU.
NO, IT'S NOT. IT REALLY WAS GREAT.
BUT THAT'S WHY IT CAN'T BE TAKEN AS A JOKE...
FLICK

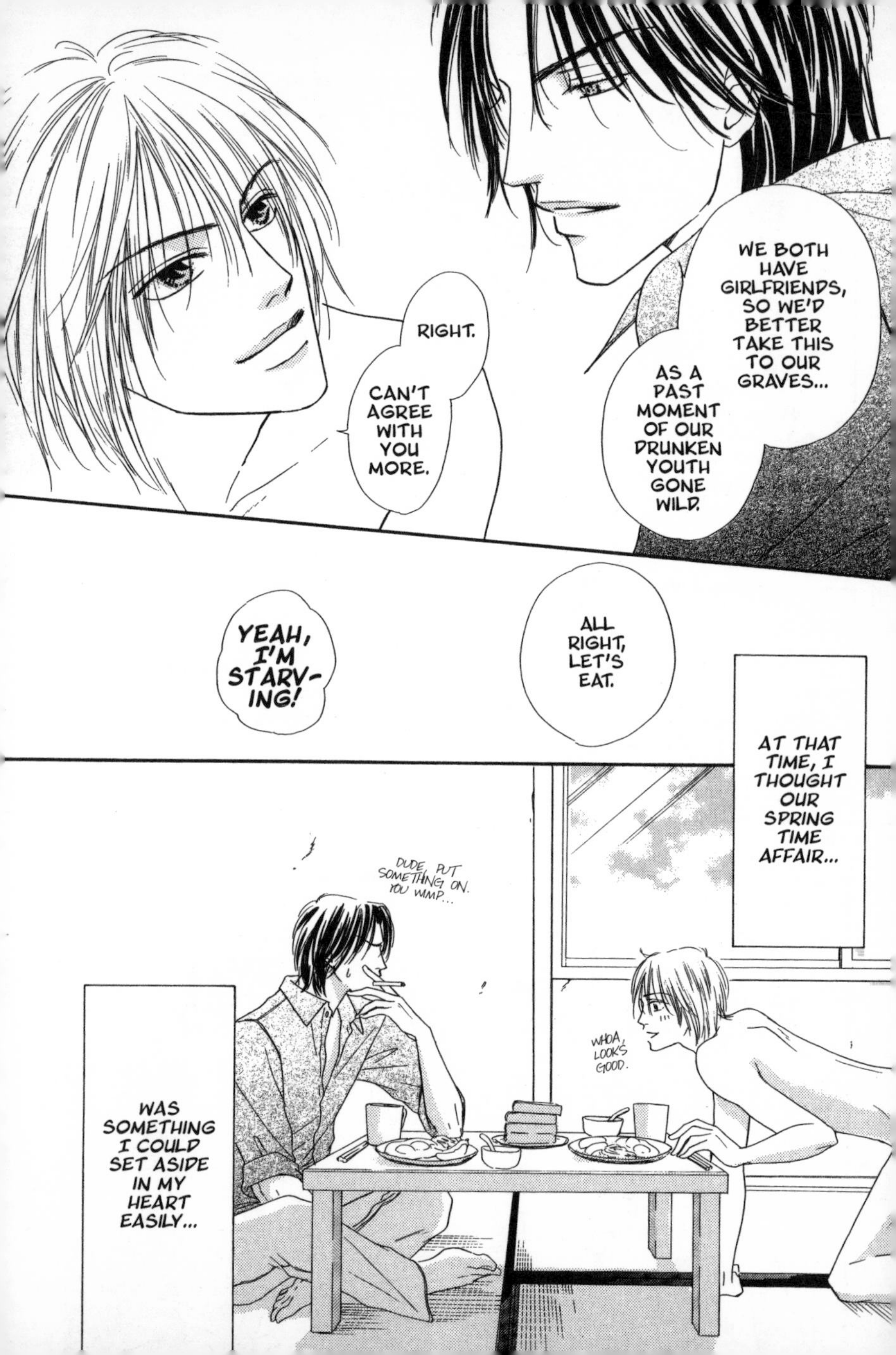
WE BOTH HAVE GIRLFRIENDS, SO WE'D BETTER TAKE THIS TO OUR GRAVES...
AS A PAST MOMENT OF OUR DRUNKEN YOUTH GONE WILD.
RIGHT.
CAN'T AGREE WITH YOU MORE.
ALL RIGHT, LET'S EAT.
YEAH, I'M STARV-ING!
AT THAT TIME, I THOUGHT OUR SPRING TIME AFFAIR...
WHOA, LOOKS GOOD.
DUDE, PUT SOMETHING ON. YOU WIMP...
WAS SOMETHING I COULD SET ASIDE IN MY HEART EASILY...

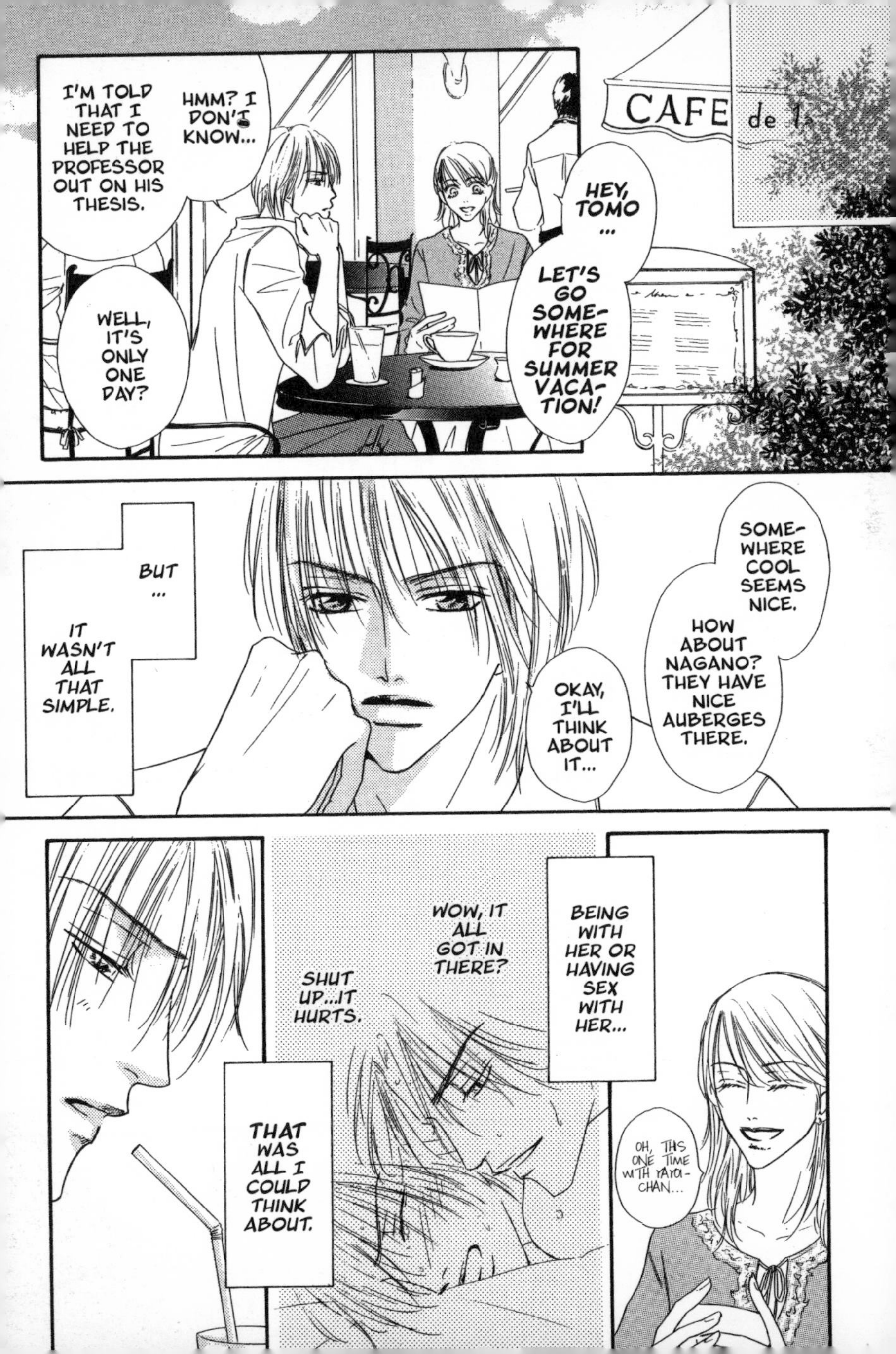
CAFE
HEY, TOMO ...
LET'S GO SOMEWHERE FOR SUMMER VACATION!
HMM? I DON'T KNOW...
I'M TOLD THAT I NEED TO HELP THE PROFESSOR OUT ON HIS THESIS.
WELL, IT'S ONLY ONE DAY?
SOMEWHERE COOL SEEMS NICE.
HOW ABOUT NAGANO? THEY HAVE NICE AUBERGES THERE.
OKAY, I'LL THINK ABOUT IT...
BUT ...
IT WASN'T ALL THAT SIMPLE.
OH, THIS ONE TIME WITH YAYOI-CHAN...
BEING WITH HER OR HAVING SEX WITH HER...
WOW, IT ALL GOT IN THERE?
SHUT UP...IT HURTS.
THAT WAS ALL I COULD THINK ABOUT.

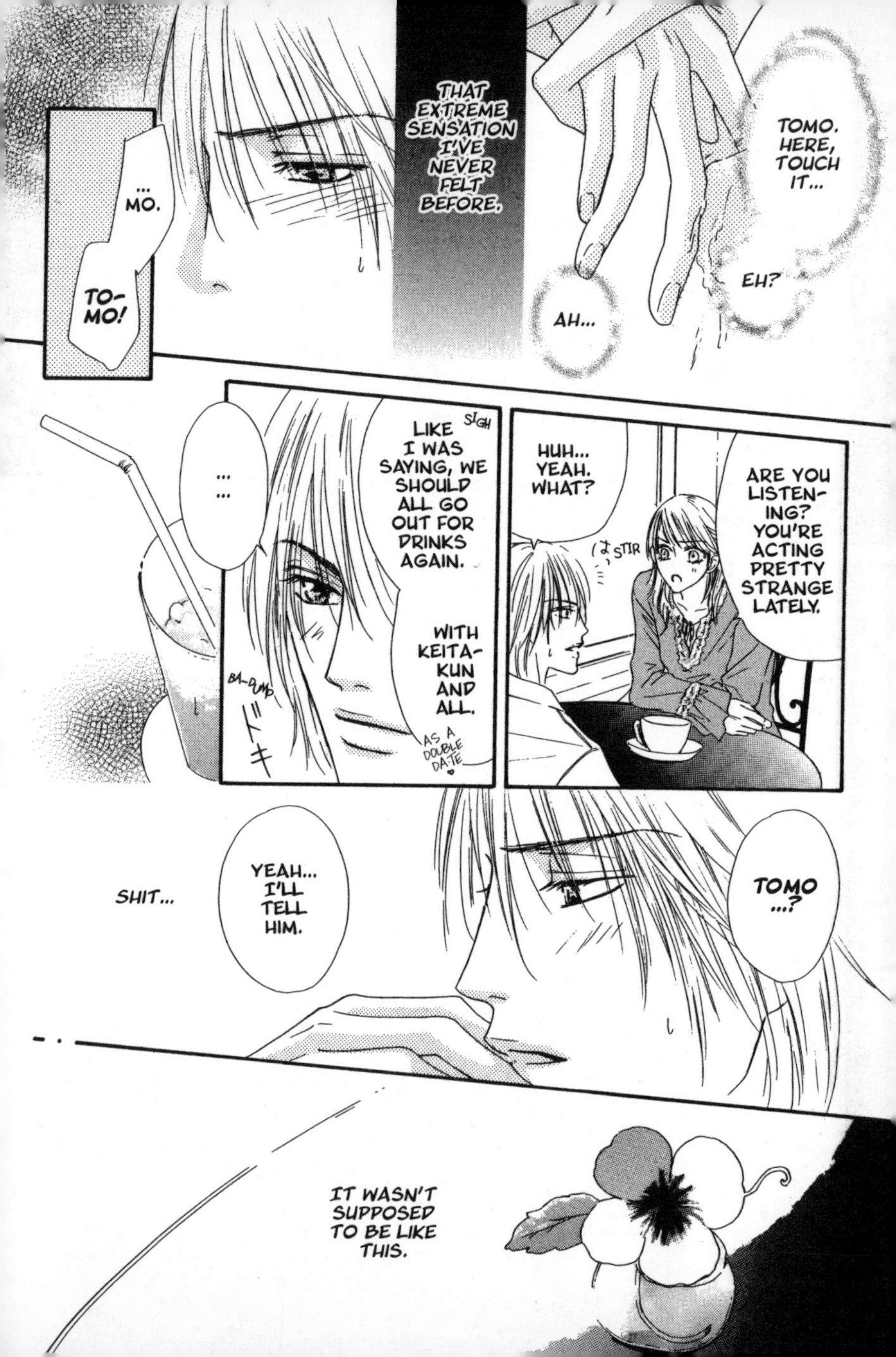
TOMO. HERE, TOUCH IT...
EH?
AH...
THAT EXTREME SENSATION I'VE NEVER FELT BEFORE.
...MO.
TO-MO!
ARE YOU LISTENING? YOU'RE ACTING PRETTY STRANGE LATELY.
HUH... YEAH. WHAT?
STIR
LIKE I WAS SAYING, WE SHOULD ALL GO OUT FOR DRINKS AGAIN.
SIGH
WITH KEITA-KUN AND ALL.
AS A DOUBLE DATE
...
...
BA-DUMP
ドキ
TOMO ...?
YEAH... I'LL TELL HIM.
SHIT...
IT WASN'T SUPPOSED TO BE LIKE THIS.

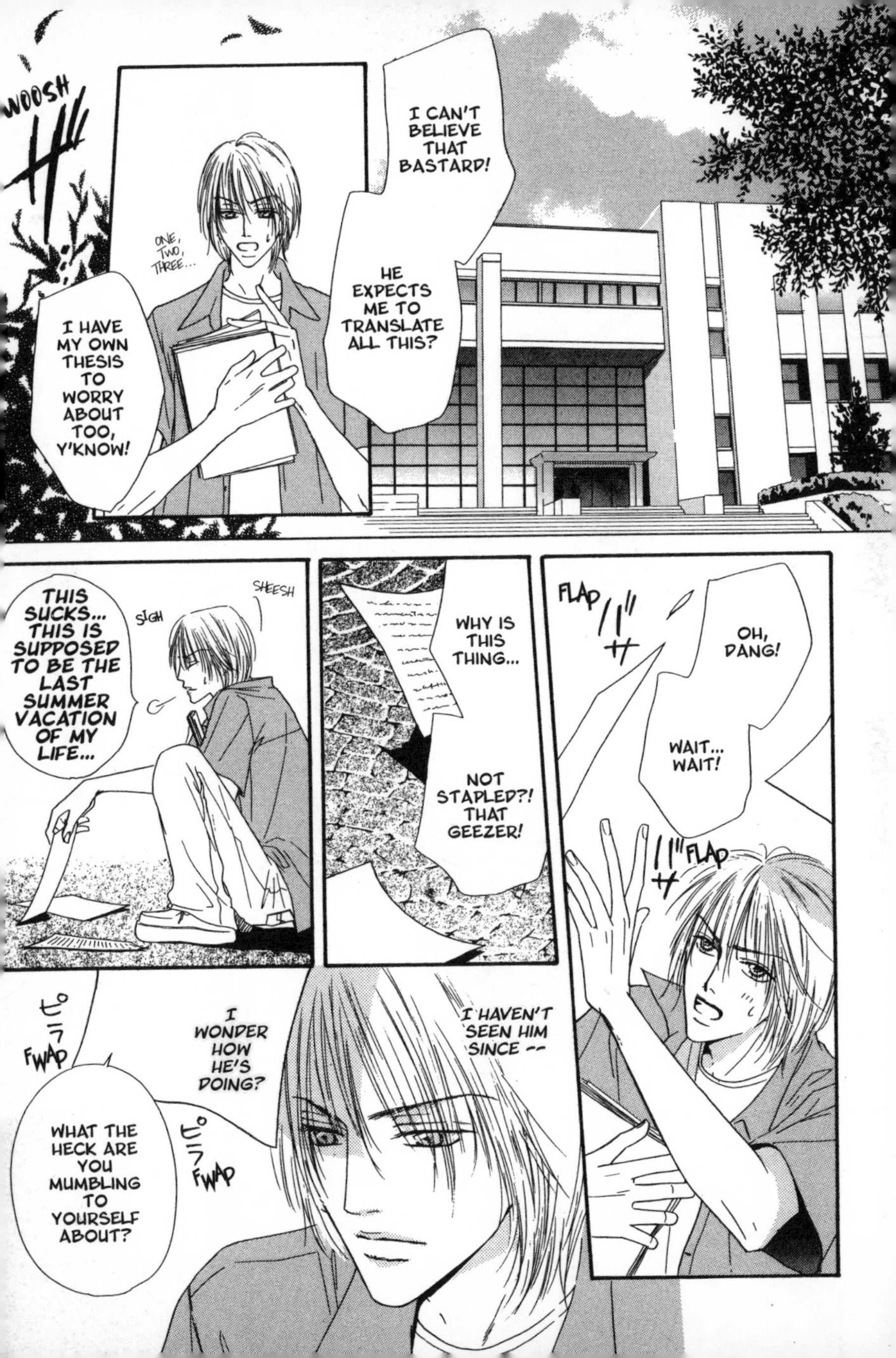
I CAN'T BELIEVE THAT BASTARD!
HE EXPECTS ME TO TRANSLATE ALL THIS?
WOOSH
ONE, TWO, THREE...
I HAVE MY OWN THESIS TO WORRY ABOUT TOO, Y'KNOW!
FLAP
OH, DANG!
WAIT... WAIT!
FLAP
WHY IS THIS THING...
NOT STAPLED?! THAT GEEZER!
SHEESH
SIGH
THIS SUCKS... THIS IS SUPPOSED TO BE THE LAST SUMMER VACATION OF MY LIFE...
I HAVEN'T SEEN HIM SINCE --
I WONDER HOW HE'S DOING?
ピラ FWAP
WHAT THE HECK ARE YOU MUMBLING TO YOURSELF ABOUT?
ピラ FWAP

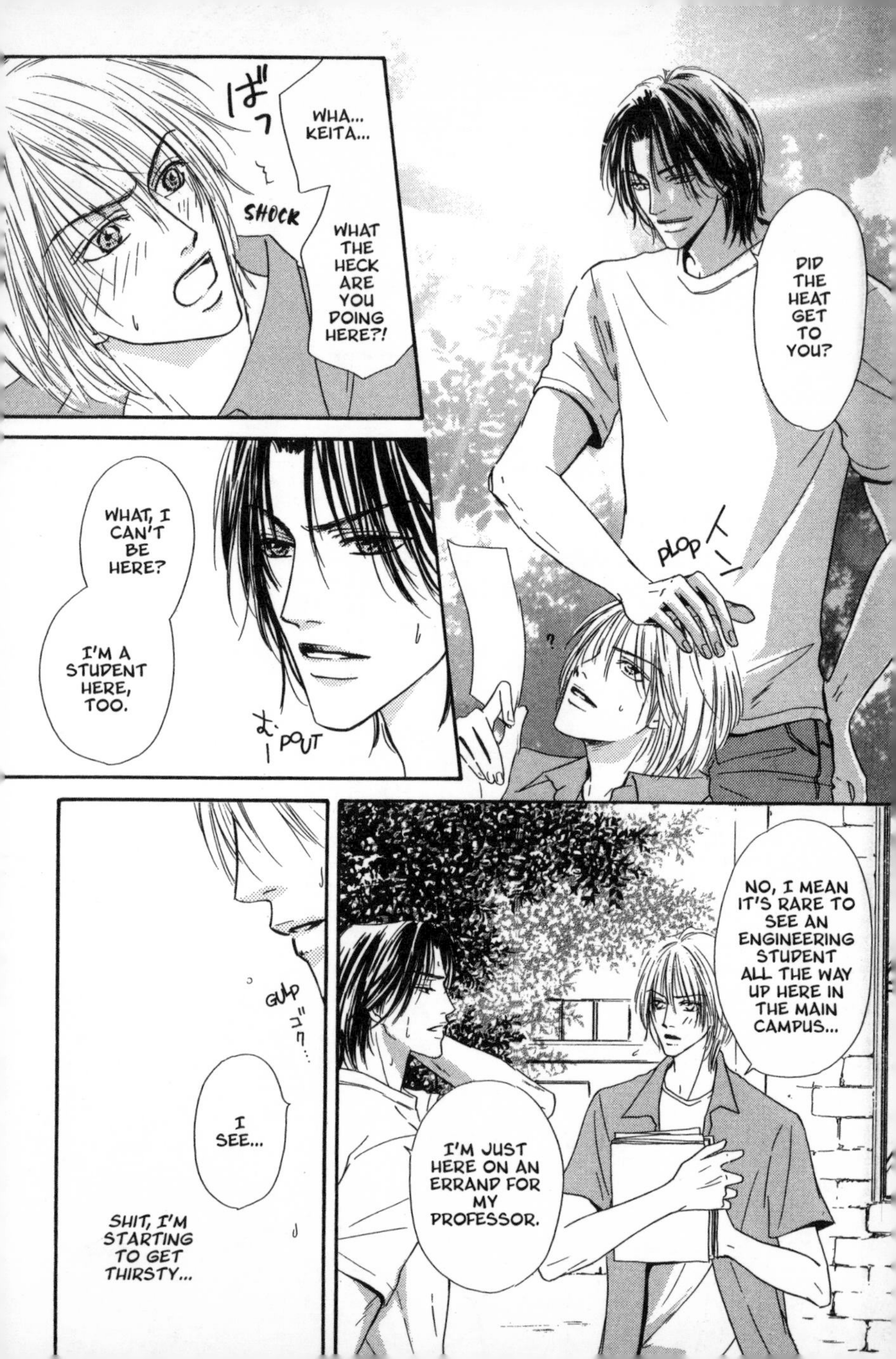
DID THE HEAT GET TO YOU?
PLOP
ばっ
SHOCK
WHA... KEITA...
WHAT THE HECK ARE YOU DOING HERE?!
WHAT, I CAN'T BE HERE?
I'M A STUDENT HERE, TOO.
POUT
NO, I MEAN IT'S RARE TO SEE AN ENGINEERING STUDENT ALL THE WAY UP HERE IN THE MAIN CAMPUS...
I'M JUST HERE ON AN ERRAND FOR MY PROFESSOR.
GULP
I SEE...
SHIT, I'M STARTING TO GET THIRSTY...

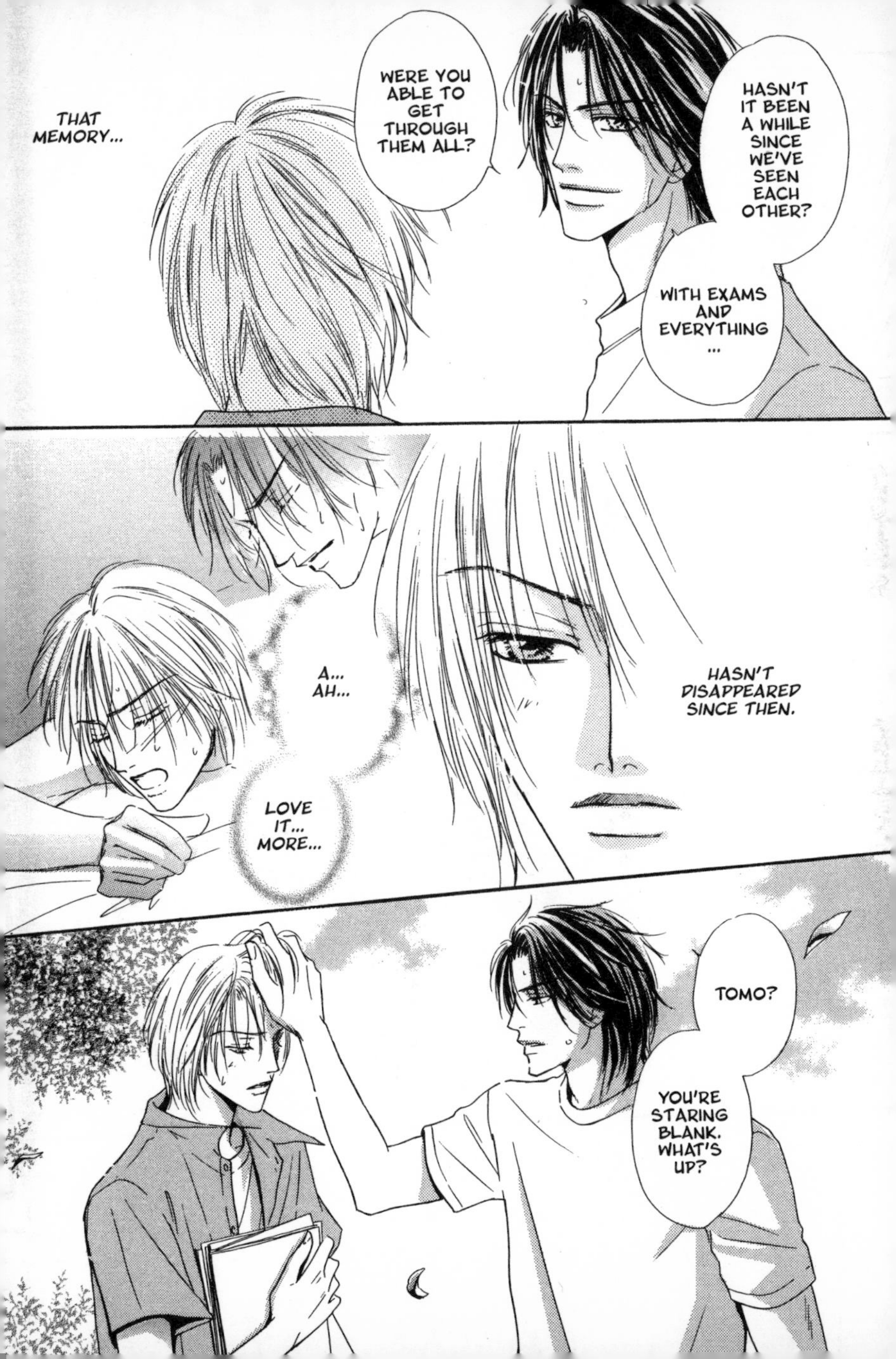
HASN'T IT BEEN A WHILE SINCE WE'VE SEEN EACH OTHER?
WITH EXAMS AND EVERYTHING ...
WERE YOU ABLE TO GET THROUGH THEM ALL?
THAT MEMORY...
HASN'T DISAPPEARED SINCE THEN.
A... AH...
LOVE IT... MORE...
TOMO?
YOU'RE STARING BLANK. WHAT'S UP?

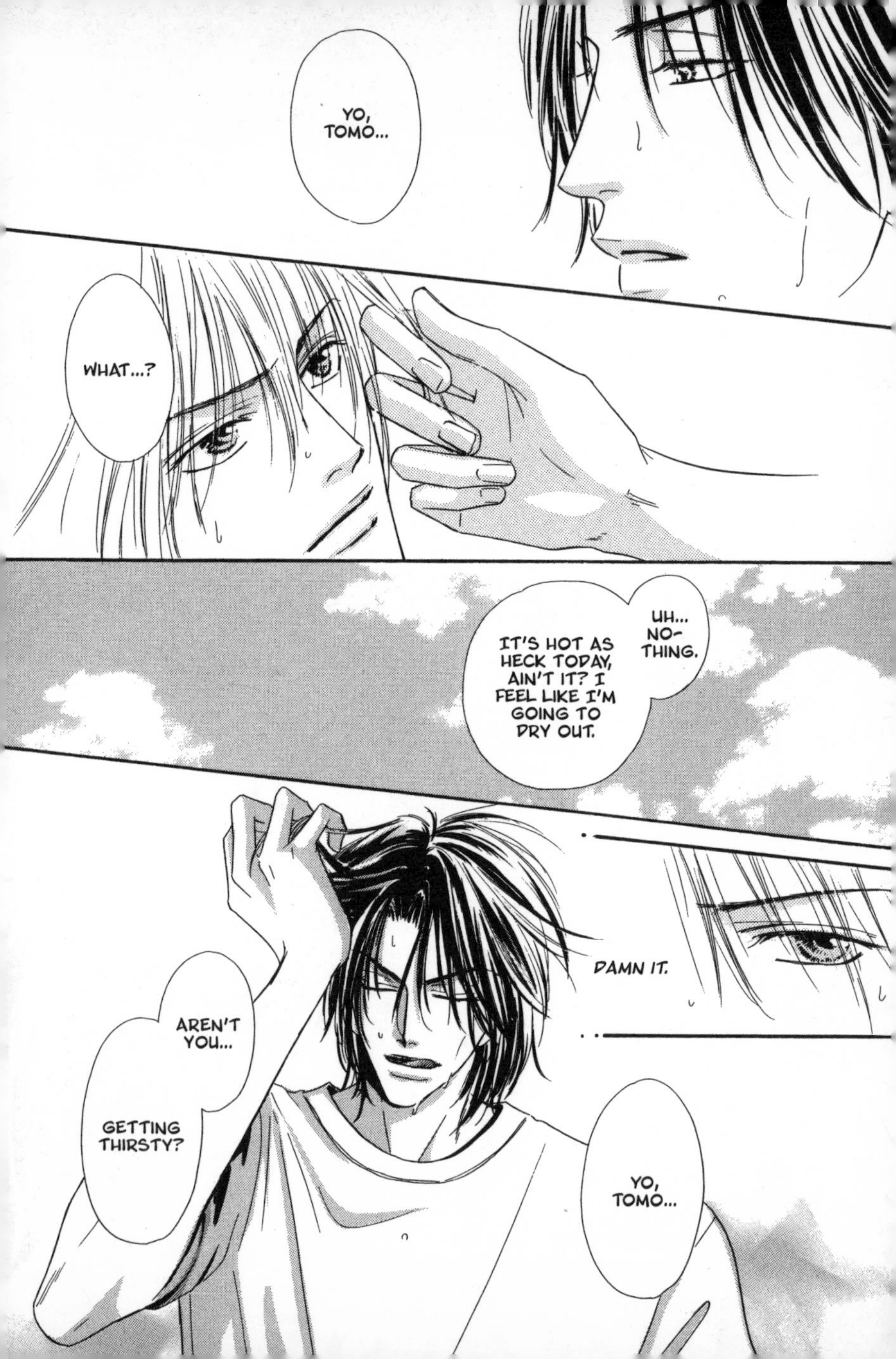
YO, TOMO...
WHAT...?
UH... NO- THING.
IT'S HOT AS HECK TODAY, AIN'T IT? I FEEL LIKE I'M GOING TO DRY OUT.
DAMN IT.
YO, TOMO...
AREN'T YOU...
GETTING THIRSTY?

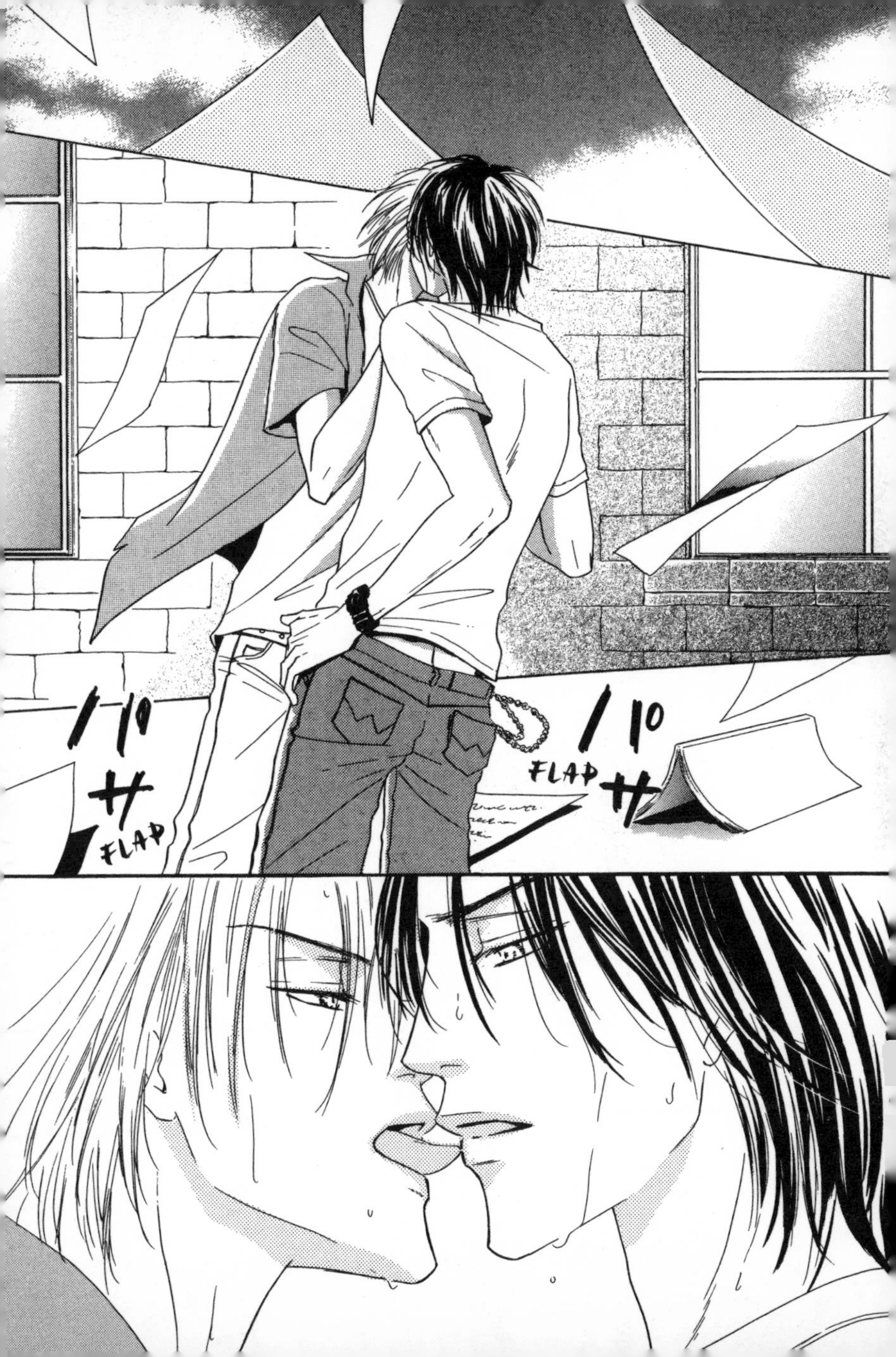
パサ
FLAP
パサ
FLAP

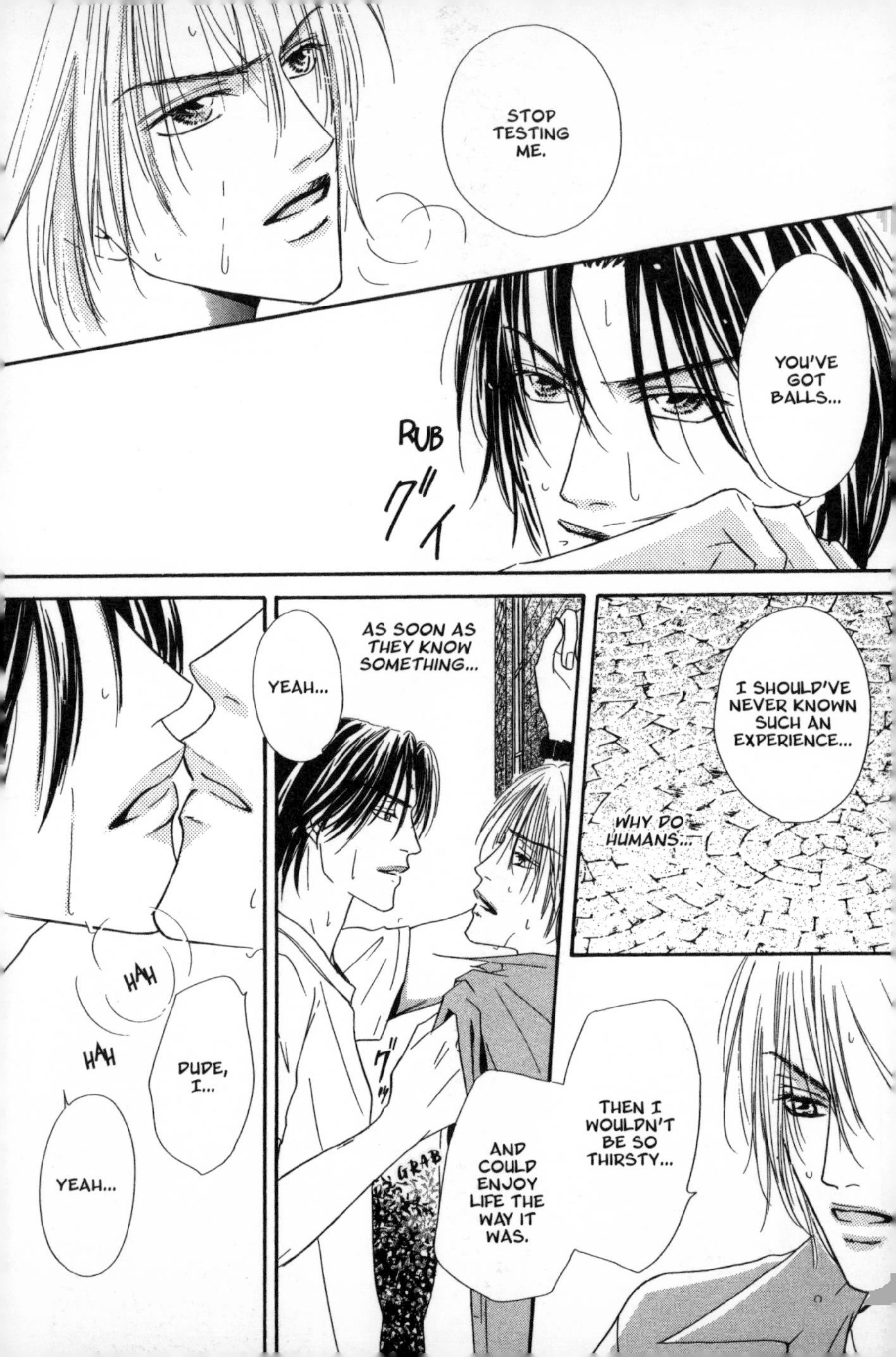
STOP TESTING ME.
YOU'VE GOT BALLS...
RUB
グイ
I SHOULD'VE NEVER KNOWN SUCH AN EXPERIENCE...
WHY DO HUMANS...
THEN I WOULDN'T BE SO THIRSTY...
AND COULD ENJOY LIFE THE WAY IT WAS.
AS SOON AS THEY KNOW SOMETHING...
YEAH...
GRAB
HAH
HAH
DUDE, I...
YEAH...

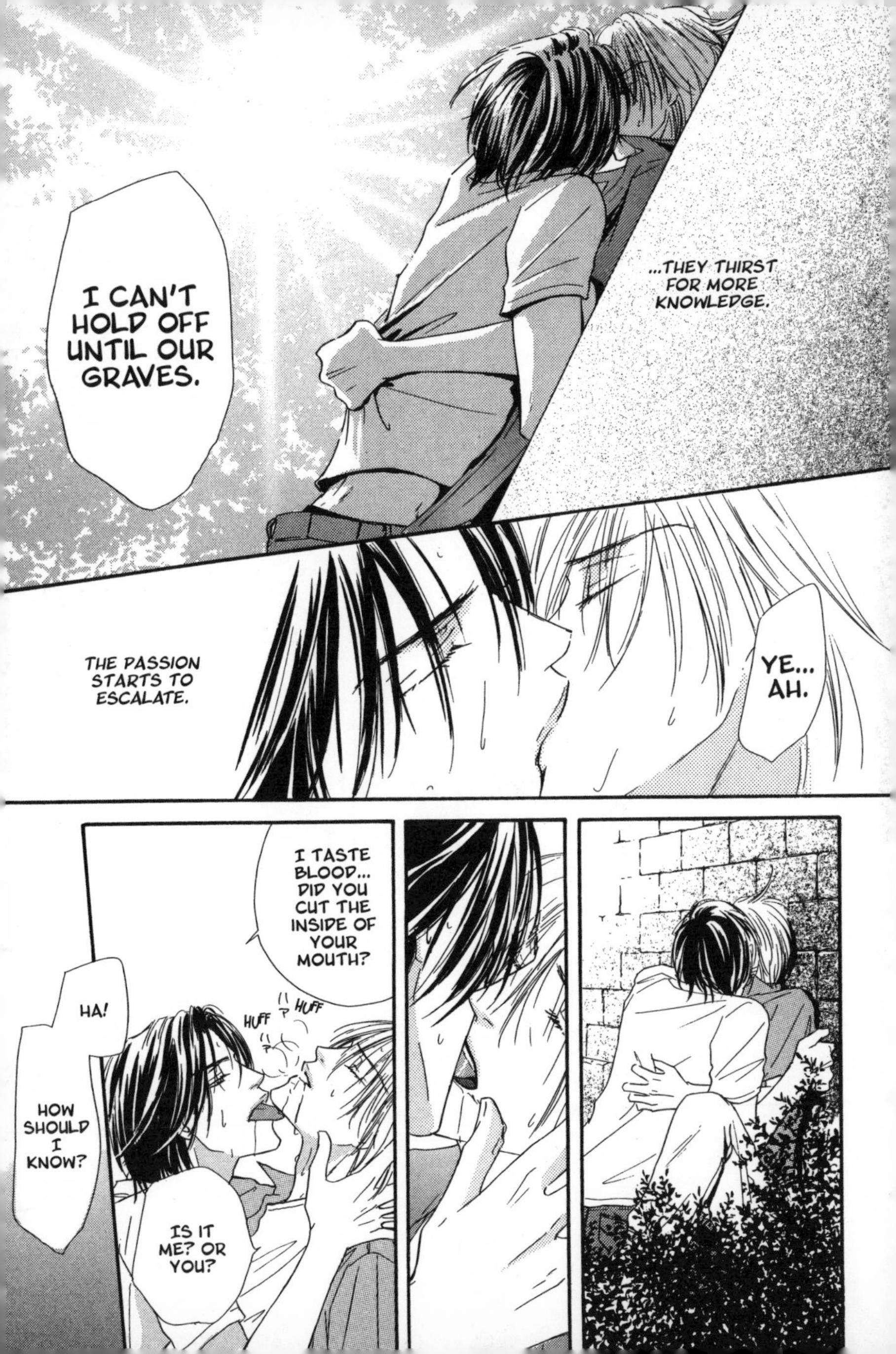

...THEY THIRST FOR MORE KNOWLEDGE.
I CAN'T HOLD OFF UNTIL OUR GRAVES.
YE... AH.
THE PASSION STARTS TO ESCALATE.
I TASTE BLOOD... DID YOU CUT THE INSIDE OF YOUR MOUTH?
HUFF
HUFF
HA!
HOW SHOULD I KNOW?
IS IT ME? OR YOU?

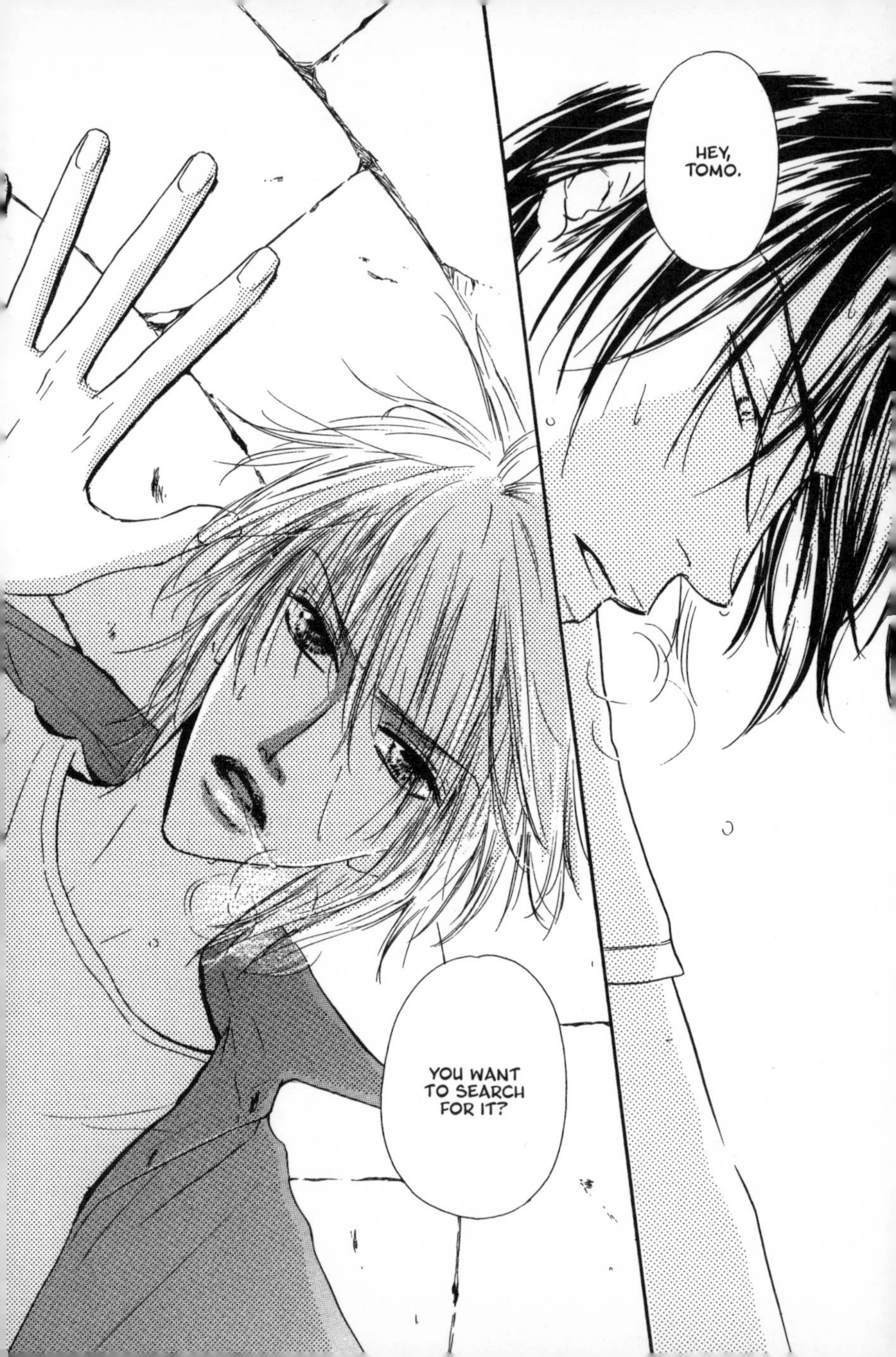
HEY, TOMO.
YOU WANT TO SEARCH FOR IT?

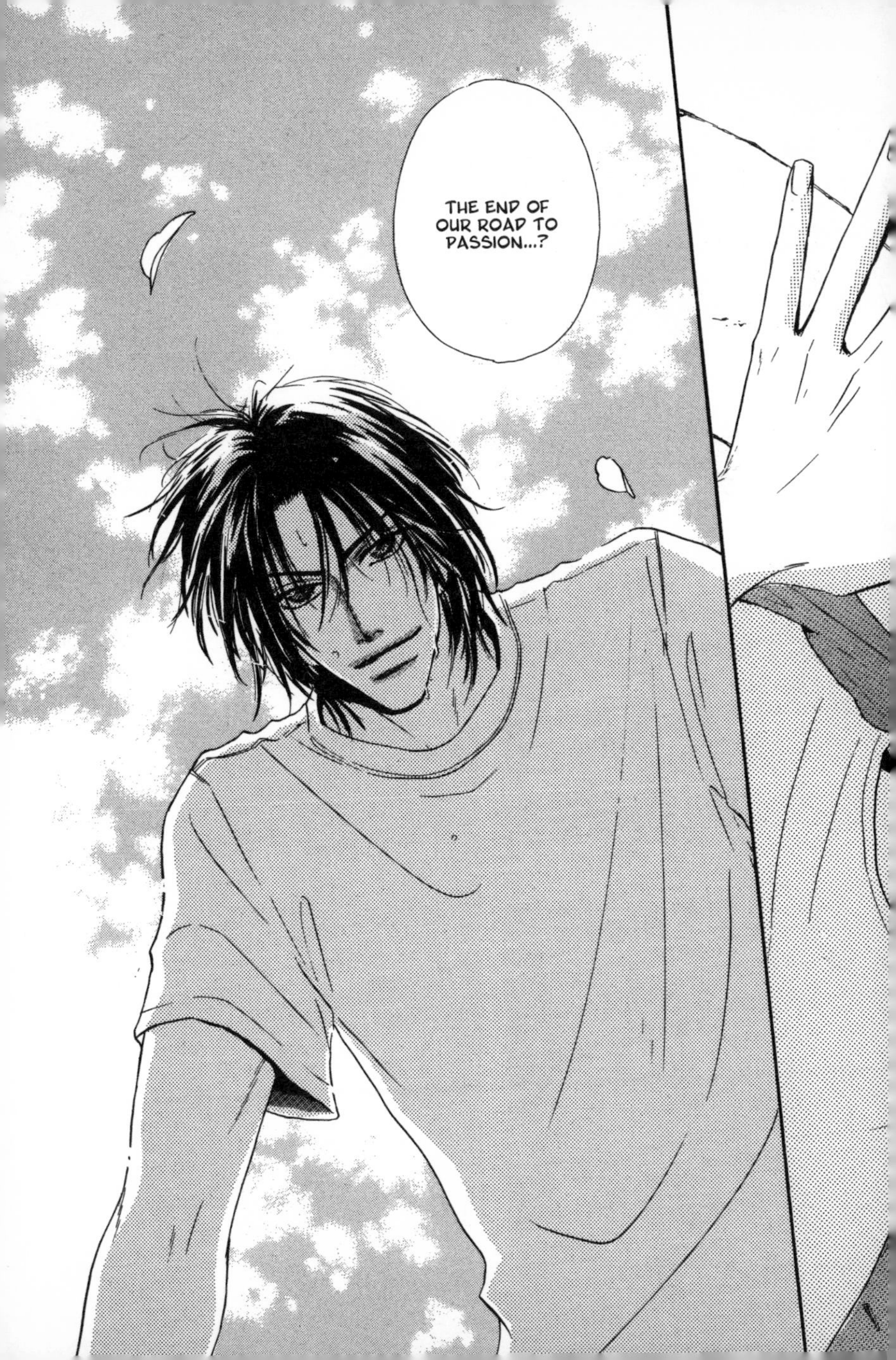
THE END OF OUR ROAD TO PASSION...?

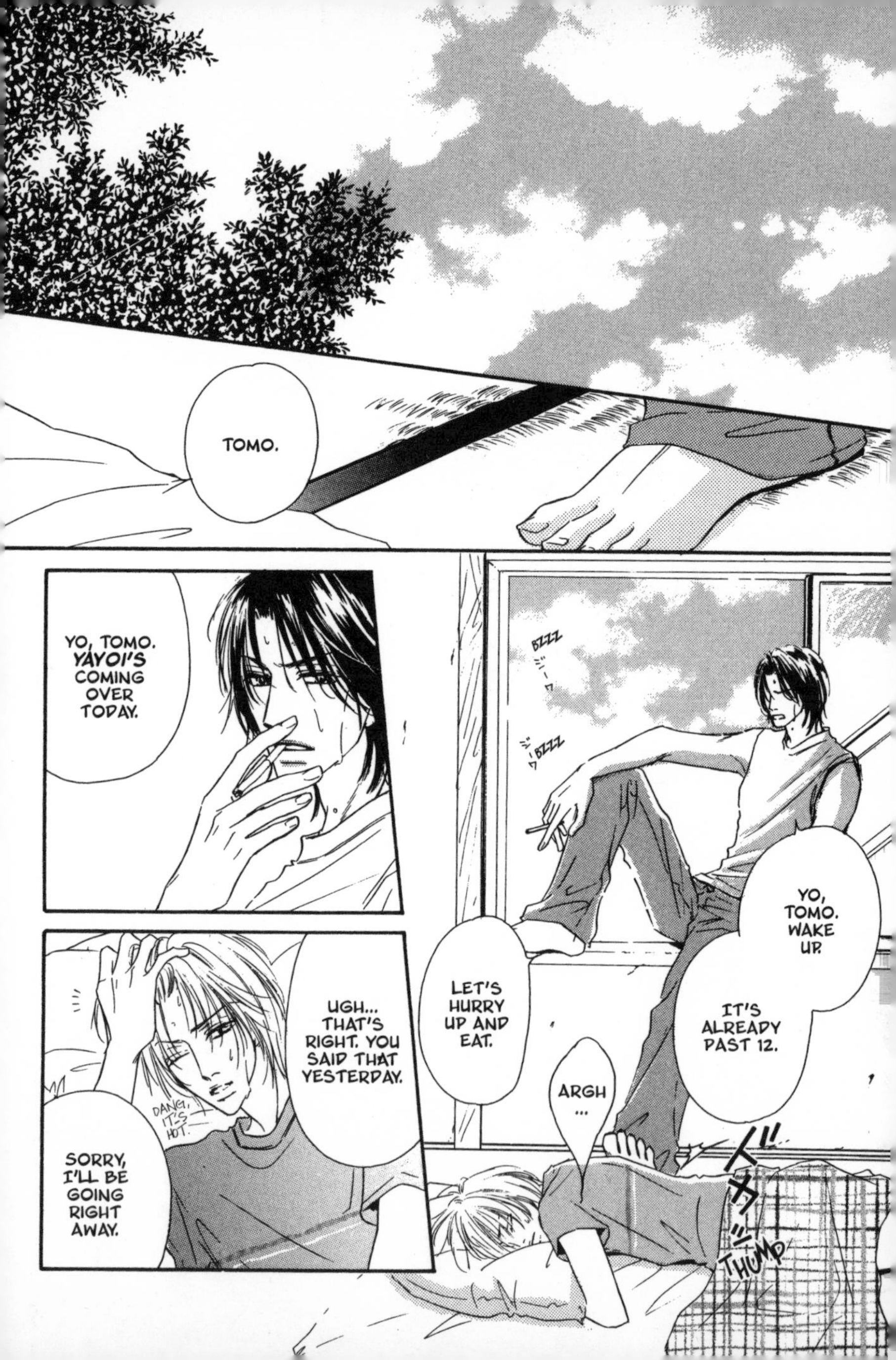
TOMO.
BZZZ
BZZZ
YO, TOMO. WAKE UP.
IT'S ALREADY PAST 12.
LET'S HURRY UP AND EAT.
ARGH...
THUMP
YO, TOMO. YAYOI'S COMING OVER TODAY.
UGH... THAT'S RIGHT. YOU SAID THAT YESTERDAY.
DANG, IT'S HOT.
SORRY, I'LL BE GOING RIGHT AWAY.

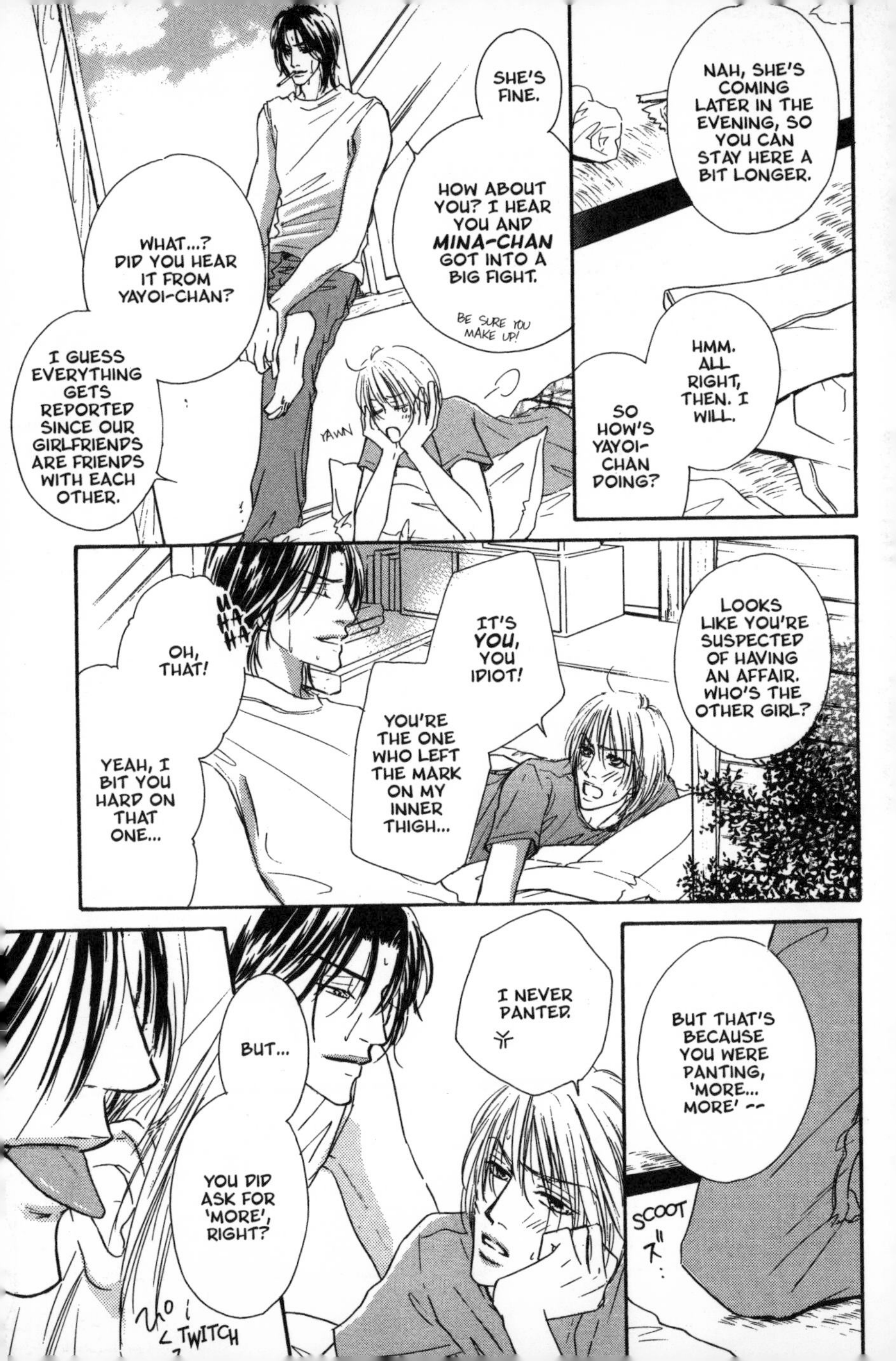

NAH, SHE'S COMING LATER IN THE EVENING, SO YOU CAN STAY HERE A BIT LONGER.
HMM. ALL RIGHT, THEN. I WILL.
SO HOW'S YAYOI-CHAN DOING?
SHE'S FINE.
HOW ABOUT YOU? I HEAR YOU AND MINA-CHAN GOT INTO A BIG FIGHT.
BE SURE YOU MAKE UP!
WHAT...? DID YOU HEAR IT FROM YAYOI-CHAN?
YAWN
I GUESS EVERYTHING GETS REPORTED SINCE OUR GIRLFRIENDS ARE FRIENDS WITH EACH OTHER.
LOOKS LIKE YOU'RE SUSPECTED OF HAVING AN AFFAIR. WHO'S THE OTHER GIRL?
IT'S YOU, YOU IDIOT!
YOU'RE THE ONE WHO LEFT THE MARK ON MY INNER THIGH...
HA HA HA
OH, THAT!
YEAH, I BIT YOU HARD ON THAT ONE...
BUT THAT'S BECAUSE YOU WERE PANTING, 'MORE... MORE' --
SCOOT
I NEVER PANTED.
BUT...
YOU DID ASK FOR 'MORE', RIGHT?
TWITCH

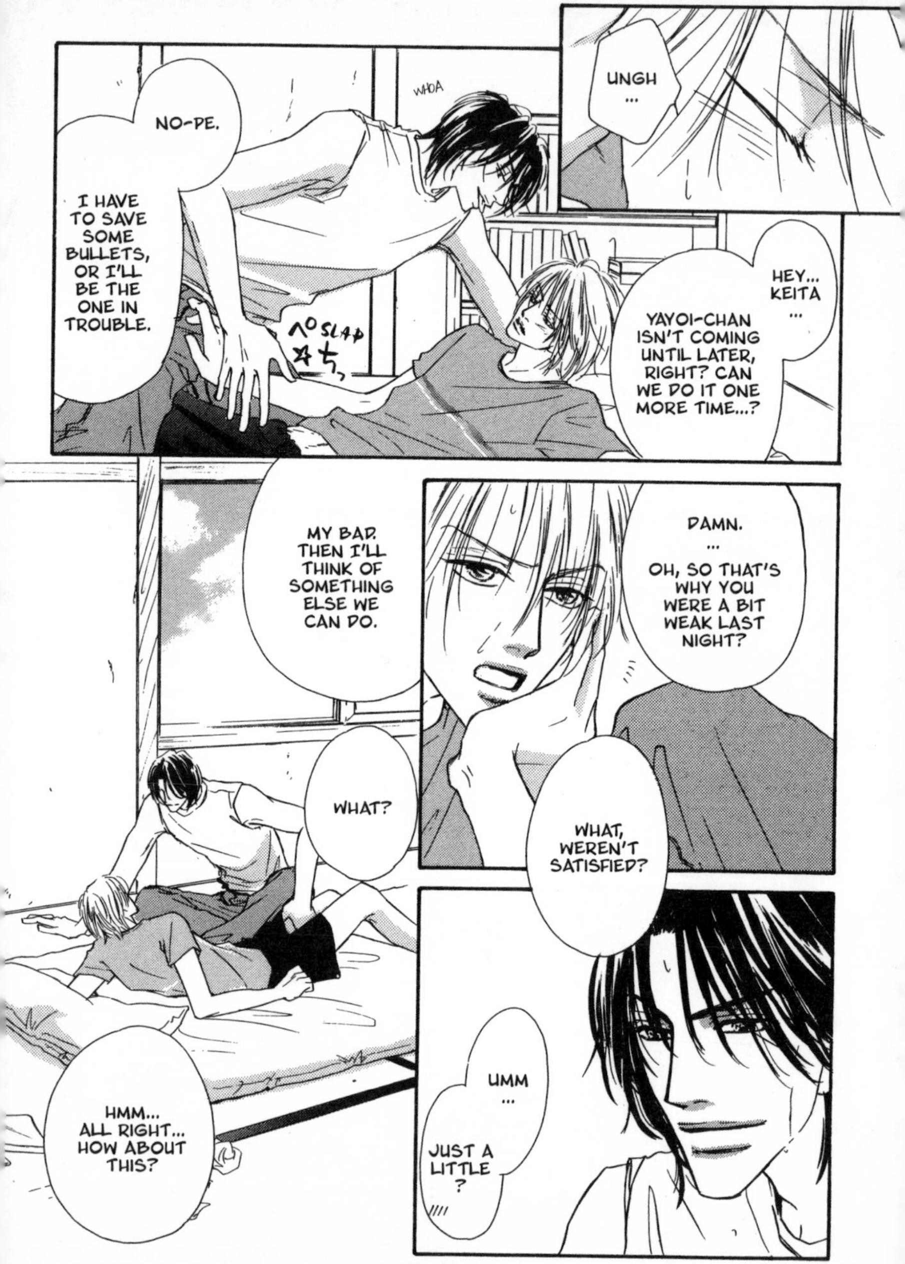
UNGH ...
HEY... KEITA ...
YAYOI-CHAN ISN'T COMING UNTIL LATER, RIGHT? CAN WE DO IT ONE MORE TIME...?
WHOA
NO-PE.
I HAVE TO SAVE SOME BULLETS, OR I'LL BE THE ONE IN TROUBLE.
SLAP
DAMN. ... OH, SO THAT'S WHY YOU WERE A BIT WEAK LAST NIGHT?
WHAT, WEREN'T SATISFIED?
UMM ...
JUST A LITTLE ?
MY BAD. THEN I'LL THINK OF SOMETHING ELSE WE CAN DO.
WHAT?
HMM... ALL RIGHT... HOW ABOUT THIS?

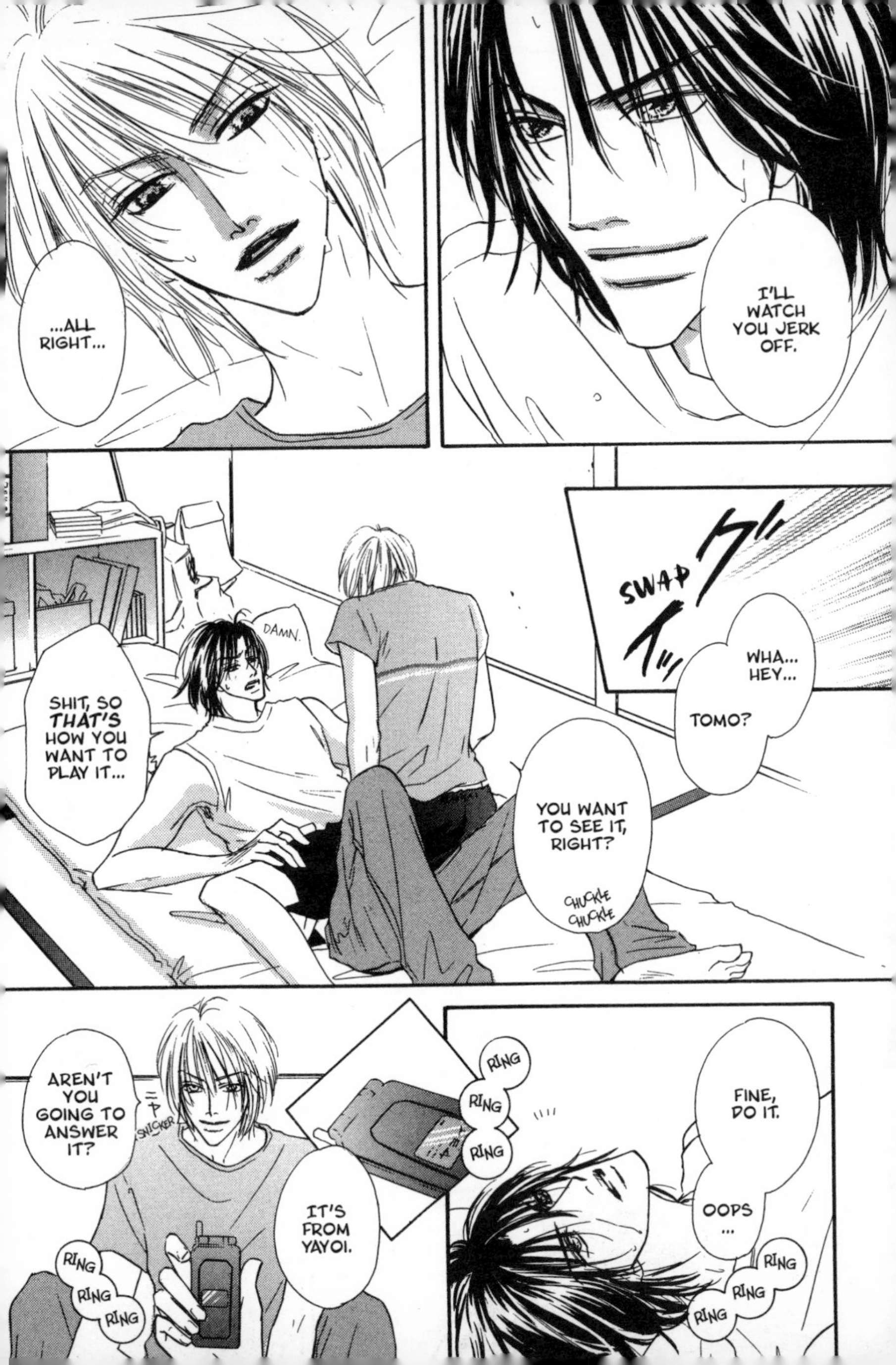

I'LL WATCH YOU JERK OFF.
...ALL RIGHT...
SWAP
WHA... HEY...
TOMO?
YOU WANT TO SEE IT, RIGHT?
CHUCKLE CHUCKLE
DAMN.
SHIT, SO *THAT'S* HOW YOU WANT TO PLAY IT...
FINE, DO IT.
OOPS ...
RING RING RING
RING RING RING
IT'S FROM YAYOI.
SNICKER
AREN'T YOU GOING TO ANSWER IT?
RING RING RING

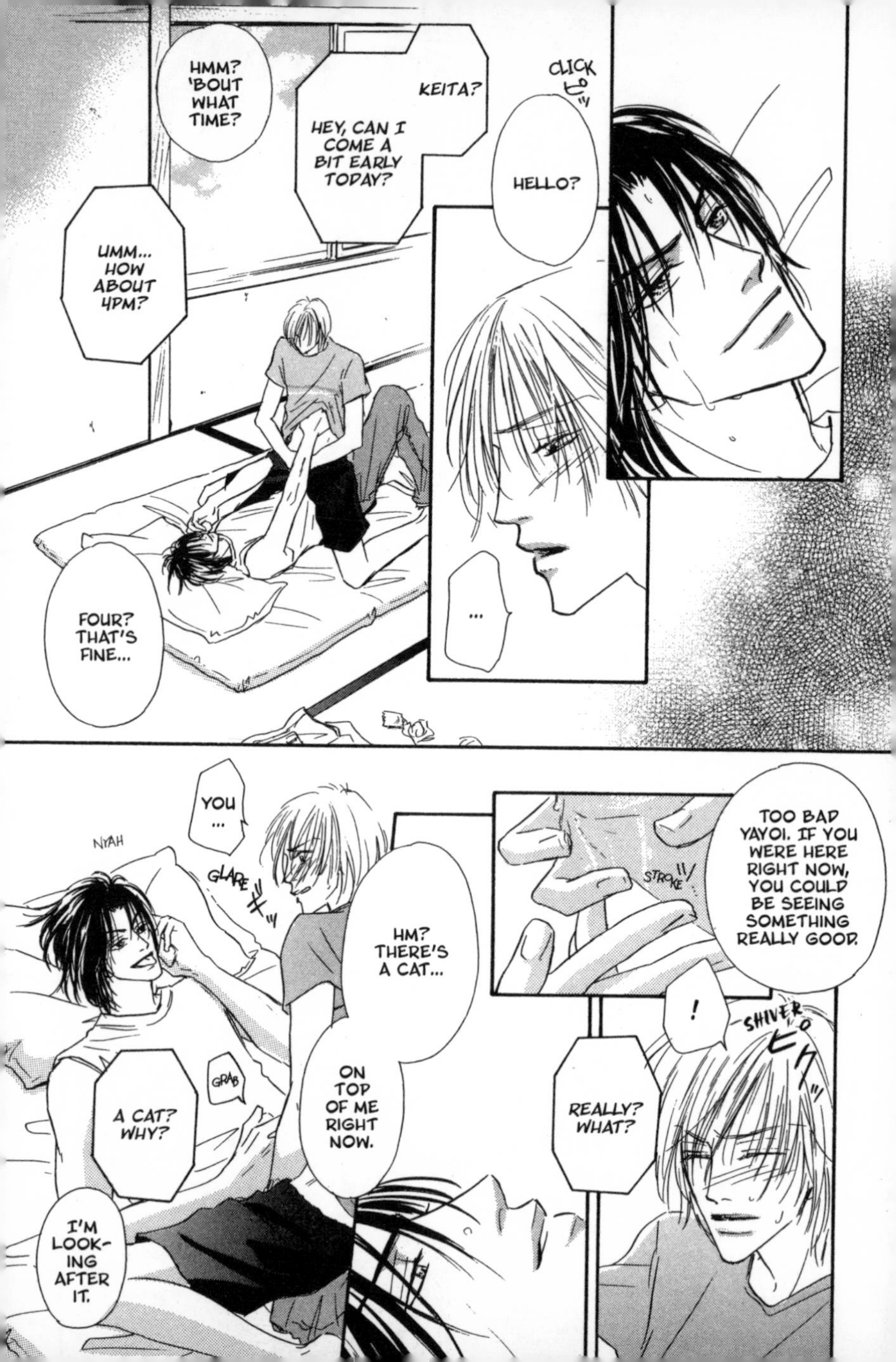

CLICK
HELLO?
...
KEITA?
HEY, CAN I COME A BIT EARLY TODAY?
HMM? 'BOUT WHAT TIME?
UMM... HOW ABOUT 4PM?
FOUR? THAT'S FINE...
TOO BAD YAYOI. IF YOU WERE HERE RIGHT NOW, YOU COULD BE SEEING SOMETHING REALLY GOOD.
STROKE
!
SHIVER
REALLY? WHAT?
YOU ...
GLARE
NYAH
HM? THERE'S A CAT...
ON TOP OF ME RIGHT NOW.
A CAT? WHY?
GRAB
I'M LOOKING AFTER IT.

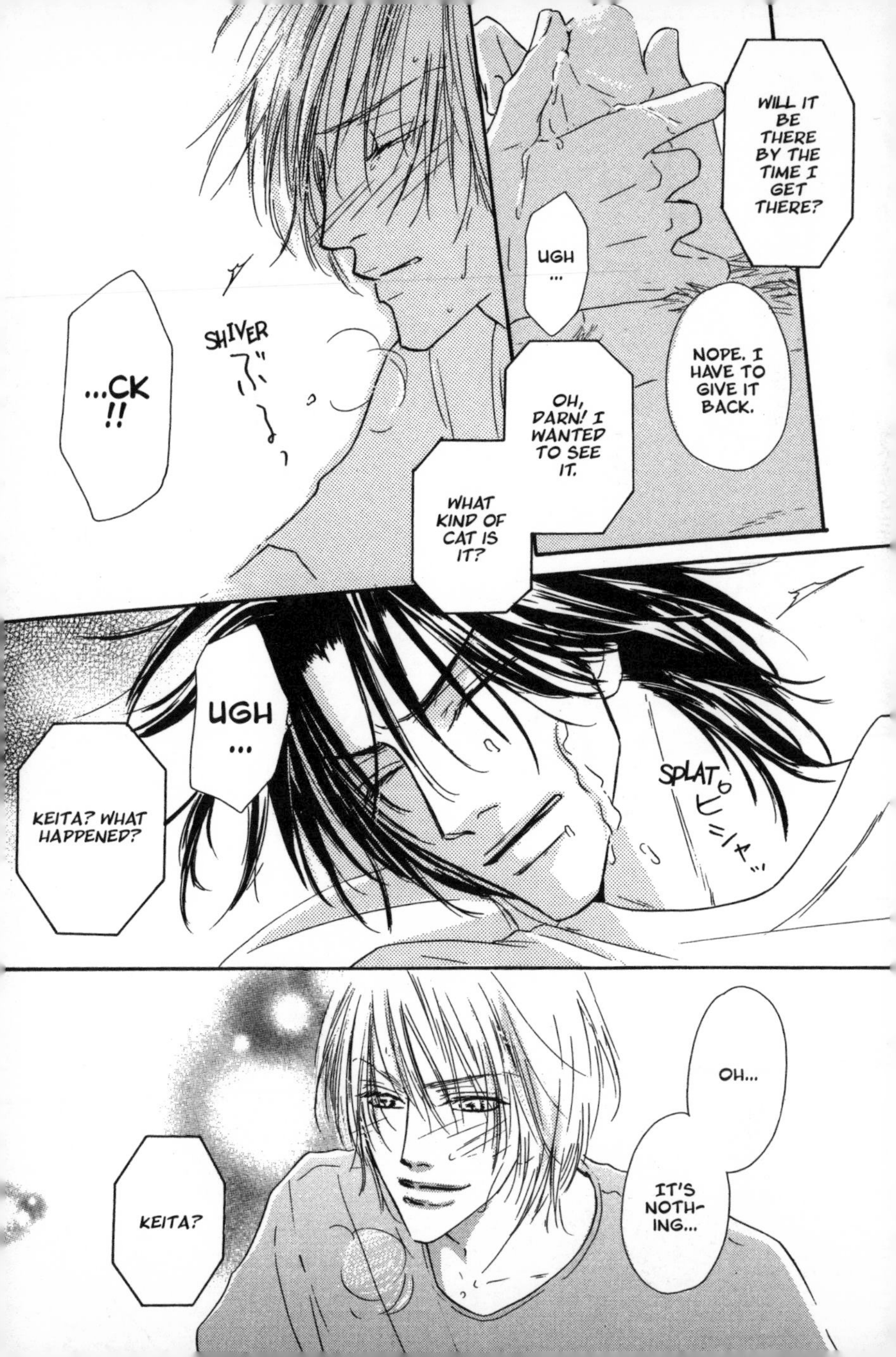
WILL IT BE THERE BY THE TIME I GET THERE?
NOPE. I HAVE TO GIVE IT BACK.
UGH...
OH, DARN! I WANTED TO SEE IT.
WHAT KIND OF CAT IS IT?
SHIVER ぶるっ
...CK!!
SPLAT ピシャッ
UGH...
KEITA? WHAT HAPPENED?
OH...
IT'S NOTHING...
KEITA?

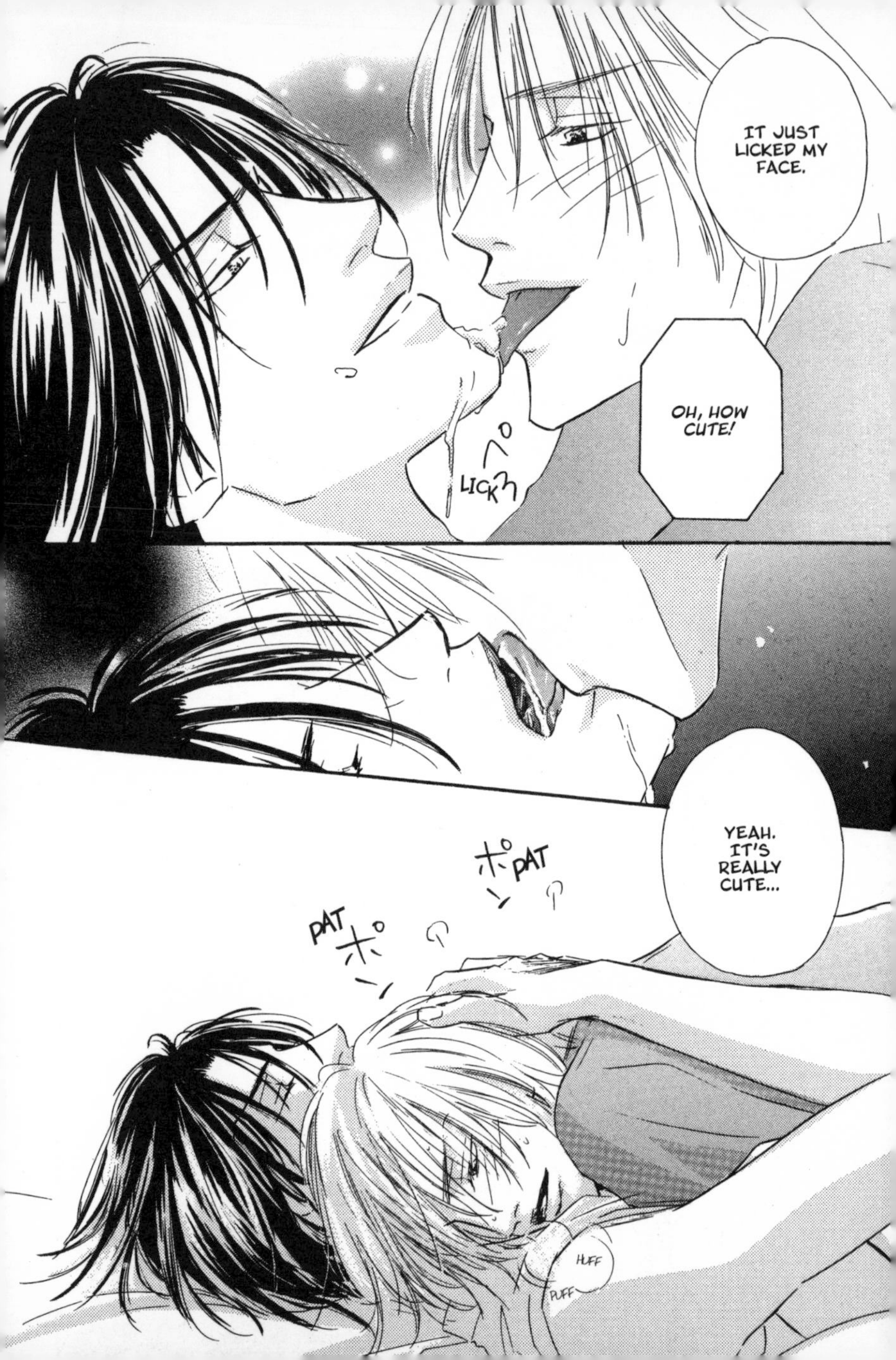
IT JUST LICKED MY FACE.
OH, HOW CUTE!
LICK
YEAH. IT'S REALLY CUTE...
PAT
PAT
HUFF
PUFF

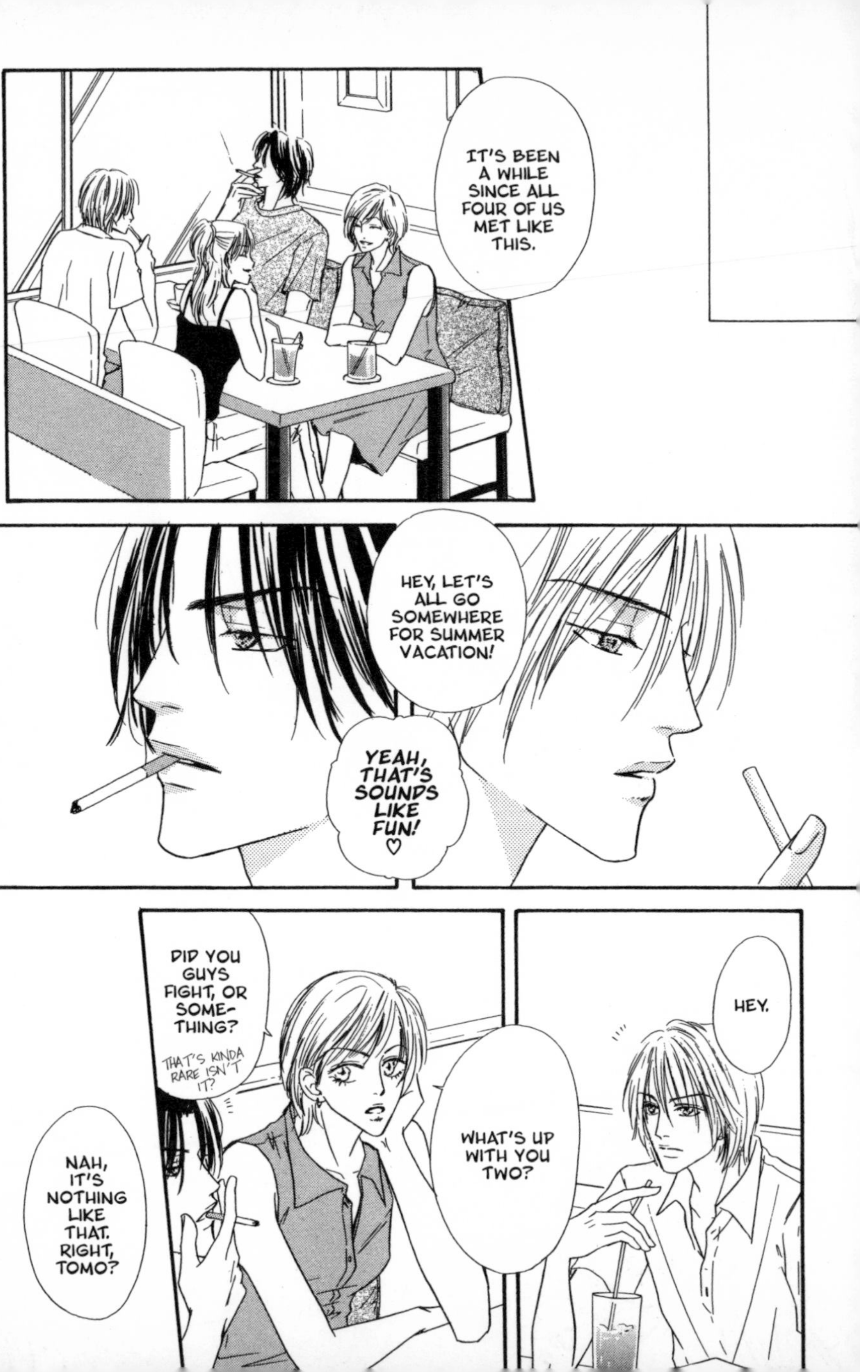
IT'S BEEN A WHILE SINCE ALL FOUR OF US MET LIKE THIS.
HEY, LET'S ALL GO SOMEWHERE FOR SUMMER VACATION!
YEAH, THAT'S SOUNDS LIKE FUN! ♡
HEY.
WHAT'S UP WITH YOU TWO?
DID YOU GUYS FIGHT, OR SOME-THING?
THAT'S KINDA RARE ISN'T IT?
NAH, IT'S NOTHING LIKE THAT. RIGHT, TOMO?

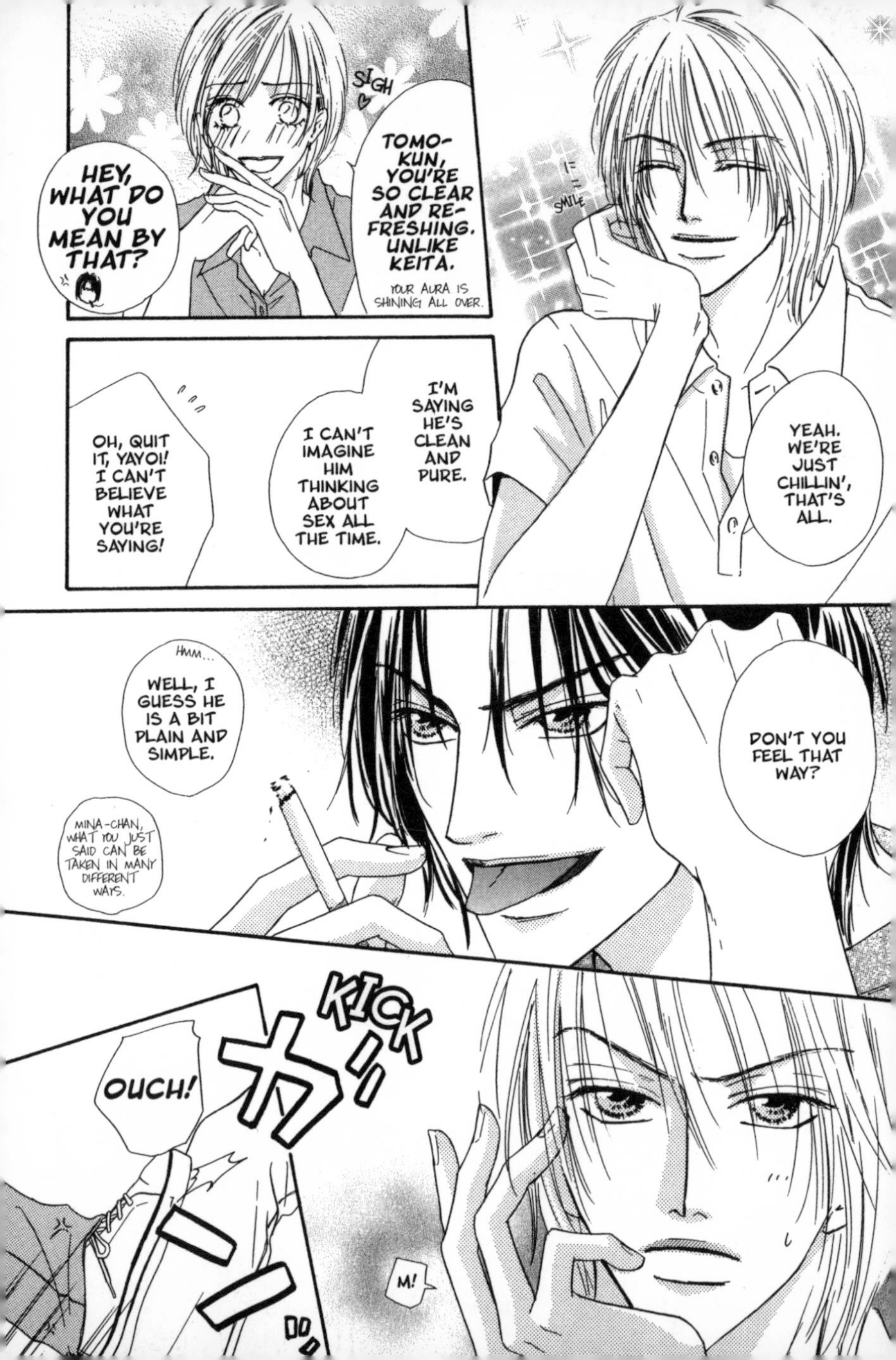
SMILE
YEAH. WE'RE JUST CHILLIN', THAT'S ALL.
SIGH
TOMO-KUN, YOU'RE SO CLEAR AND RE-FRESHING. UNLIKE KEITA.
YOUR AURA IS SHINING ALL OVER.
HEY, WHAT DO YOU MEAN BY THAT?
I'M SAYING HE'S CLEAN AND PURE.
I CAN'T IMAGINE HIM THINKING ABOUT SEX ALL THE TIME.
OH, QUIT IT, YAYOI! I CAN'T BELIEVE WHAT YOU'RE SAYING!
DON'T YOU FEEL THAT WAY?
HMM...
WELL, I GUESS HE IS A BIT PLAIN AND SIMPLE.
MINA-CHAN, WHAT YOU JUST SAID CAN BE TAKEN IN MANY DIFFERENT WAYS.
M!
KICK
OUCH!

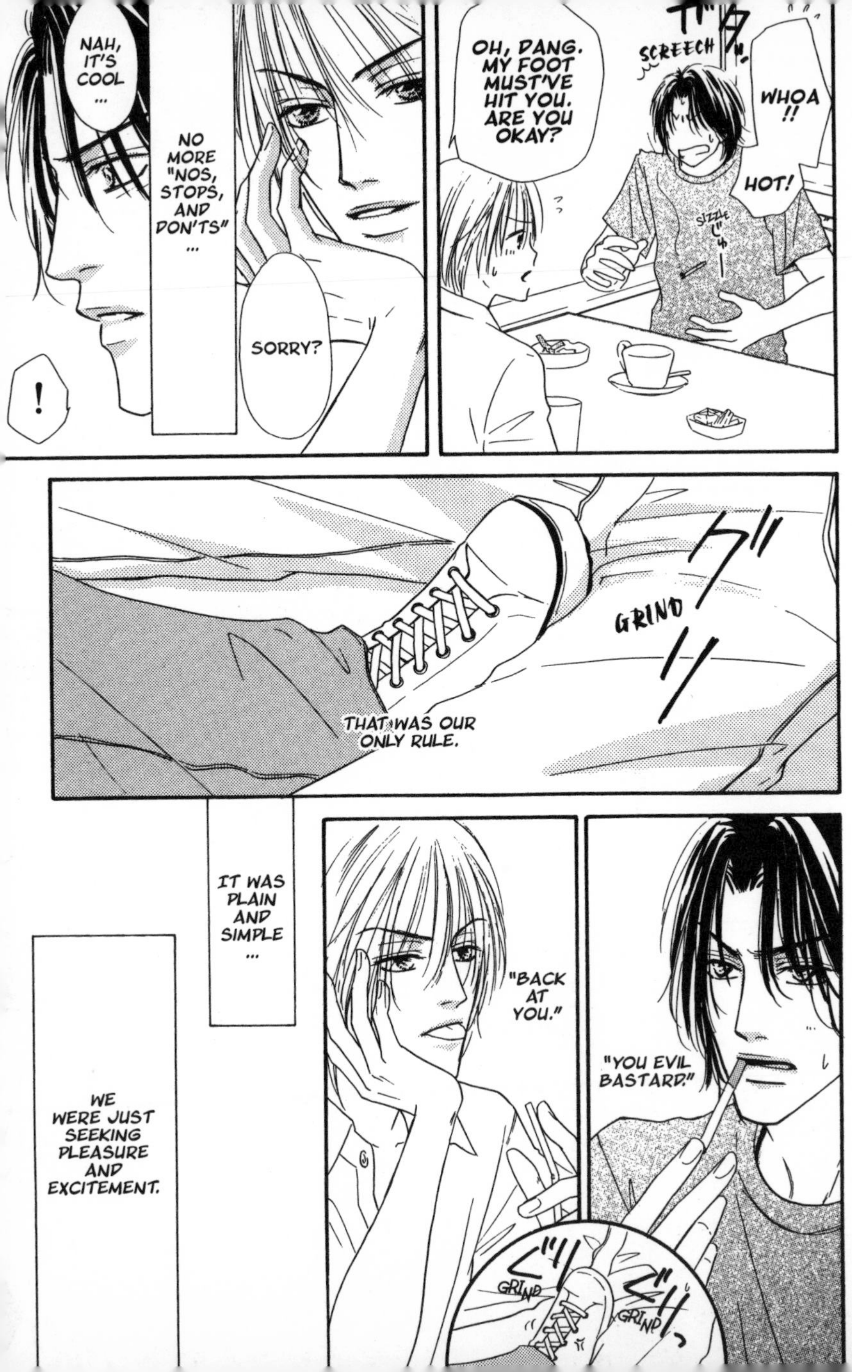
WHOA!!
SCREECH
OH, DANG. MY FOOT MUST'VE HIT YOU. ARE YOU OKAY?
HOT!
SIZZLE
NO MORE "NOS, STOPS, AND DON'TS"...
SORRY?
NAH, IT'S COOL...
!
GRIND
THAT WAS OUR ONLY RULE.
"YOU EVIL BASTARD."
"BACK AT YOU."
IT WAS PLAIN AND SIMPLE...
GRIND
GRIND
WE WERE JUST SEEKING PLEASURE AND EXCITEMENT.

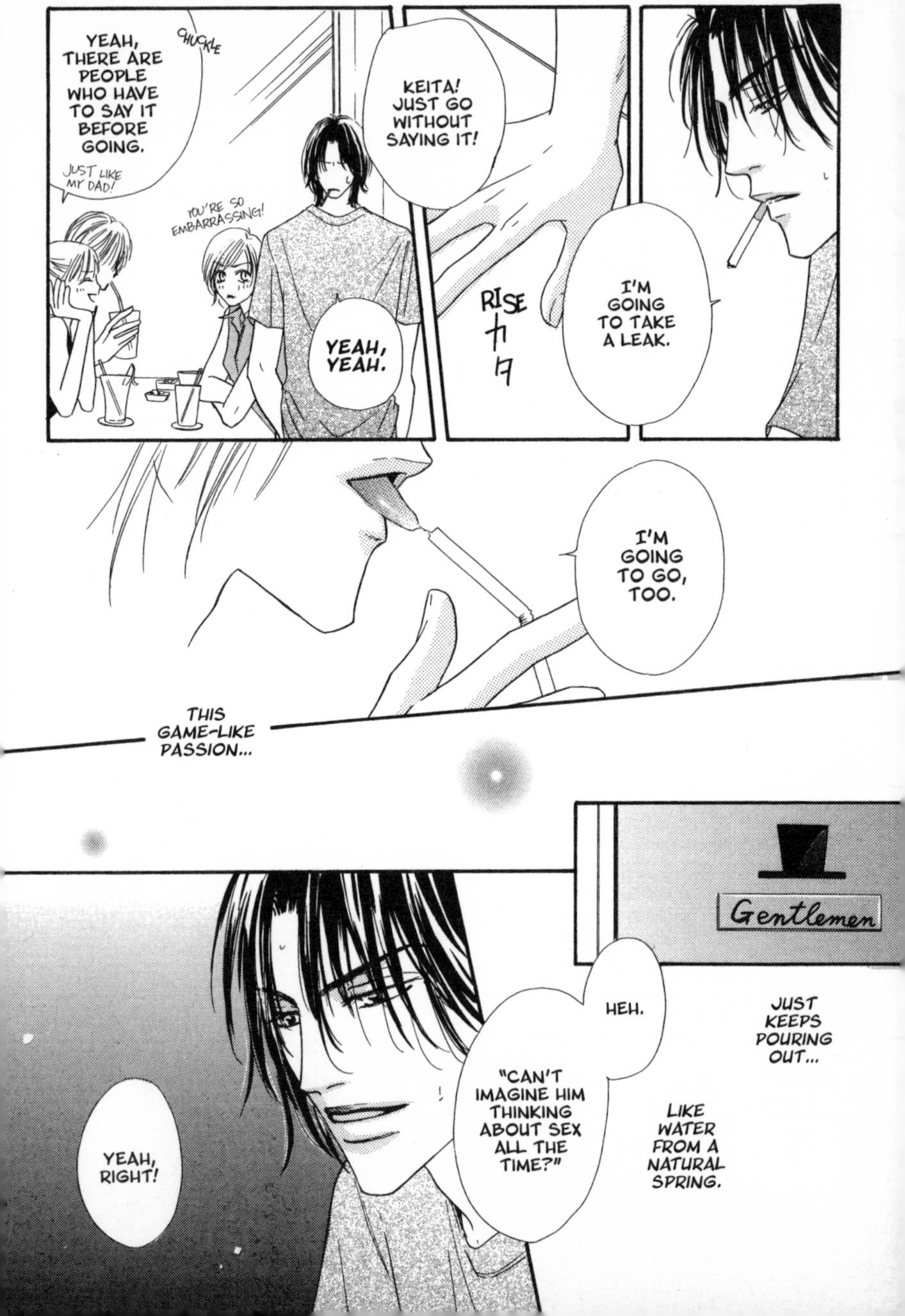
I'M GOING TO TAKE A LEAK.
KEITA! JUST GO WITHOUT SAYING IT!
RISE
カク
YEAH, THERE ARE PEOPLE WHO HAVE TO SAY IT BEFORE GOING.
CHUCKLE
JUST LIKE MY DAD!
YOU'RE SO EMBARRASSING!
YEAH, YEAH.
I'M GOING TO GO, TOO.
THIS GAME-LIKE PASSION...
JUST KEEPS POURING OUT...
LIKE WATER FROM A NATURAL SPRING.
Gentlemen
HEH.
"CAN'T IMAGINE HIM THINKING ABOUT SEX ALL THE TIME?"
YEAH, RIGHT!

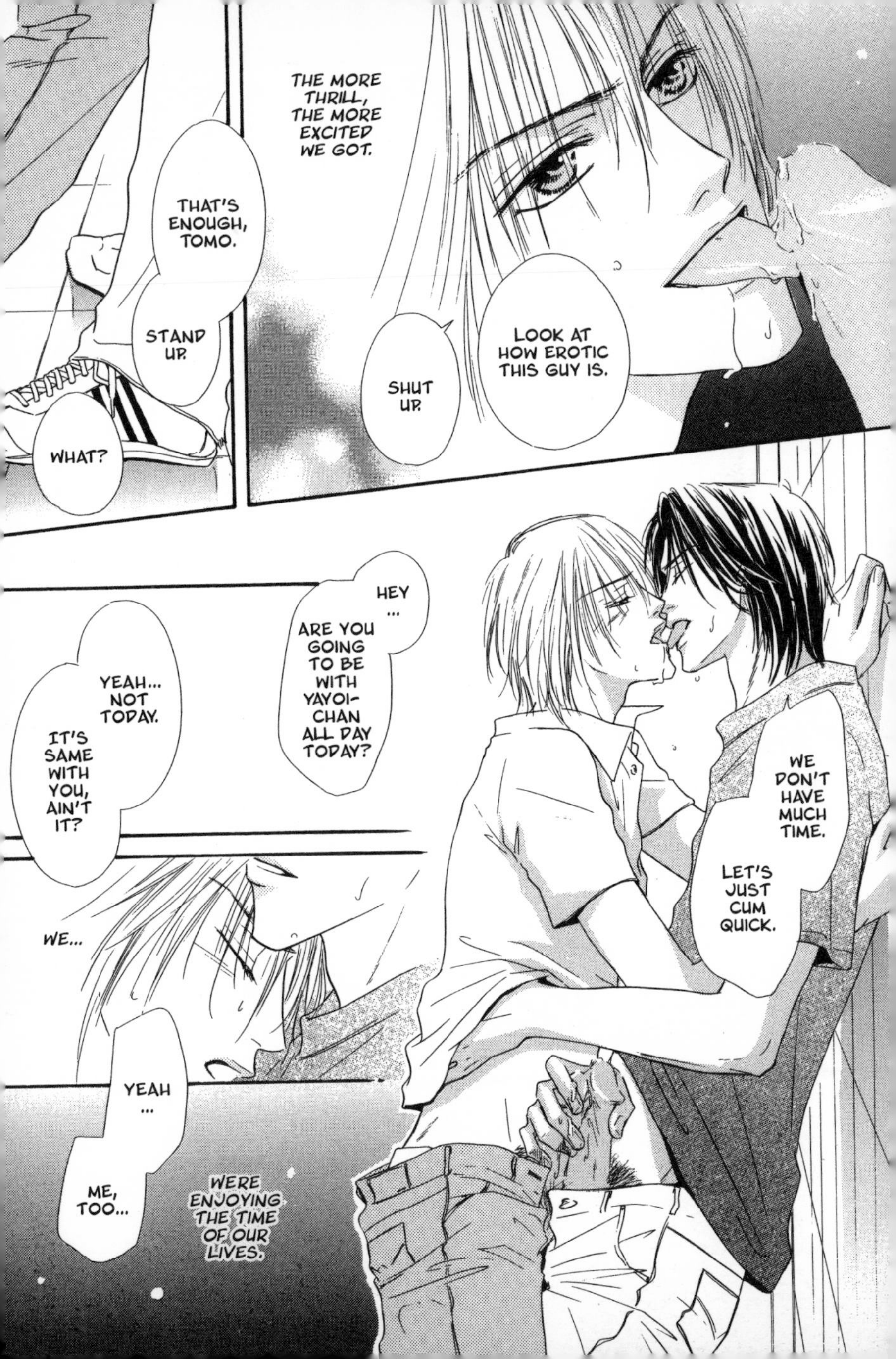
THE MORE THRILL, THE MORE EXCITED WE GOT.
LOOK AT HOW EROTIC THIS GUY IS.
SHUT UP.
THAT'S ENOUGH, TOMO.
STAND UP.
WHAT?
HEY ... ARE YOU GOING TO BE WITH YAYOI-CHAN ALL DAY TODAY?
YEAH... NOT TODAY.
IT'S SAME WITH YOU, AIN'T IT?
WE DON'T HAVE MUCH TIME.
LET'S JUST CUM QUICK.
WE...
YEAH ...
ME, TOO...
WERE ENJOYING THE TIME OF OUR LIVES.

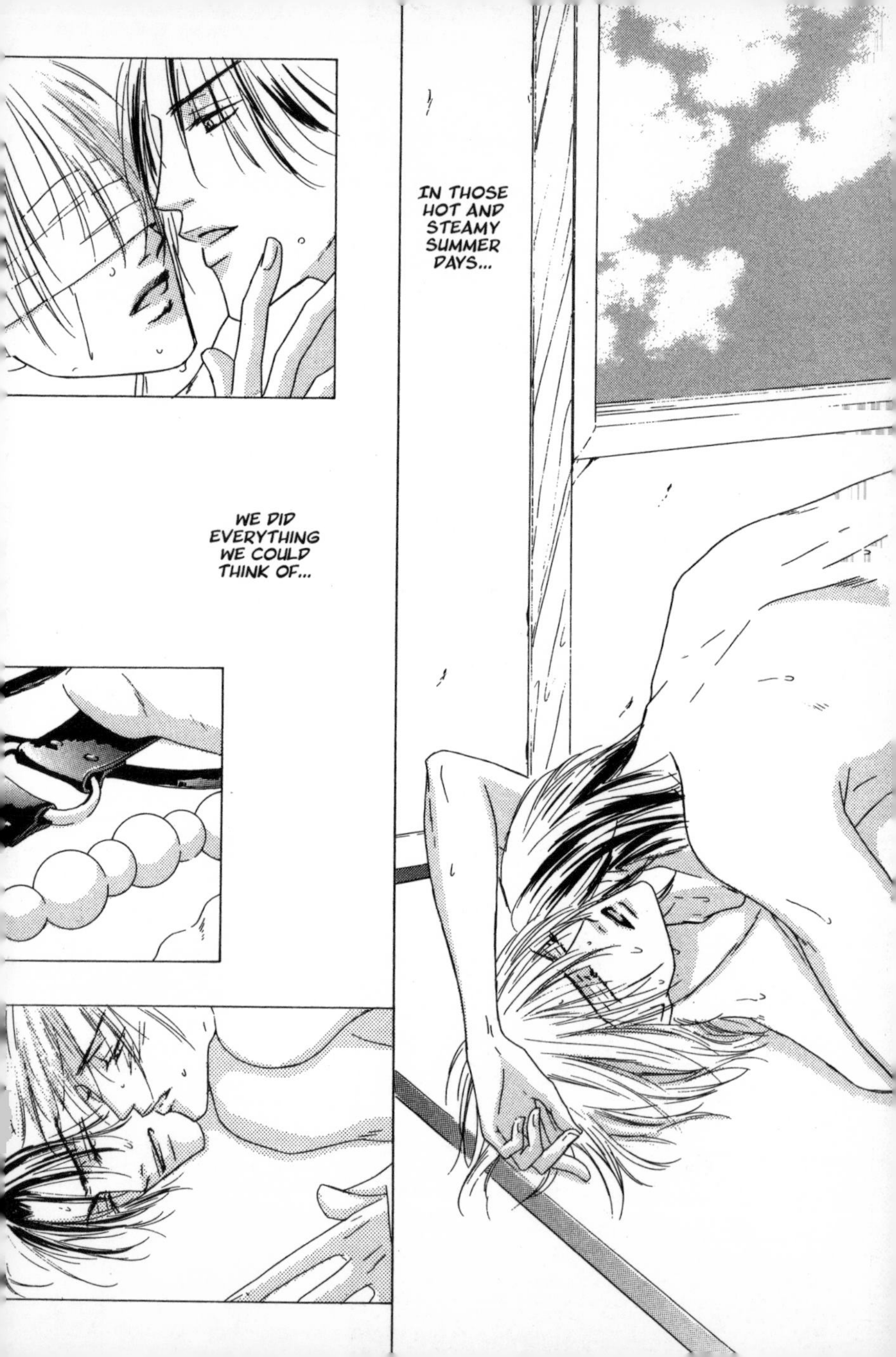
IN THOSE HOT AND STEAMY SUMMER DAYS...
WE DID EVERYTHING WE COULD THINK OF...

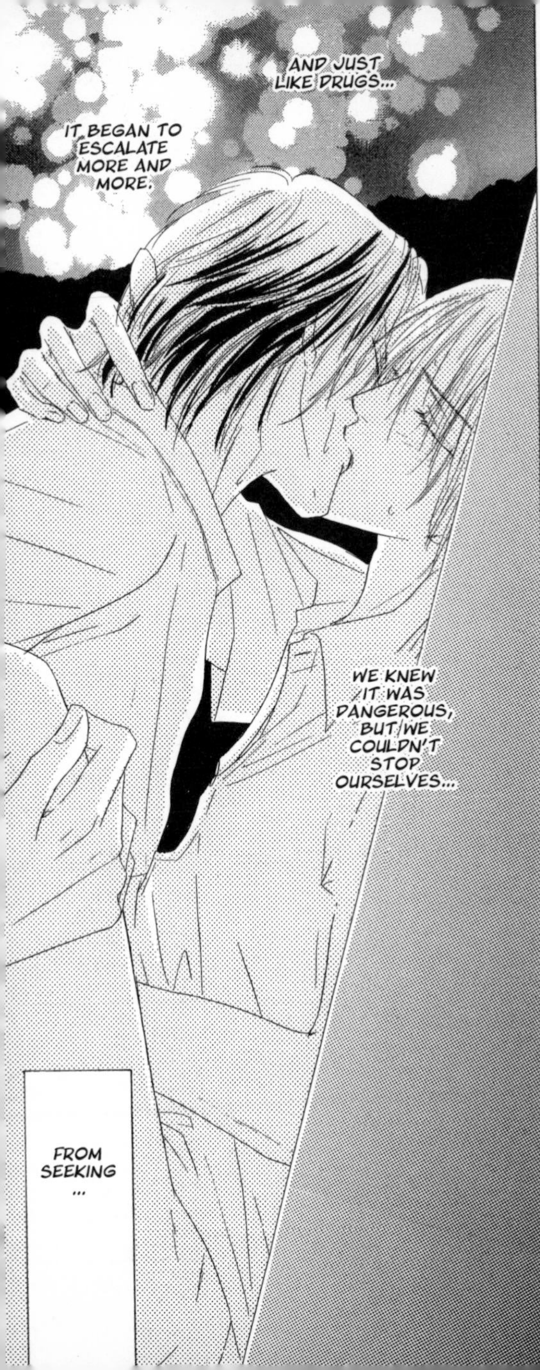
AND JUST LIKE DRUGS...
IT BEGAN TO ESCALATE MORE AND MORE.
WE KNEW IT WAS DANGEROUS, BUT WE COULDN'T STOP OURSELVES...
FROM SEEKING ...

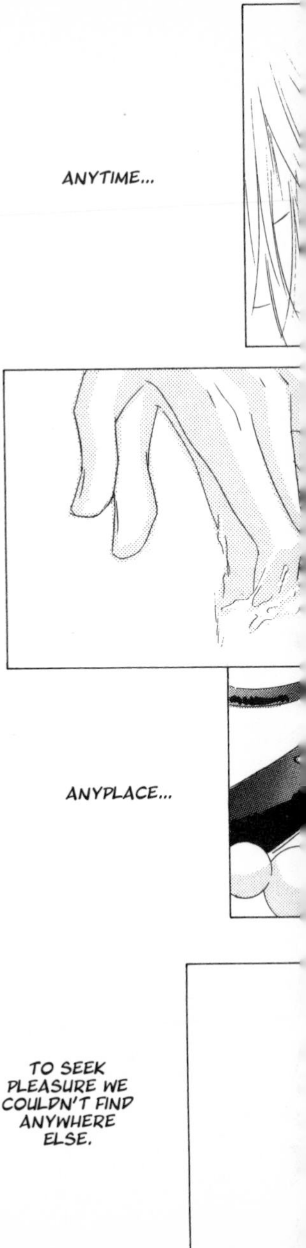
ANYTIME...
ANYPLACE...
TO SEEK PLEASURE WE COULDN'T FIND ANYWHERE ELSE.

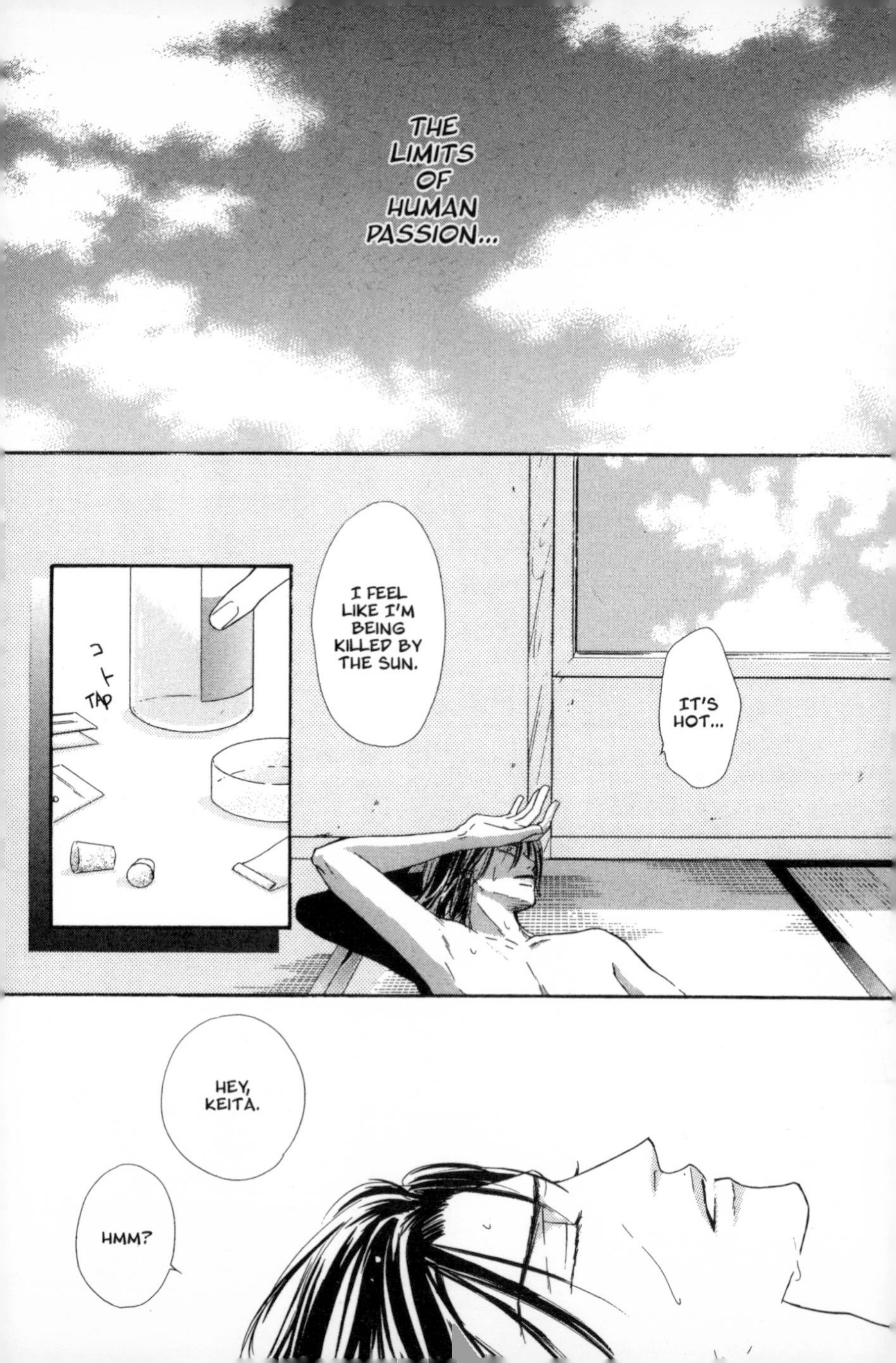
THE LIMITS OF HUMAN PASSION...
IT'S HOT...
I FEEL LIKE I'M BEING KILLED BY THE SUN.
コト
TAP
HEY, KEITA.
HMM?

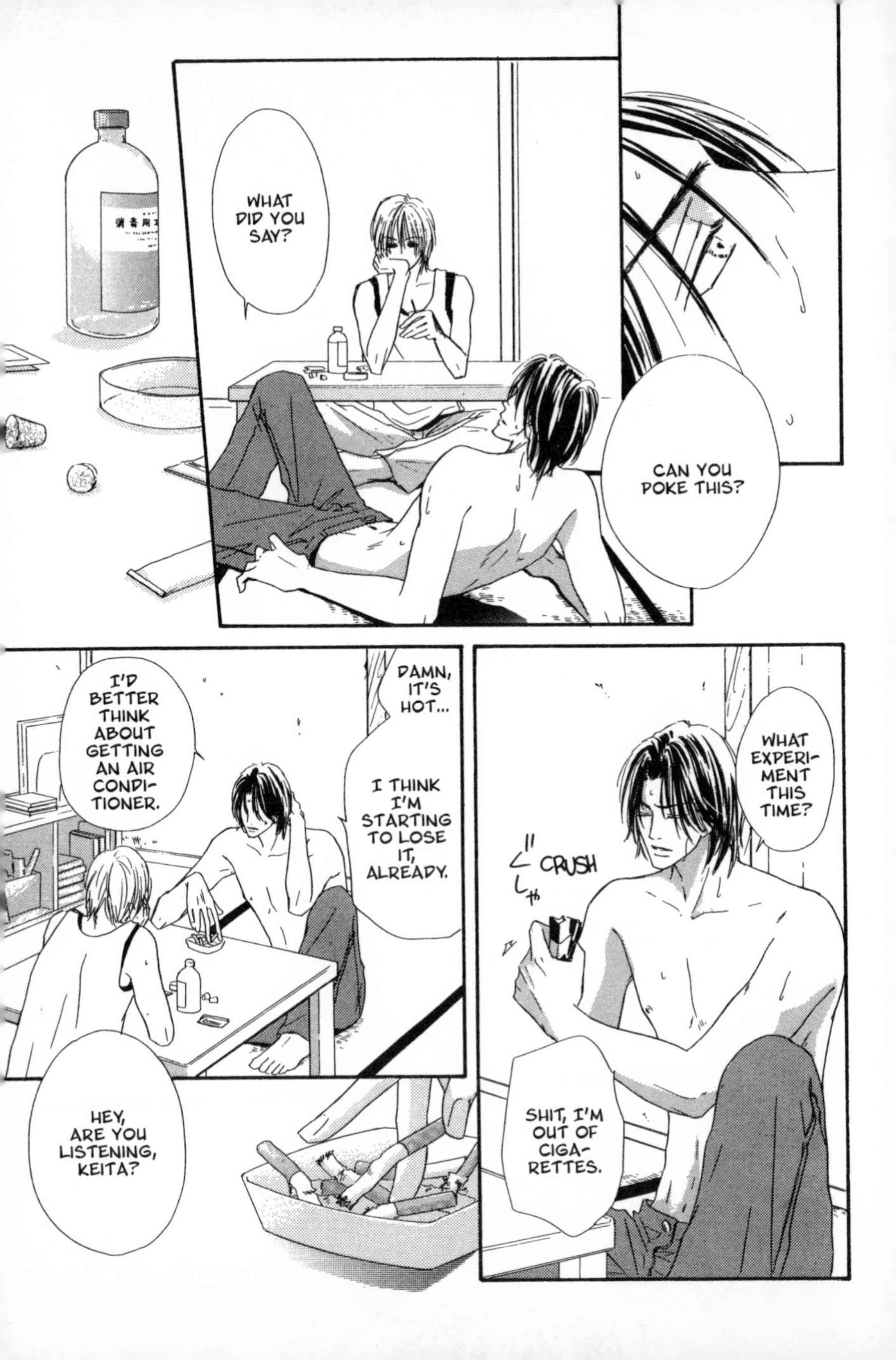

CAN YOU POKE THIS?
WHAT DID YOU SAY?
WHAT EXPERIMENT THIS TIME?
CRUSH
SHIT, I'M OUT OF CIGARETTES.
DAMN, IT'S HOT...
I THINK I'M STARTING TO LOSE IT, ALREADY.
I'D BETTER THINK ABOUT GETTING AN AIR CONDITIONER.
HEY, ARE YOU LISTENING, KEITA?

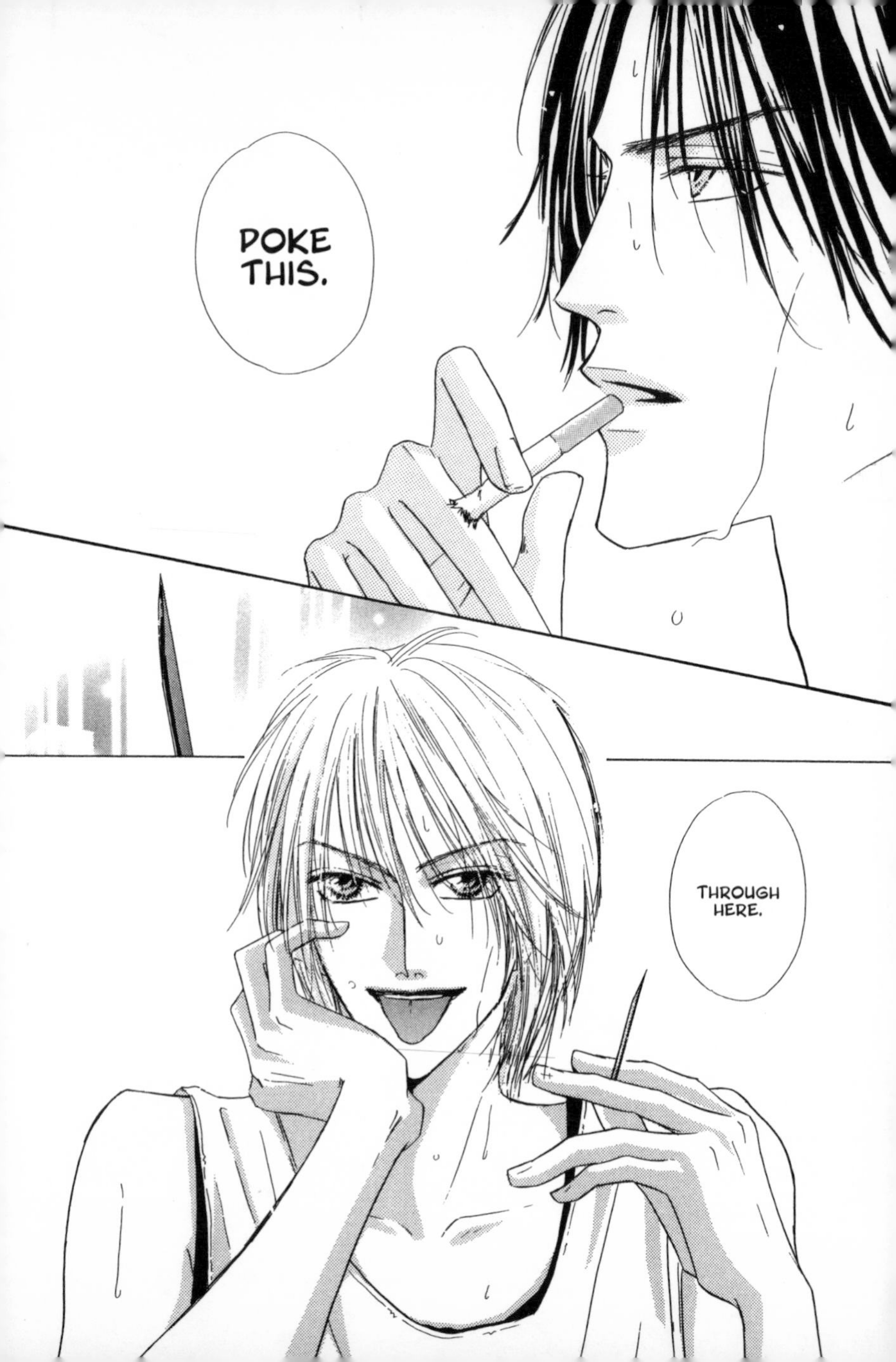
POKE THIS.
THROUGH HERE.

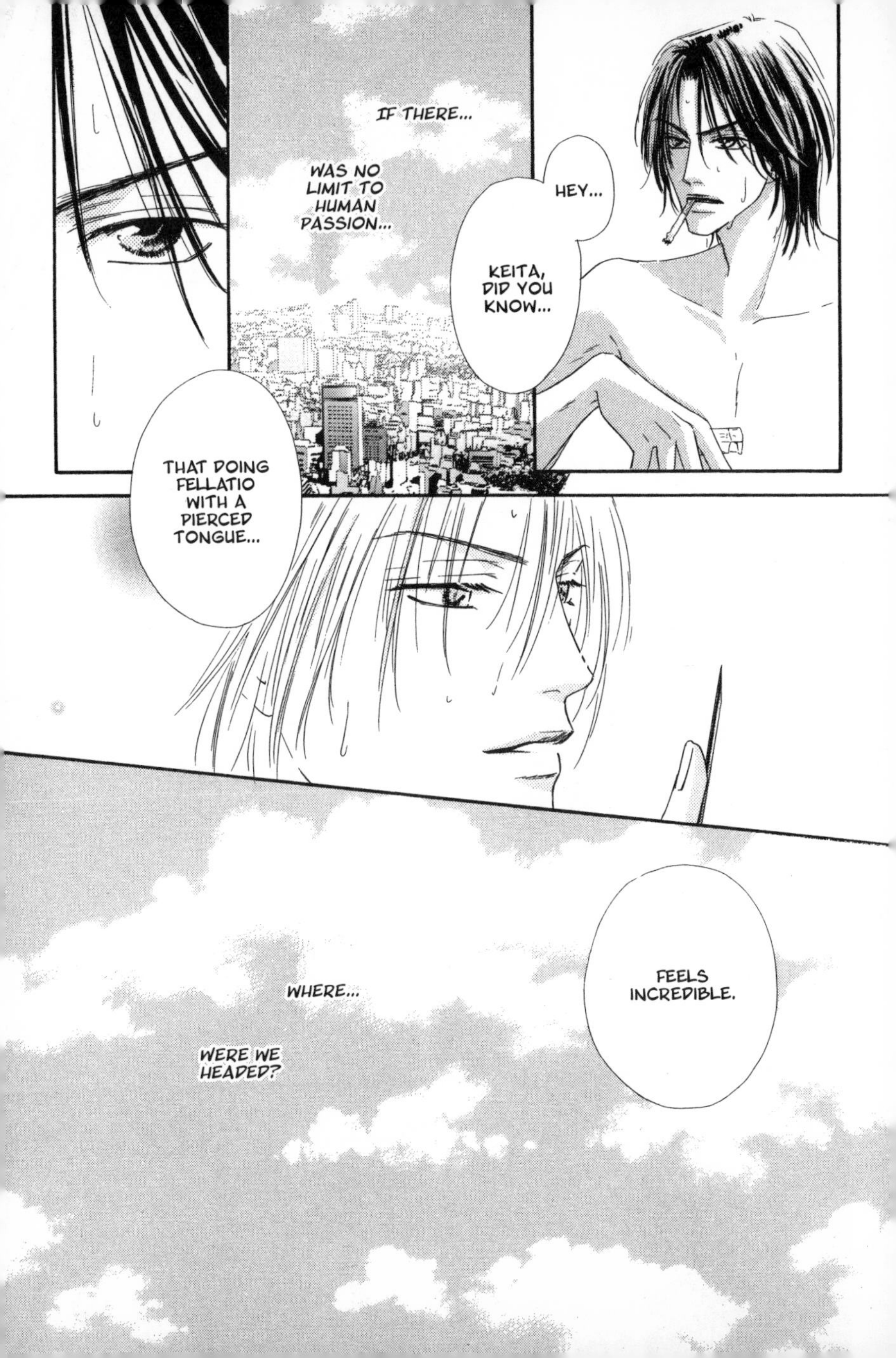
HEY...
KEITA, DID YOU KNOW...
IF THERE...
WAS NO LIMIT TO HUMAN PASSION...
THAT DOING FELLATIO WITH A PIERCED TONGUE...
FEELS INCREDIBLE.
WHERE...
WERE WE HEADED?

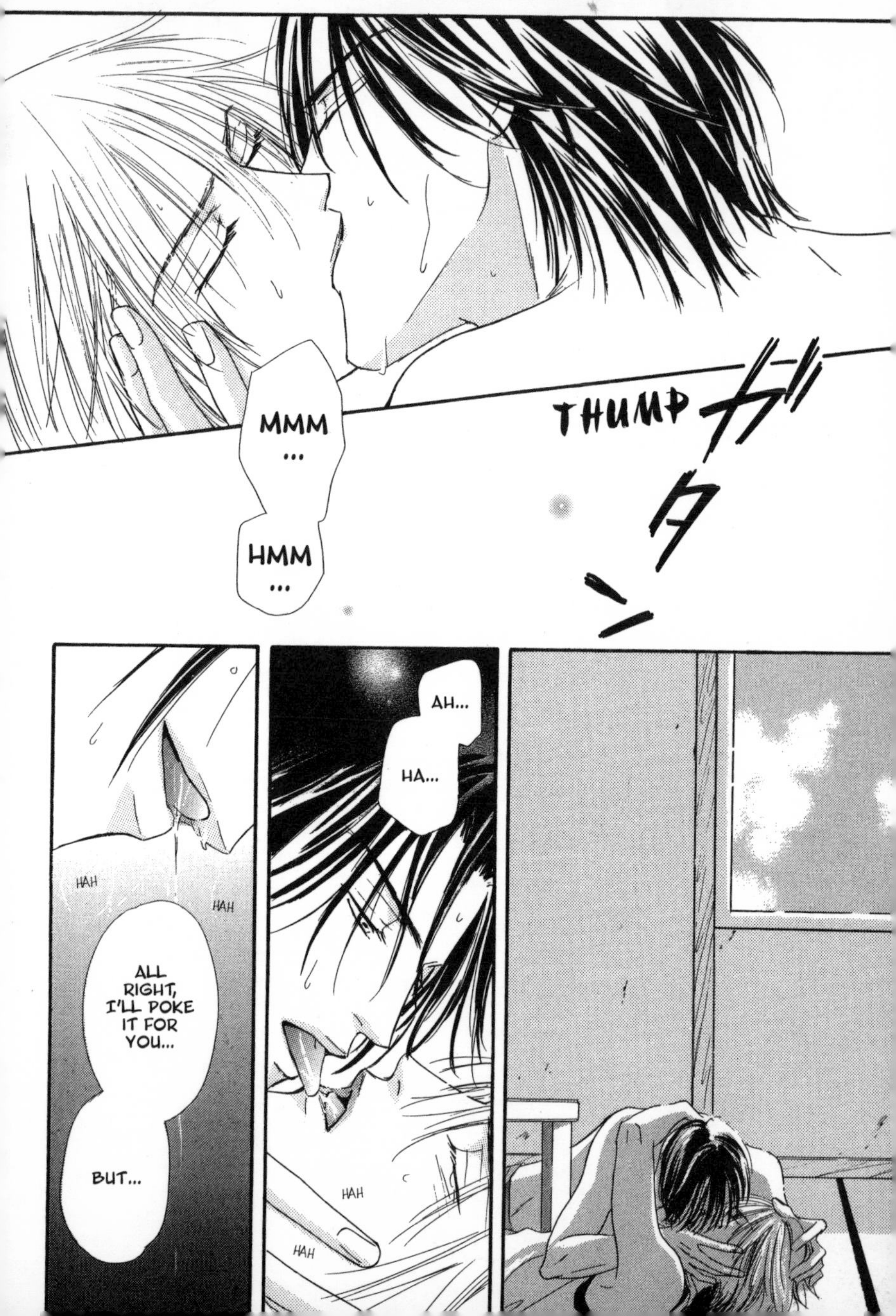
THUMP
ガタン
MMM...
HMM...
AH...
HA...
HAH
HAH
HAH
HAH
ALL RIGHT, I'LL POKE IT FOR YOU...
BUT...

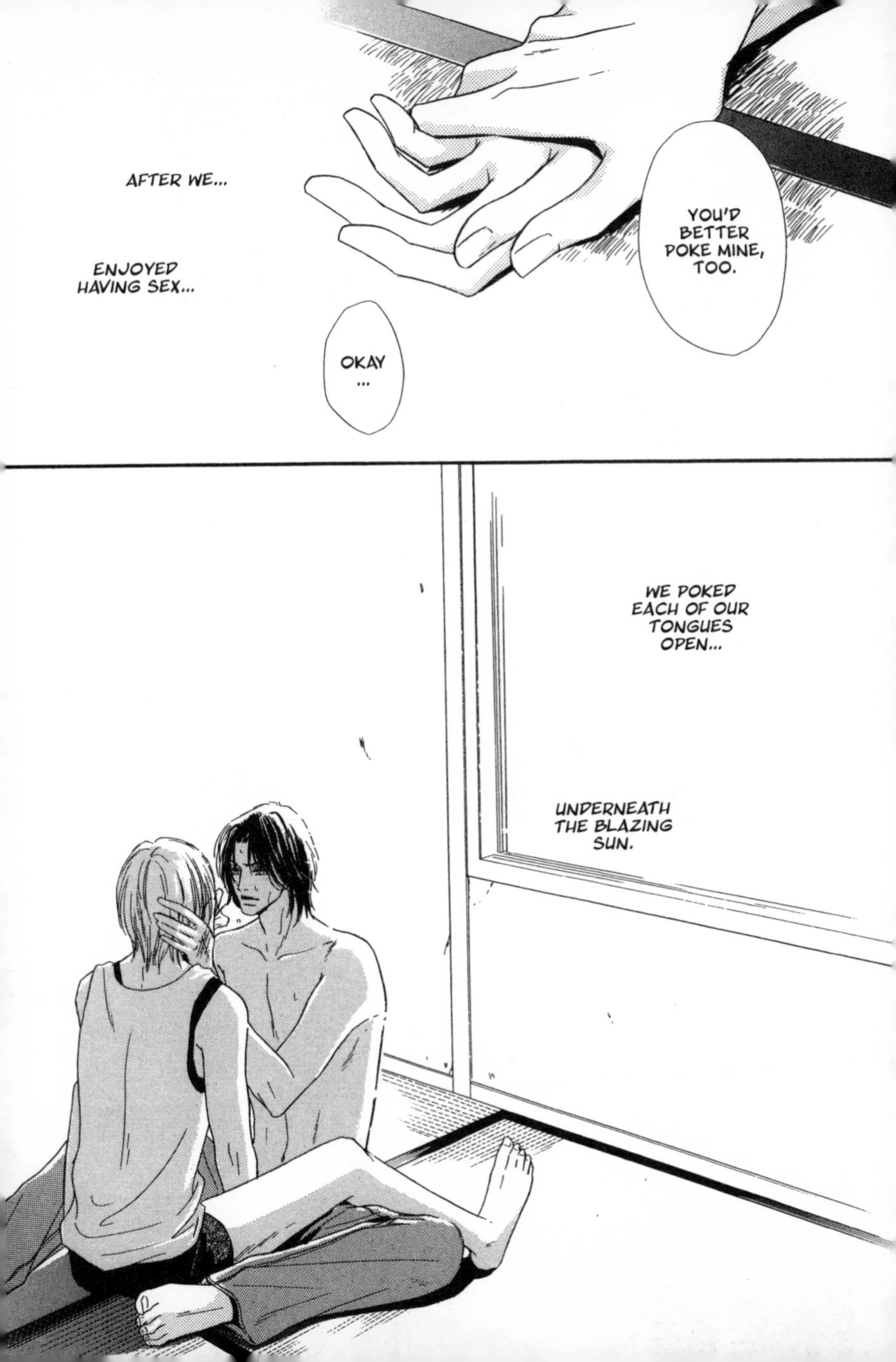
YOU'D BETTER POKE MINE, TOO.
OKAY ...
AFTER WE...
ENJOYED HAVING SEX...
WE POKED EACH OF OUR TONGUES OPEN...
UNDERNEATH THE BLAZING SUN.

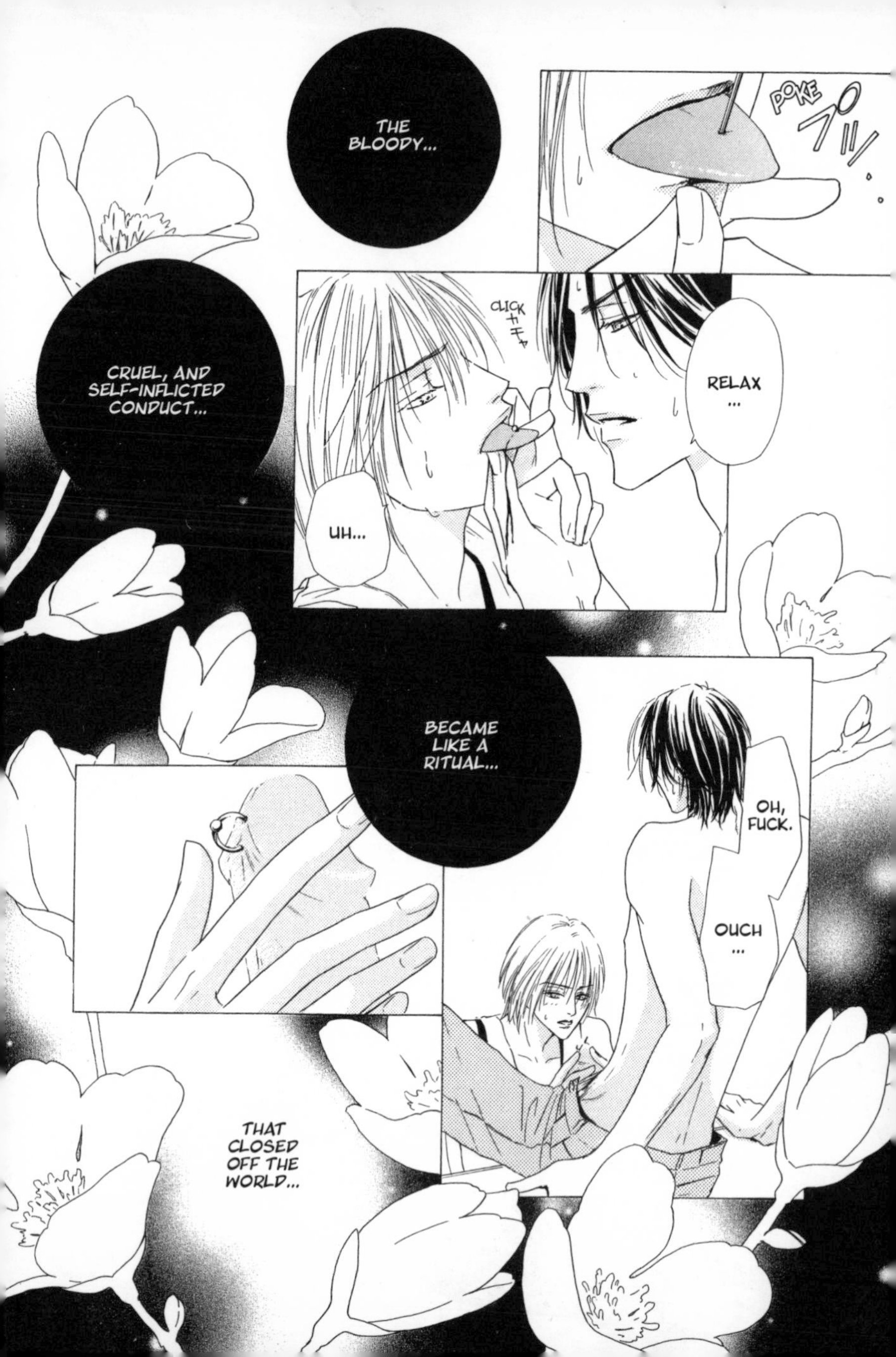
POKE
THE BLOODY...
RELAX ...
CLICK
UH...
CRUEL, AND SELF-INFLICTED CONDUCT...
BECAME LIKE A RITUAL...
OH, FUCK.
OUCH ...
THAT CLOSED OFF THE WORLD...

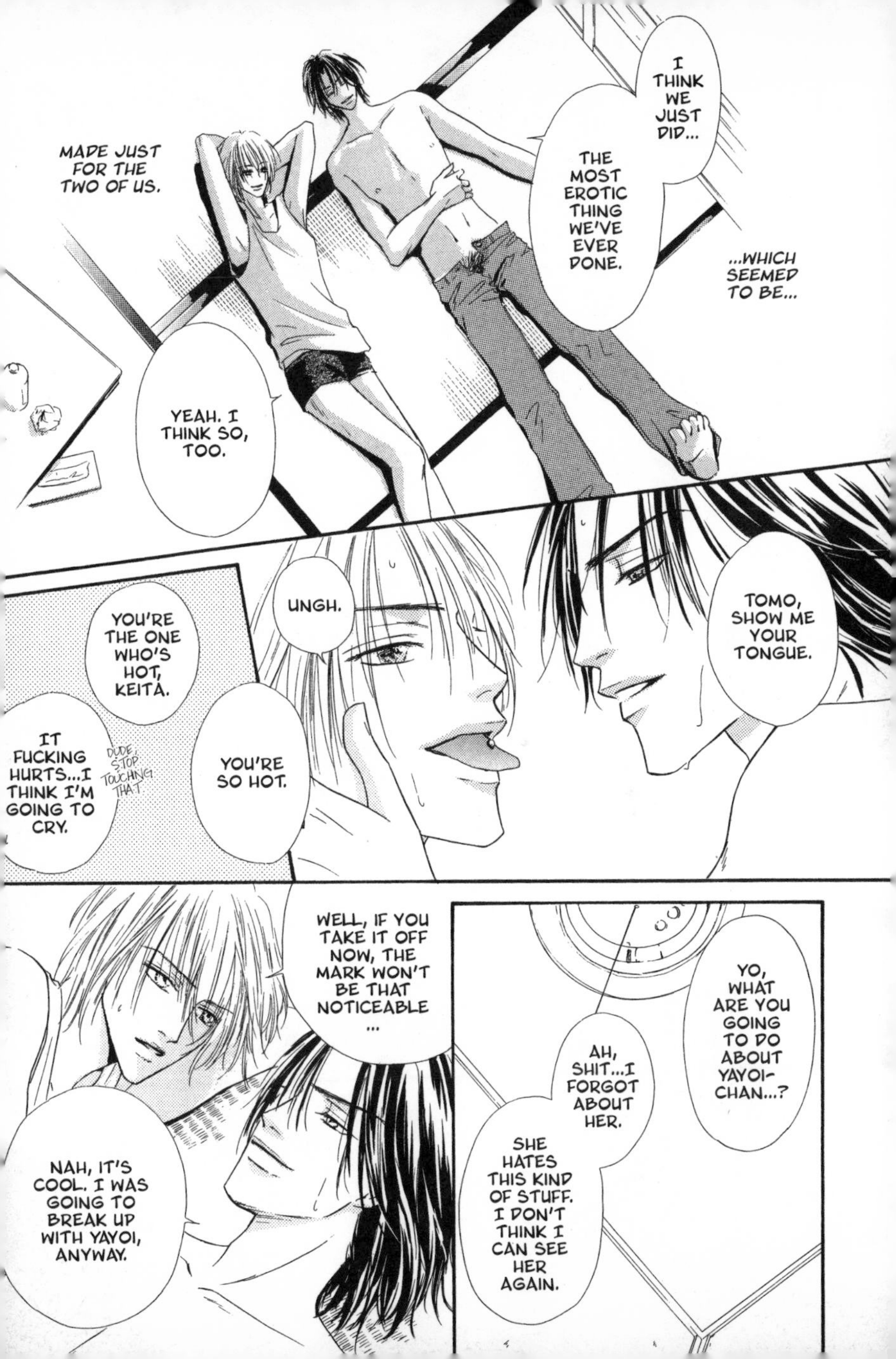
I THINK WE JUST DID...
THE MOST EROTIC THING WE'VE EVER DONE.
...WHICH SEEMED TO BE...
MADE JUST FOR THE TWO OF US.
YEAH. I THINK SO, TOO.
TOMO, SHOW ME YOUR TONGUE.
UNGH.
YOU'RE SO HOT.
YOU'RE THE ONE WHO'S HOT, KEITA.
IT FUCKING HURTS...I THINK I'M GOING TO CRY.
DUDE, STOP TOUCHING THAT
YO, WHAT ARE YOU GOING TO DO ABOUT YAYOI-CHAN...?
AH, SHIT...I FORGOT ABOUT HER.
SHE HATES THIS KIND OF STUFF. I DON'T THINK I CAN SEE HER AGAIN.
WELL, IF YOU TAKE IT OFF NOW, THE MARK WON'T BE THAT NOTICEABLE...
NAH, IT'S COOL. I WAS GOING TO BREAK UP WITH YAYOI, ANYWAY.

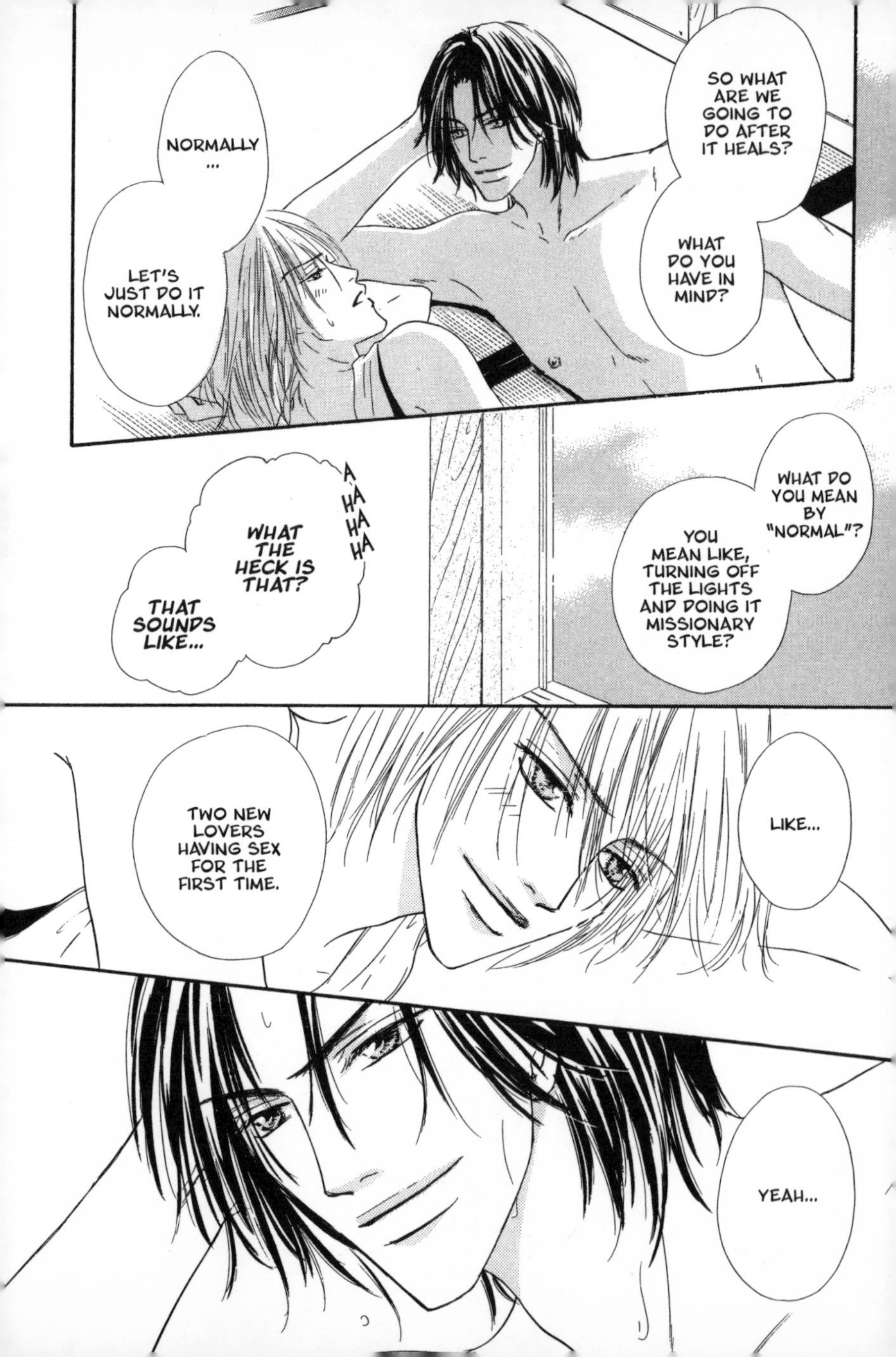
SO WHAT ARE WE GOING TO DO AFTER IT HEALS?
WHAT DO YOU HAVE IN MIND?
NORMALLY ...
LET'S JUST DO IT NORMALLY.
WHAT DO YOU MEAN BY "NORMAL"?
YOU MEAN LIKE, TURNING OFF THE LIGHTS AND DOING IT MISSIONARY STYLE?
AHAHAHA
WHAT THE HECK IS THAT?
THAT SOUNDS LIKE...
LIKE...
TWO NEW LOVERS HAVING SEX FOR THE FIRST TIME.
YEAH...

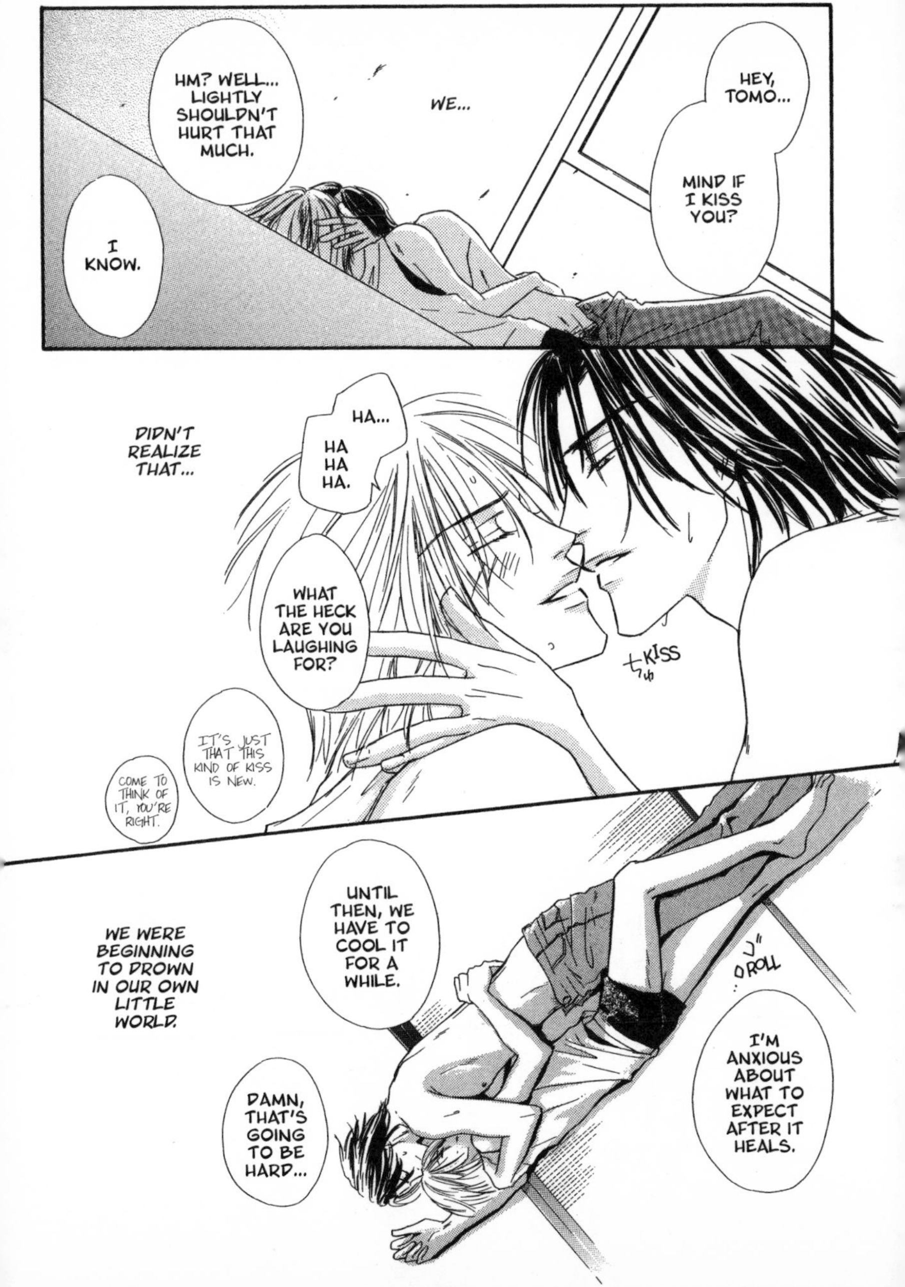
HEY, TOMO...
MIND IF I KISS YOU?
WE...
HM? WELL... LIGHTLY SHOULDN'T HURT THAT MUCH.
I KNOW.
HA... HA HA HA.
DIDN'T REALIZE THAT...
KISS
WHAT THE HECK ARE YOU LAUGHING FOR?
IT'S JUST THAT THIS KIND OF KISS IS NEW.
COME TO THINK OF IT, YOU'RE RIGHT.
ROLL
I'M ANXIOUS ABOUT WHAT TO EXPECT AFTER IT HEALS.
UNTIL THEN, WE HAVE TO COOL IT FOR A WHILE.
DAMN, THAT'S GOING TO BE HARD...
WE WERE BEGINNING TO DROWN IN OUR OWN LITTLE WORLD.

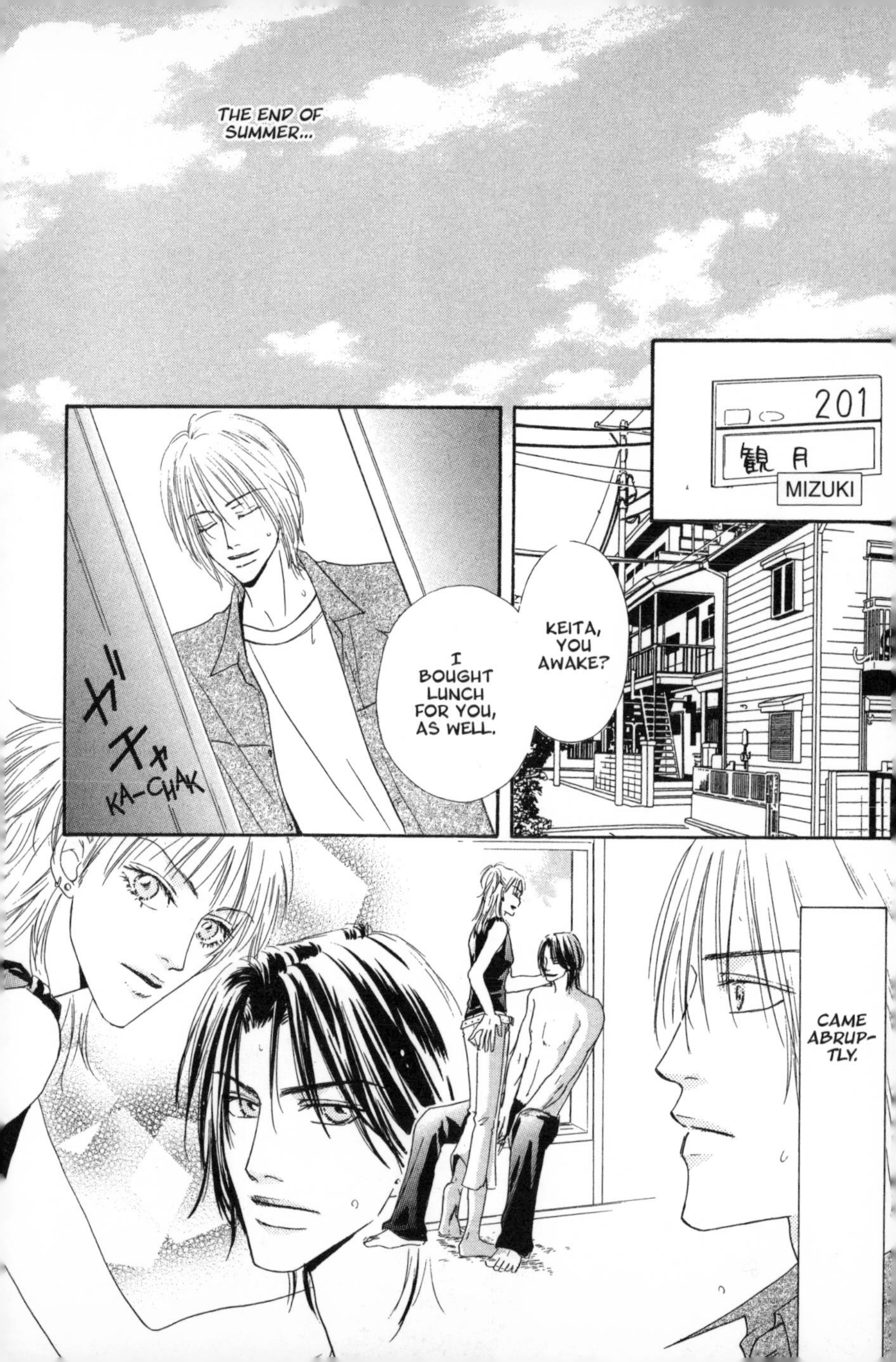
THE END OF SUMMER...
201
観月
MIZUKI
KEITA, YOU AWAKE?
I BOUGHT LUNCH FOR YOU, AS WELL.
ガチャ
KA-CHAK
CAME ABRUP-TLY.

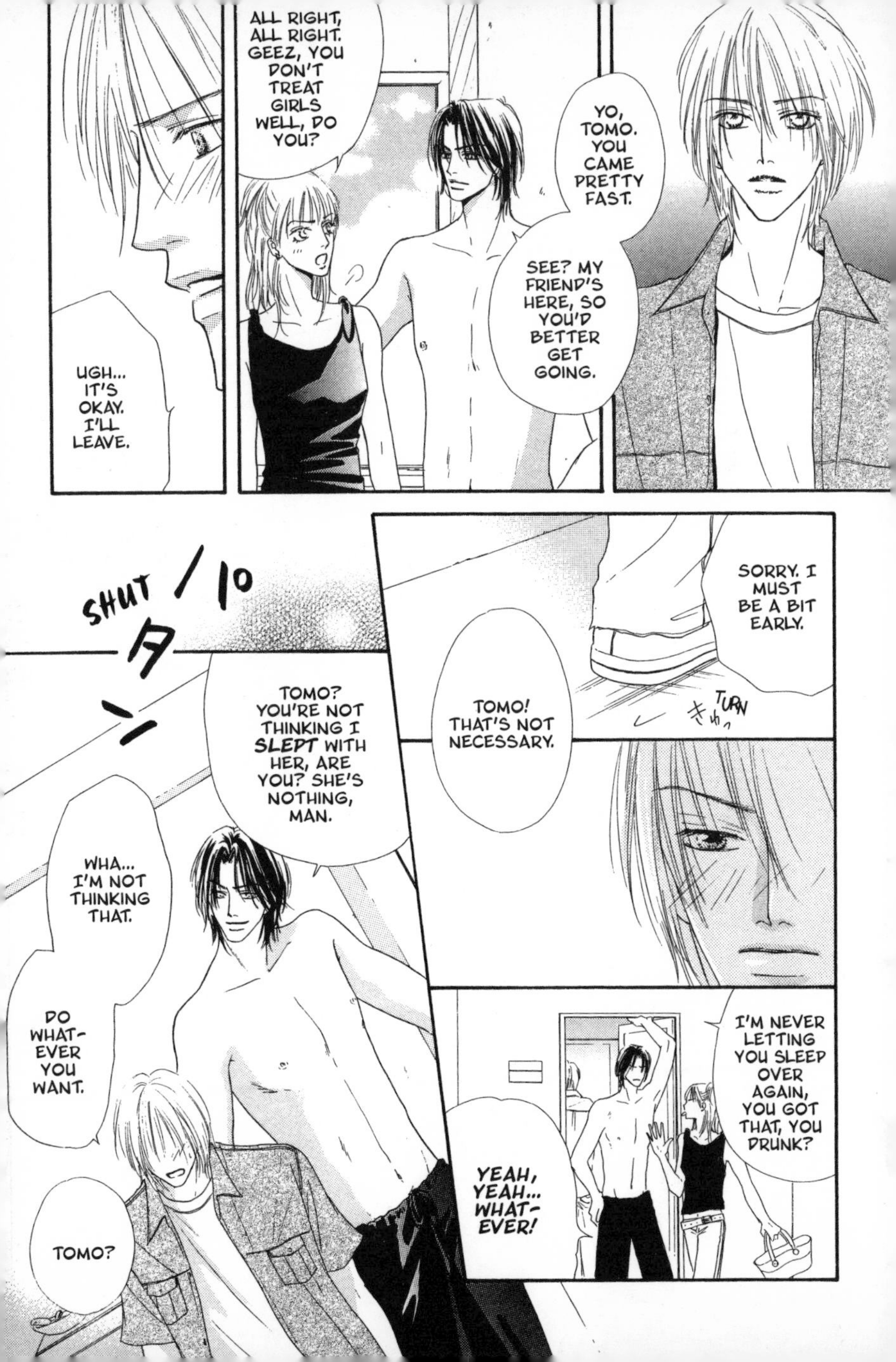
YO, TOMO. YOU CAME PRETTY FAST.
SEE? MY FRIEND'S HERE, SO YOU'D BETTER GET GOING.
ALL RIGHT, ALL RIGHT. GEEZ, YOU DON'T TREAT GIRLS WELL, DO YOU?
UGH... IT'S OKAY. I'LL LEAVE.
SORRY. I MUST BE A BIT EARLY.
TOMO! THAT'S NOT NECESSARY.
TURN
I'M NEVER LETTING YOU SLEEP OVER AGAIN, YOU GOT THAT, YOU DRUNK?
YEAH, YEAH... WHAT-EVER!
SHUT
TOMO? YOU'RE NOT THINKING I **SLEPT** WITH HER, ARE YOU? SHE'S NOTHING, MAN.
WHA... I'M NOT THINKING THAT.
DO WHAT-EVER YOU WANT.
TOMO?

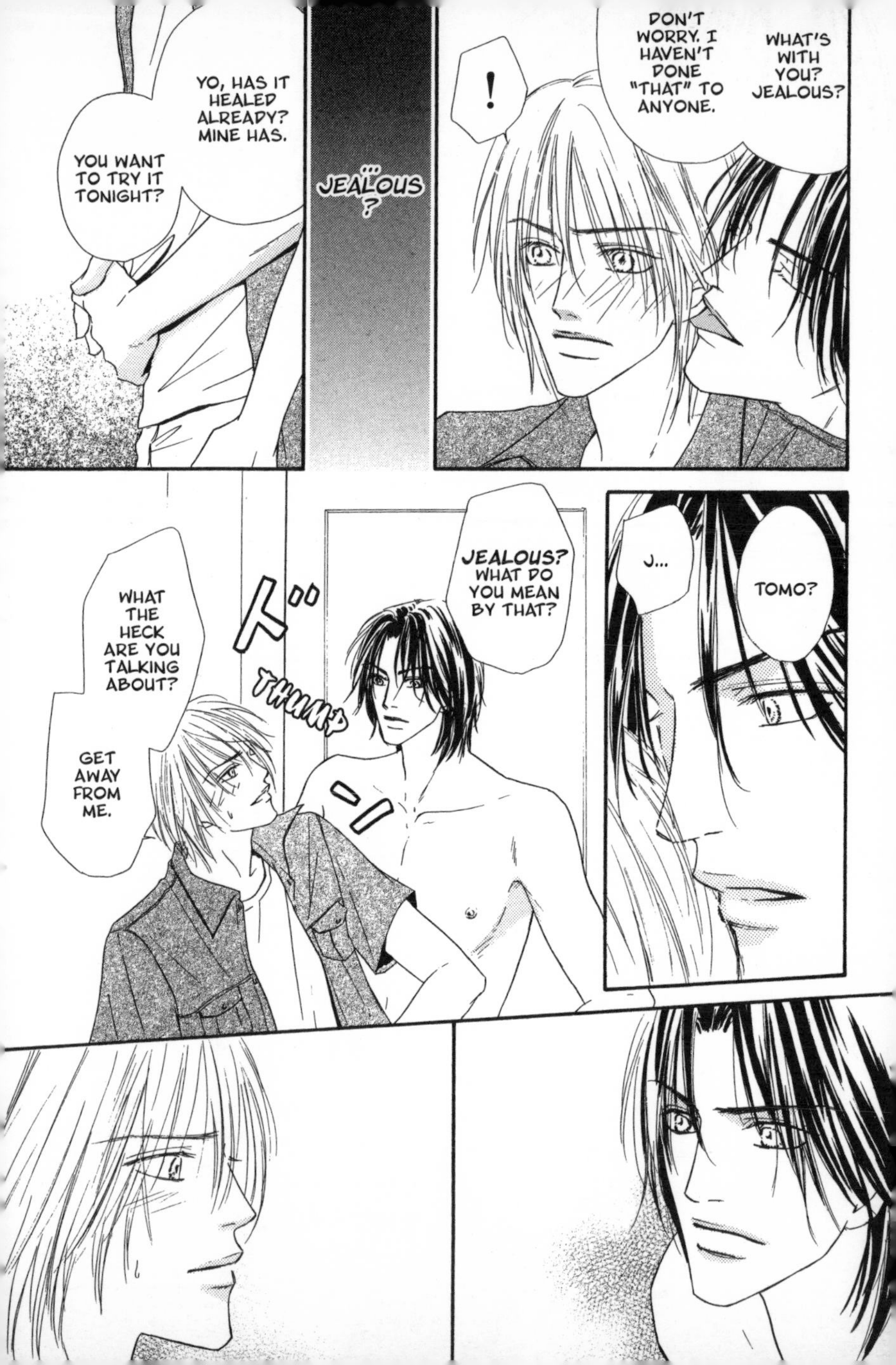
WHAT'S WITH YOU? JEALOUS?
DON'T WORRY. I HAVEN'T DONE "THAT" TO ANYONE.
!
...JEALOUS?
YO, HAS IT HEALED ALREADY? MINE HAS.
YOU WANT TO TRY IT TONIGHT?
TOMO?
J...
JEALOUS? WHAT DO YOU MEAN BY THAT?
THUMP
WHAT THE HECK ARE YOU TALKING ABOUT?
GET AWAY FROM ME.

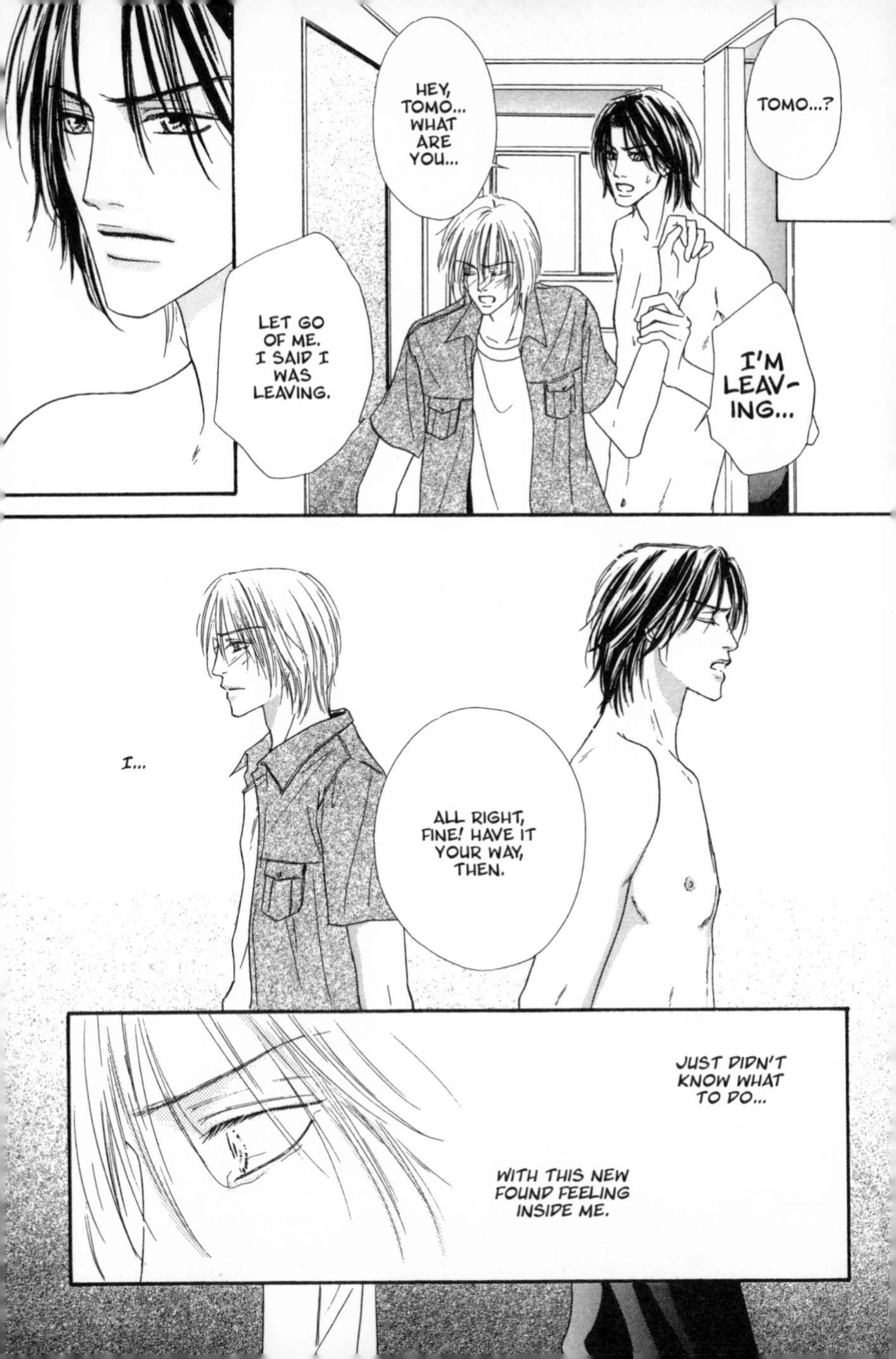
TOMO...?
HEY, TOMO... WHAT ARE YOU...
I'M LEAV-ING...
LET GO OF ME. I SAID I WAS LEAVING.
ALL RIGHT, FINE! HAVE IT YOUR WAY, THEN.
I...
JUST DIDN'T KNOW WHAT TO DO...
WITH THIS NEW FOUND FEELING INSIDE ME.

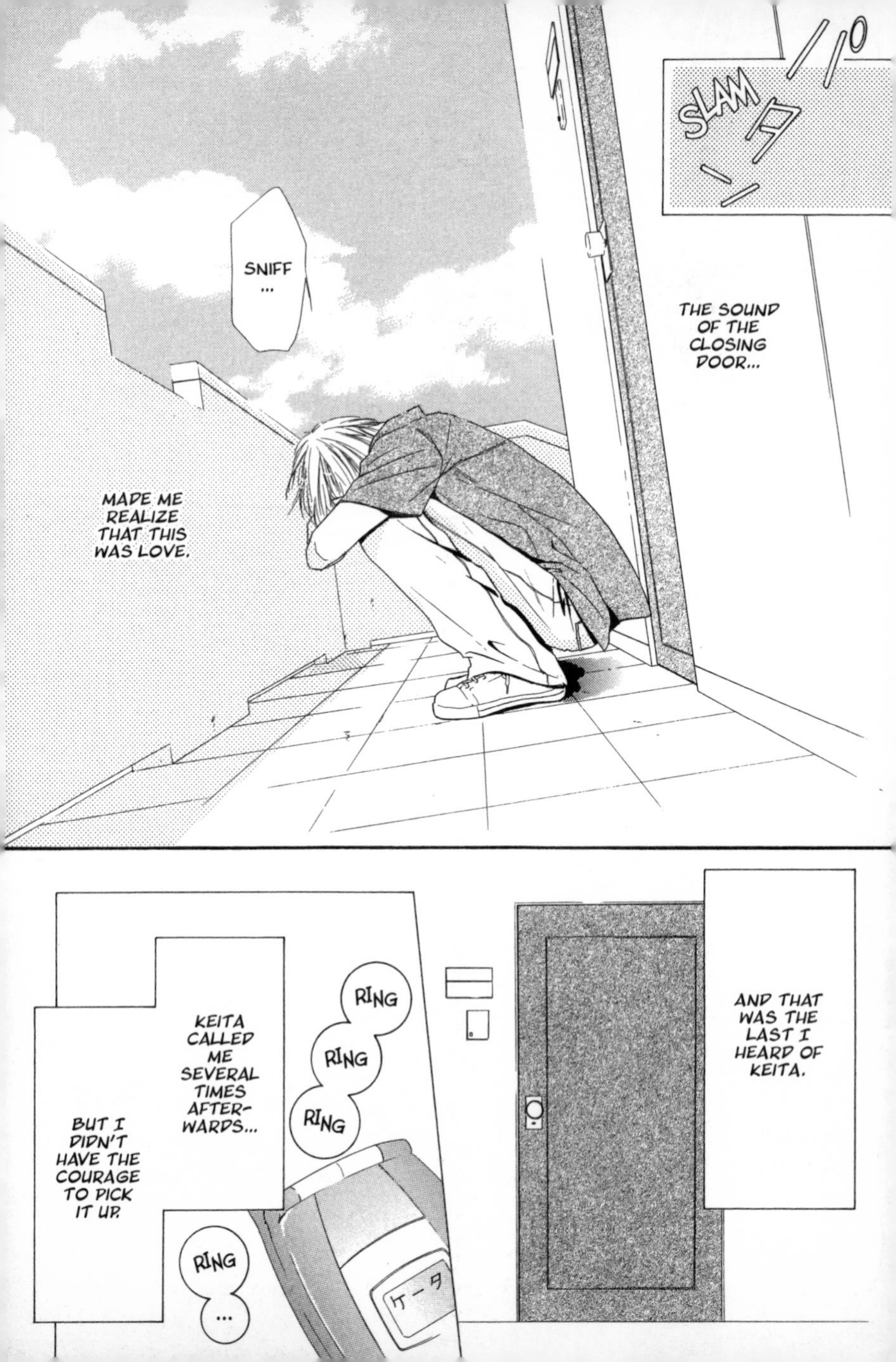

SLAM
THE SOUND OF THE CLOSING DOOR...
SNIFF ...
MADE ME REALIZE THAT THIS WAS LOVE.
AND THAT WAS THE LAST I HEARD OF KEITA.
RING
RING
RING
KEITA CALLED ME SEVERAL TIMES AFTERWARDS...
BUT I DIDN'T HAVE THE COURAGE TO PICK IT UP.
ケータ
RING
...

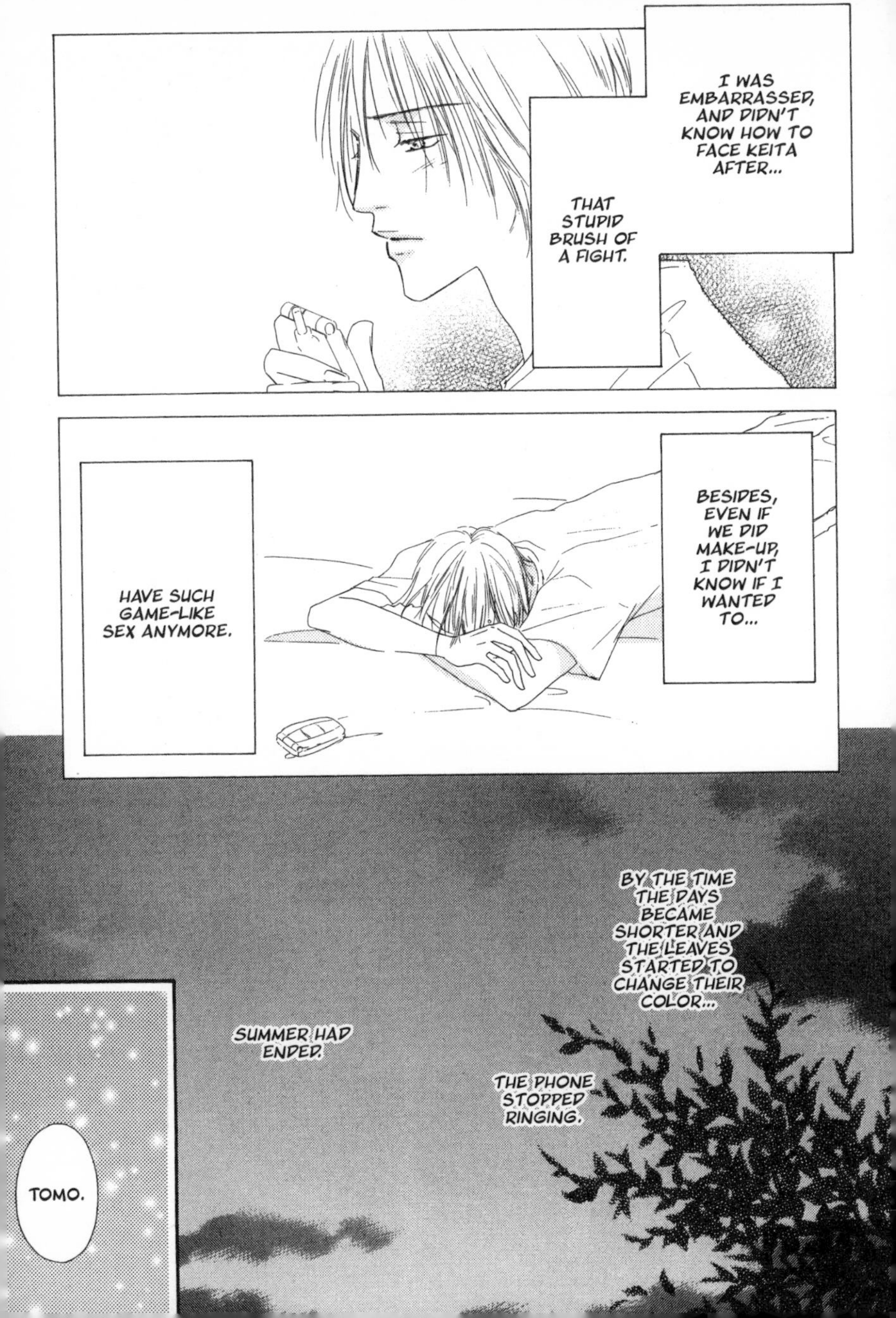
I WAS EMBARRASSED, AND DIDN'T KNOW HOW TO FACE KEITA AFTER...
THAT STUPID BRUSH OF A FIGHT.
BESIDES, EVEN IF WE DID MAKE-UP, I DIDN'T KNOW IF I WANTED TO...
HAVE SUCH GAME-LIKE SEX ANYMORE.
BY THE TIME THE DAYS BECAME SHORTER AND THE LEAVES STARTED TO CHANGE THEIR COLOR...
SUMMER HAD ENDED.
THE PHONE STOPPED RINGING.
TOMO.

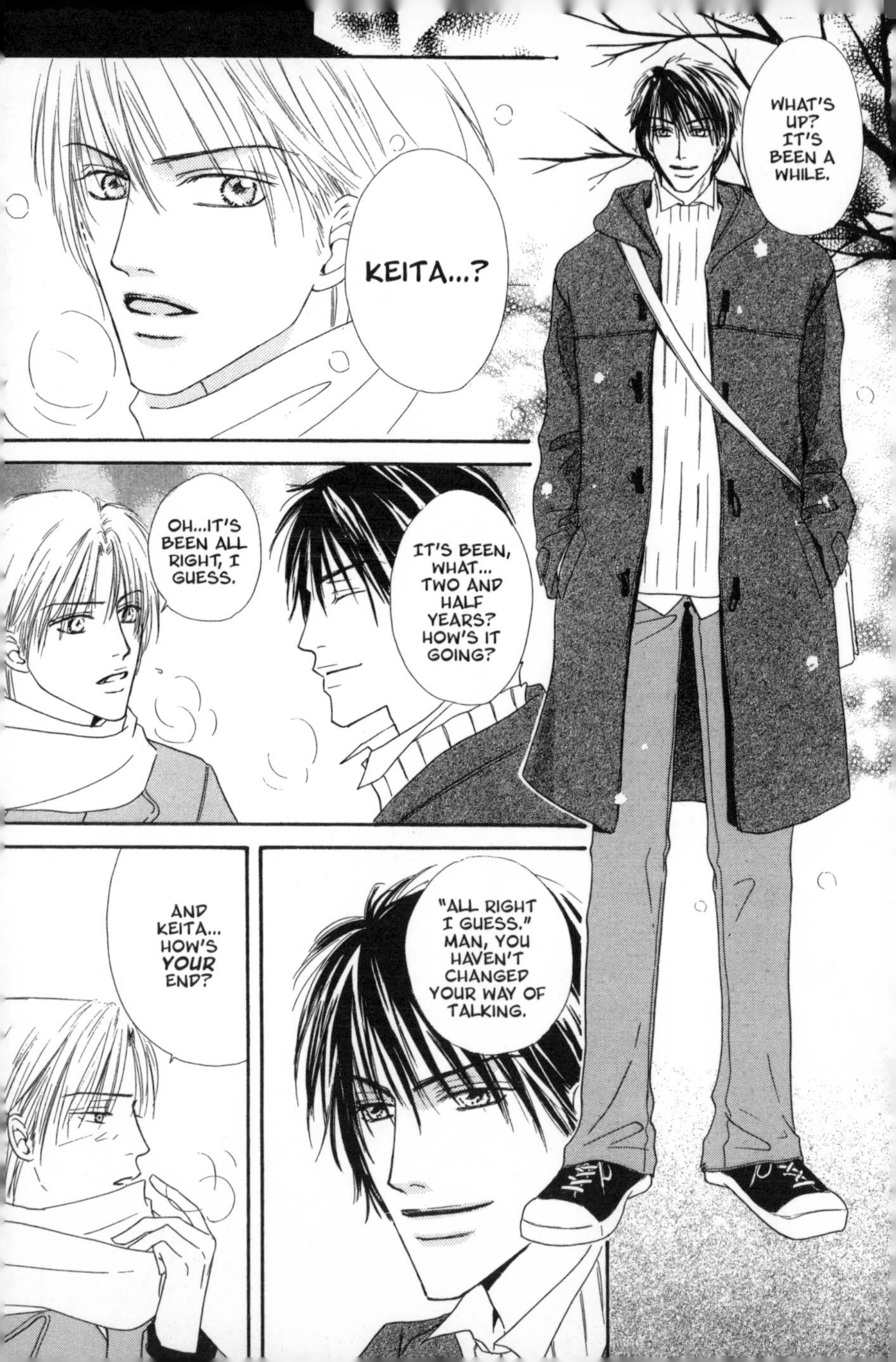
WHAT'S UP? IT'S BEEN A WHILE.
KEITA...?
IT'S BEEN, WHAT... TWO AND HALF YEARS? HOW'S IT GOING?
OH...IT'S BEEN ALL RIGHT, I GUESS.
"ALL RIGHT I GUESS." MAN, YOU HAVEN'T CHANGED YOUR WAY OF TALKING.
AND KEITA... HOW'S YOUR END?

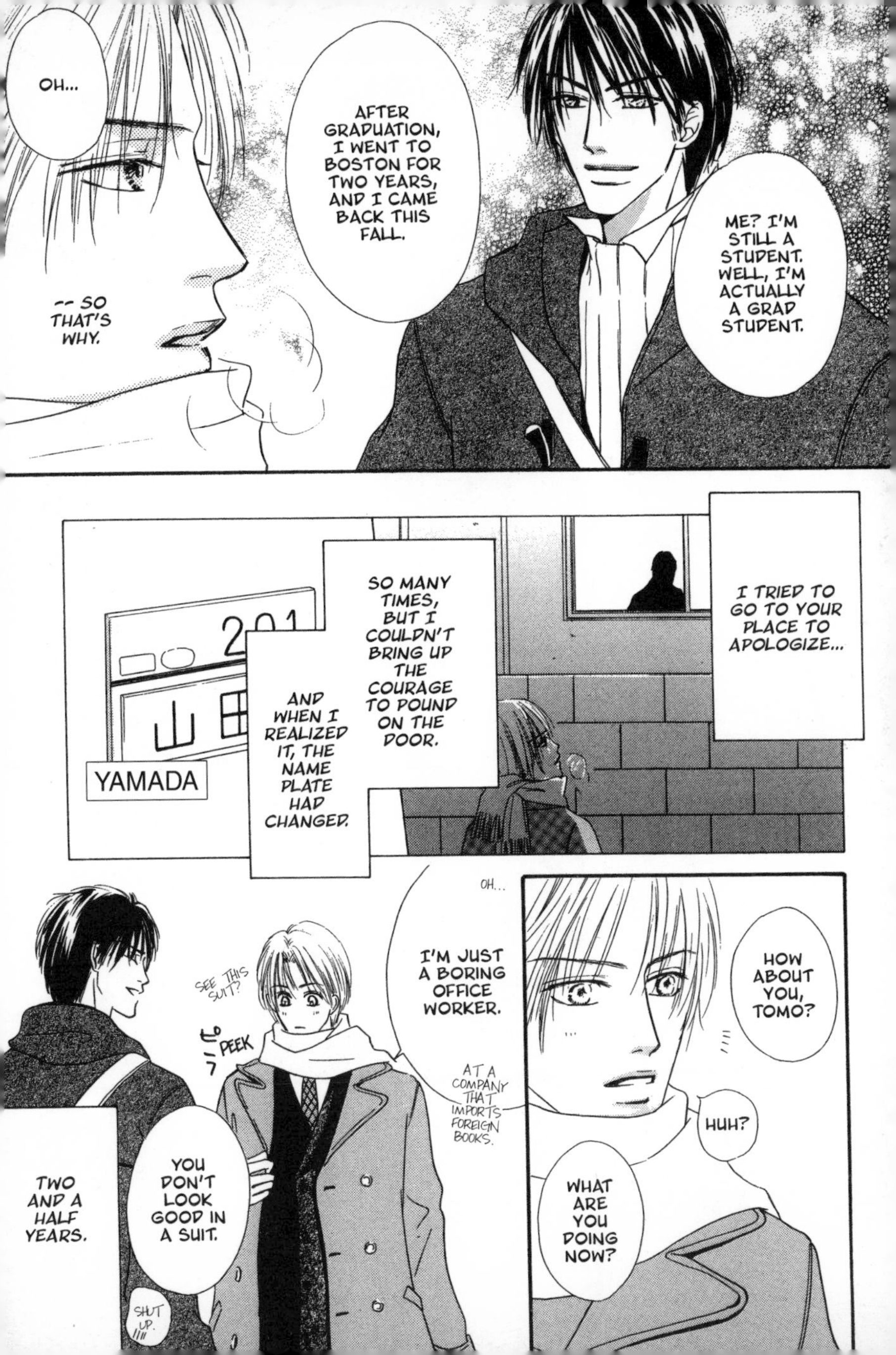
ME? I'M STILL A STUDENT. WELL, I'M ACTUALLY A GRAD STUDENT.
AFTER GRADUATION, I WENT TO BOSTON FOR TWO YEARS, AND I CAME BACK THIS FALL.
OH...
-- SO THAT'S WHY.
I TRIED TO GO TO YOUR PLACE TO APOLOGIZE...
SO MANY TIMES, BUT I COULDN'T BRING UP THE COURAGE TO POUND ON THE DOOR.
AND WHEN I REALIZED IT, THE NAME PLATE HAD CHANGED.
201
YAMADA
HOW ABOUT YOU, TOMO?
HUH?
WHAT ARE YOU DOING NOW?
OH...
I'M JUST A BORING OFFICE WORKER.
AT A COMPANY THAT IMPORTS FOREIGN BOOKS.
SEE THIS SUIT?
PEEK
YOU DON'T LOOK GOOD IN A SUIT.
SHUT UP.
TWO AND A HALF YEARS.

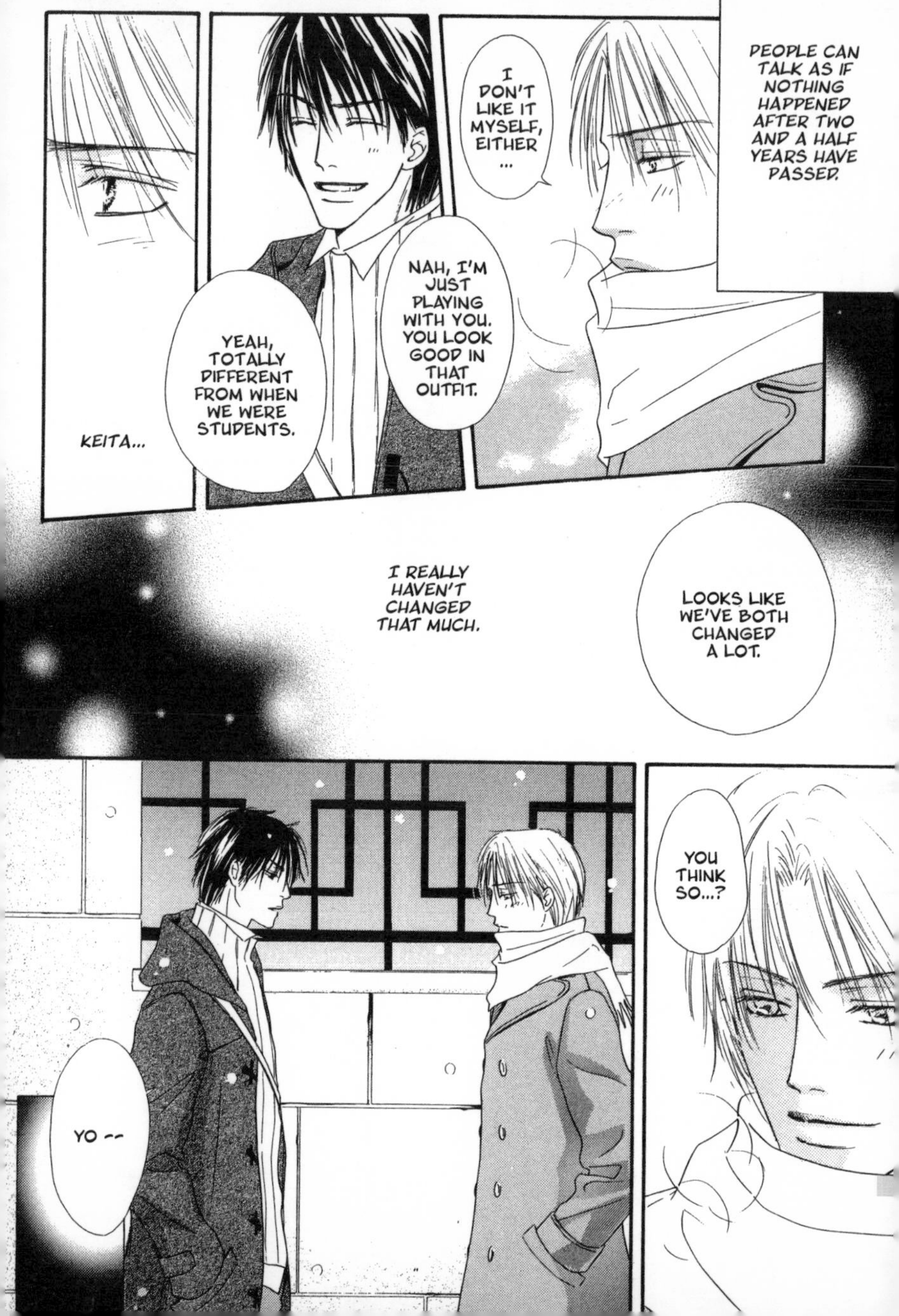
PEOPLE CAN TALK AS IF NOTHING HAPPENED AFTER TWO AND A HALF YEARS HAVE PASSED.
I DON'T LIKE IT MYSELF, EITHER ...
NAH, I'M JUST PLAYING WITH YOU. YOU LOOK GOOD IN THAT OUTFIT.
YEAH, TOTALLY DIFFERENT FROM WHEN WE WERE STUDENTS.
KEITA...
LOOKS LIKE WE'VE BOTH CHANGED A LOT.
I REALLY HAVEN'T CHANGED THAT MUCH.
YOU THINK SO...?
YO --

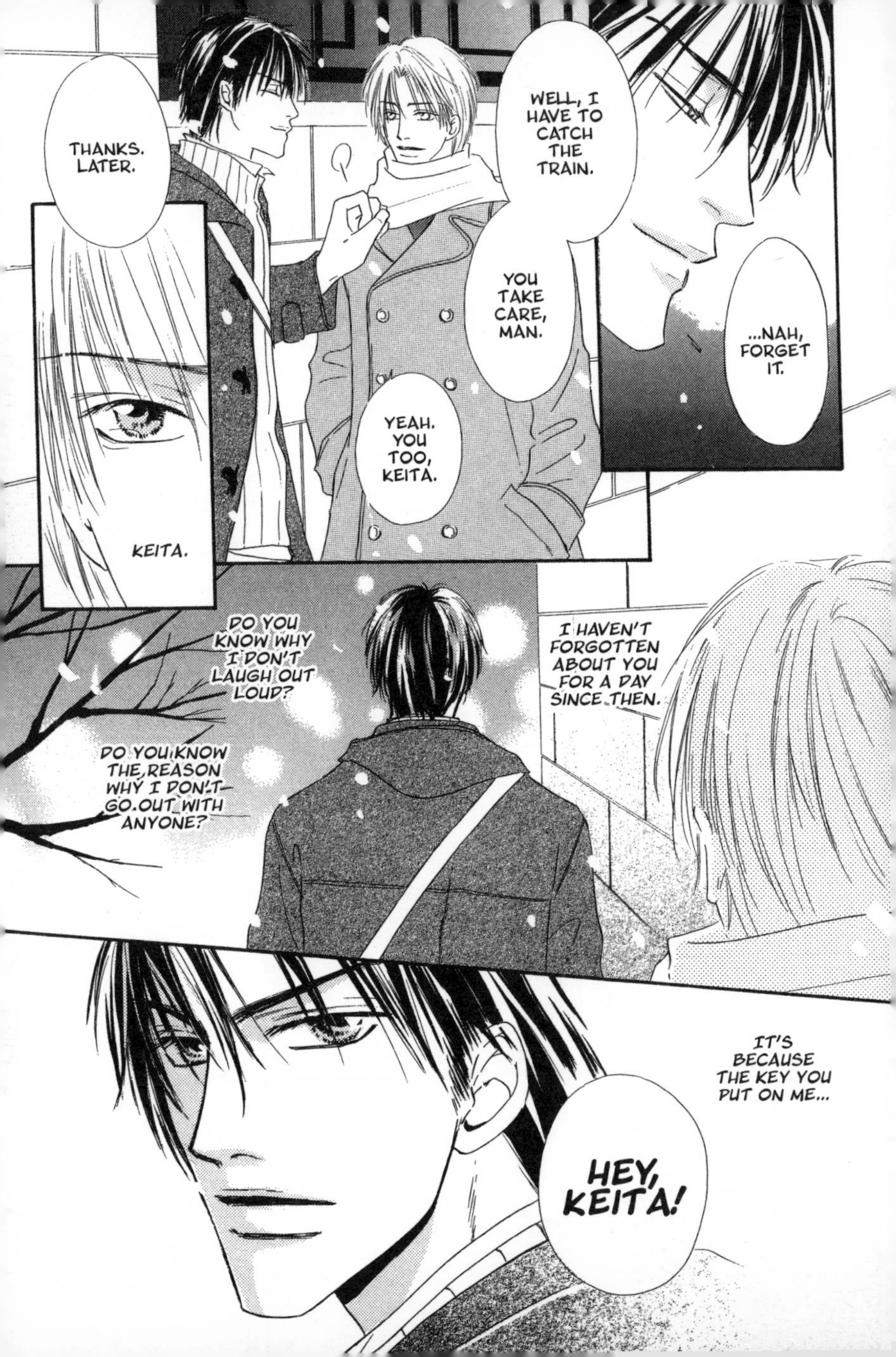
...NAH, FORGET IT.
WELL, I HAVE TO CATCH THE TRAIN.
THANKS. LATER.
YOU TAKE CARE, MAN.
YEAH. YOU TOO, KEITA.
KEITA.
I HAVEN'T FORGOTTEN ABOUT YOU FOR A DAY SINCE THEN.
DO YOU KNOW WHY I DON'T LAUGH OUT LOUD?
DO YOU KNOW THE REASON WHY I DON'T GO OUT WITH ANYONE?
IT'S BECAUSE THE KEY YOU PUT ON ME...
HEY, KEITA!

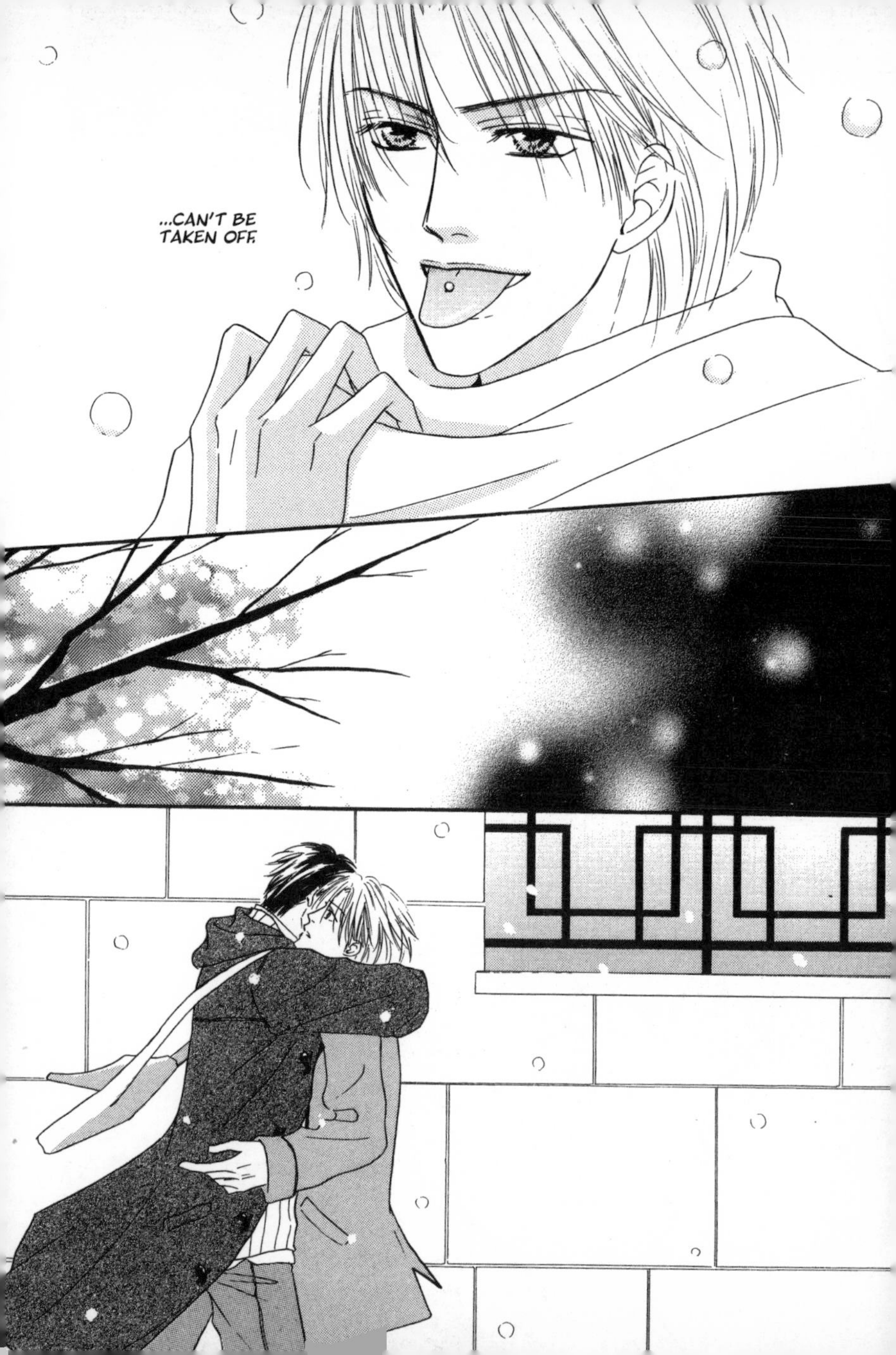
...CAN'T BE
TAKEN OFF.

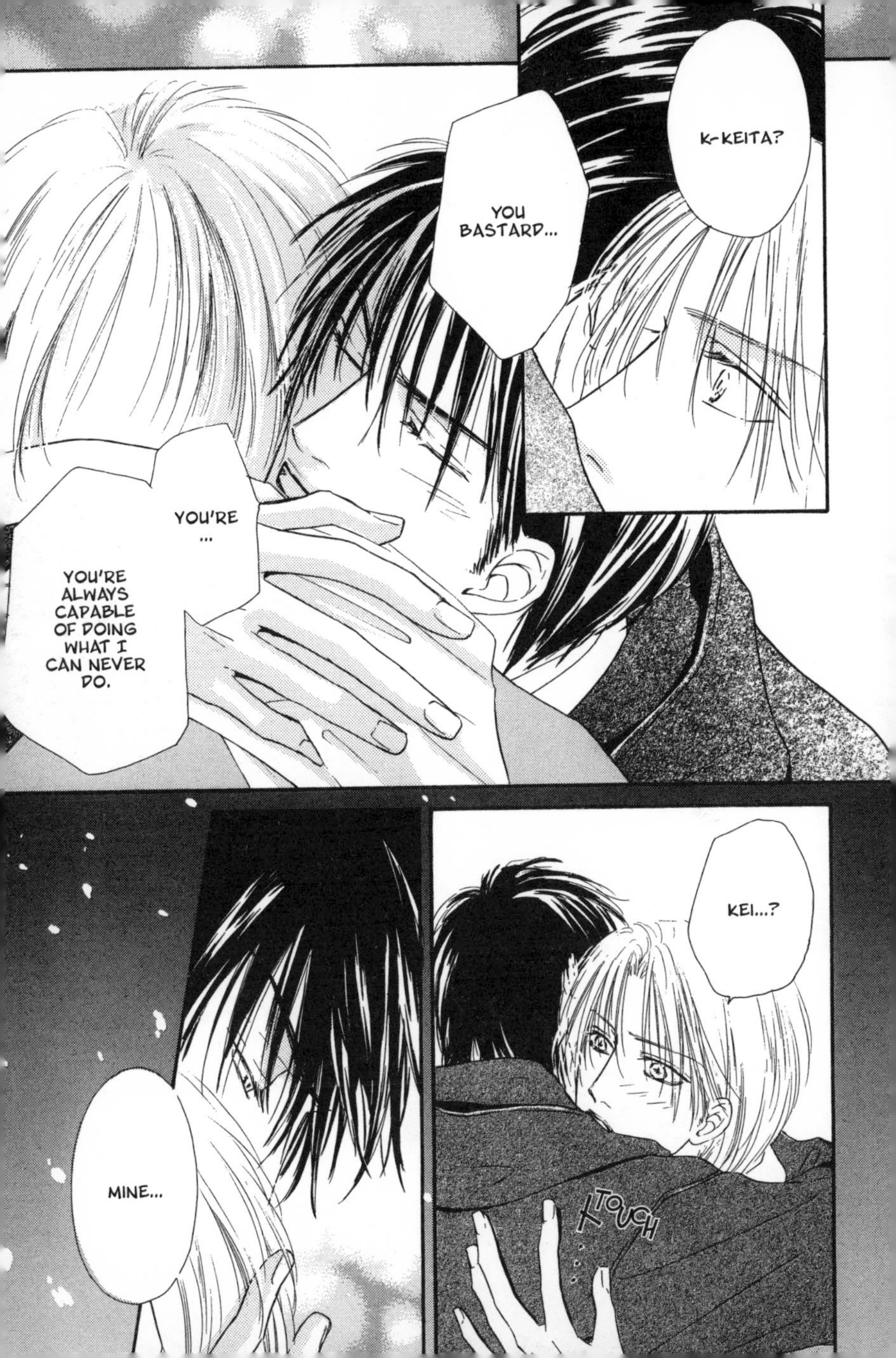
K-KEITA?
YOU BASTARD...
YOU'RE ...
YOU'RE ALWAYS CAPABLE OF DOING WHAT I CAN NEVER DO.
KEI...?
TOUCH
MINE...

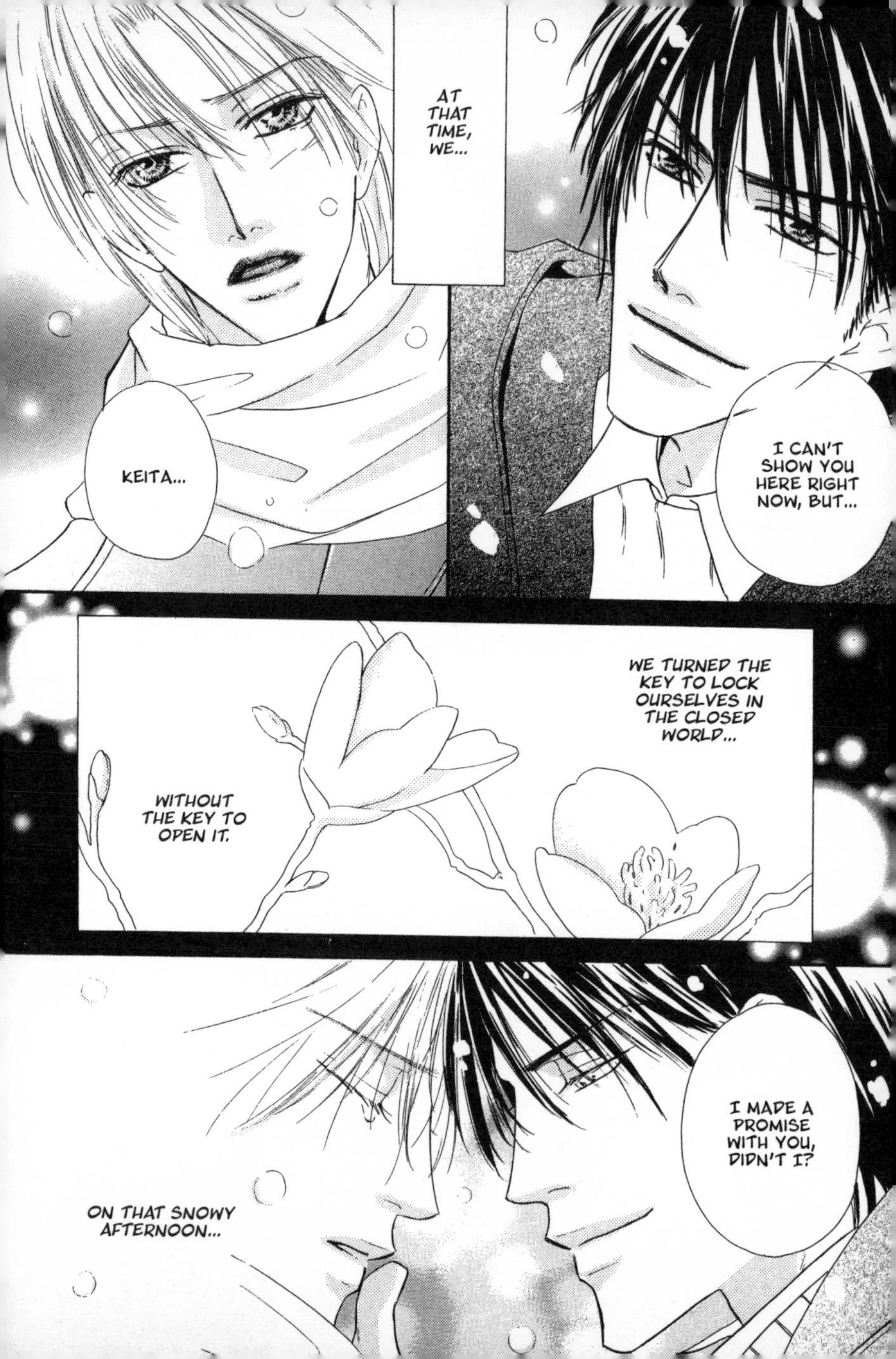
I CAN'T SHOW YOU HERE RIGHT NOW, BUT...
AT THAT TIME, WE...
KEITA...
WE TURNED THE KEY TO LOCK OURSELVES IN THE CLOSED WORLD...
WITHOUT THE KEY TO OPEN IT.
I MADE A PROMISE WITH YOU, DIDN'T I?
ON THAT SNOWY AFTERNOON...

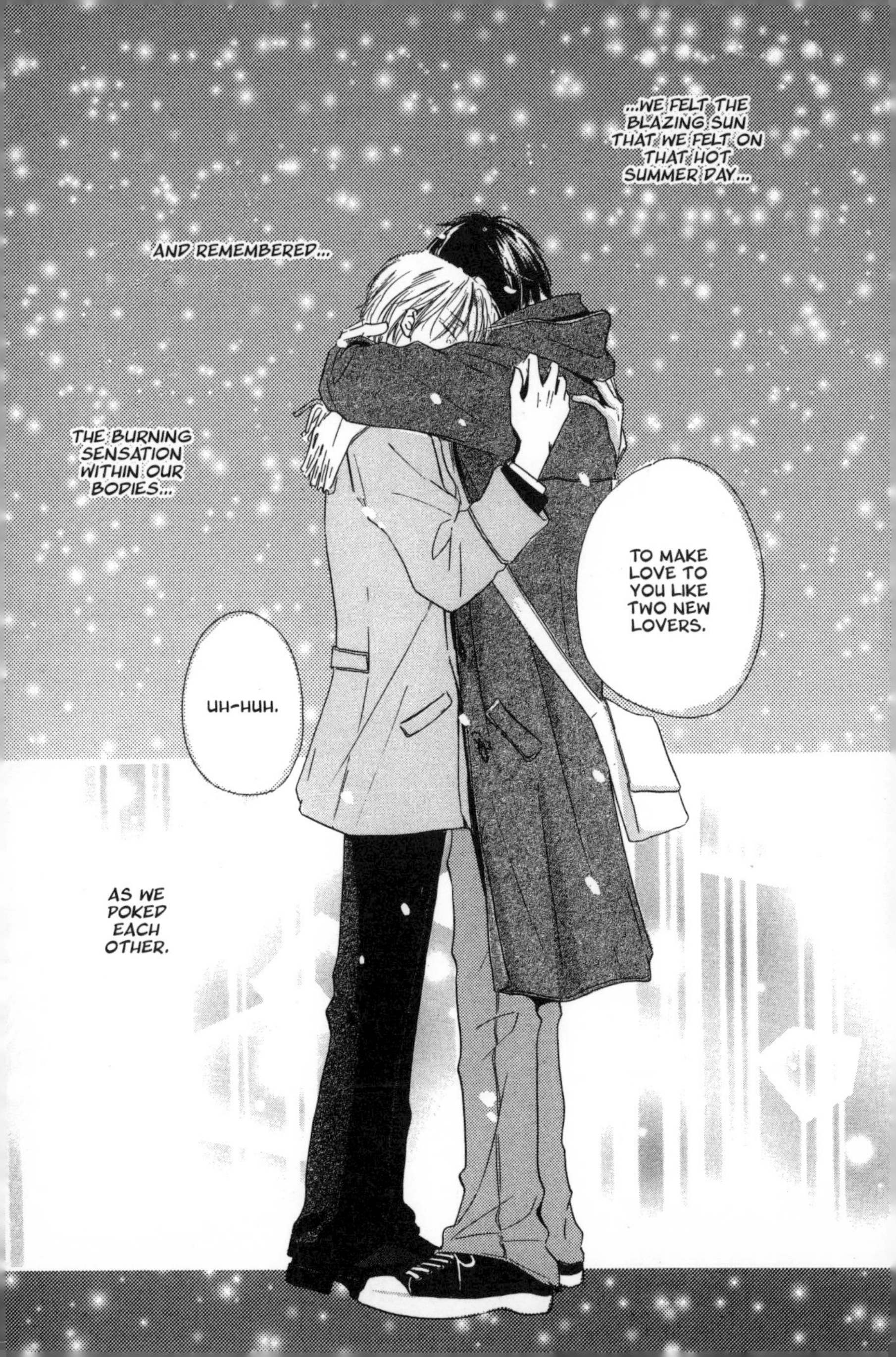
...WE FELT THE BLAZING SUN THAT WE FELT ON THAT HOT SUMMER DAY...
AND REMEMBERED...
THE BURNING SENSATION WITHIN OUR BODIES...
TO MAKE LOVE TO YOU LIKE TWO NEW LOVERS.
UH-HUH.
AS WE POKED EACH OTHER.

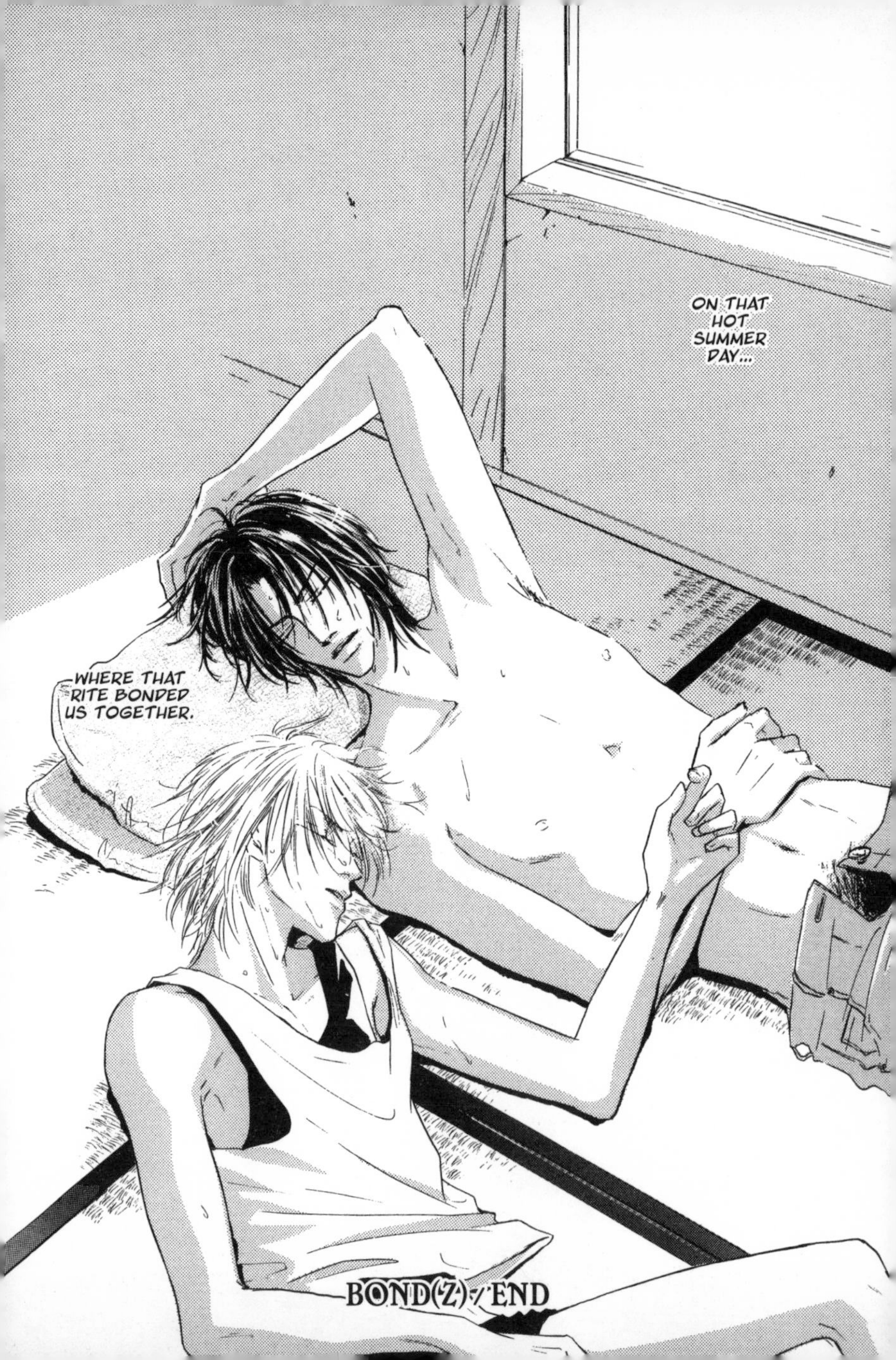
ON THAT HOT SUMMER DAY...
WHERE THAT RITE BONDED US TOGETHER.
BOND(Z) / END

Bond [bond] (noun)
1. (by love or for profit) a connection, tie, to unite
2. [used as plural] restrain, bind
3. a contract, an agreement
4. [used as singular] join, stick together (condition of;)
5. glue

Taken from Kenkyusha's LIGHT HOUSE dictionary.

bonds

...

situation

...

KITAN garden

...

sakura

Presented by Tōko Kawai

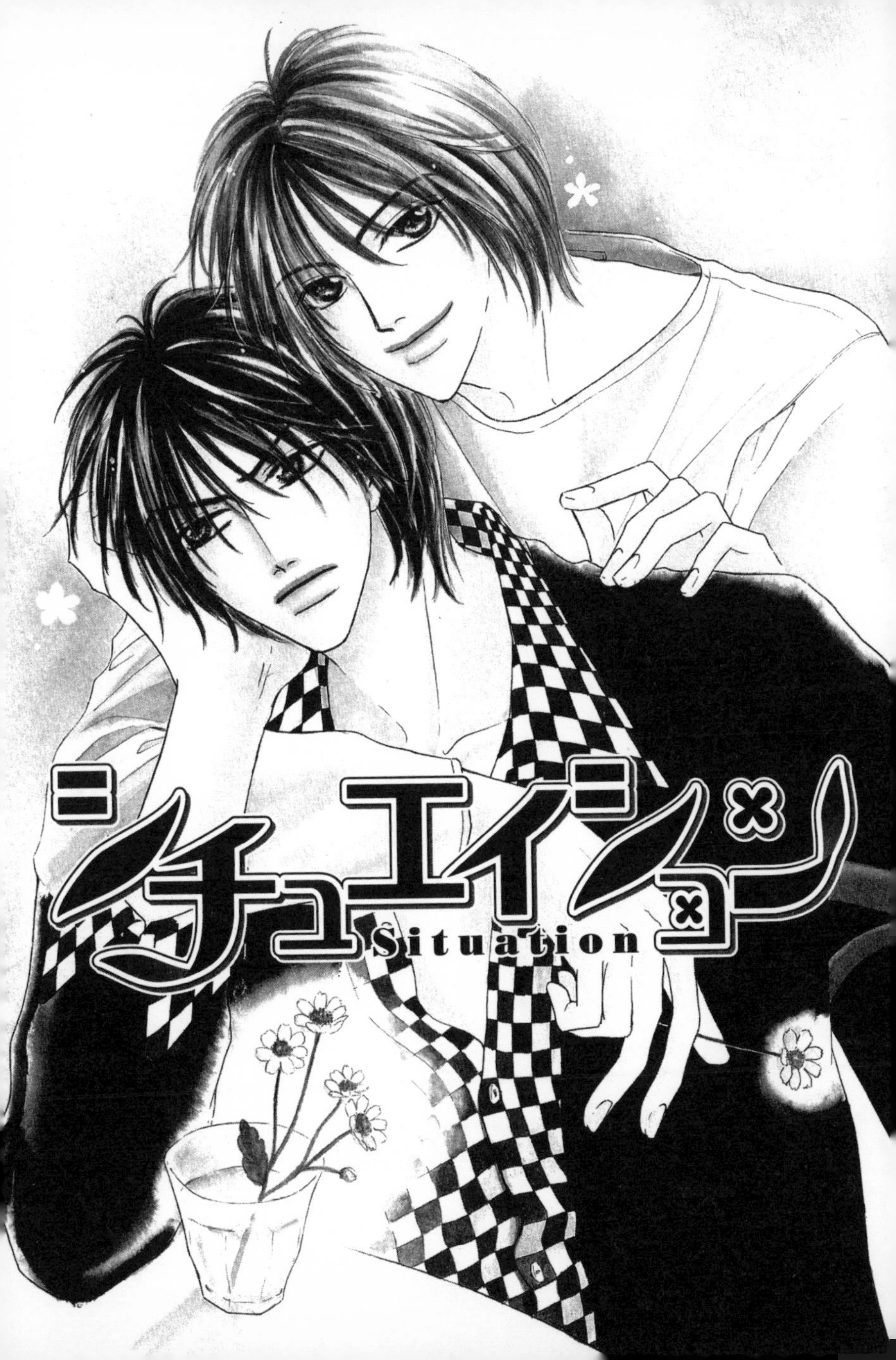
シチュエイション
Situation

bonds

...

situation

...

KITAN garden

...

sakura

Presented by Tōko Kawai

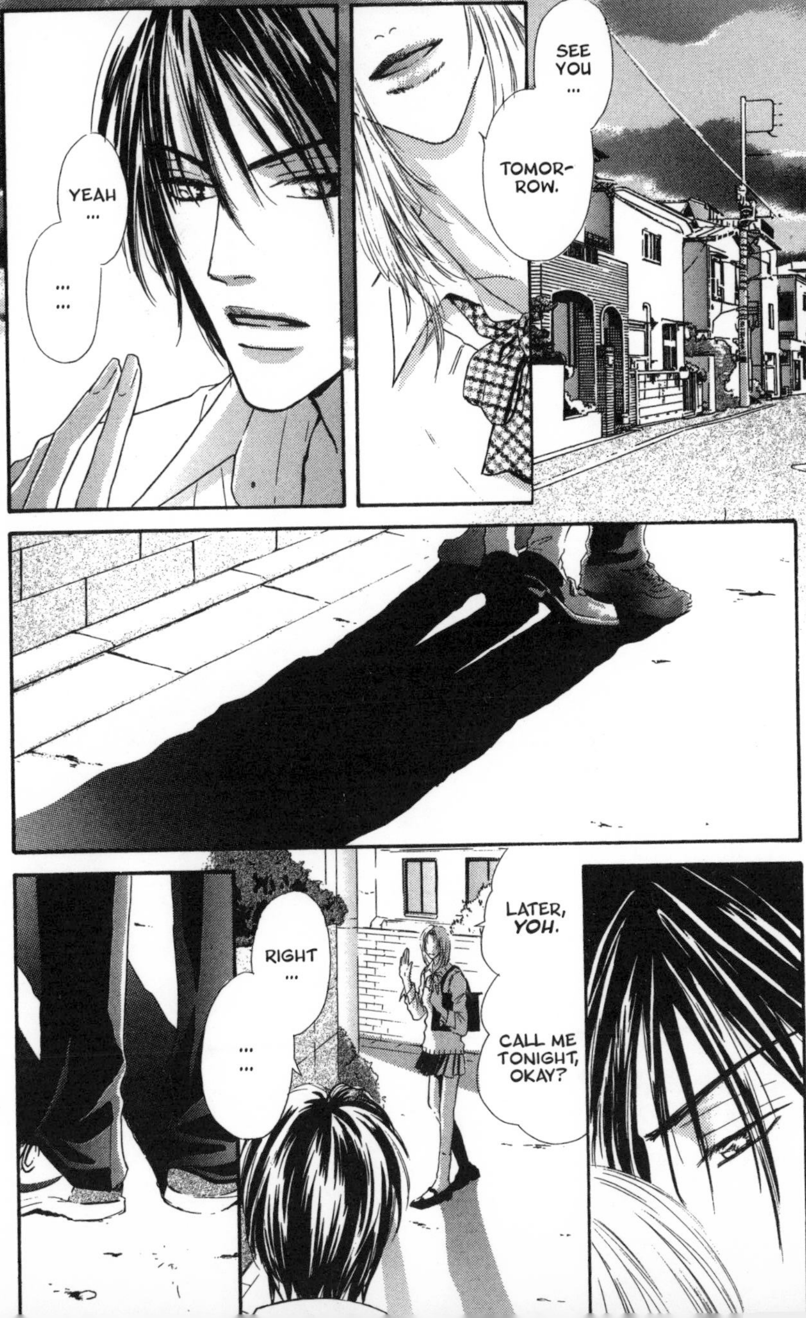
SEE YOU ...
TOMOR-ROW.
YEAH ...
... ...
LATER, YOH.
CALL ME TONIGHT, OKAY?
RIGHT ...
... ...

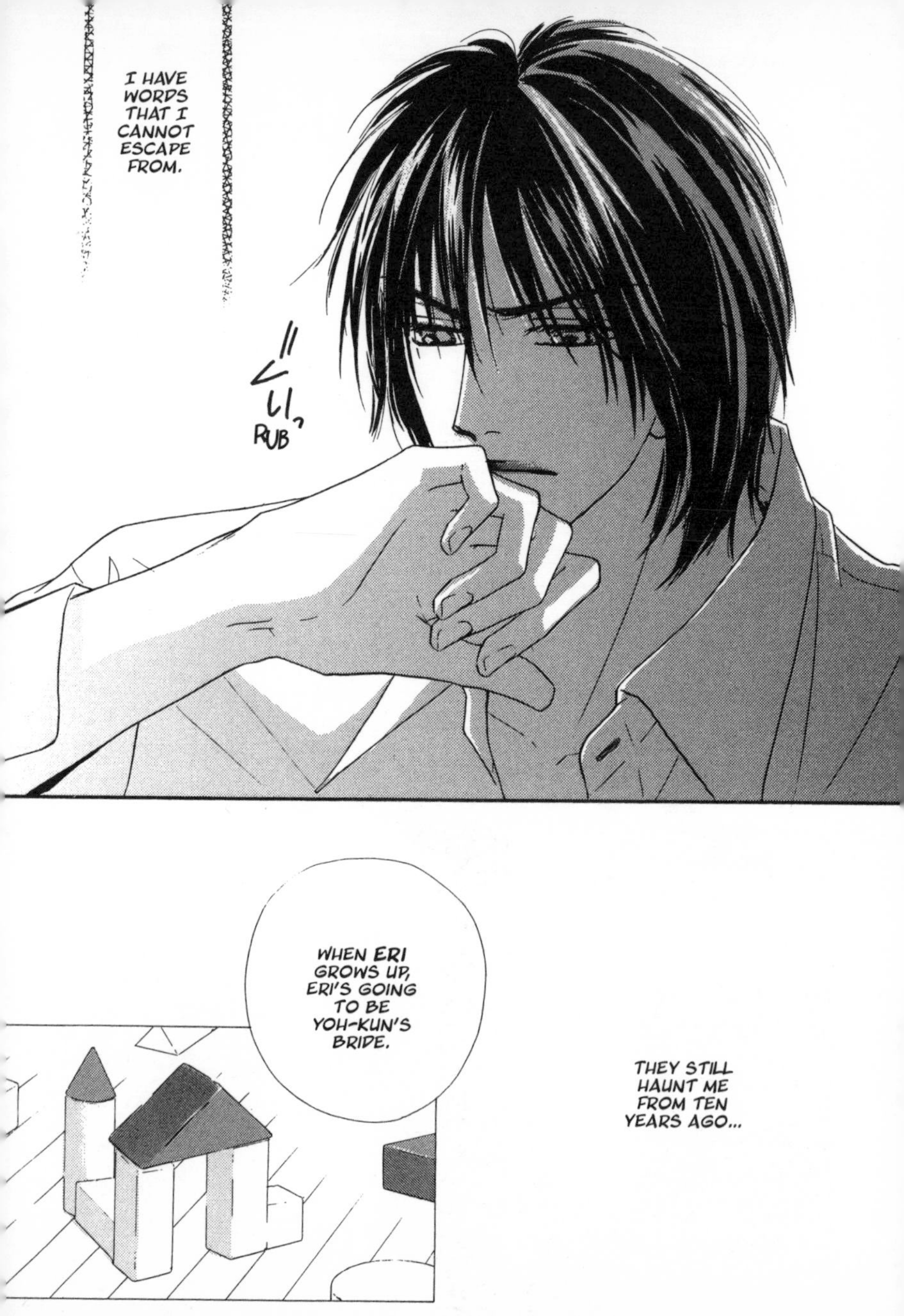
I HAVE WORDS THAT I CANNOT ESCAPE FROM.
RUB
WHEN ERI GROWS UP, ERI'S GOING TO BE YOH-KUN'S BRIDE.
THEY STILL HAUNT ME FROM TEN YEARS AGO...

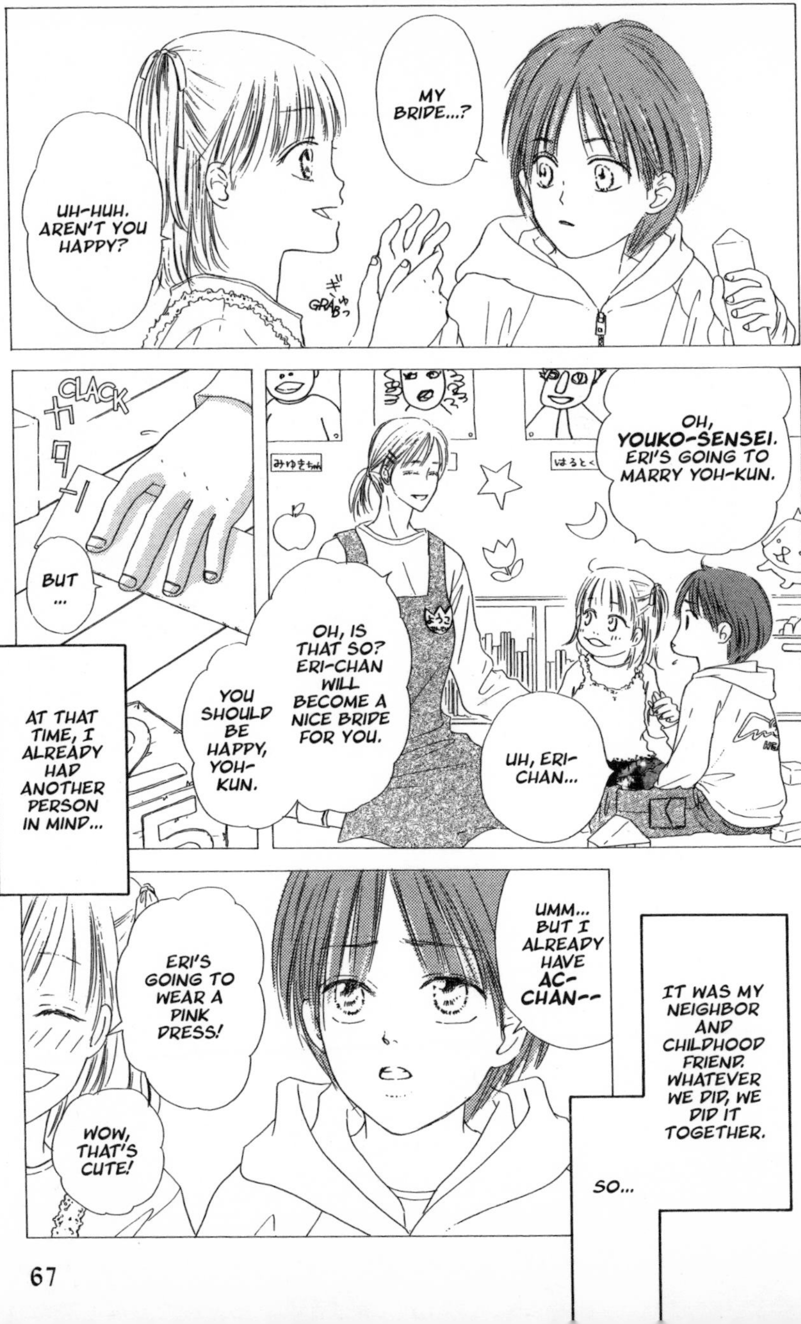

MY BRIDE...?
UH-HUH. AREN'T YOU HAPPY?
GRAB
OH, YOUKO-SENSEI. ERI'S GOING TO MARRY YOH-KUN.
OH, IS THAT SO? ERI-CHAN WILL BECOME A NICE BRIDE FOR YOU.
YOU SHOULD BE HAPPY, YOH-KUN.
UH, ERI-CHAN...
CLACK
BUT ...
AT THAT TIME, I ALREADY HAD ANOTHER PERSON IN MIND...
IT WAS MY NEIGHBOR AND CHILDHOOD FRIEND. WHATEVER WE DID, WE DID IT TOGETHER.
SO...
UMM... BUT I ALREADY HAVE AC-CHAN--
ERI'S GOING TO WEAR A PINK DRESS!
WOW, THAT'S CUTE!

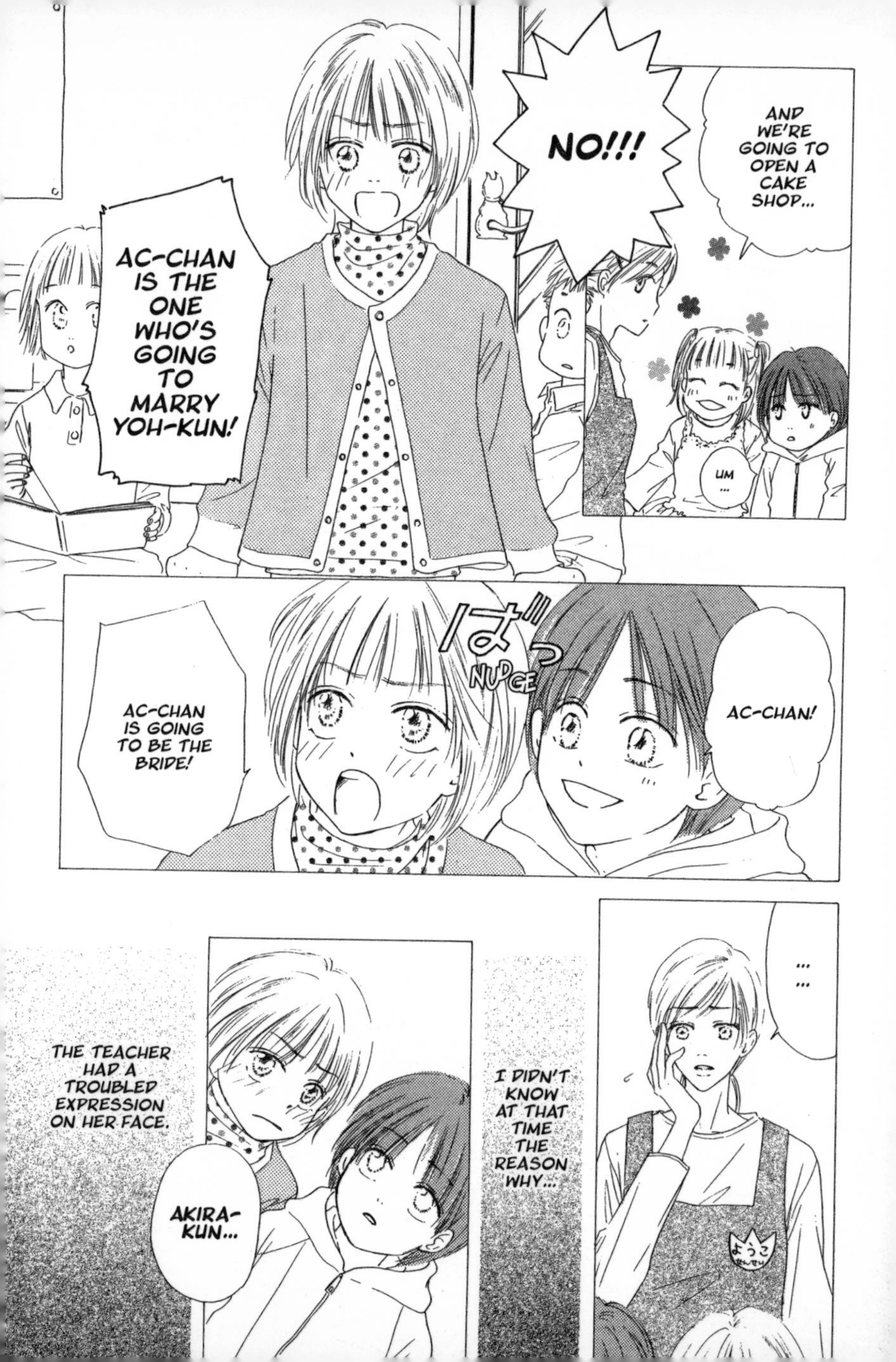
AND WE'RE GOING TO OPEN A CAKE SHOP...
UM ...
NO!!!
AC-CHAN IS THE ONE WHO'S GOING TO MARRY YOH-KUN!
AC-CHAN!
ばっ
NUDGE
AC-CHAN IS GOING TO BE THE BRIDE!
... ...
ようこ せんせい
I DIDN'T KNOW AT THAT TIME THE REASON WHY...
THE TEACHER HAD A TROUBLED EXPRESSION ON HER FACE.
AKIRA-KUN...

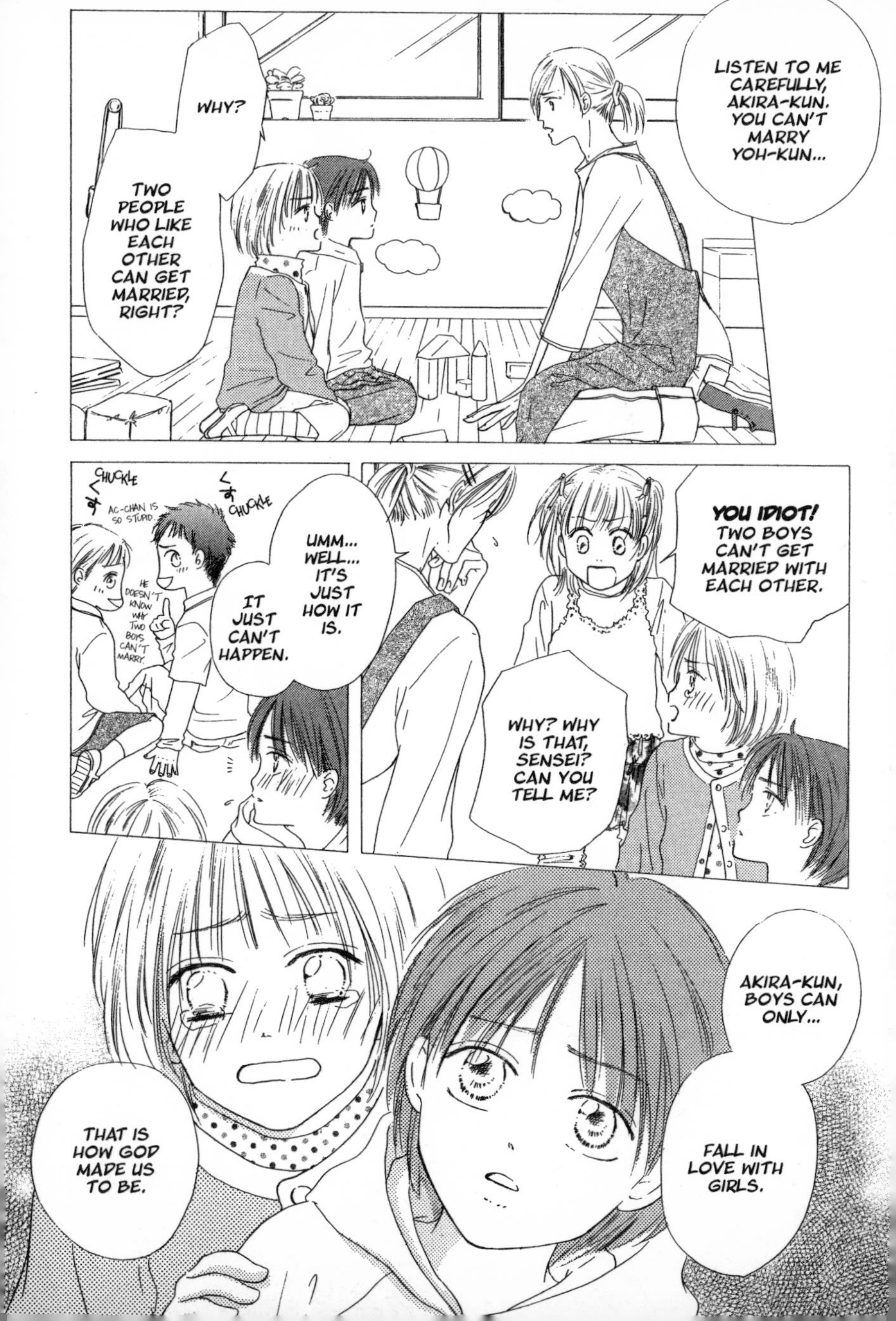
LISTEN TO ME CAREFULLY, AKIRA-KUN. YOU CAN'T MARRY YOH-KUN...
WHY?
TWO PEOPLE WHO LIKE EACH OTHER CAN GET MARRIED, RIGHT?
YOU IDIOT! TWO BOYS CAN'T GET MARRIED WITH EACH OTHER.
WHY? WHY IS THAT, SENSEI? CAN YOU TELL ME?
くす CHUCKLE
UMM... WELL... IT'S JUST HOW IT IS.
IT JUST CAN'T HAPPEN.
くす CHUCKLE
AC-CHAN IS SO STUPID.
HE DOESN'T KNOW WHY TWO BOYS CAN'T MARRY.
AKIRA-KUN, BOYS CAN ONLY...
FALL IN LOVE WITH GIRLS.
THAT IS HOW GOD MADE US TO BE.

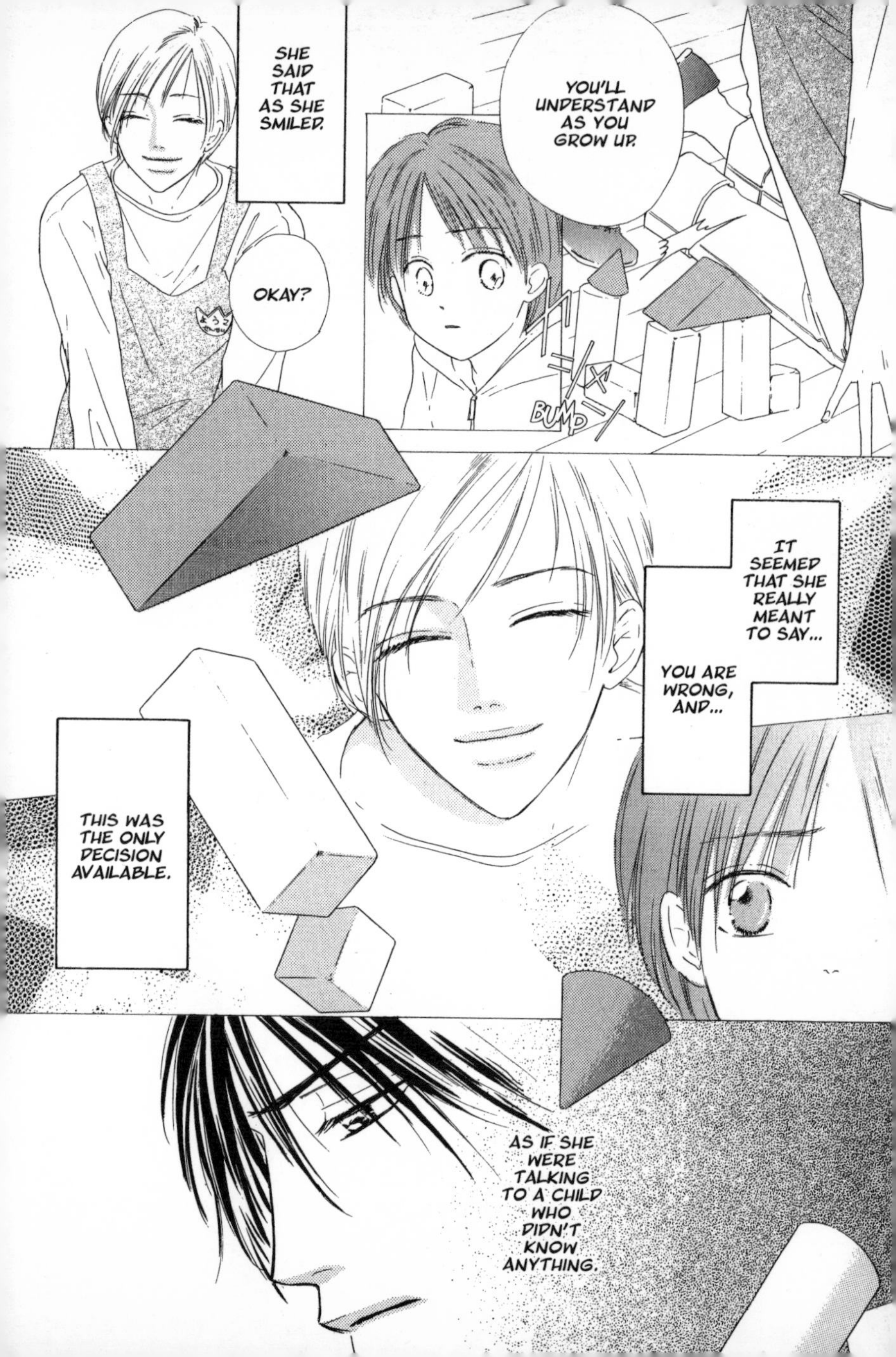
YOU'LL UNDERSTAND AS YOU GROW UP.
BUMP
SHE SAID THAT AS SHE SMILED.
OKAY?
IT SEEMED THAT SHE REALLY MEANT TO SAY...
YOU ARE WRONG, AND...
THIS WAS THE ONLY DECISION AVAILABLE.
AS IF SHE WERE TALKING TO A CHILD WHO DIDN'T KNOW ANYTHING.

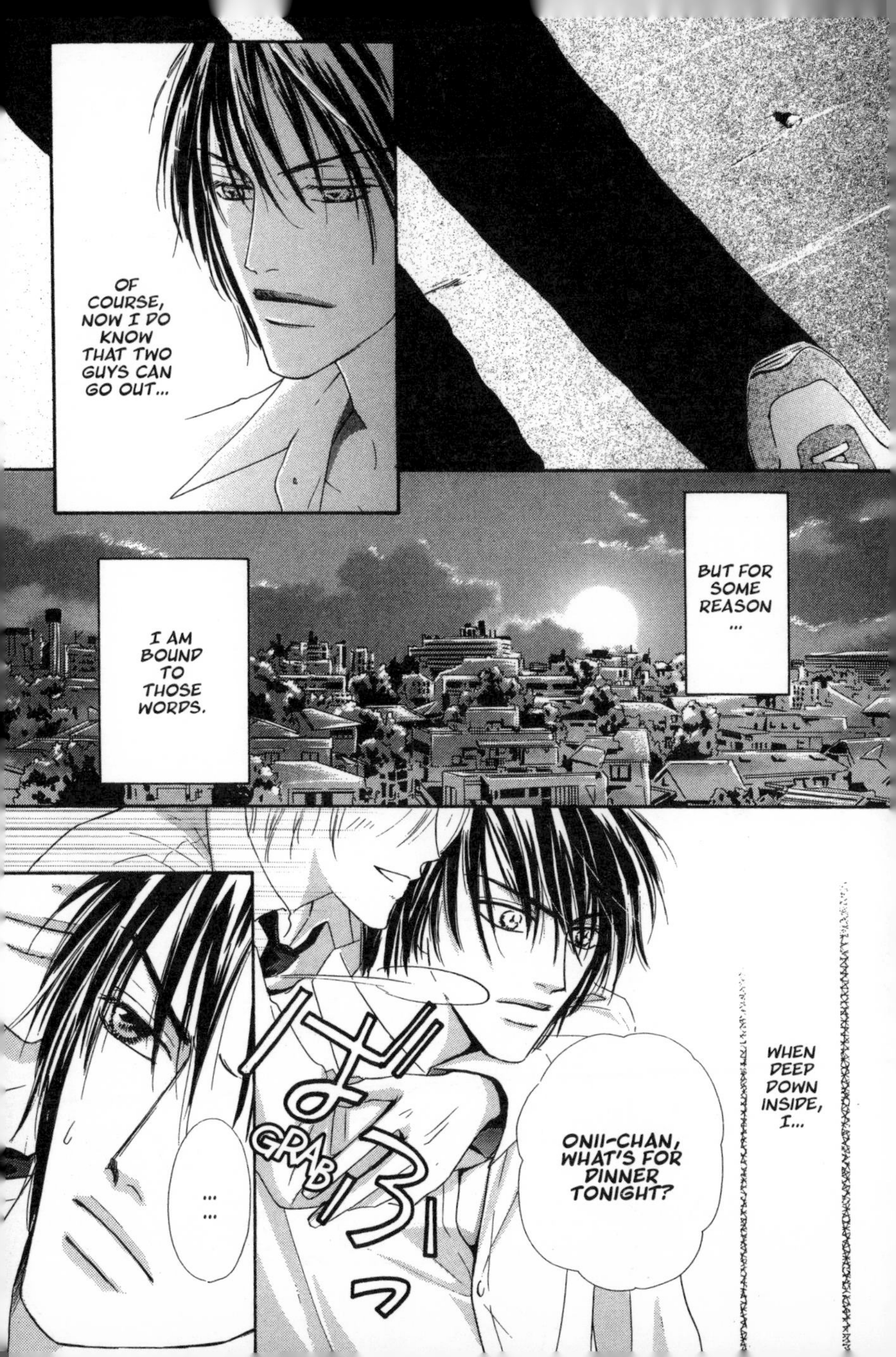
OF COURSE, NOW I DO KNOW THAT TWO GUYS CAN GO OUT...
BUT FOR SOME REASON ...
I AM BOUND TO THOSE WORDS.
WHEN DEEP DOWN INSIDE, I...
ONII-CHAN, WHAT'S FOR DINNER TONIGHT?
GRAB
... ...

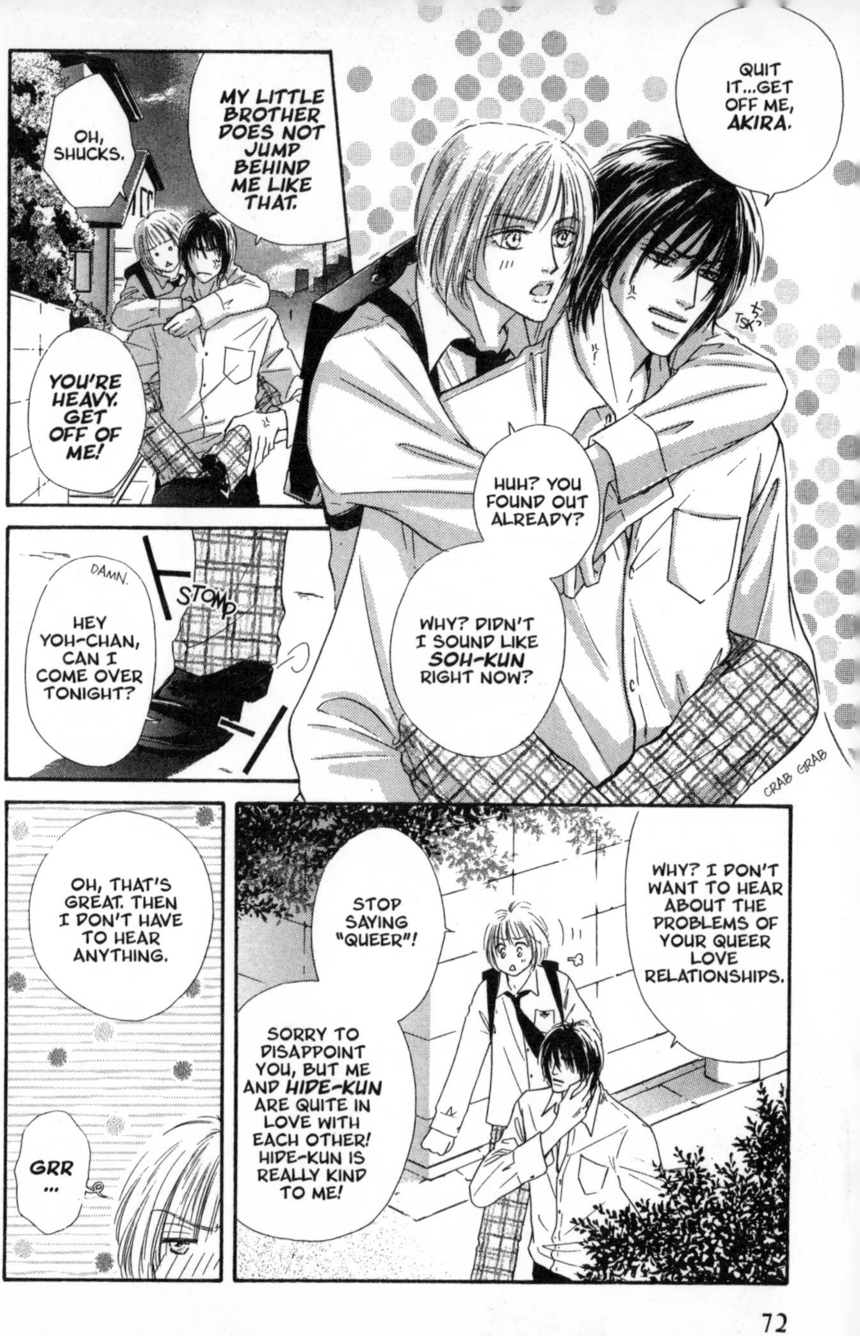
QUIT IT...GET OFF ME, AKIRA.
TSK
HUH? YOU FOUND OUT ALREADY?
WHY? DIDN'T I SOUND LIKE SOH-KUN RIGHT NOW?
GRAB GRAB
MY LITTLE BROTHER DOES NOT JUMP BEHIND ME LIKE THAT.
OH, SHUCKS.
YOU'RE HEAVY. GET OFF OF ME!
STOMP
DAMN.
HEY YOH-CHAN, CAN I COME OVER TONIGHT?
WHY? I DON'T WANT TO HEAR ABOUT THE PROBLEMS OF YOUR QUEER LOVE RELATIONSHIPS.
STOP SAYING "QUEER"!
SORRY TO DISAPPOINT YOU, BUT ME AND HIDE-KUN ARE QUITE IN LOVE WITH EACH OTHER! HIDE-KUN IS REALLY KIND TO ME!
OH, THAT'S GREAT. THEN I DON'T HAVE TO HEAR ANYTHING.
GRR ...

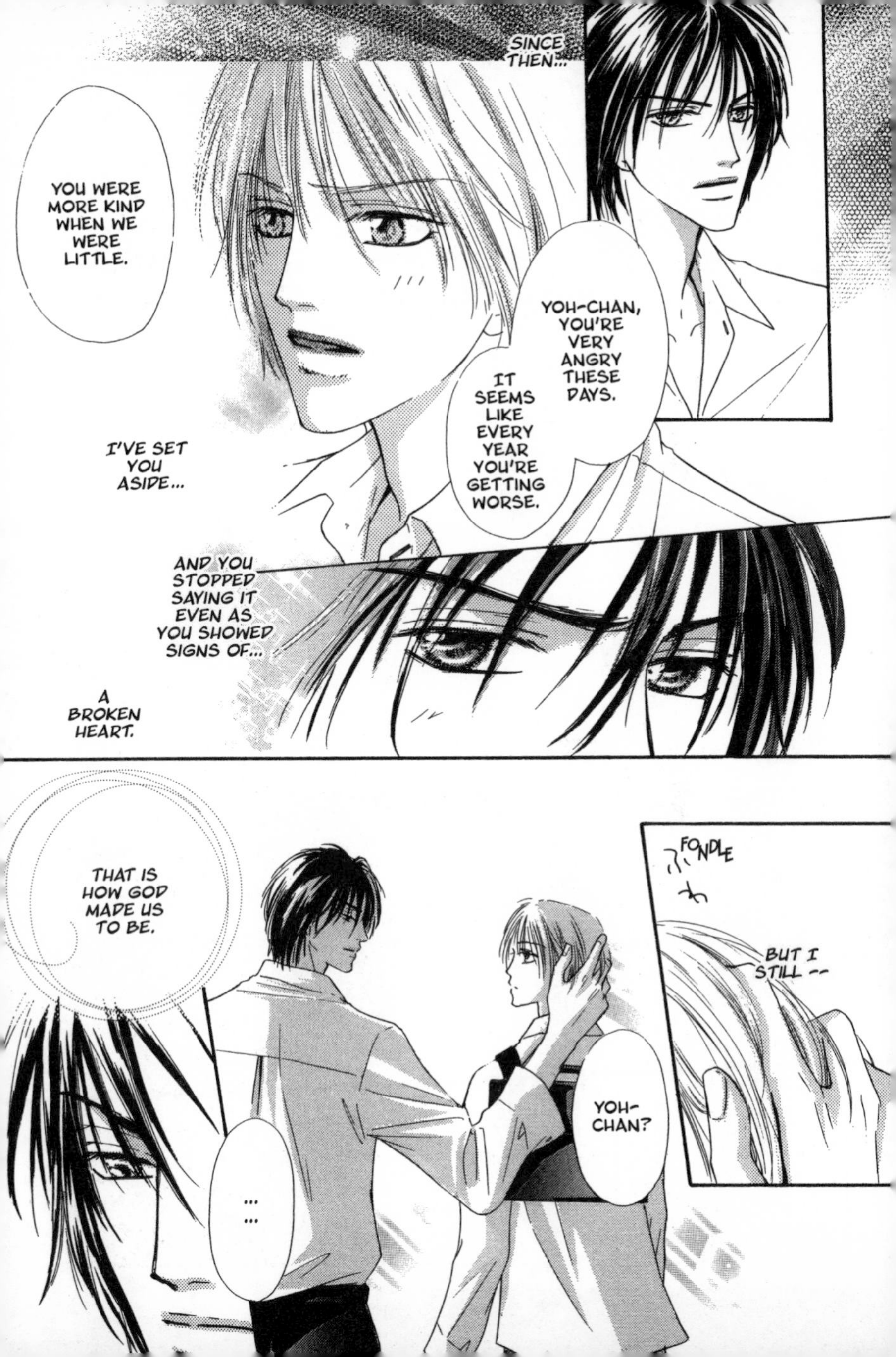

SINCE THEN...
YOH-CHAN, YOU'RE VERY ANGRY THESE DAYS.
IT SEEMS LIKE EVERY YEAR YOU'RE GETTING WORSE.
YOU WERE MORE KIND WHEN WE WERE LITTLE.
I'VE SET YOU ASIDE...
AND YOU STOPPED SAYING IT EVEN AS YOU SHOWED SIGNS OF...
A BROKEN HEART.
ふわ FONDLE
BUT I STILL --
YOH-CHAN?
... ...
THAT IS HOW GOD MADE US TO BE.

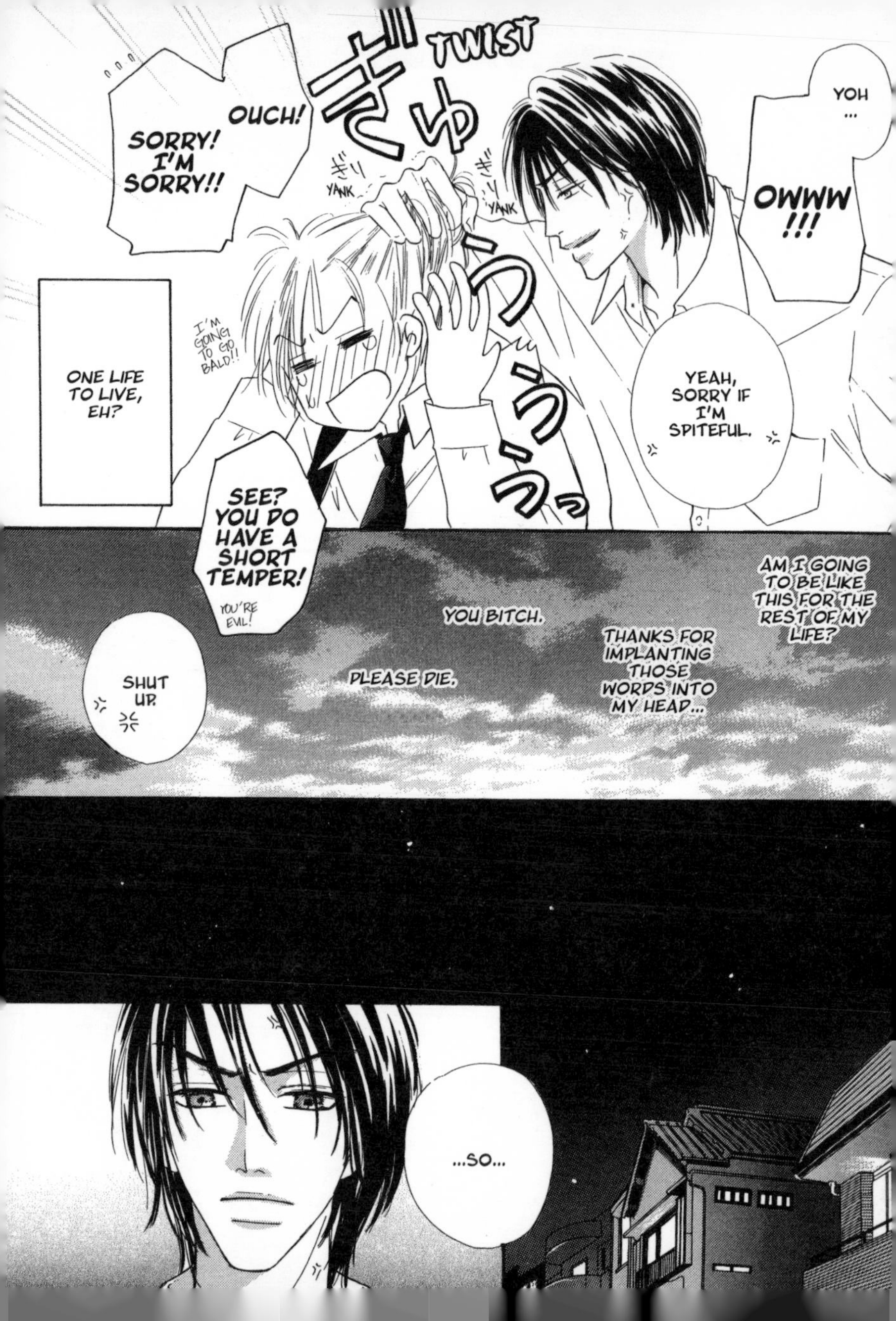
YOH...
OWWW!!!
TWIST
YANK
YANK
YEAH, SORRY IF I'M SPITEFUL.
OUCH!
SORRY! I'M SORRY!!
I'M GOING TO GO BALD!!
ONE LIFE TO LIVE, EH?
SEE? YOU DO HAVE A SHORT TEMPER!
YOU'RE EVIL!
AM I GOING TO BE LIKE THIS FOR THE REST OF MY LIFE?
THANKS FOR IMPLANTING THOSE WORDS INTO MY HEAD...
YOU BITCH.
PLEASE DIE.
SHUT UP.
...SO...

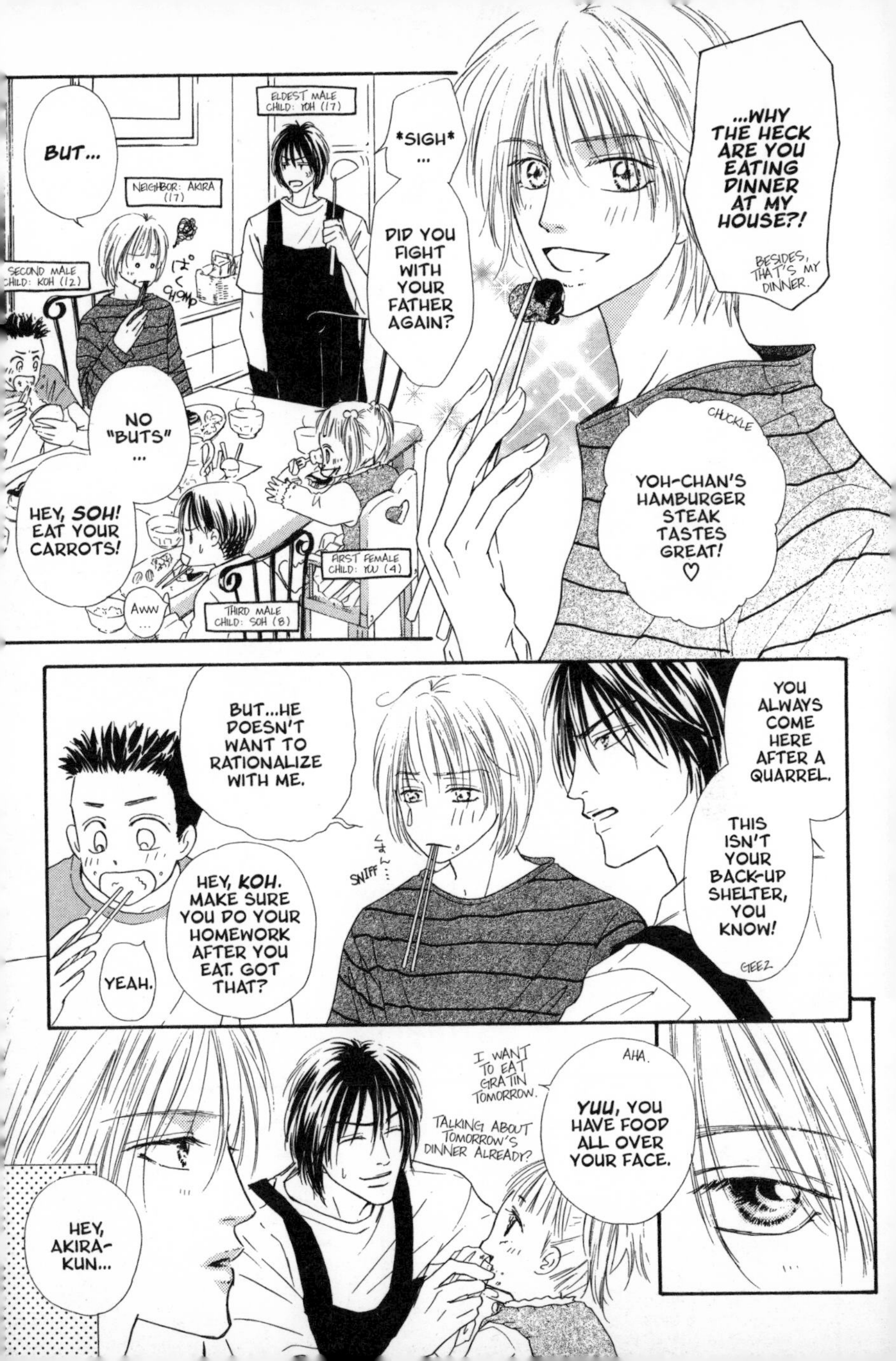
...WHY THE HECK ARE YOU EATING DINNER AT MY HOUSE?!
BESIDES, THAT'S MY DINNER.
SIGH ...
DID YOU FIGHT WITH YOUR FATHER AGAIN?
CHUCKLE
YOH-CHAN'S HAMBURGER STEAK TASTES GREAT! ♡
ELDEST MALE CHILD: YOH (17)
BUT...
NEIGHBOR: AKIRA (17)
ぱく
CHOMP
SECOND MALE CHILD: KOH (12)
NO "BUTS" ...
HEY, SOH! EAT YOUR CARROTS!
FIRST FEMALE CHILD: YOU (4)
THIRD MALE CHILD: SOH (8)
AWW ...
YOU ALWAYS COME HERE AFTER A QUARREL.
THIS ISN'T YOUR BACK-UP SHELTER, YOU KNOW!
GEEZ
BUT...HE DOESN'T WANT TO RATIONALIZE WITH ME.
くすん...
SNIFF
HEY, KOH. MAKE SURE YOU DO YOUR HOMEWORK AFTER YOU EAT. GOT THAT?
YEAH.
...
AHA.
YUU, YOU HAVE FOOD ALL OVER YOUR FACE.
I WANT TO EAT GRATIN TOMORROW.
TALKING ABOUT TOMORROW'S DINNER ALREADY?
HEY, AKIRA-KUN...

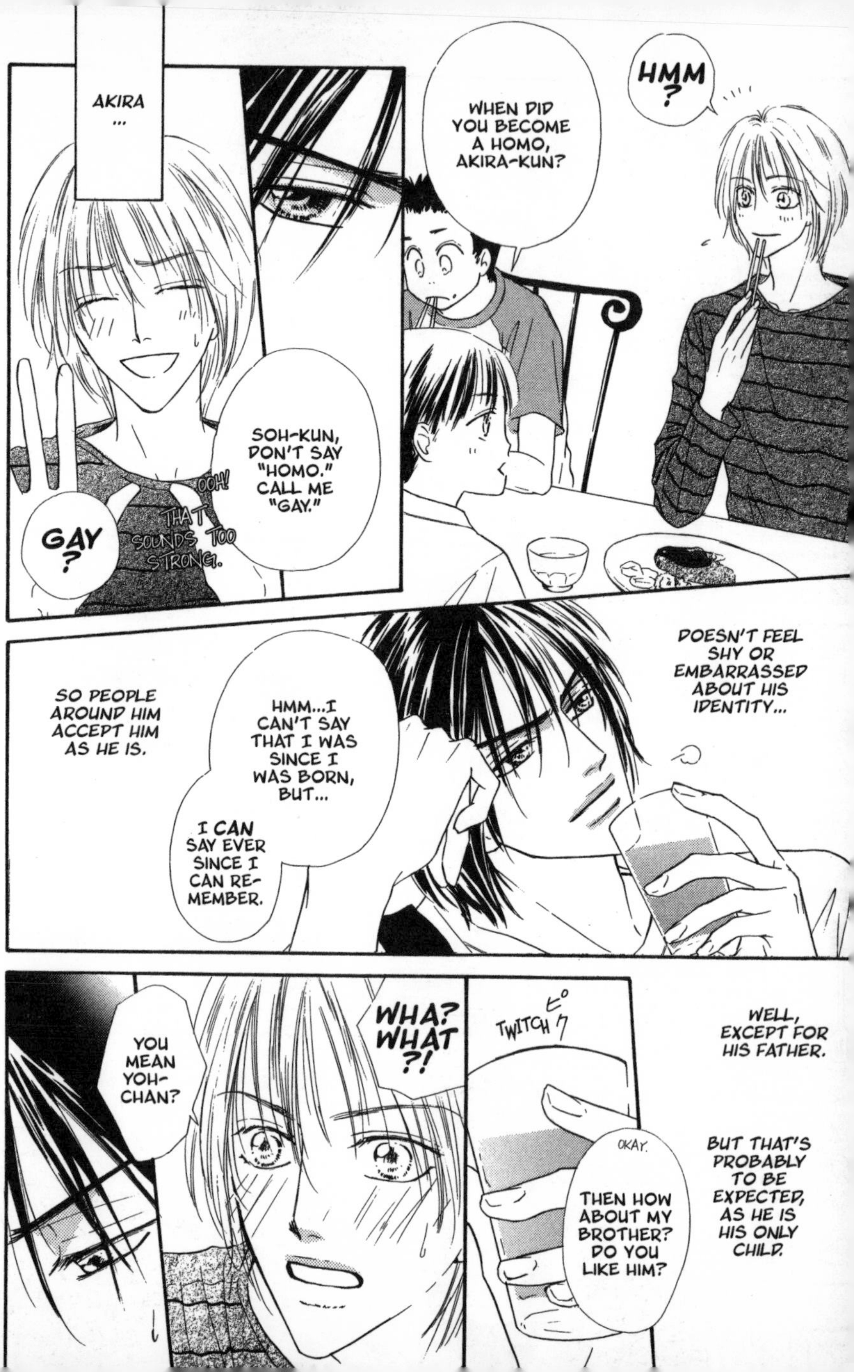

HMM?
WHEN DID YOU BECOME A HOMO, AKIRA-KUN?
AKIRA...
SOH-KUN, DON'T SAY "HOMO." CALL ME "GAY."
OOH! THAT SOUNDS TOO STRONG.
GAY?
DOESN'T FEEL SHY OR EMBARRASSED ABOUT HIS IDENTITY...
HMM...I CAN'T SAY THAT I WAS SINCE I WAS BORN, BUT...
I CAN SAY EVER SINCE I CAN RE-MEMBER.
SO PEOPLE AROUND HIM ACCEPT HIM AS HE IS.
WELL, EXCEPT FOR HIS FATHER.
BUT THAT'S PROBABLY TO BE EXPECTED, AS HE IS HIS ONLY CHILD.
TWITCH ピク
OKAY.
THEN HOW ABOUT MY BROTHER? DO YOU LIKE HIM?
WHA? WHAT?!
YOU MEAN YOH-CHAN?

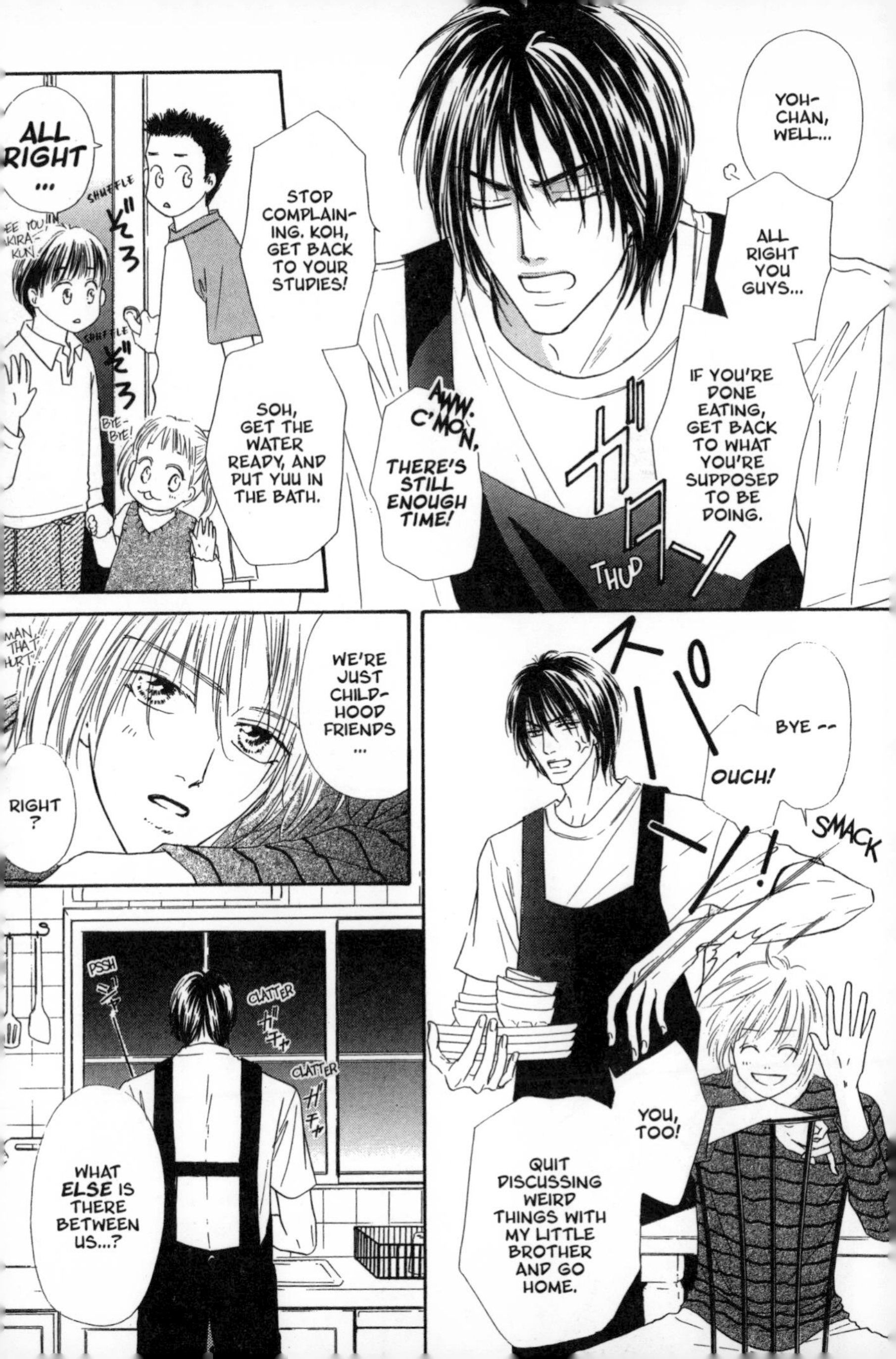
YOH-CHAN, WELL...
ALL RIGHT YOU GUYS...
IF YOU'RE DONE EATING, GET BACK TO WHAT YOU'RE SUPPOSED TO BE DOING.
AWW. C'MON, THERE'S STILL ENOUGH TIME!
THUD
STOP COMPLAINING. KOH, GET BACK TO YOUR STUDIES!
SOH, GET THE WATER READY, AND PUT YUU IN THE BATH.
ALL RIGHT ...
SHUFFLE
SHUFFLE
EE YOU, KIRA-KUN
BYE-BYE!
BYE --
OUCH!
SMACK
YOU, TOO!
QUIT DISCUSSING WEIRD THINGS WITH MY LITTLE BROTHER AND GO HOME.
WE'RE JUST CHILDHOOD FRIENDS ...
RIGHT ?
MAN THAT HURT...
PSSH
CLATTER
CLATTER
WHAT ELSE IS THERE BETWEEN US...?

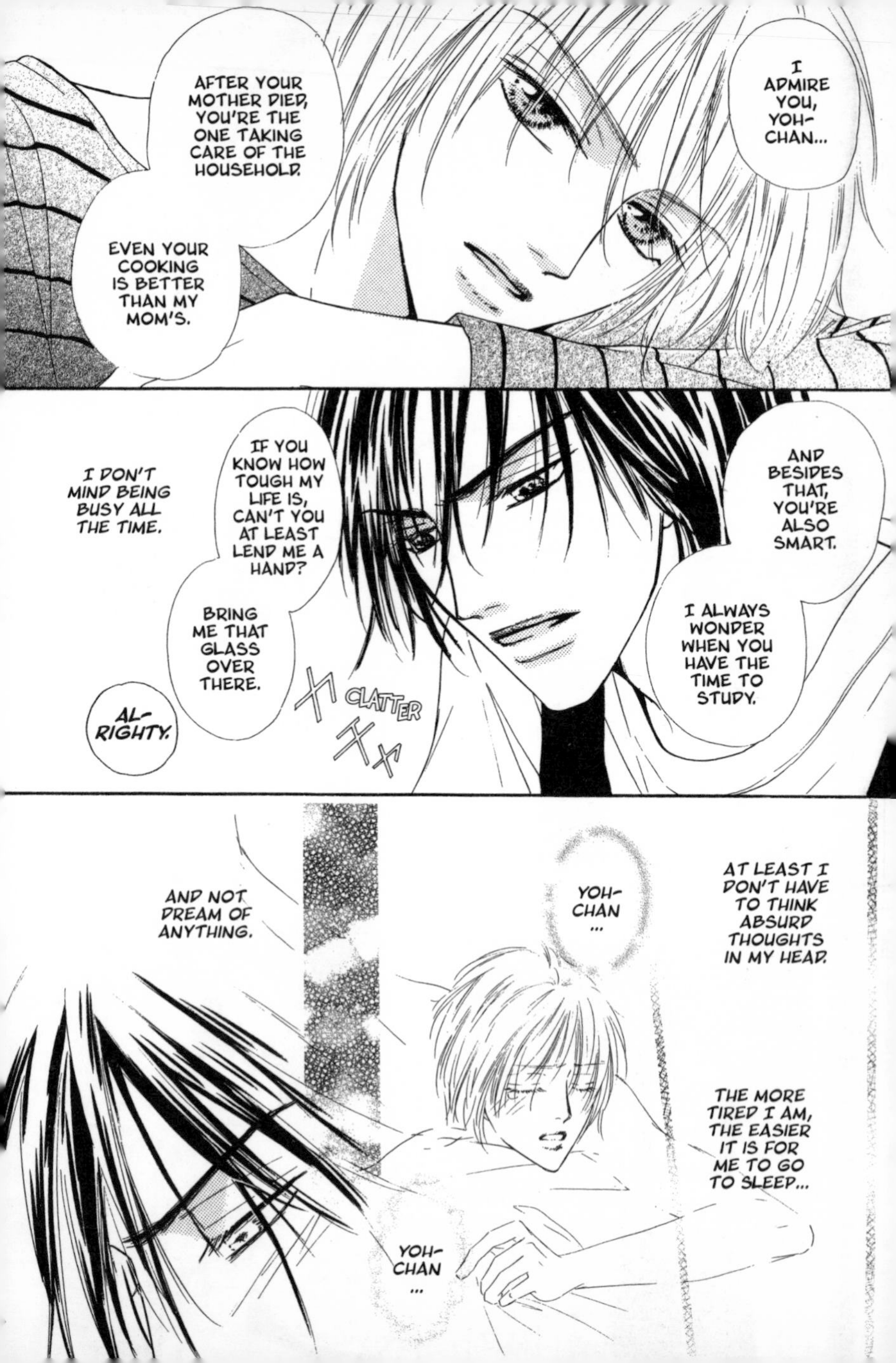
I ADMIRE YOU, YOH-CHAN...
AFTER YOUR MOTHER DIED, YOU'RE THE ONE TAKING CARE OF THE HOUSEHOLD.
EVEN YOUR COOKING IS BETTER THAN MY MOM'S.
AND BESIDES THAT, YOU'RE ALSO SMART.
I ALWAYS WONDER WHEN YOU HAVE THE TIME TO STUDY.
IF YOU KNOW HOW TOUGH MY LIFE IS, CAN'T YOU AT LEAST LEND ME A HAND?
BRING ME THAT GLASS OVER THERE.
CLATTER
I DON'T MIND BEING BUSY ALL THE TIME.
AL-RIGHTY.
AT LEAST I DON'T HAVE TO THINK ABSURD THOUGHTS IN MY HEAD.
YOH-CHAN...
THE MORE TIRED I AM, THE EASIER IT IS FOR ME TO GO TO SLEEP...
AND NOT DREAM OF ANYTHING.
YOH-CHAN...

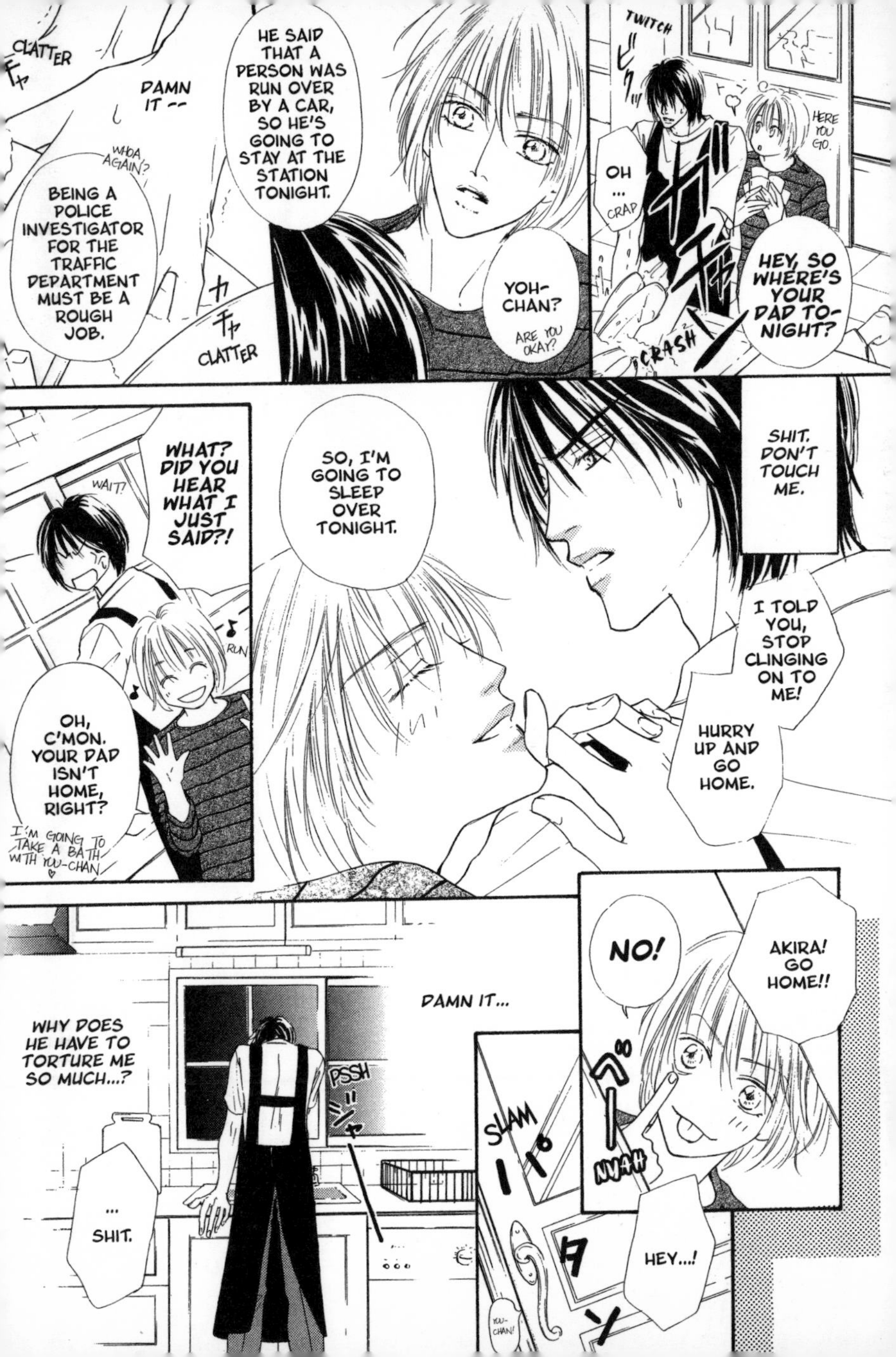
TWITCH
HERE YOU GO.
HEY, SO WHERE'S YOUR DAD TO-NIGHT?
OH ... CRAP
CRASH
HE SAID THAT A PERSON WAS RUN OVER BY A CAR, SO HE'S GOING TO STAY AT THE STATION TONIGHT.
YOH-CHAN?
ARE YOU OKAY?
CLATTER
DAMN IT --
WHOA AGAIN?
BEING A POLICE INVESTIGATOR FOR THE TRAFFIC DEPARTMENT MUST BE A ROUGH JOB.
CLATTER
SHIT. DON'T TOUCH ME.
SO, I'M GOING TO SLEEP OVER TONIGHT.
I TOLD YOU, STOP CLINGING ON TO ME!
HURRY UP AND GO HOME.
WHAT? DID YOU HEAR WHAT I JUST SAID?!
WAIT!
RUN
OH, C'MON. YOUR DAD ISN'T HOME, RIGHT?
I'M GOING TO TAKE A BATH WITH YOU-CHAN ♡
AKIRA! GO HOME!!
NO!
NYAH
SLAM
HEY...!
YOU-CHAN!
DAMN IT...
WHY DOES HE HAVE TO TORTURE ME SO MUCH...?
PSSH
... SHIT.

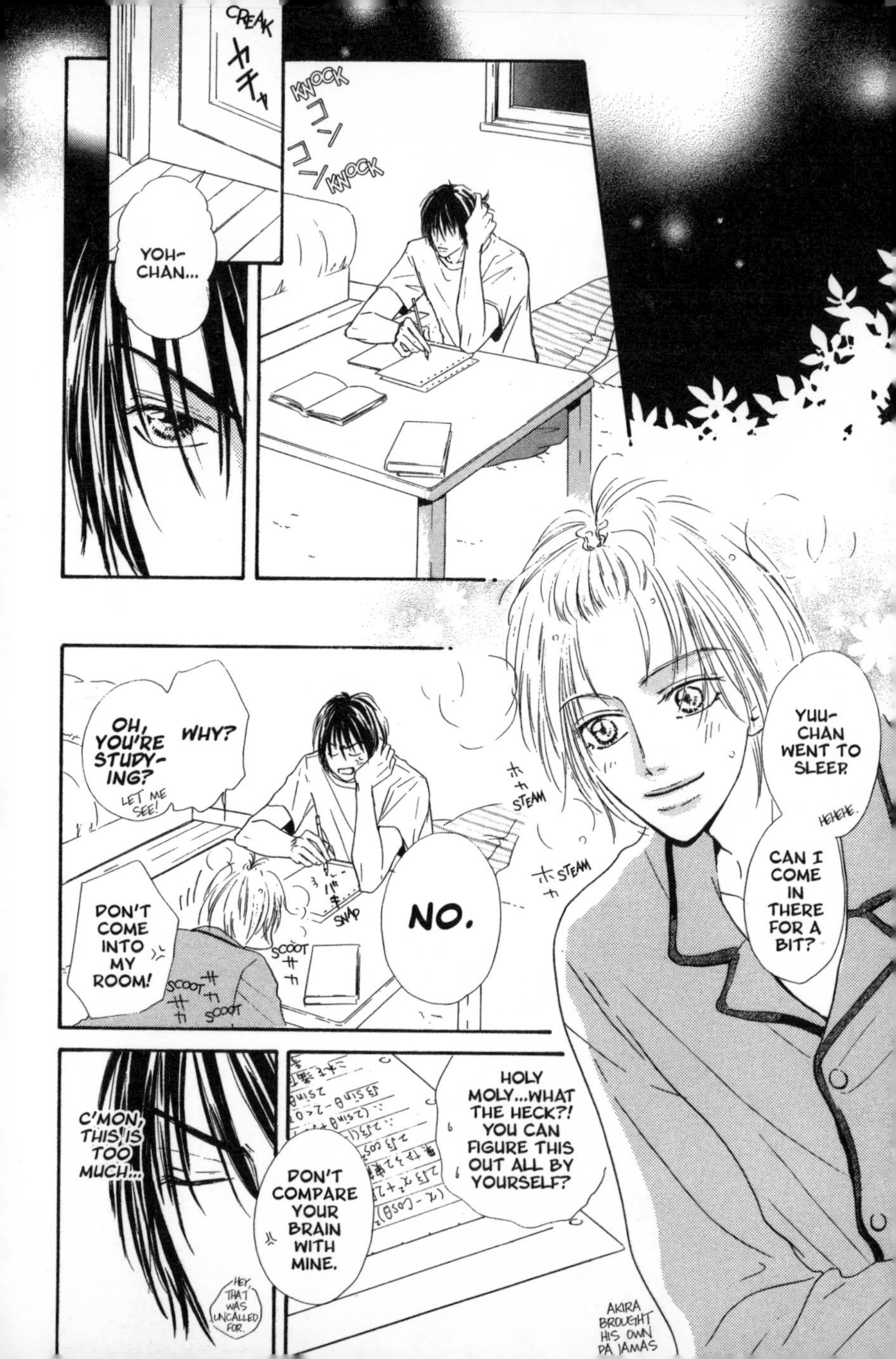

KNOCK
コン
コン
KNOCK
CREAK
カチャ
YOH-CHAN...
YUU-CHAN WENT TO SLEEP.
HEHEHE.
CAN I COME IN THERE FOR A BIT?
STEAM
STEAM
AKIRA BROUGHT HIS OWN PAJAMAS
OH, YOU'RE STUDYING?
LET ME SEE!
WHY?
NO.
SNAP
DON'T COME INTO MY ROOM!
SCOOT
SCOOT
SCOOT
HOLY MOLY...WHAT THE HECK?! YOU CAN FIGURE THIS OUT ALL BY YOURSELF?
DON'T COMPARE YOUR BRAIN WITH MINE.
C'MON, THIS IS TOO MUCH...
HEY, THAT WAS UNCALLED FOR.

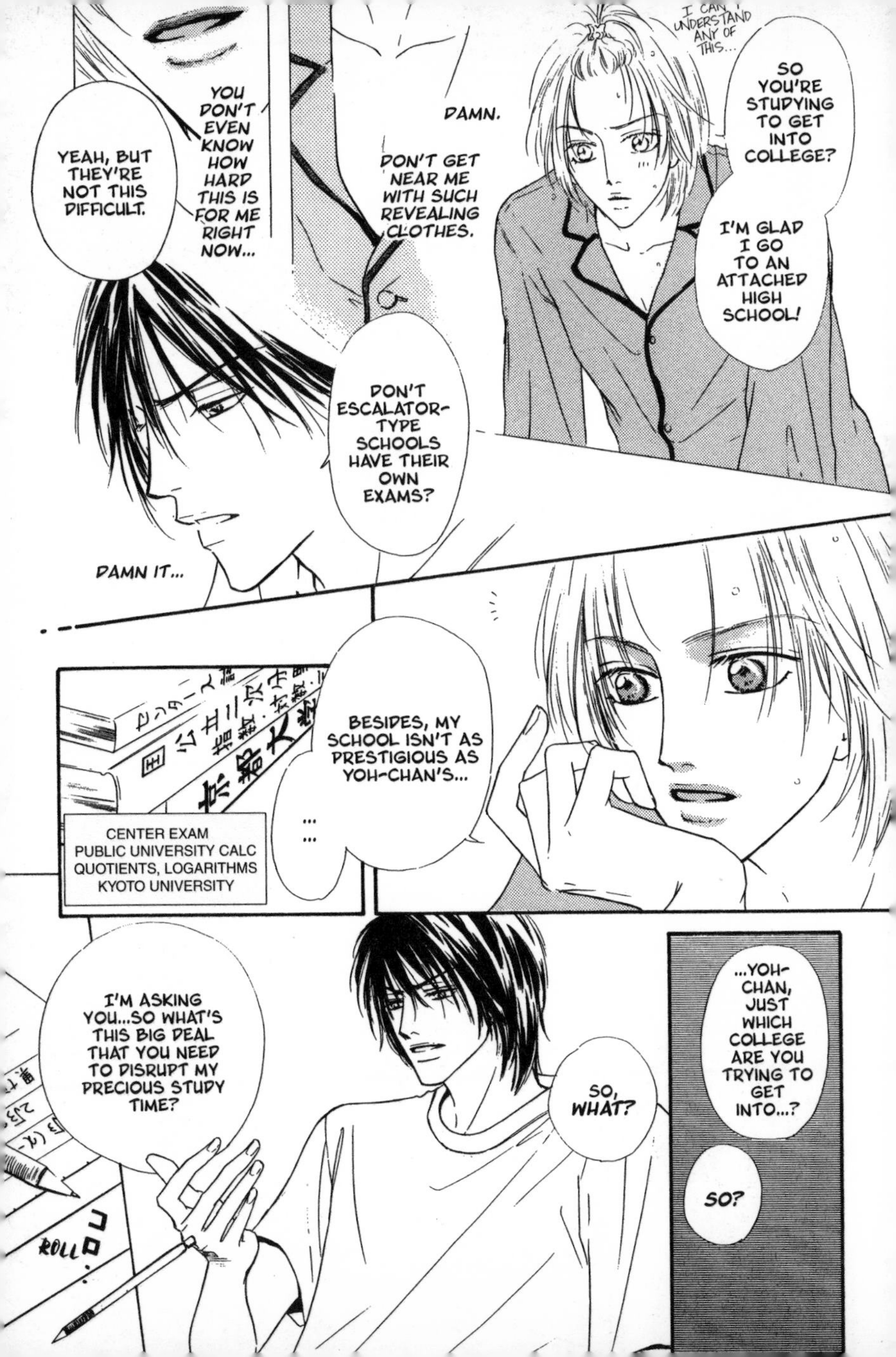

I CAN'T UNDERSTAND ANY OF THIS...
SO YOU'RE STUDYING TO GET INTO COLLEGE?
I'M GLAD I GO TO AN ATTACHED HIGH SCHOOL!
DAMN.
DON'T GET NEAR ME WITH SUCH REVEALING CLOTHES.
YOU DON'T EVEN KNOW HOW HARD THIS IS FOR ME RIGHT NOW...
DON'T ESCALATOR-TYPE SCHOOLS HAVE THEIR OWN EXAMS?
YEAH, BUT THEY'RE NOT THIS DIFFICULT.
DAMN IT...
BESIDES, MY SCHOOL ISN'T AS PRESTIGIOUS AS YOH-CHAN'S...
... ...
CENTER EXAM
PUBLIC UNIVERSITY CALC
QUOTIENTS, LOGARITHMS
KYOTO UNIVERSITY
...YOH-CHAN, JUST WHICH COLLEGE ARE YOU TRYING TO GET INTO...?
SO?
SO, WHAT?
I'M ASKING YOU...SO WHAT'S THIS BIG DEAL THAT YOU NEED TO DISRUPT MY PRECIOUS STUDY TIME?
ROLL
コロ

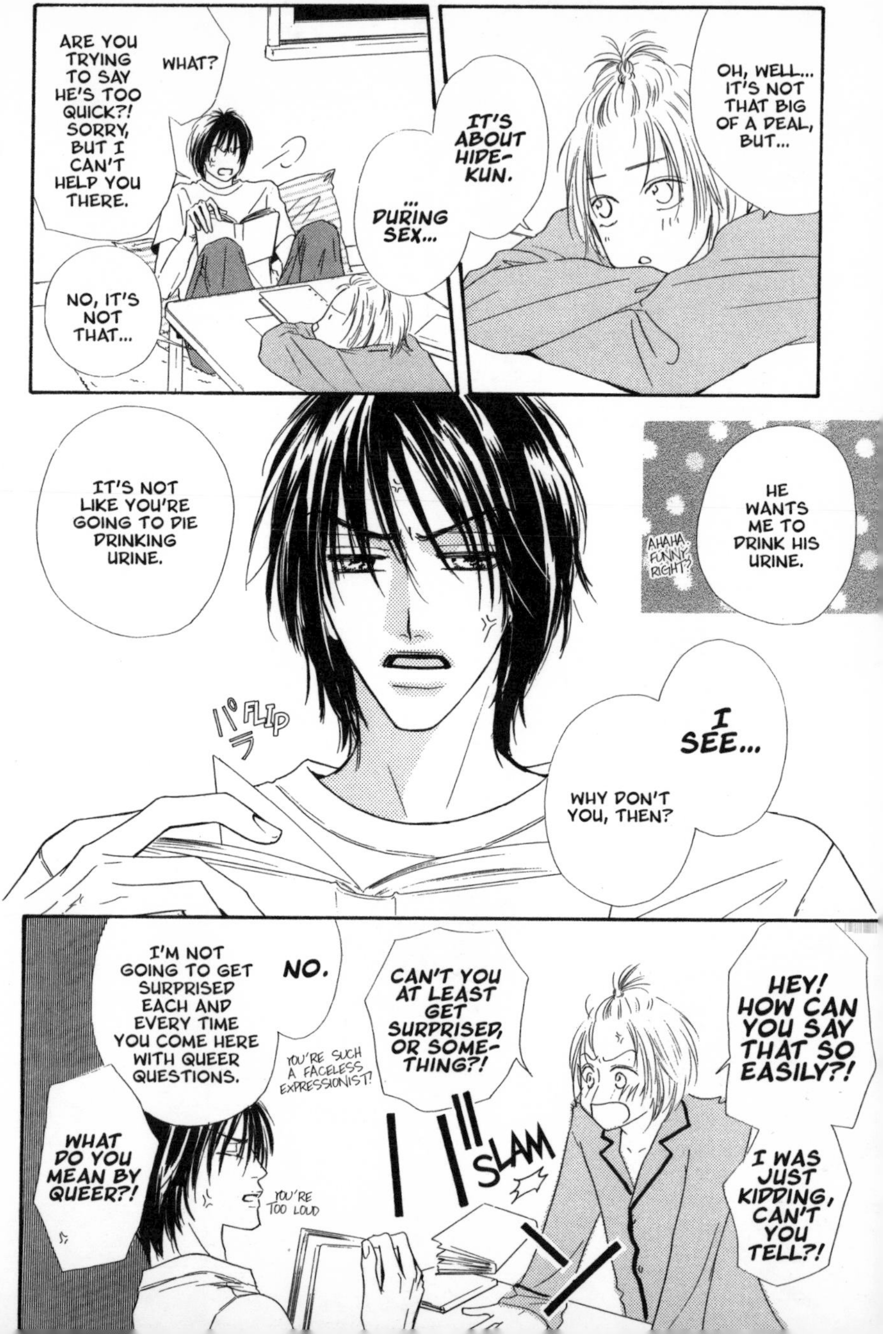
OH, WELL... IT'S NOT THAT BIG OF A DEAL, BUT...
IT'S ABOUT HIDE-KUN.
... DURING SEX...
WHAT?
ARE YOU TRYING TO SAY HE'S TOO QUICK?! SORRY, BUT I CAN'T HELP YOU THERE.
NO, IT'S NOT THAT...
HE WANTS ME TO DRINK HIS URINE.
AHAHA FUNNY, RIGHT?
I SEE...
WHY DON'T YOU, THEN?
パラ FLIP
IT'S NOT LIKE YOU'RE GOING TO DIE DRINKING URINE.
HEY! HOW CAN YOU SAY THAT SO EASILY?!
I WAS JUST KIDDING, CAN'T YOU TELL?!
CAN'T YOU AT LEAST GET SURPRISED, OR SOMETHING?!
YOU'RE SUCH A FACELESS EXPRESSIONIST!
SLAM
NO.
I'M NOT GOING TO GET SURPRISED EACH AND EVERY TIME YOU COME HERE WITH QUEER QUESTIONS.
WHAT DO YOU MEAN BY QUEER?!
YOU'RE TOO LOUD

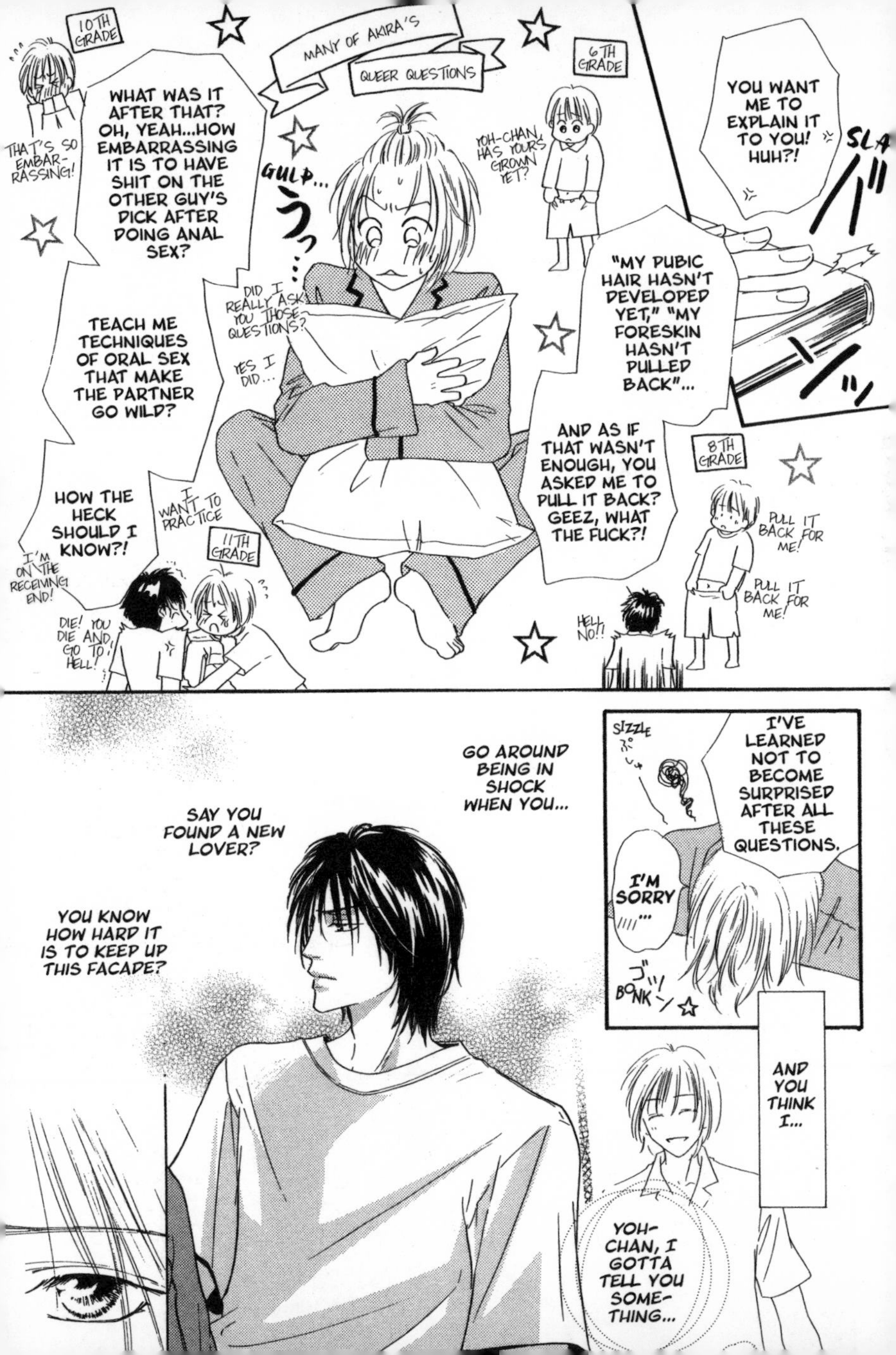

MANY OF AKIRA'S QUEER QUESTIONS
YOU WANT ME TO EXPLAIN IT TO YOU! HUH?!
SLA
6TH GRADE
YOH-CHAN, HAS YOURS GROWN YET?
"MY PUBIC HAIR HASN'T DEVELOPED YET," "MY FORESKIN HASN'T PULLED BACK"...
AND AS IF THAT WASN'T ENOUGH, YOU ASKED ME TO PULL IT BACK? GEEZ, WHAT THE FUCK?!
8TH GRADE
PULL IT BACK FOR ME!
PULL IT BACK FOR ME!
HELL NO!!
GULP...
DID I REALLY ASK YOU THOSE QUESTIONS?
YES I DID...
10TH GRADE
THAT'S SO EMBARRASSING!
WHAT WAS IT AFTER THAT? OH, YEAH...HOW EMBARRASSING IT IS TO HAVE SHIT ON THE OTHER GUY'S DICK AFTER DOING ANAL SEX?
TEACH ME TECHNIQUES OF ORAL SEX THAT MAKE THE PARTNER GO WILD?
HOW THE HECK SHOULD I KNOW?!
I WANT TO PRACTICE
11TH GRADE
I'M ON THE RECEIVING END!
DIE! YOU DIE AND GO TO HELL!
I'VE LEARNED NOT TO BECOME SURPRISED AFTER ALL THESE QUESTIONS.
SIZZLE
I'M SORRY...
BONK
AND YOU THINK I...
YOH-CHAN, I GOTTA TELL YOU SOMETHING...
GO AROUND BEING IN SHOCK WHEN YOU...
SAY YOU FOUND A NEW LOVER?
YOU KNOW HOW HARD IT IS TO KEEP UP THIS FACADE?

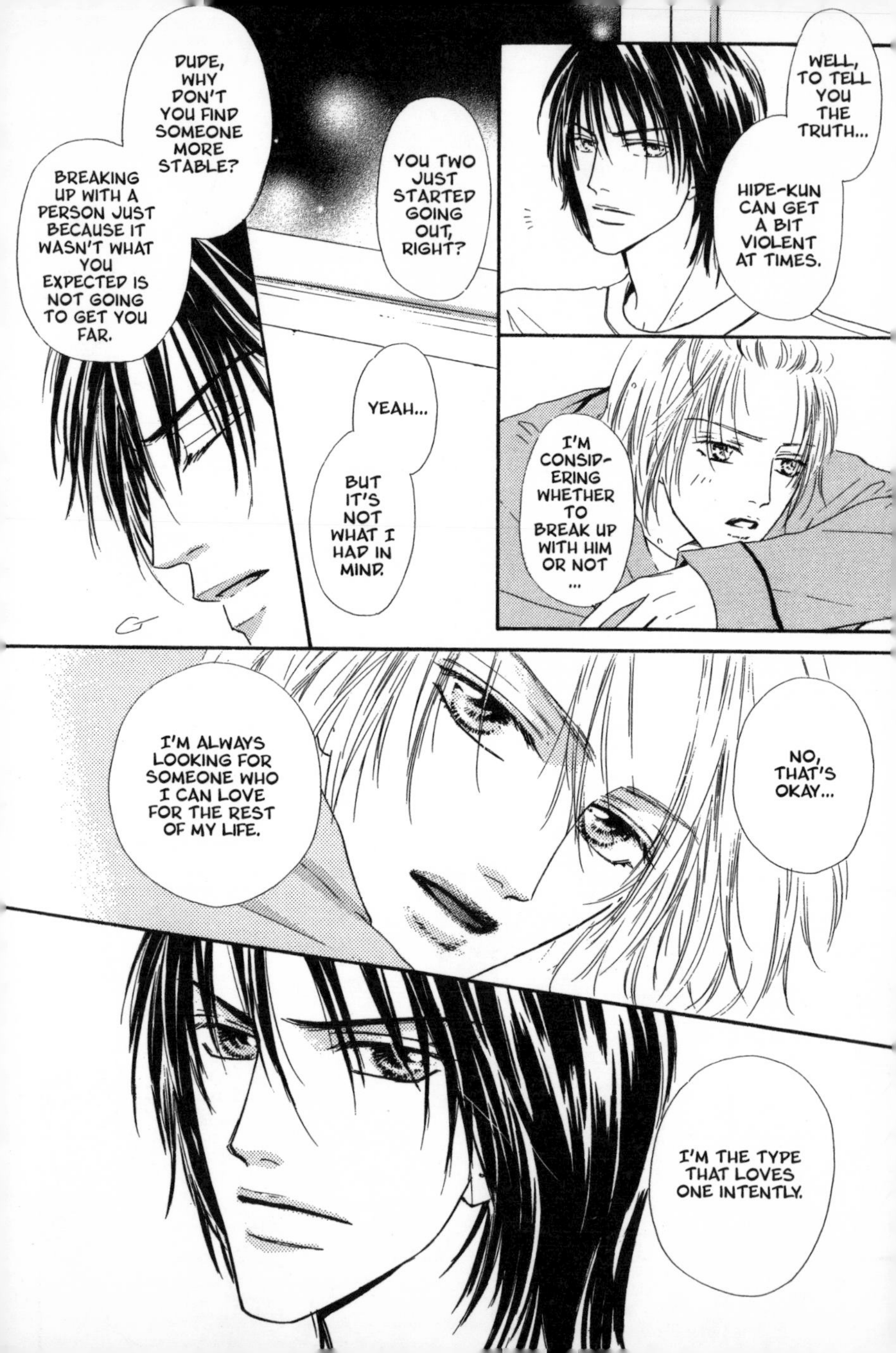
WELL, TO TELL YOU THE TRUTH...
HIDE-KUN CAN GET A BIT VIOLENT AT TIMES.
I'M CONSID-ERING WHETHER TO BREAK UP WITH HIM OR NOT ...
YOU TWO JUST STARTED GOING OUT, RIGHT?
YEAH...
BUT IT'S NOT WHAT I HAD IN MIND.
DUDE, WHY DON'T YOU FIND SOMEONE MORE STABLE?
BREAKING UP WITH A PERSON JUST BECAUSE IT WASN'T WHAT YOU EXPECTED IS NOT GOING TO GET YOU FAR.
NO, THAT'S OKAY...
I'M ALWAYS LOOKING FOR SOMEONE WHO I CAN LOVE FOR THE REST OF MY LIFE.
I'M THE TYPE THAT LOVES ONE INTENTLY.

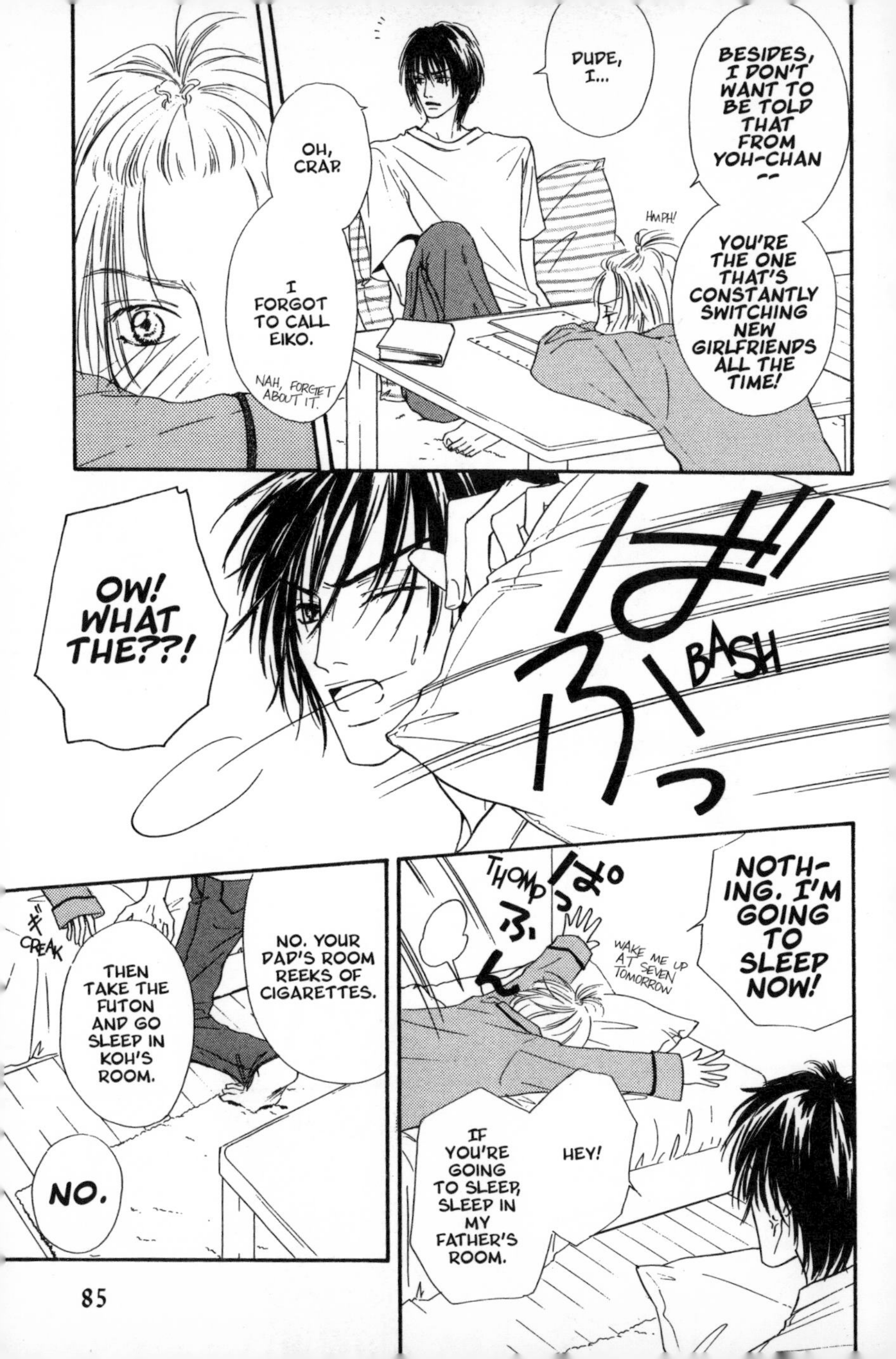
BESIDES, I DON'T WANT TO BE TOLD THAT FROM YOH-CHAN --
YOU'RE THE ONE THAT'S CONSTANTLY SWITCHING NEW GIRLFRIENDS ALL THE TIME!
HMPH!
DUDE, I...
OH, CRAP.
I FORGOT TO CALL EIKO.
NAH, FORGET ABOUT IT.
ばふっ
BASH
OW! WHAT THE??!
NOTH-ING. I'M GOING TO SLEEP NOW!
WAKE ME UP AT SEVEN TOMORROW
ぽふん
THOMP
HEY!
IF YOU'RE GOING TO SLEEP, SLEEP IN MY FATHER'S ROOM.
NO. YOUR DAD'S ROOM REEKS OF CIGARETTES.
THEN TAKE THE FUTON AND GO SLEEP IN KOH'S ROOM.
ギ
CREAK
NO.

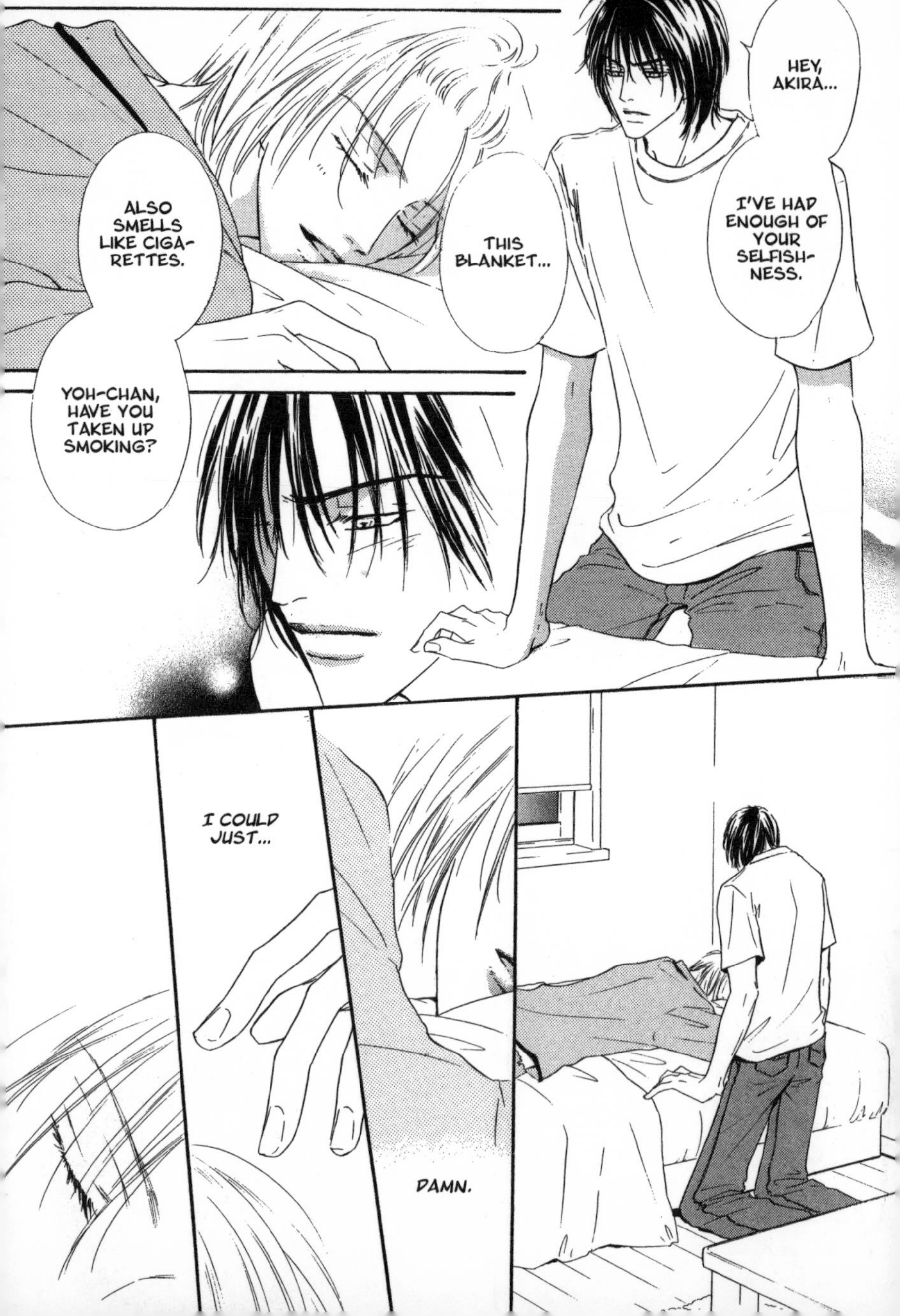
HEY, AKIRA...
I'VE HAD ENOUGH OF YOUR SELFISH-NESS.
THIS BLANKET...
ALSO SMELLS LIKE CIGA-RETTES.
YOH-CHAN, HAVE YOU TAKEN UP SMOKING?
DAMN.
I COULD JUST...

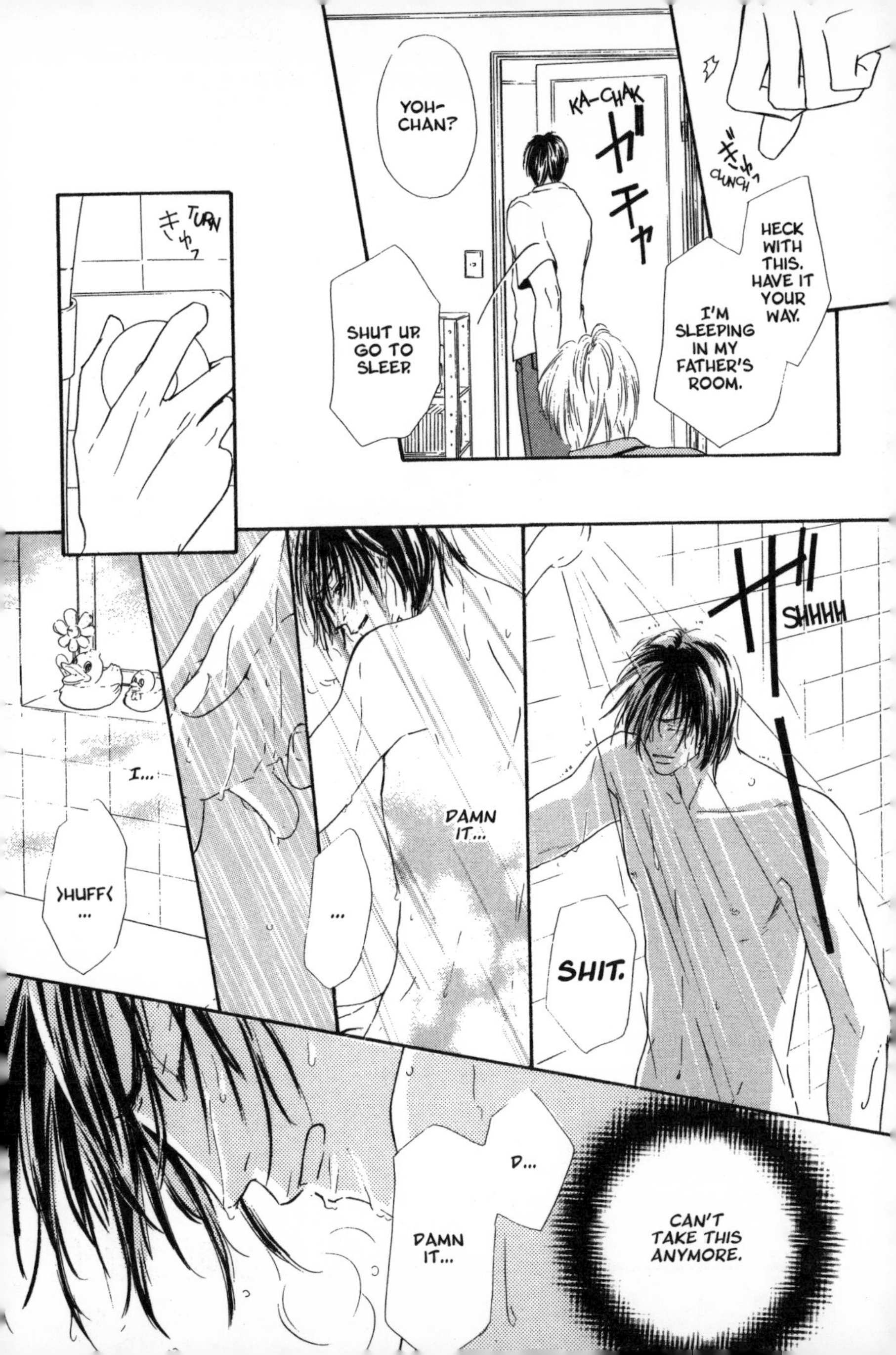
ギュッ
CLUNCH
HECK WITH THIS. HAVE IT YOUR WAY.
I'M SLEEPING IN MY FATHER'S ROOM.
KA-CHAK
ガチャ
YOH-CHAN?
SHUT UP. GO TO SLEEP.
TURN
きゅっ
SHHHH
SHIT.
DAMN IT...
...
I...
>HUFF< ...
CAN'T TAKE THIS ANYMORE.
D...
DAMN IT...

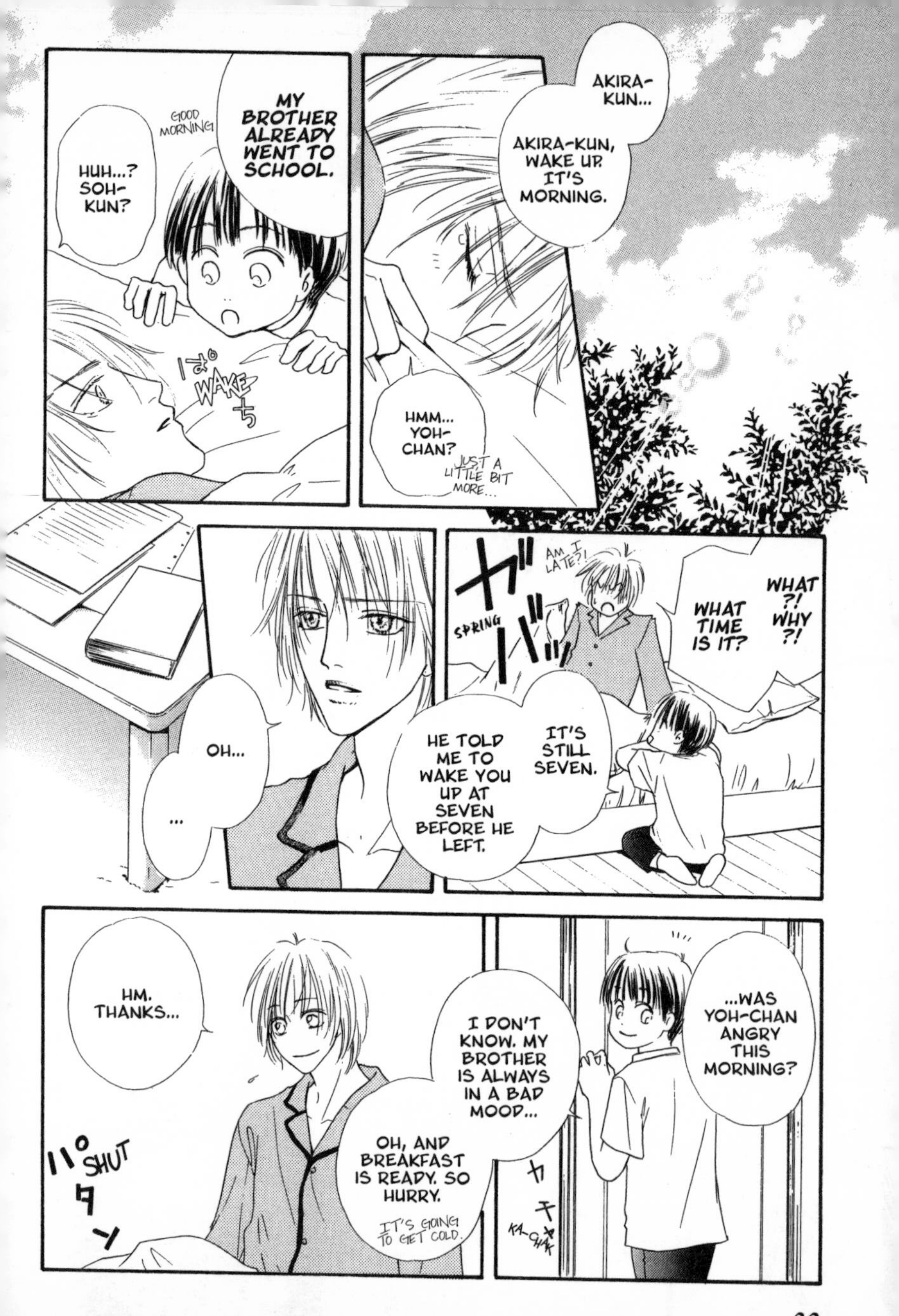
AKIRA-KUN...
AKIRA-KUN, WAKE UP. IT'S MORNING.
HMM... YOH-CHAN?
JUST A LITTLE BIT MORE...
MY BROTHER ALREADY WENT TO SCHOOL.
GOOD MORNING
HUH...? SOH-KUN?
ぱち WAKE
WHAT?! WHY?!
WHAT TIME IS IT?
AM I LATE?!
ガバッ SPRING
IT'S STILL SEVEN.
HE TOLD ME TO WAKE YOU UP AT SEVEN BEFORE HE LEFT.
OH...
...
...WAS YOH-CHAN ANGRY THIS MORNING?
I DON'T KNOW. MY BROTHER IS ALWAYS IN A BAD MOOD...
カチャ KA-CHAK
OH, AND BREAKFAST IS READY. SO HURRY.
IT'S GOING TO GET COLD.
HM. THANKS...
パタン SHUT

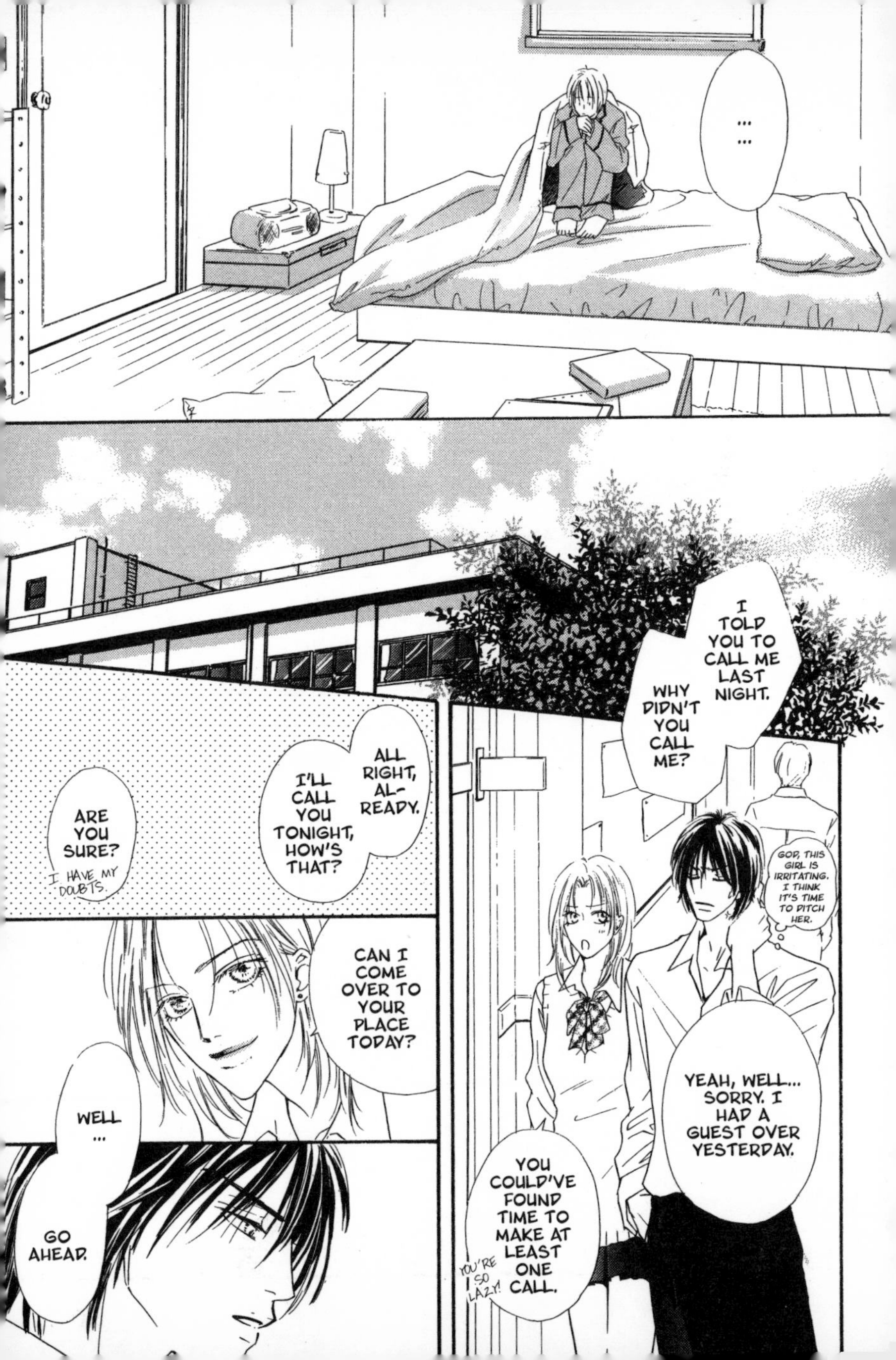
......
I TOLD YOU TO CALL ME LAST NIGHT.
WHY DIDN'T YOU CALL ME?
GOD, THIS GIRL IS IRRITATING. I THINK IT'S TIME TO PITCH HER.
YEAH, WELL... SORRY. I HAD A GUEST OVER YESTERDAY.
YOU COULD'VE FOUND TIME TO MAKE AT LEAST ONE CALL.
YOU'RE SO LAZY!
ALL RIGHT, AL-READY.
I'LL CALL YOU TONIGHT, HOW'S THAT?
ARE YOU SURE?
I HAVE MY DOUBTS.
CAN I COME OVER TO YOUR PLACE TODAY?
WELL ...
GO AHEAD.

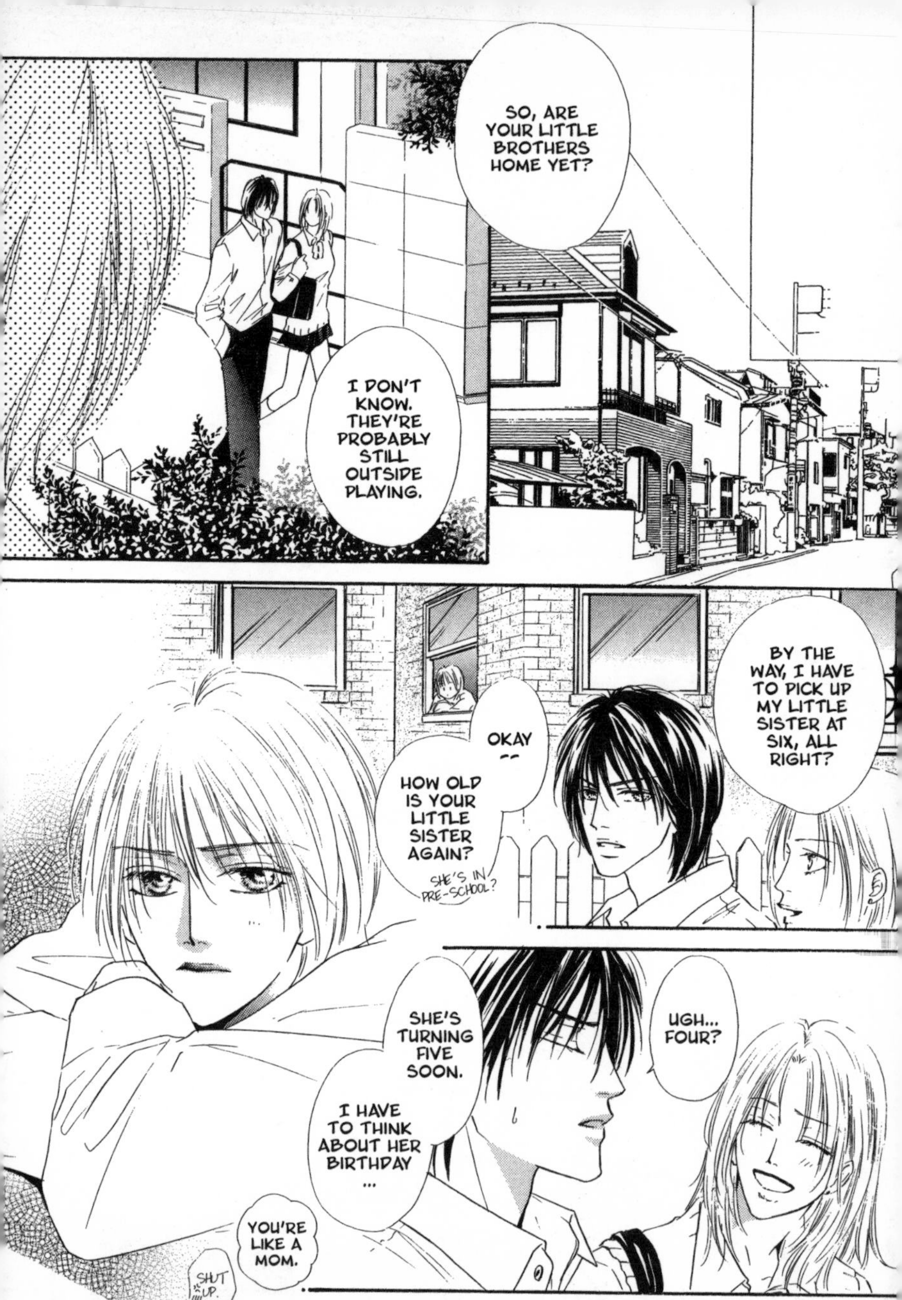
SO, ARE YOUR LITTLE BROTHERS HOME YET?
I DON'T KNOW. THEY'RE PROBABLY STILL OUTSIDE PLAYING.
BY THE WAY, I HAVE TO PICK UP MY LITTLE SISTER AT SIX, ALL RIGHT?
OKAY --
HOW OLD IS YOUR LITTLE SISTER AGAIN?
SHE'S IN PRE-SCHOOL?
UGH... FOUR?
SHE'S TURNING FIVE SOON.
I HAVE TO THINK ABOUT HER BIRTHDAY ...
YOU'RE LIKE A MOM.
SHUT UP.

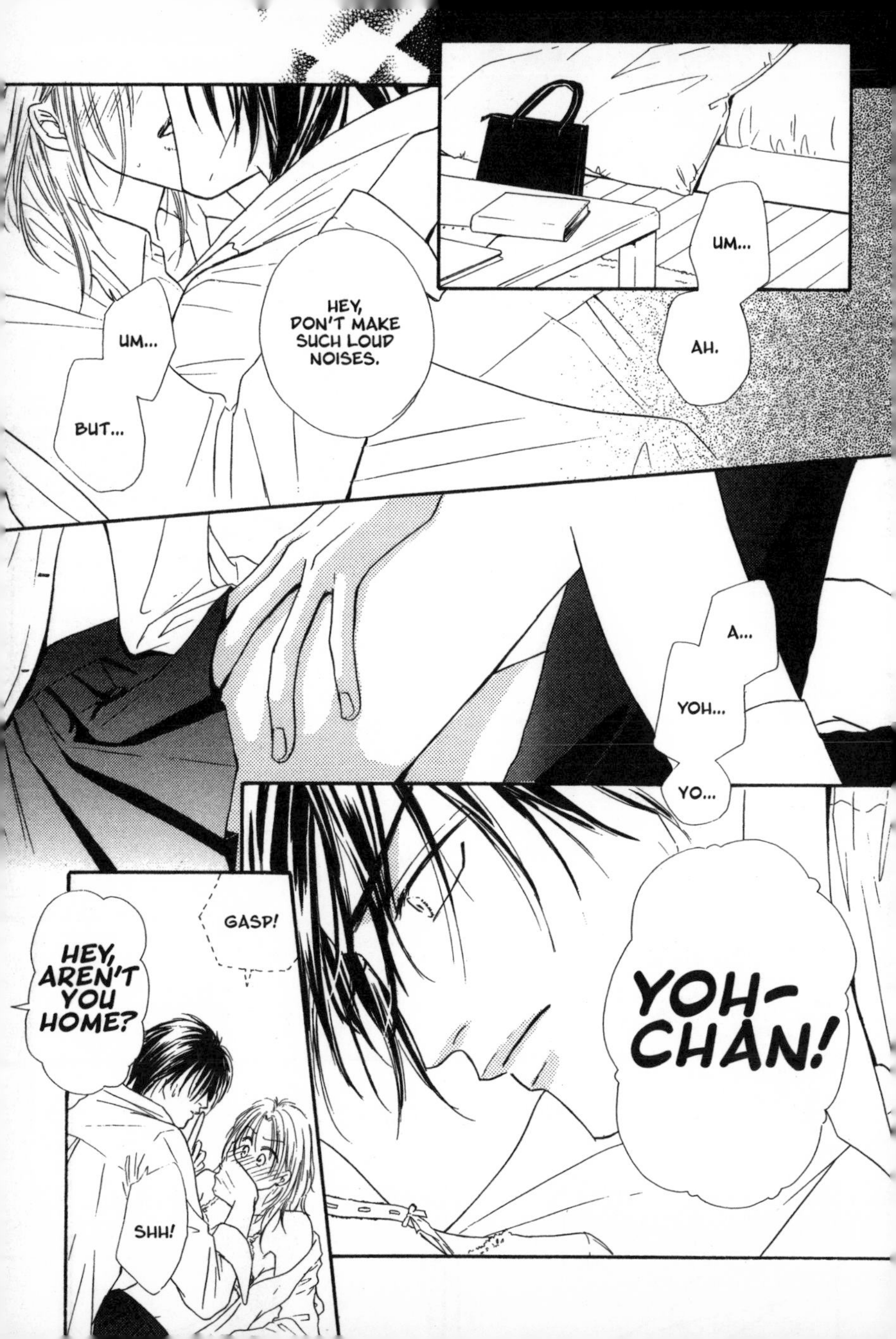
UM...
AH.
HEY, DON'T MAKE SUCH LOUD NOISES.
UM...
BUT...
A...
YOH...
YO...
YOH-CHAN!
GASP!
HEY, AREN'T YOU HOME?
SHH!

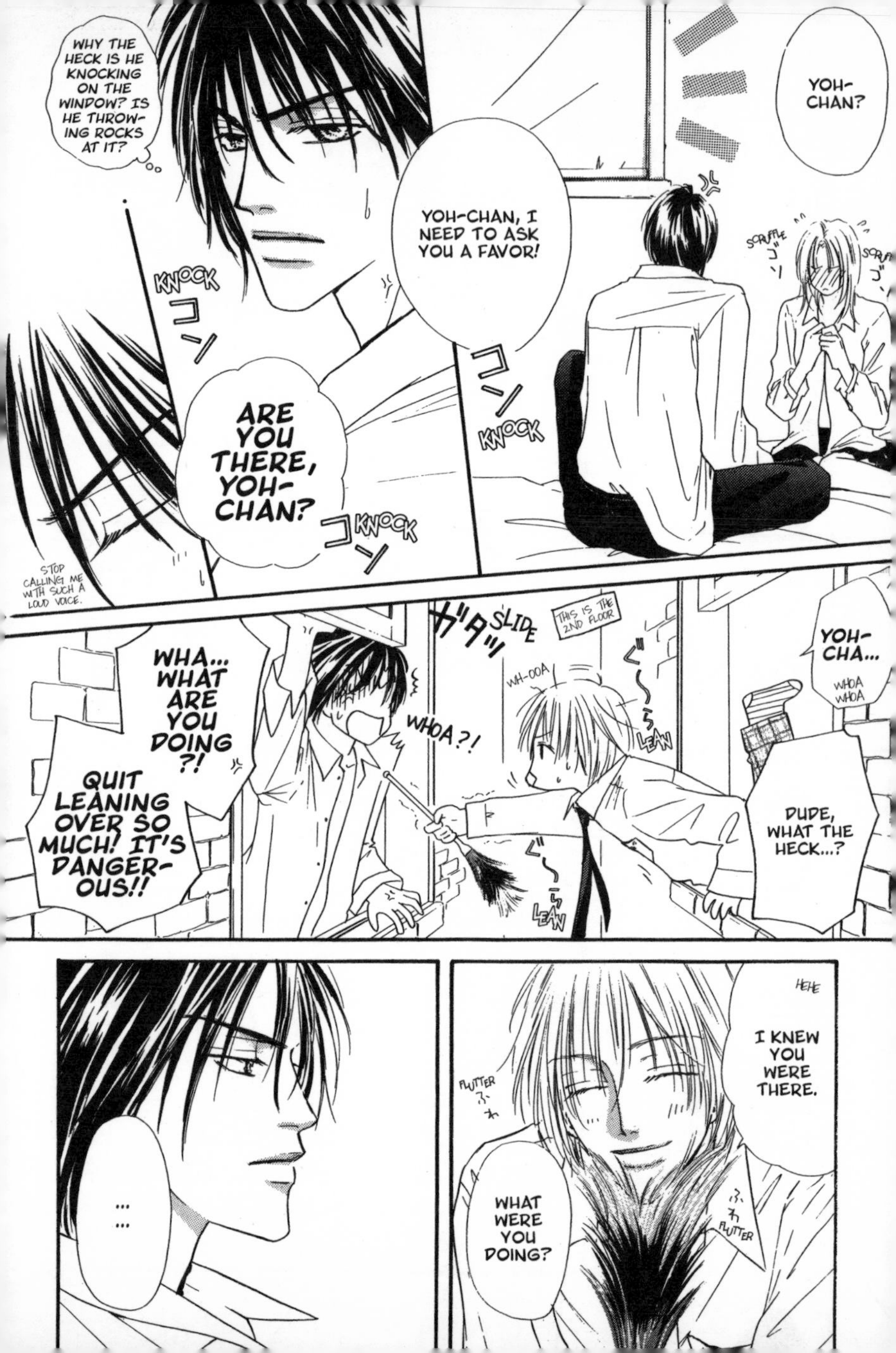

YOH-CHAN?
SCRUFFLE
SCRUFFLE
YOH-CHAN, I NEED TO ASK YOU A FAVOR!
KNOCK
WHY THE HECK IS HE KNOCKING ON THE WINDOW? IS HE THROWING ROCKS AT IT?
KNOCK
ARE YOU THERE, YOH-CHAN?
KNOCK
STOP CALLING ME WITH SUCH A LOUD VOICE.
YOH-CHA...
WHOA WHOA
DUDE, WHAT THE HECK...?
LEAN
THIS IS THE 2ND FLOOR
WH-OOA
SLIDE
WHOA?!
WHA... WHAT ARE YOU DOING?!
QUIT LEANING OVER SO MUCH! IT'S DANGEROUS!!
LEAN
HEHE
I KNEW YOU WERE THERE.
FLUTTER
WHAT WERE YOU DOING?
FLUTTER
... ...

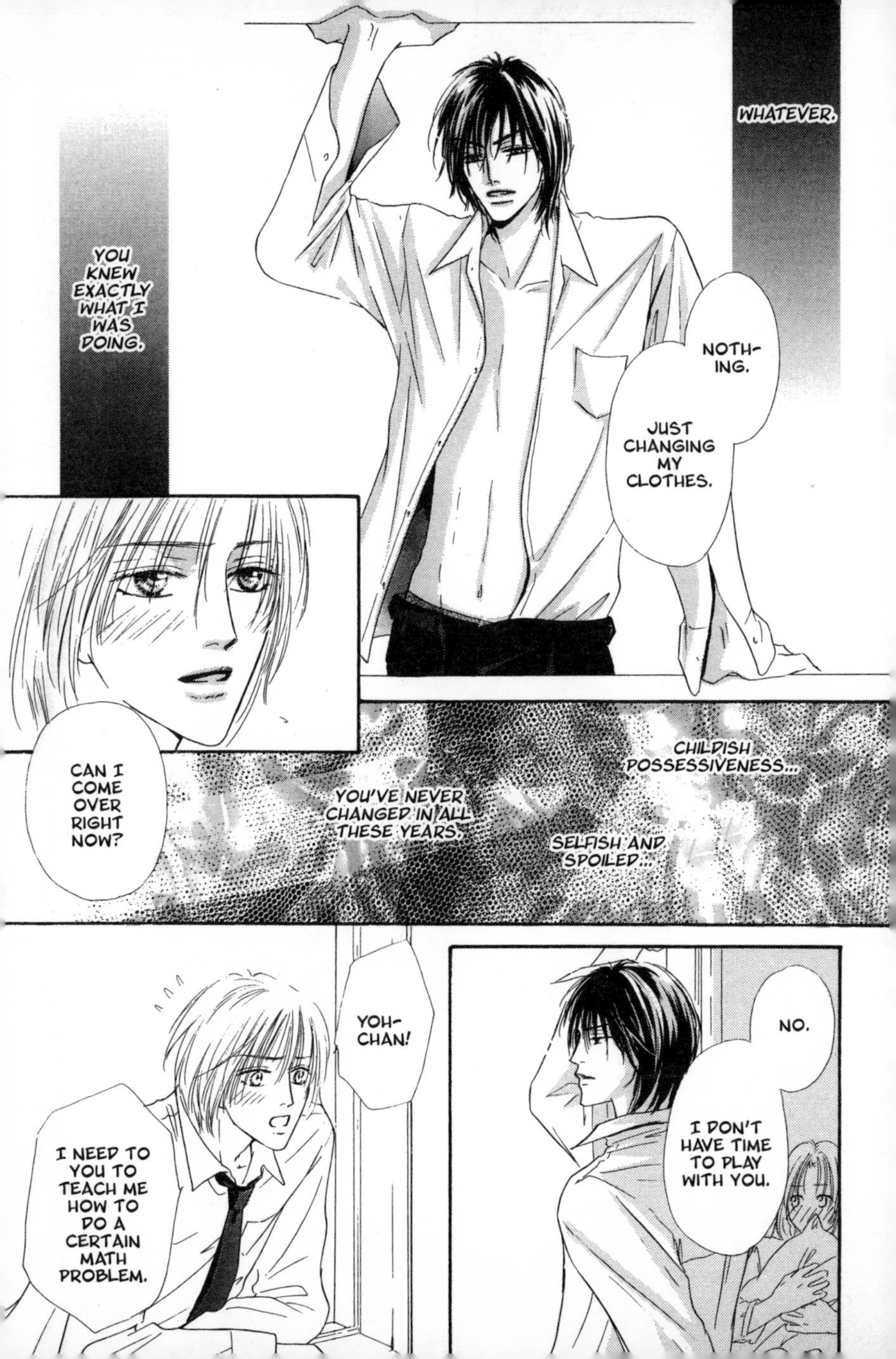
WHATEVER.
NOTH-ING.
JUST CHANGING MY CLOTHES.
YOU KNEW EXACTLY WHAT I WAS DOING.
CAN I COME OVER RIGHT NOW?
CHILDISH POSSESSIVENESS...
SELFISH AND SPOILED...
YOU'VE NEVER CHANGED IN ALL THESE YEARS.
NO.
I DON'T HAVE TIME TO PLAY WITH YOU.
YOH-CHAN!
I NEED TO YOU TO TEACH ME HOW TO DO A CERTAIN MATH PROBLEM.

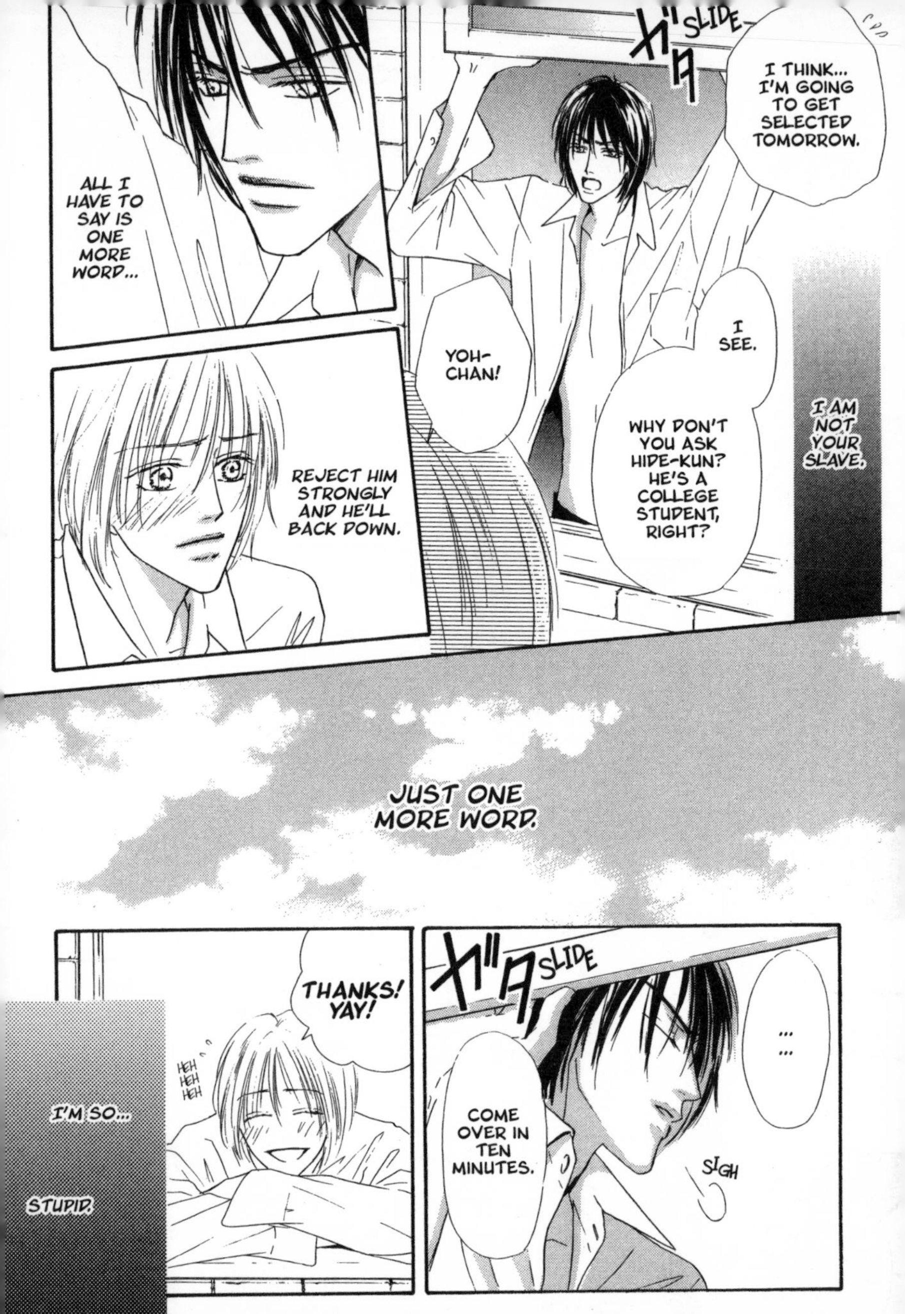
SLIDE
I THINK... I'M GOING TO GET SELECTED TOMORROW.
I SEE.
I AM NOT YOUR SLAVE.
WHY DON'T YOU ASK HIDE-KUN? HE'S A COLLEGE STUDENT, RIGHT?
YOH-CHAN!
ALL I HAVE TO SAY IS ONE MORE WORD...
REJECT HIM STRONGLY AND HE'LL BACK DOWN.
JUST ONE MORE WORD.
SLIDE
......
COME OVER IN TEN MINUTES.
SIGH
THANKS! YAY!
HEH HEH HEH
I'M SO...
STUPID.

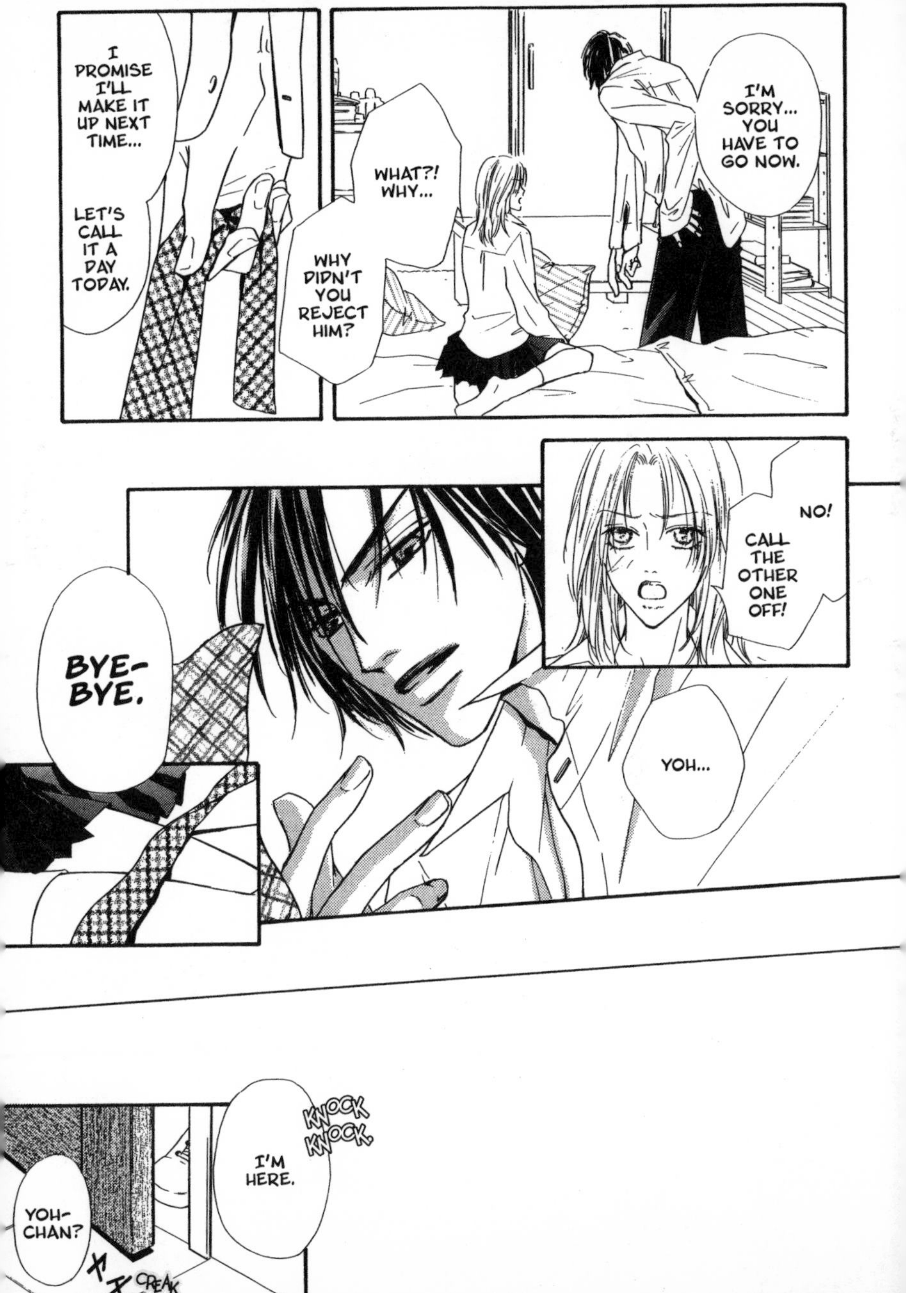
I'M SORRY... YOU HAVE TO GO NOW.
WHAT?! WHY...
WHY DIDN'T YOU REJECT HIM?
I PROMISE I'LL MAKE IT UP NEXT TIME...
LET'S CALL IT A DAY TODAY.
NO!
CALL THE OTHER ONE OFF!
YOH...
BYE-BYE.
KNOCK KNOCK.
I'M HERE.
YOH-CHAN?
CREAK

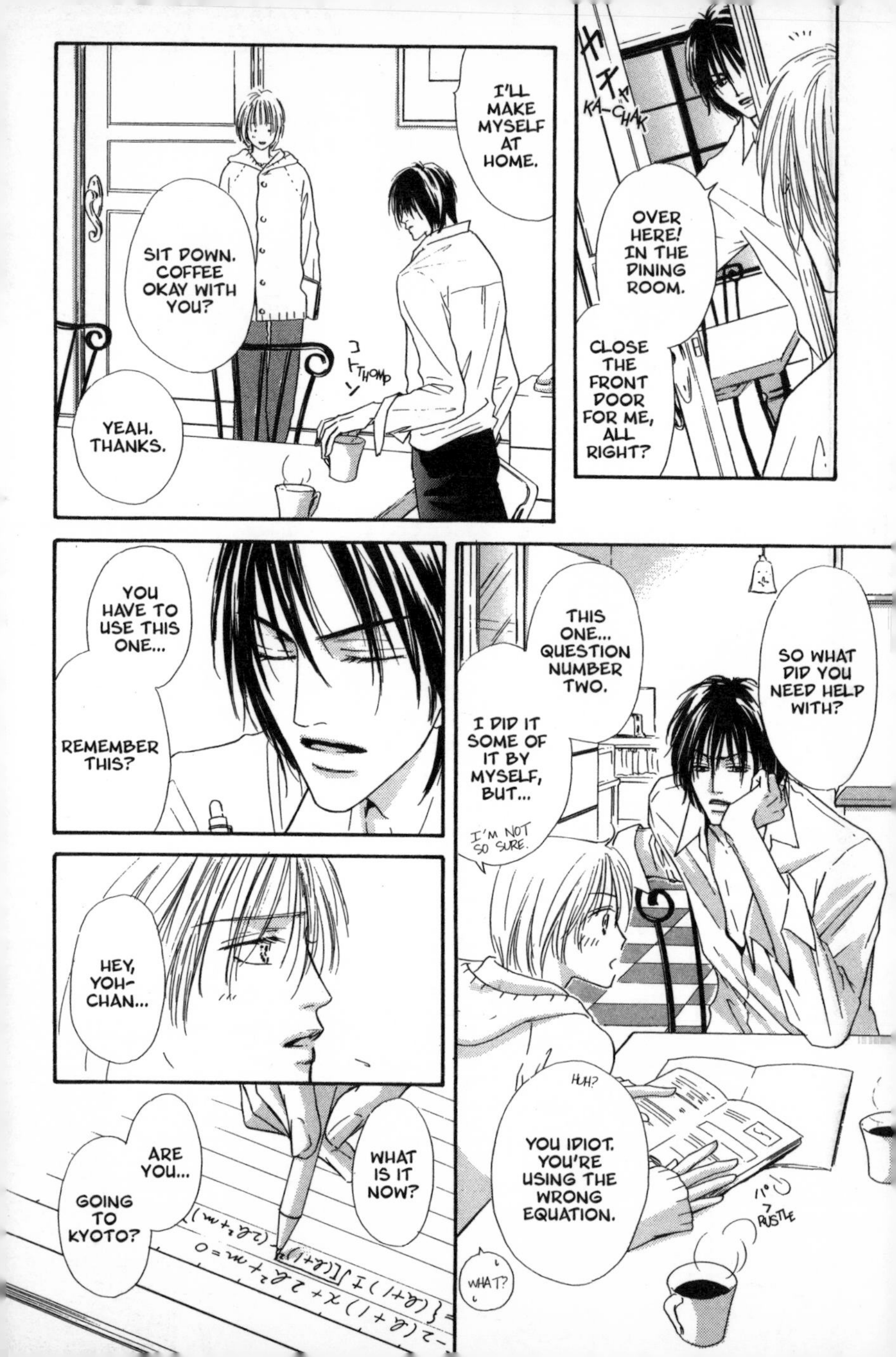
KA-CHAK
OVER HERE! IN THE DINING ROOM.
CLOSE THE FRONT DOOR FOR ME, ALL RIGHT?
I'LL MAKE MYSELF AT HOME.
SIT DOWN. COFFEE OKAY WITH YOU?
THOMP
YEAH. THANKS.
SO WHAT DID YOU NEED HELP WITH?
THIS ONE... QUESTION NUMBER TWO.
I DID IT SOME OF IT BY MYSELF, BUT...
I'M NOT SO SURE.
HUH?
YOU IDIOT. YOU'RE USING THE WRONG EQUATION.
RUSTLE
WHAT?
YOU HAVE TO USE THIS ONE...
REMEMBER THIS?
HEY, YOH-CHAN...
WHAT IS IT NOW?
ARE YOU...
GOING TO KYOTO?

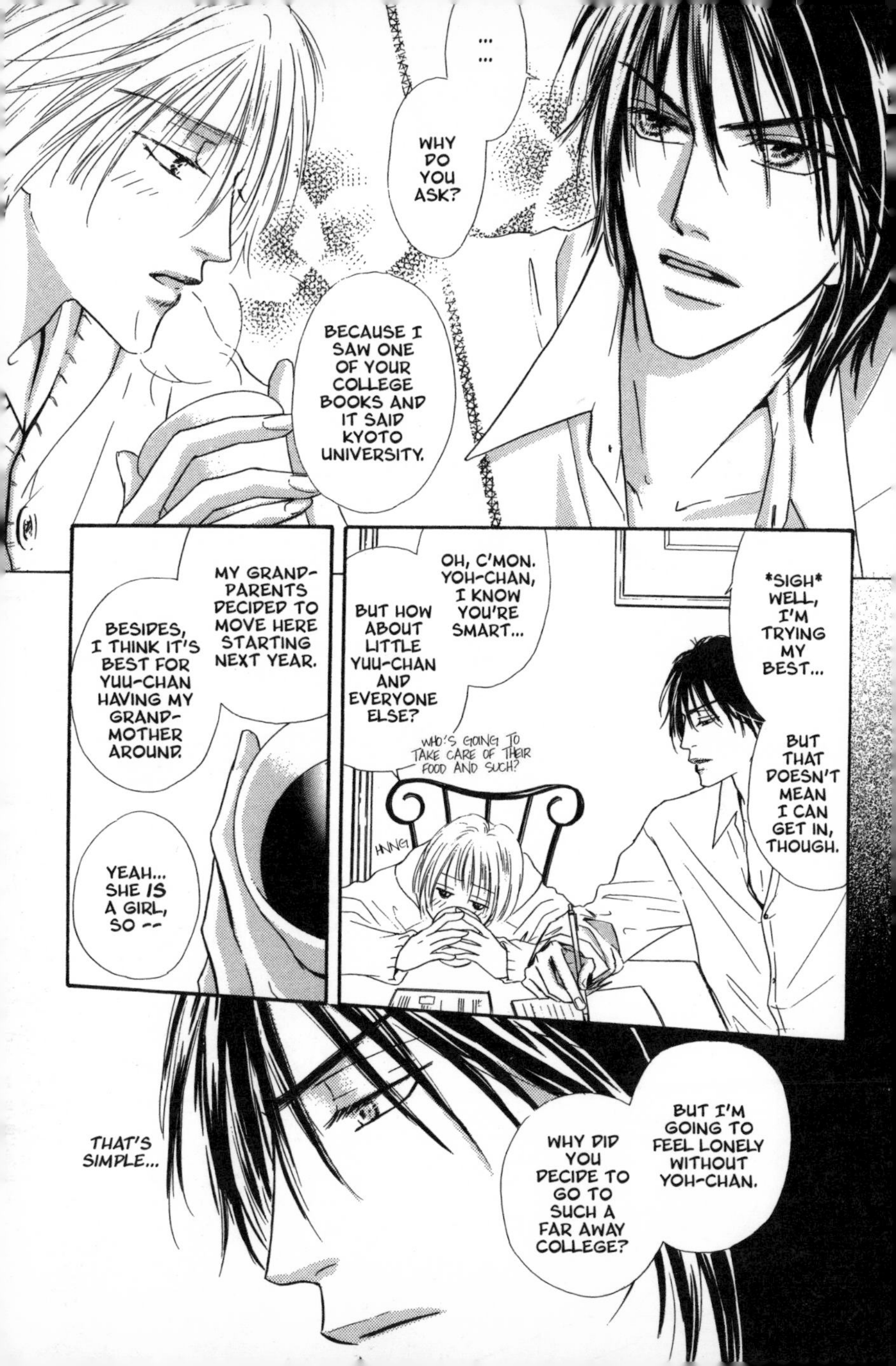
... ...
WHY DO YOU ASK?
BECAUSE I SAW ONE OF YOUR COLLEGE BOOKS AND IT SAID KYOTO UNIVERSITY.
SIGH WELL, I'M TRYING MY BEST...
BUT THAT DOESN'T MEAN I CAN GET IN, THOUGH.
OH, C'MON. YOH-CHAN, I KNOW YOU'RE SMART...
BUT HOW ABOUT LITTLE YUU-CHAN AND EVERYONE ELSE?
WHO'S GOING TO TAKE CARE OF THEIR FOOD AND SUCH?
HNNG
MY GRAND-PARENTS DECIDED TO MOVE HERE STARTING NEXT YEAR.
BESIDES, I THINK IT'S BEST FOR YUU-CHAN HAVING MY GRAND-MOTHER AROUND.
YEAH... SHE IS A GIRL, SO --
BUT I'M GOING TO FEEL LONELY WITHOUT YOH-CHAN.
WHY DID YOU DECIDE TO GO TO SUCH A FAR AWAY COLLEGE?
THAT'S SIMPLE...

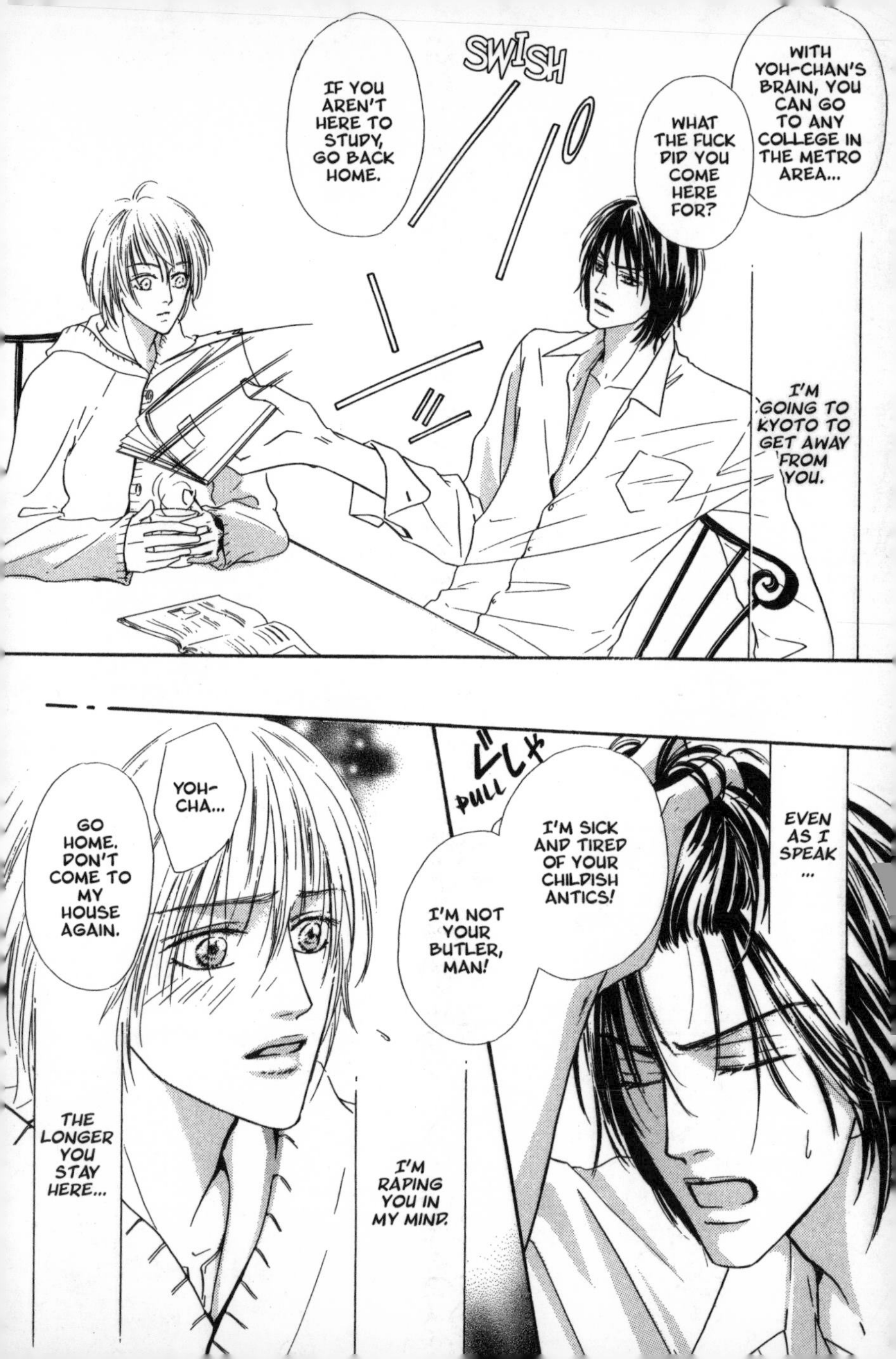
WITH YOH-CHAN'S BRAIN, YOU CAN GO TO ANY COLLEGE IN THE METRO AREA...
WHAT THE FUCK DID YOU COME HERE FOR?
SWISH
IF YOU AREN'T HERE TO STUDY, GO BACK HOME.
I'M GOING TO KYOTO TO GET AWAY FROM YOU.
EVEN AS I SPEAK ...
PULL
I'M SICK AND TIRED OF YOUR CHILDISH ANTICS!
I'M NOT YOUR BUTLER, MAN!
YOH-CHA...
GO HOME. DON'T COME TO MY HOUSE AGAIN.
I'M RAPING YOU IN MY MIND.
THE LONGER YOU STAY HERE...

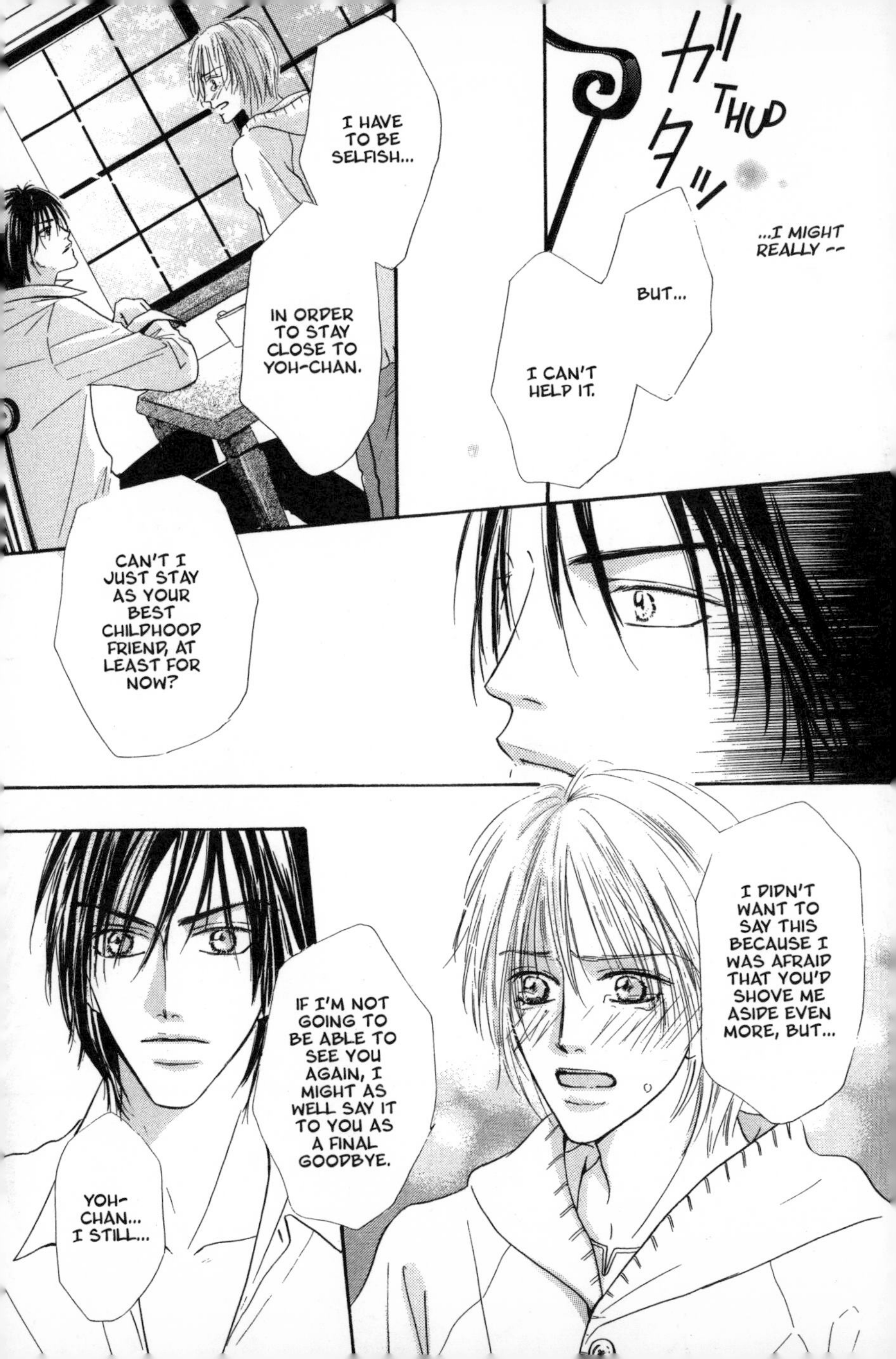
ガタッ
THUD
...I MIGHT REALLY --
BUT...
I CAN'T HELP IT.
I HAVE TO BE SELFISH...
IN ORDER TO STAY CLOSE TO YOH-CHAN.
CAN'T I JUST STAY AS YOUR BEST CHILDHOOD FRIEND, AT LEAST FOR NOW?
I DIDN'T WANT TO SAY THIS BECAUSE I WAS AFRAID THAT YOU'D SHOVE ME ASIDE EVEN MORE, BUT...
IF I'M NOT GOING TO BE ABLE TO SEE YOU AGAIN, I MIGHT AS WELL SAY IT TO YOU AS A FINAL GOODBYE.
YOH-CHAN... I STILL...

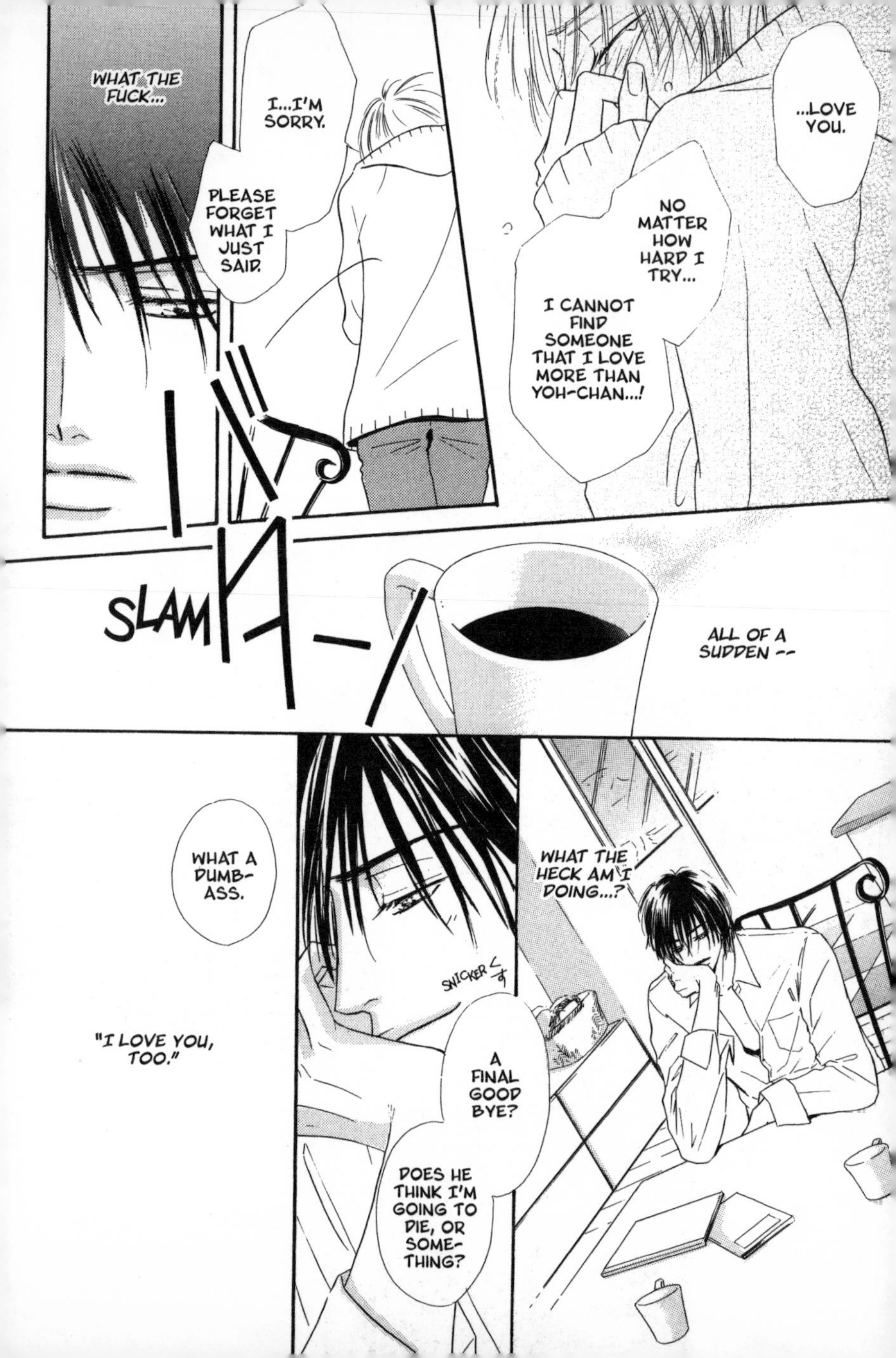
...LOVE YOU.
NO MATTER HOW HARD I TRY...
I CANNOT FIND SOMEONE THAT I LOVE MORE THAN YOH-CHAN...!
I...I'M SORRY.
PLEASE FORGET WHAT I JUST SAID.
WHAT THE FUCK...
ALL OF A SUDDEN --
SLAM
WHAT THE HECK AM I DOING...?
SNICKER
A FINAL GOOD BYE?
DOES HE THINK I'M GOING TO DIE, OR SOME-THING?
WHAT A DUMB-ASS.
"I LOVE YOU, TOO."

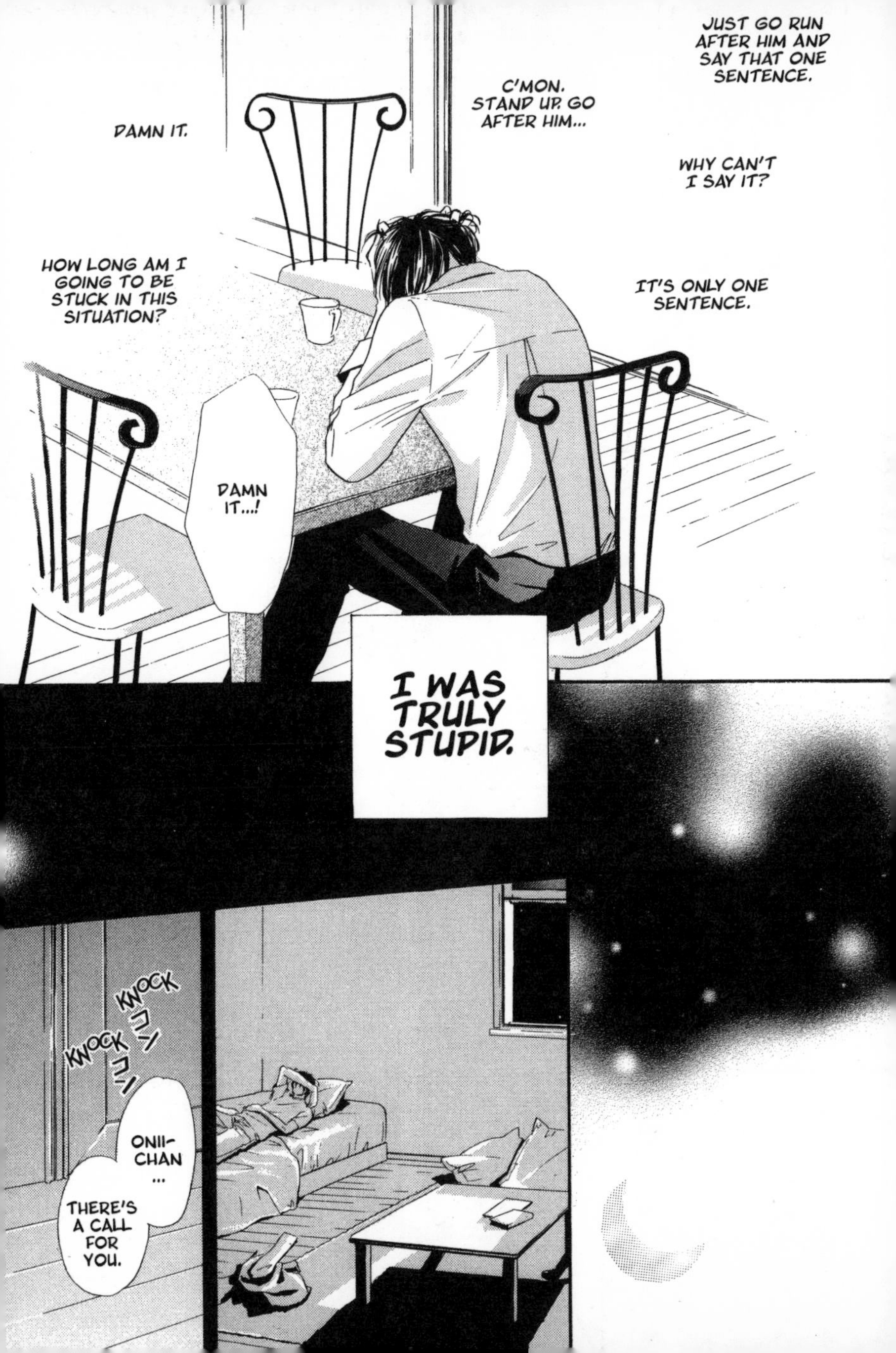
JUST GO RUN AFTER HIM AND SAY THAT ONE SENTENCE.
C'MON. STAND UP. GO AFTER HIM...
DAMN IT.
WHY CAN'T I SAY IT?
IT'S ONLY ONE SENTENCE.
HOW LONG AM I GOING TO BE STUCK IN THIS SITUATION?
DAMN IT...!
I WAS TRULY STUPID.
KNOCK
KNOCK
ONII-CHAN ... THERE'S A CALL FOR YOU.

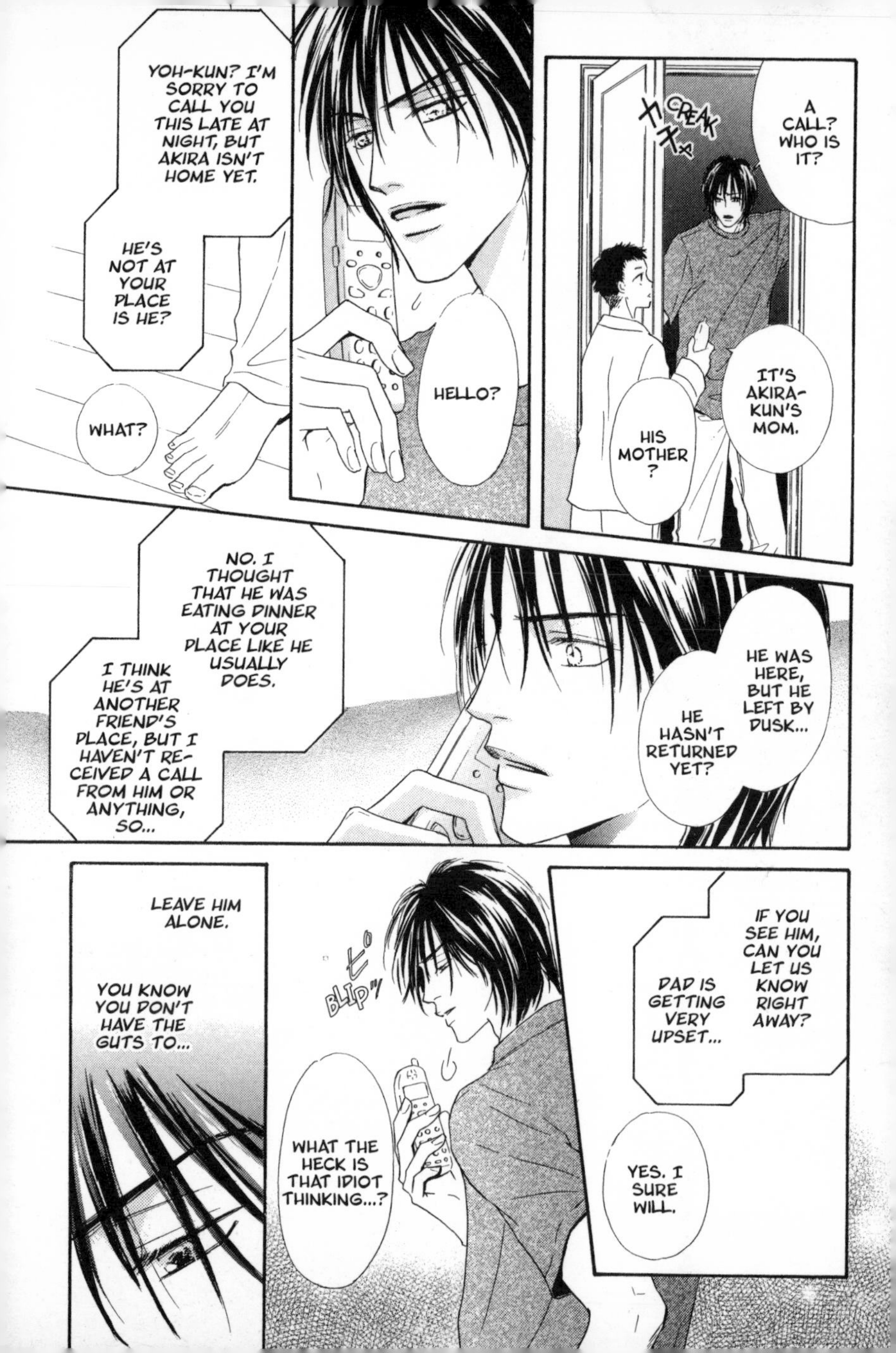
A CALL? WHO IS IT?
CREAK
IT'S AKIRA-KUN'S MOM.
HIS MOTHER?
HELLO?
YOH-KUN? I'M SORRY TO CALL YOU THIS LATE AT NIGHT, BUT AKIRA ISN'T HOME YET.
HE'S NOT AT YOUR PLACE IS HE?
WHAT?
HE WAS HERE, BUT HE LEFT BY DUSK...
HE HASN'T RETURNED YET?
NO. I THOUGHT THAT HE WAS EATING DINNER AT YOUR PLACE LIKE HE USUALLY DOES.
I THINK HE'S AT ANOTHER FRIEND'S PLACE, BUT I HAVEN'T RE-CEIVED A CALL FROM HIM OR ANYTHING, SO...
IF YOU SEE HIM, CAN YOU LET US KNOW RIGHT AWAY?
DAD IS GETTING VERY UPSET...
YES. I SURE WILL.
BLIP
WHAT THE HECK IS THAT IDIOT THINKING...?
LEAVE HIM ALONE.
YOU KNOW YOU DON'T HAVE THE GUTS TO...

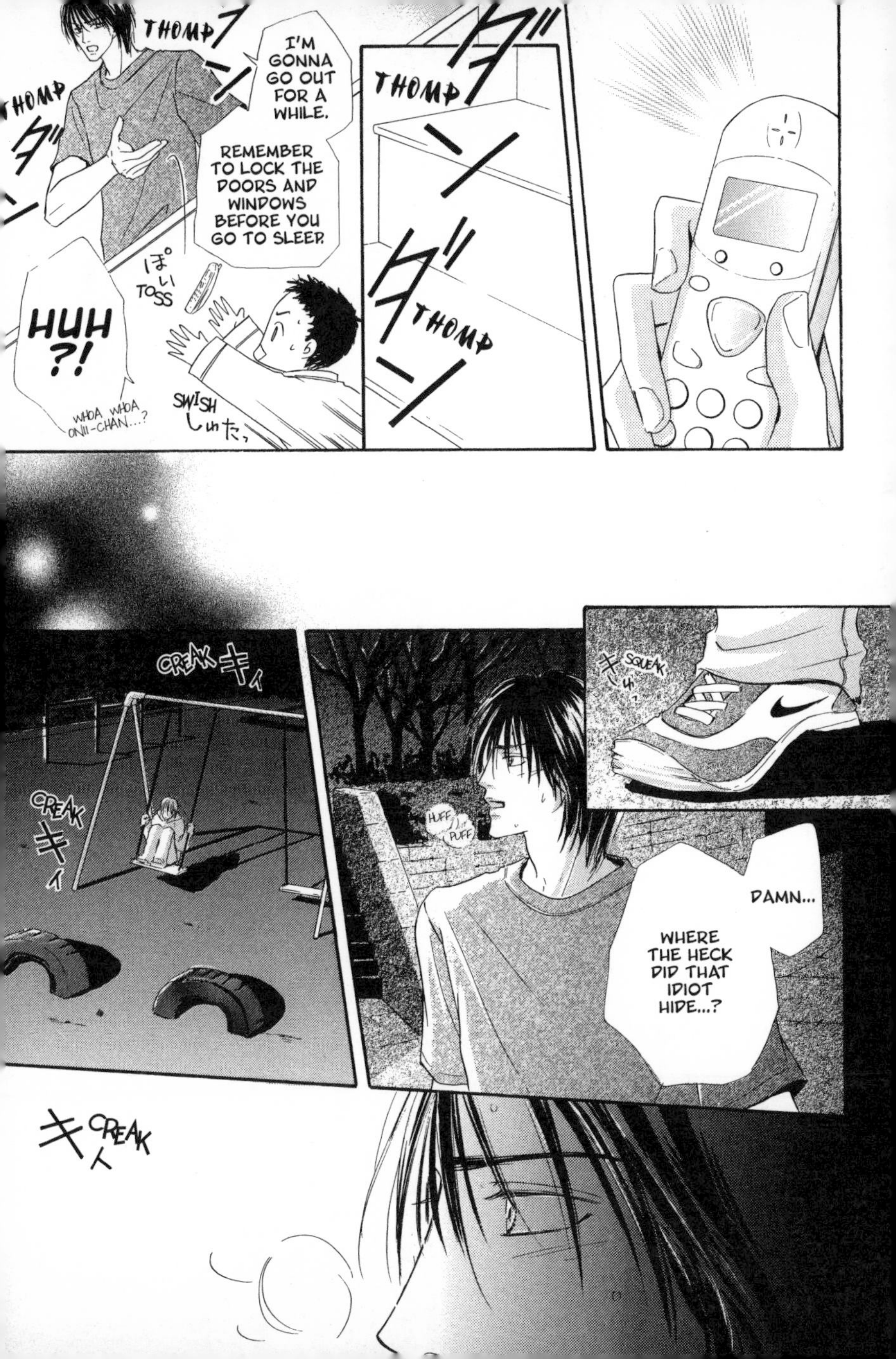

THOMP
THOMP
I'M GONNA GO OUT FOR A WHILE.
REMEMBER TO LOCK THE DOORS AND WINDOWS BEFORE YOU GO TO SLEEP.
THOMP
THOMP
ぽい TOSS
HUH ?!
WHOA WHOA ONII-CHAN...?
SWISH しゅたっ
SQUEAK
HUFF PUFF
DAMN...
WHERE THE HECK DID THAT IDIOT HIDE...?
CREAK キィ
CREAK キィ
キィ CREAK

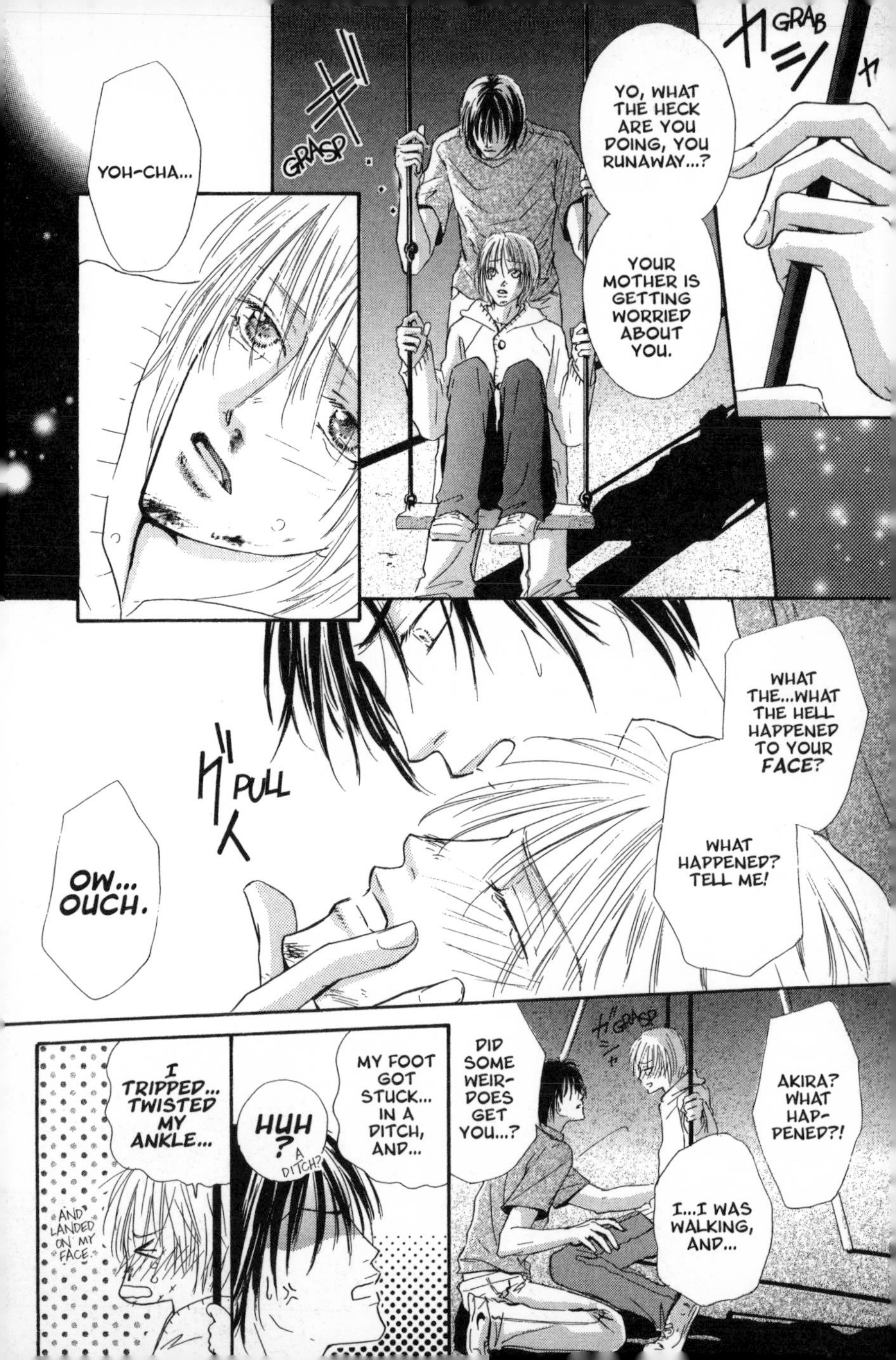
GRAB
YO, WHAT THE HECK ARE YOU DOING, YOU RUNAWAY...?
YOUR MOTHER IS GETTING WORRIED ABOUT YOU.
GRASP
YOH-CHA...
WHAT THE...WHAT THE HELL HAPPENED TO YOUR FACE?
WHAT HAPPENED? TELL ME!
PULL
OW... OUCH.
AKIRA? WHAT HAP-PENED?!
I...I WAS WALKING, AND...
GRASP
DID SOME WEIR-DOES GET YOU...?
MY FOOT GOT STUCK... IN A DITCH, AND...
HUH?
A DITCH?
I TRIPPED... TWISTED MY ANKLE...
AND LANDED ON MY FACE.

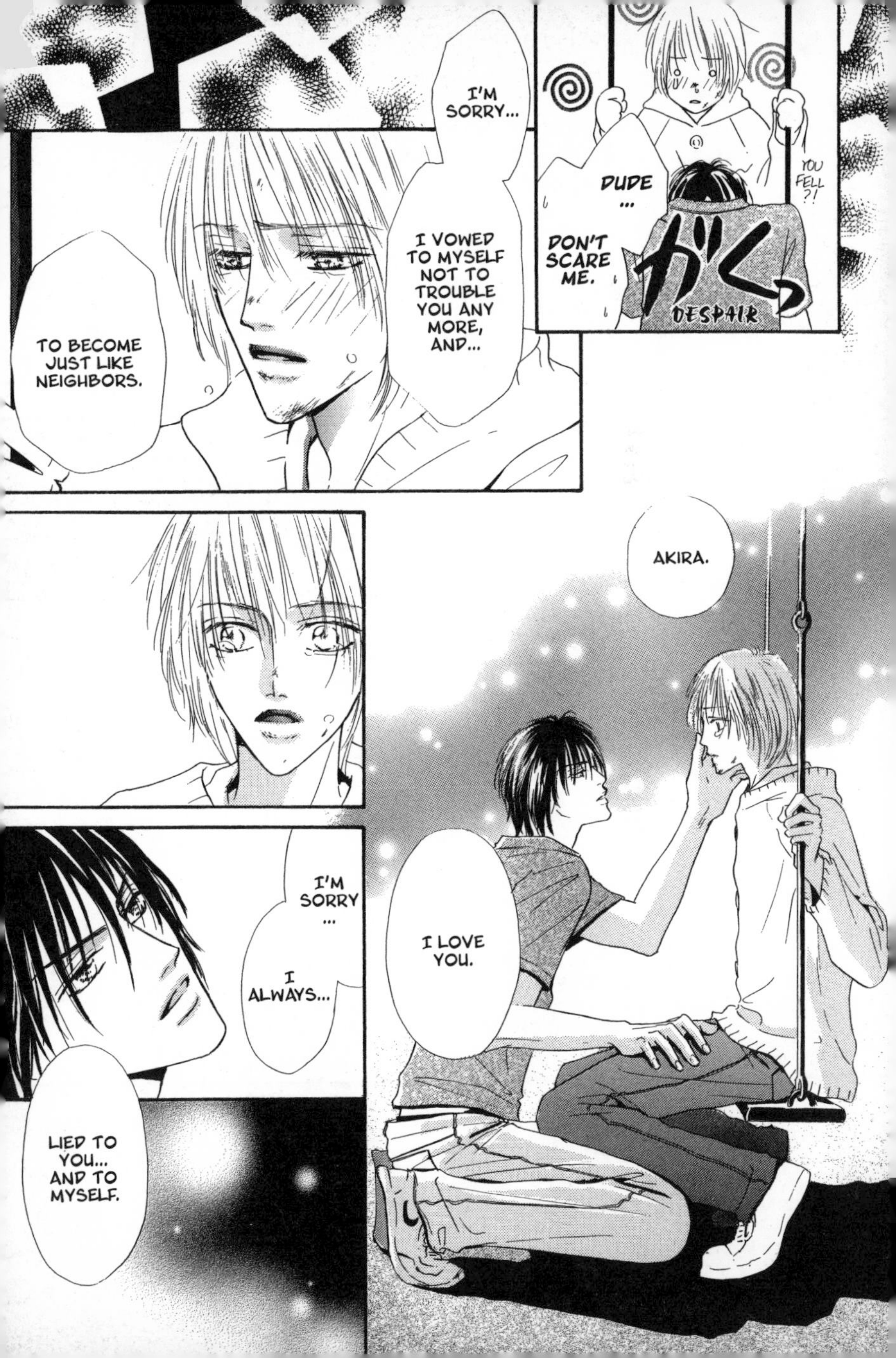
YOU FELL ?!
DUDE ...
DON'T SCARE ME.
がくっ
DESPAIR
I'M SORRY...
I VOWED TO MYSELF NOT TO TROUBLE YOU ANY MORE, AND...
TO BECOME JUST LIKE NEIGHBORS.
AKIRA.
I LOVE YOU.
I'M SORRY ...
I ALWAYS...
LIED TO YOU... AND TO MYSELF.

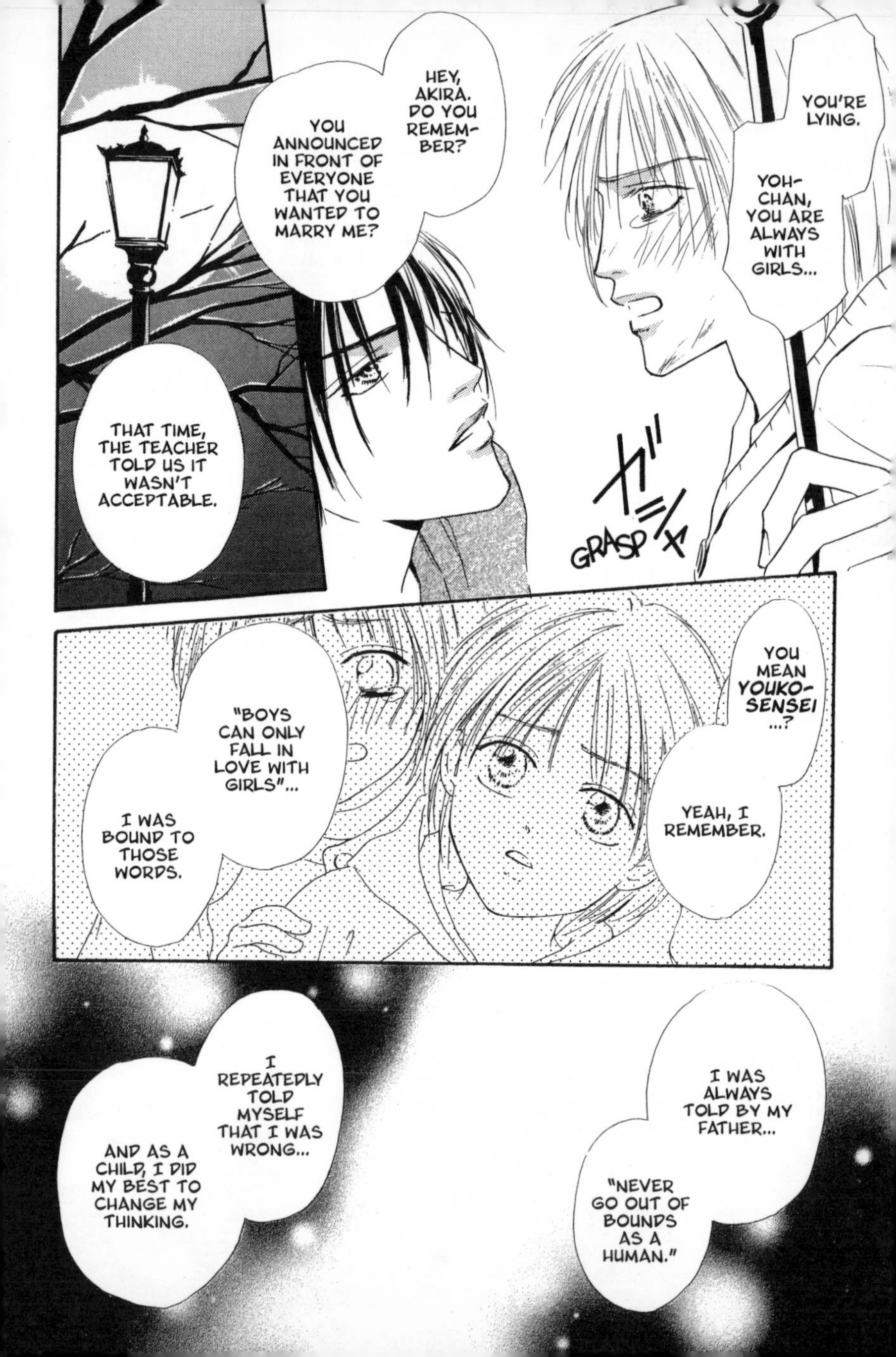
YOU'RE LYING.
YOH-CHAN, YOU ARE ALWAYS WITH GIRLS...
HEY, AKIRA. DO YOU REMEM-BER?
YOU ANNOUNCED IN FRONT OF EVERYONE THAT YOU WANTED TO MARRY ME?
GRASP
THAT TIME, THE TEACHER TOLD US IT WASN'T ACCEPTABLE.
YOU MEAN YOUKO-SENSEI ...?
YEAH, I REMEMBER.
"BOYS CAN ONLY FALL IN LOVE WITH GIRLS"...
I WAS BOUND TO THOSE WORDS.
I WAS ALWAYS TOLD BY MY FATHER...
"NEVER GO OUT OF BOUNDS AS A HUMAN."
I REPEATEDLY TOLD MYSELF THAT I WAS WRONG...
AND AS A CHILD, I DID MY BEST TO CHANGE MY THINKING.

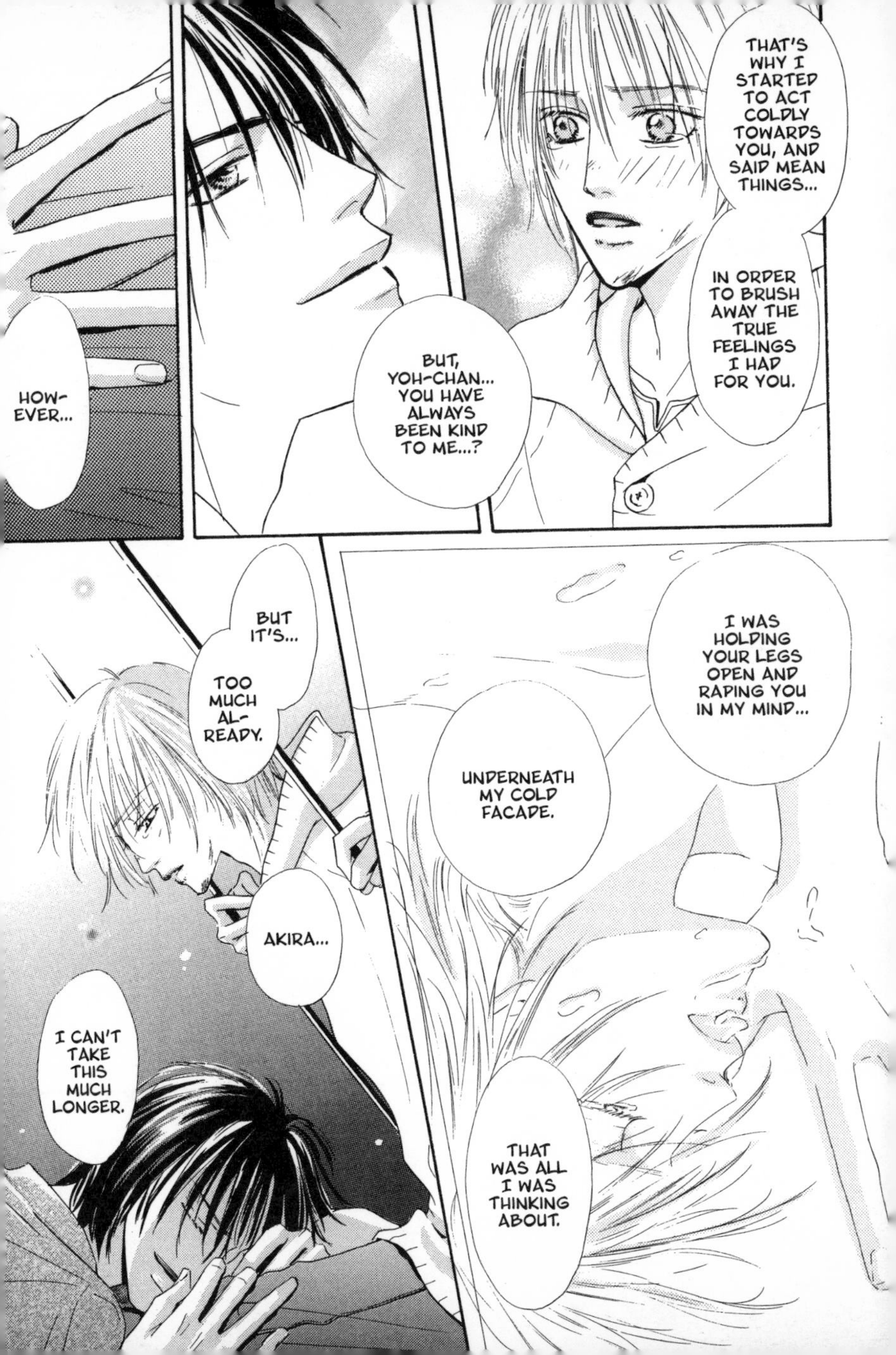
THAT'S WHY I STARTED TO ACT COLDLY TOWARDS YOU, AND SAID MEAN THINGS...
IN ORDER TO BRUSH AWAY THE TRUE FEELINGS I HAD FOR YOU.
BUT, YOH-CHAN... YOU HAVE ALWAYS BEEN KIND TO ME...?
HOW-EVER...
I WAS HOLDING YOUR LEGS OPEN AND RAPING YOU IN MY MIND...
UNDERNEATH MY COLD FACADE.
THAT WAS ALL I WAS THINKING ABOUT.
BUT IT'S...
TOO MUCH AL-READY.
AKIRA...
I CAN'T TAKE THIS MUCH LONGER.

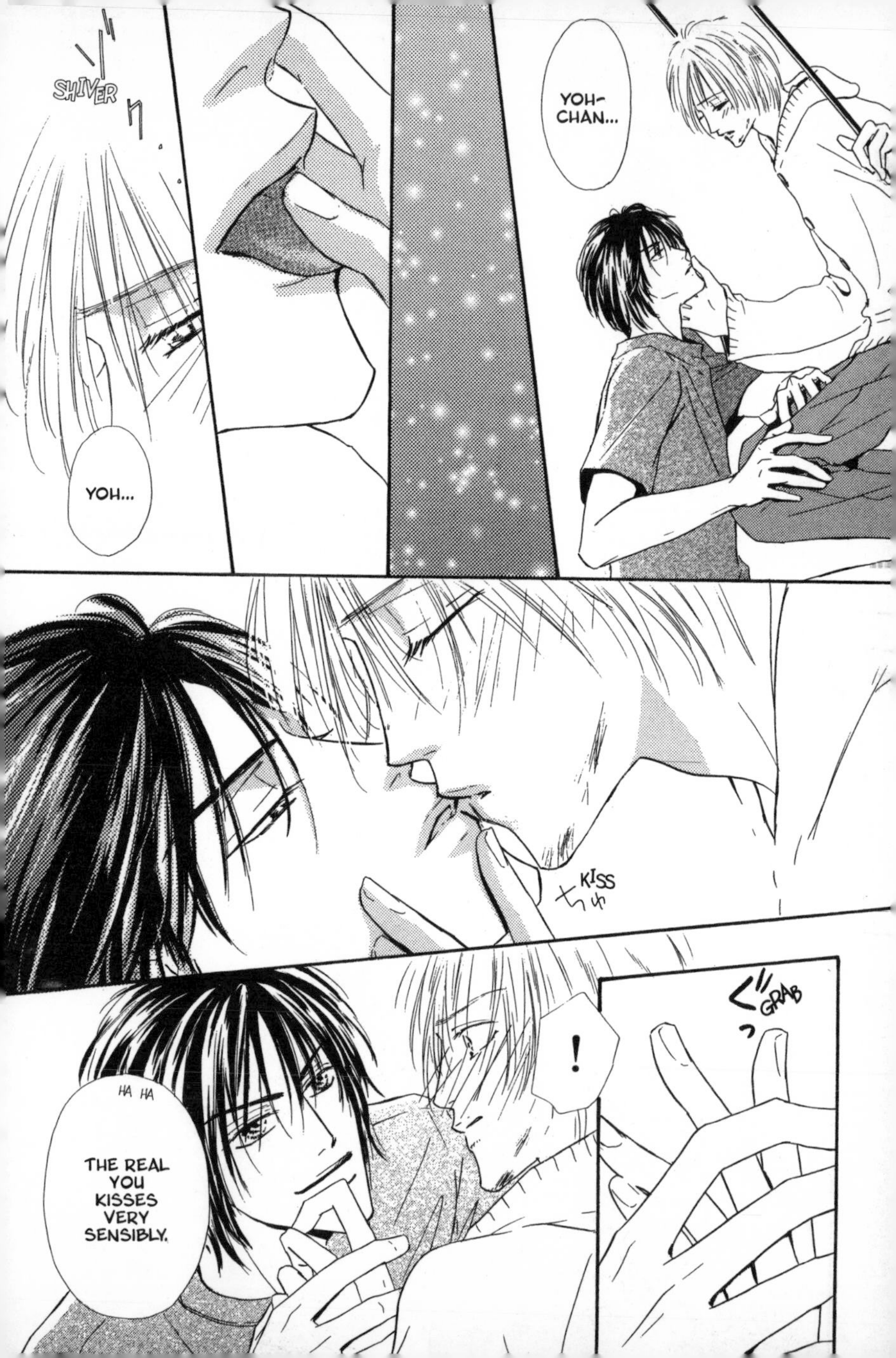
YOH-CHAN...
SHIVER
YOH...
KISS
GRAB
!
HA HA
THE REAL YOU KISSES VERY SENSIBLY.

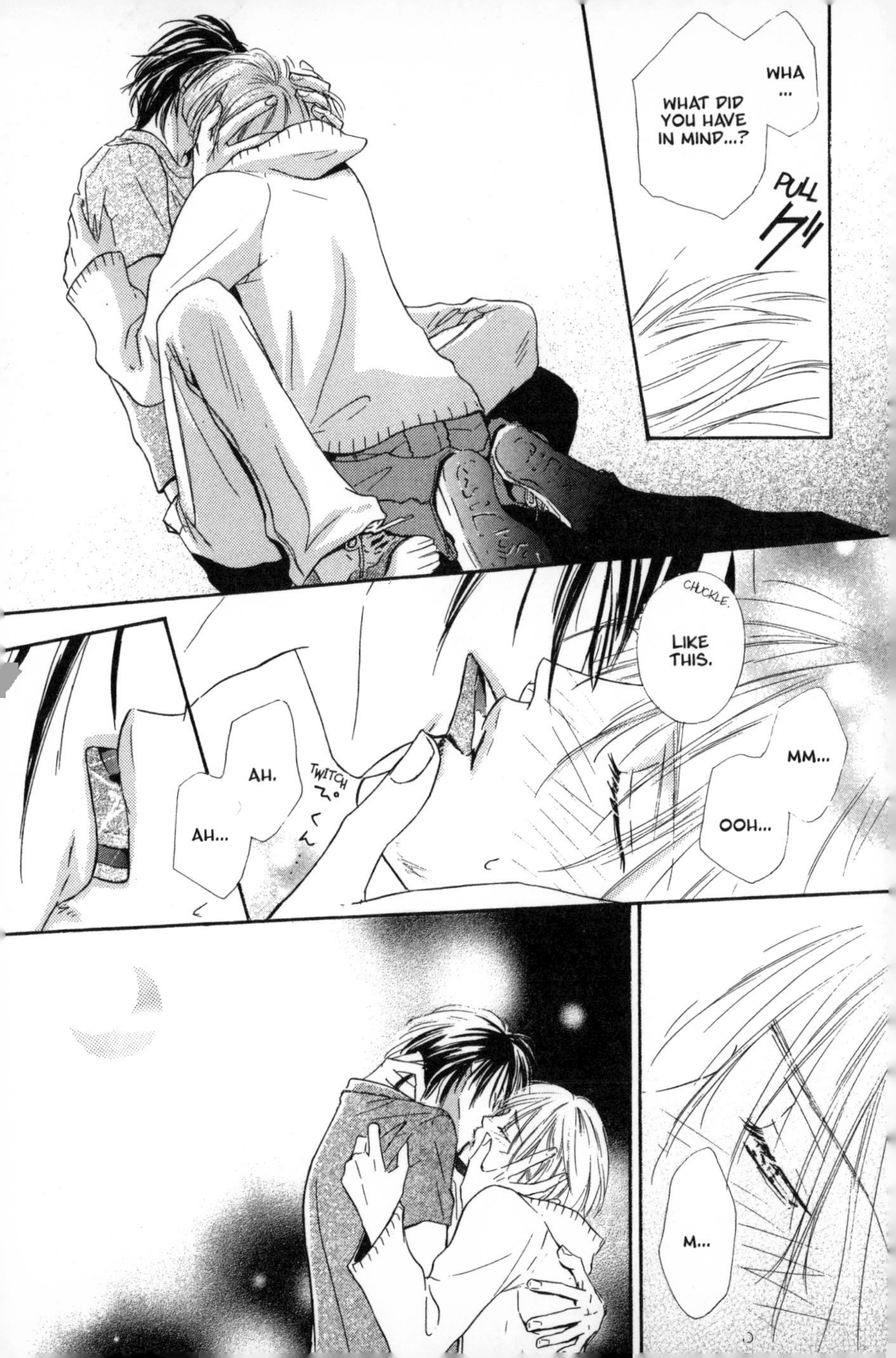
WHA ...
WHAT DID YOU HAVE IN MIND...?
PULL
CHUCKLE.
LIKE THIS.
MM...
OOH...
AH.
AH...
TWITCH
M...

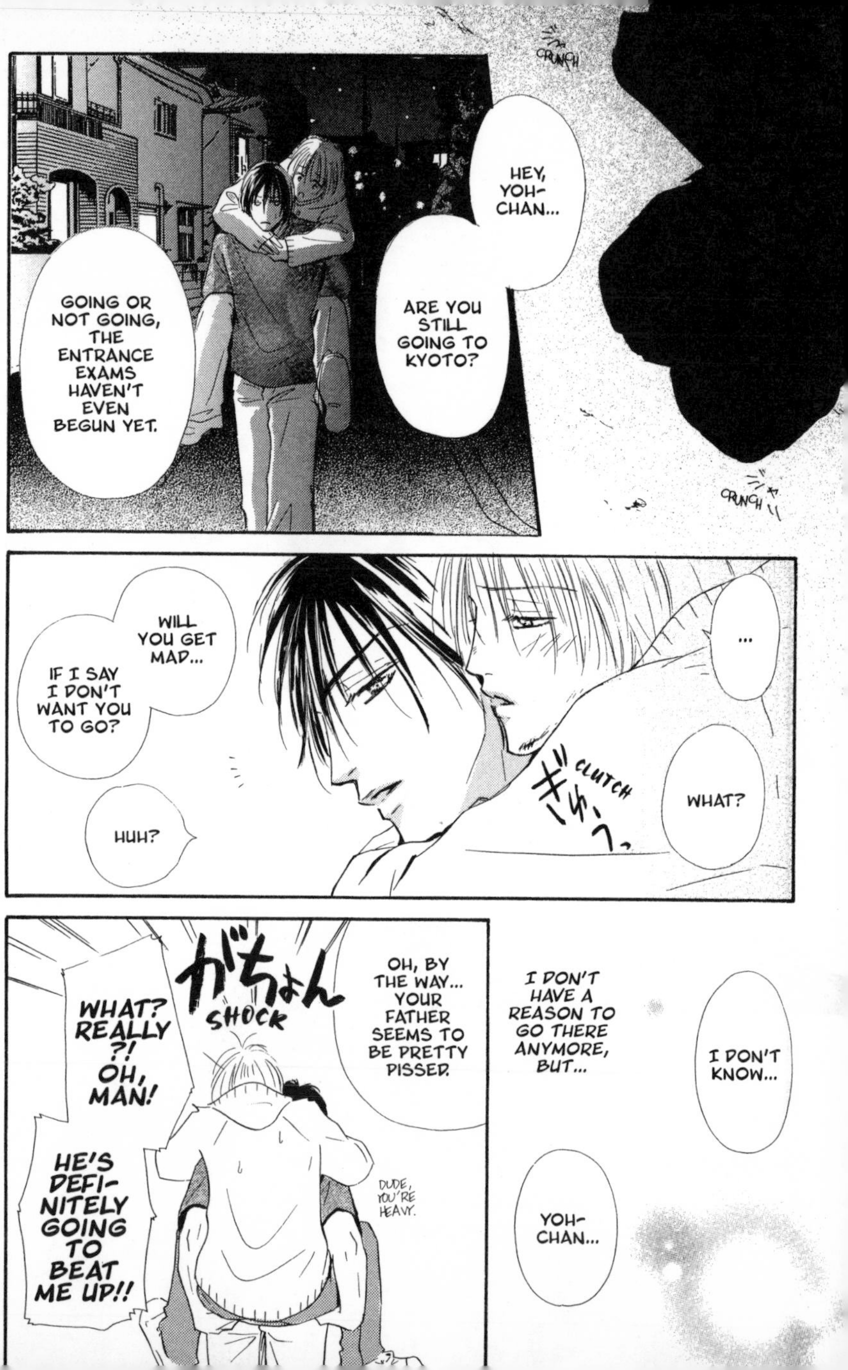
CRUNCH
HEY, YOH-CHAN...
ARE YOU STILL GOING TO KYOTO?
GOING OR NOT GOING, THE ENTRANCE EXAMS HAVEN'T EVEN BEGUN YET.
CRUNCH
...
WHAT?
CLUTCH
WILL YOU GET MAD...
IF I SAY I DON'T WANT YOU TO GO?
HUH?
I DON'T KNOW...
YOH-CHAN...
I DON'T HAVE A REASON TO GO THERE ANYMORE, BUT...
OH, BY THE WAY... YOUR FATHER SEEMS TO BE PRETTY PISSED.
がちょん
SHOCK
WHAT? REALLY?! OH, MAN!
HE'S DEFI-NITELY GOING TO BEAT ME UP!!
DUDE, YOU'RE HEAVY.

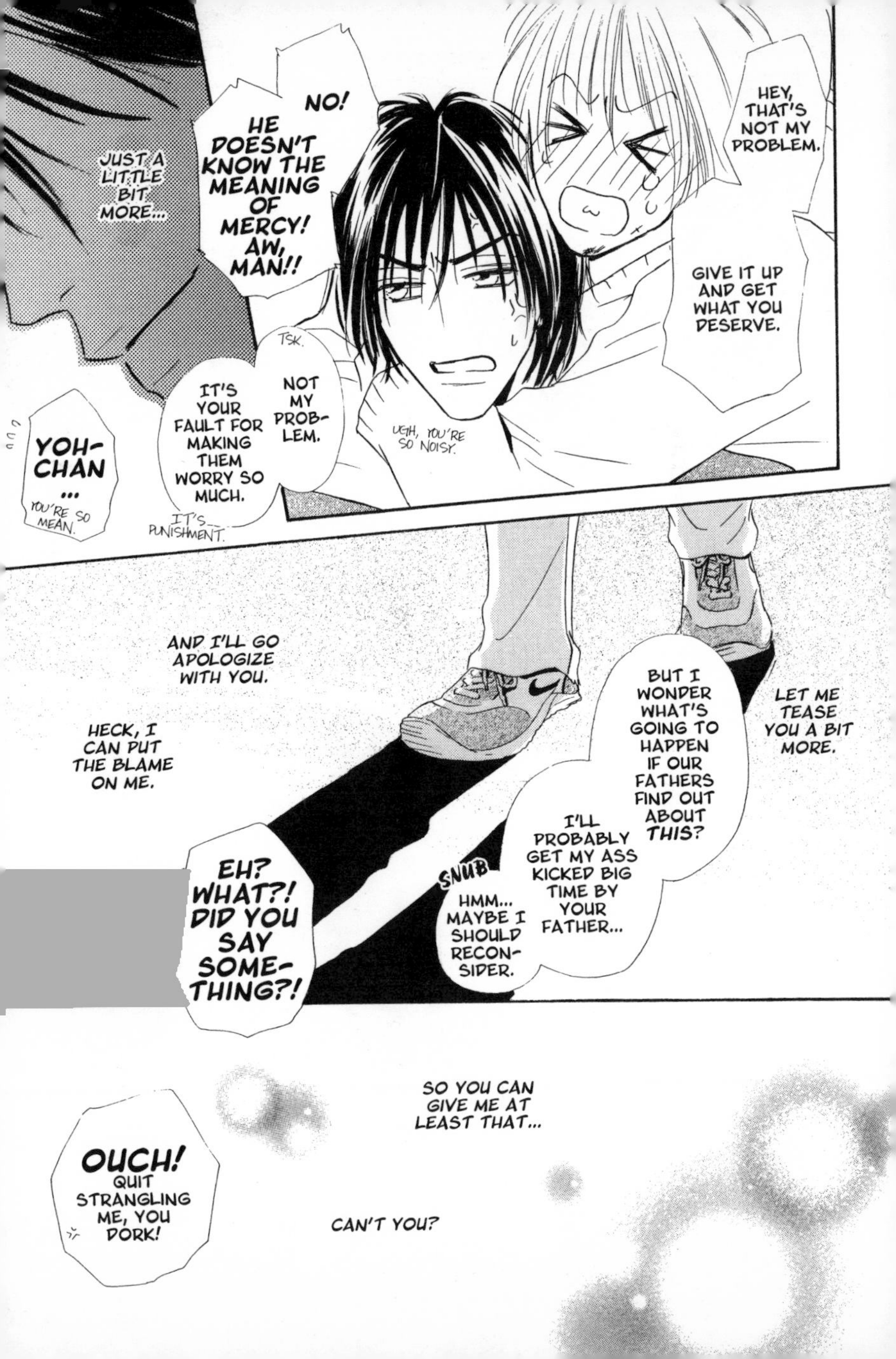
HEY, THAT'S NOT MY PROBLEM.
GIVE IT UP AND GET WHAT YOU DESERVE.
NO! HE DOESN'T KNOW THE MEANING OF MERCY! AW, MAN!!
UGH, YOU'RE SO NOISY.
TSK.
NOT MY PROB-LEM.
IT'S YOUR FAULT FOR MAKING THEM WORRY SO MUCH.
IT'S PUNISHMENT.
JUST A LITTLE BIT MORE...
YOH-CHAN...
YOU'RE SO MEAN.
LET ME TEASE YOU A BIT MORE.
BUT I WONDER WHAT'S GOING TO HAPPEN IF OUR FATHERS FIND OUT ABOUT THIS?
I'LL PROBABLY GET MY ASS KICKED BIG TIME BY YOUR FATHER...
SNUB
HMM... MAYBE I SHOULD RECON-SIDER.
AND I'LL GO APOLOGIZE WITH YOU.
HECK, I CAN PUT THE BLAME ON ME.
EH? WHAT?! DID YOU SAY SOME-THING?!
SO YOU CAN GIVE ME AT LEAST THAT...
CAN'T YOU?
OUCH! QUIT STRANGLING ME, YOU DORK!

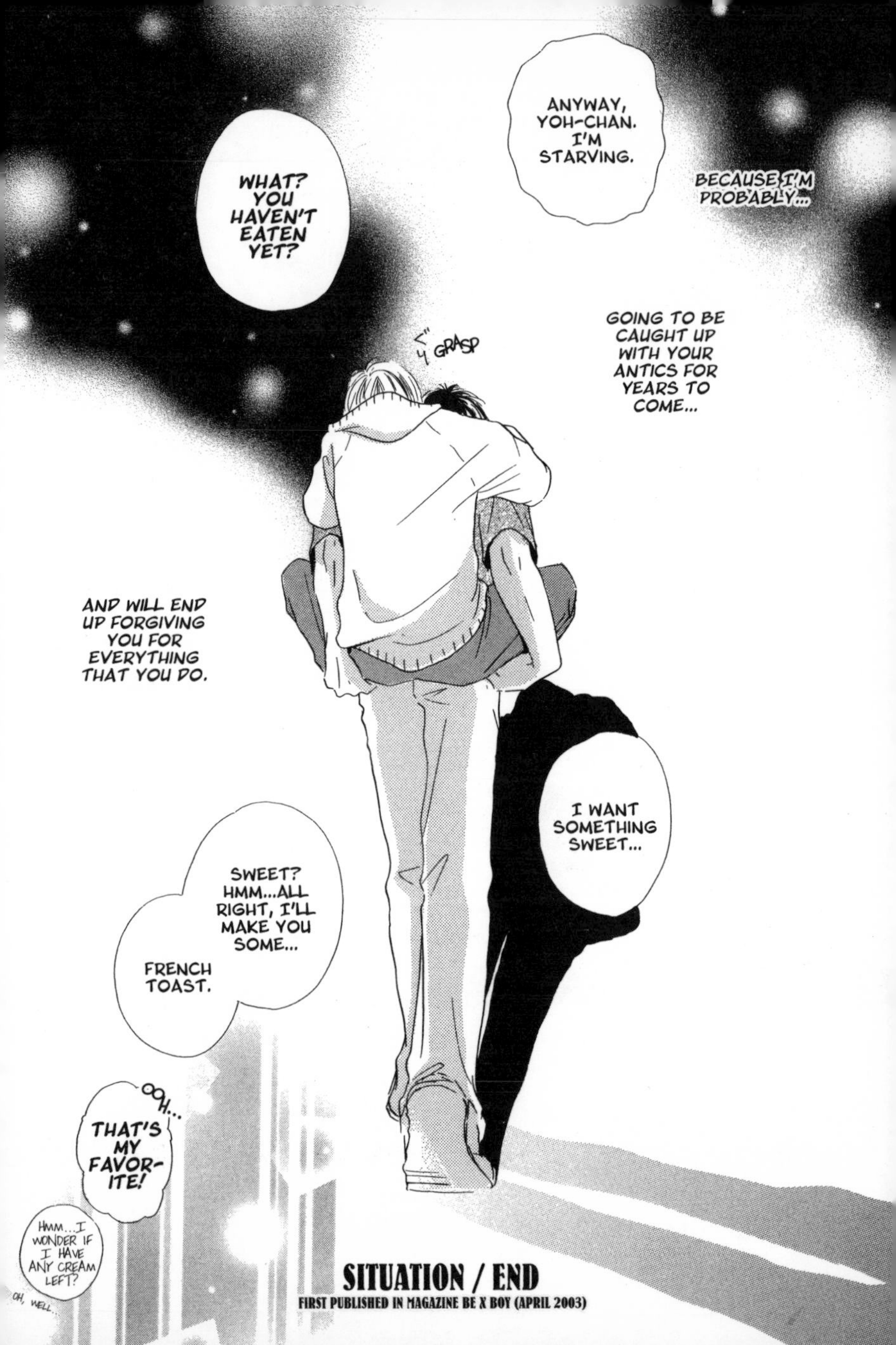
ANYWAY, YOH-CHAN. I'M STARVING.
WHAT? YOU HAVEN'T EATEN YET?
BECAUSE I'M PROBABLY...
GOING TO BE CAUGHT UP WITH YOUR ANTICS FOR YEARS TO COME...
GRASP
AND WILL END UP FORGIVING YOU FOR EVERYTHING THAT YOU DO.
I WANT SOMETHING SWEET...
SWEET? HMM...ALL RIGHT, I'LL MAKE YOU SOME...
FRENCH TOAST.
OOH...
THAT'S MY FAVOR-ITE!
HMM...I WONDER IF I HAVE ANY CREAM LEFT?
OH, WELL...

SITUATION / END

FIRST PUBLISHED IN MAGAZINE BE X BOY (APRIL 2003)

bonds

...

situation

...

KITAN garden

...

sakura

Presented by Tōko Kawai

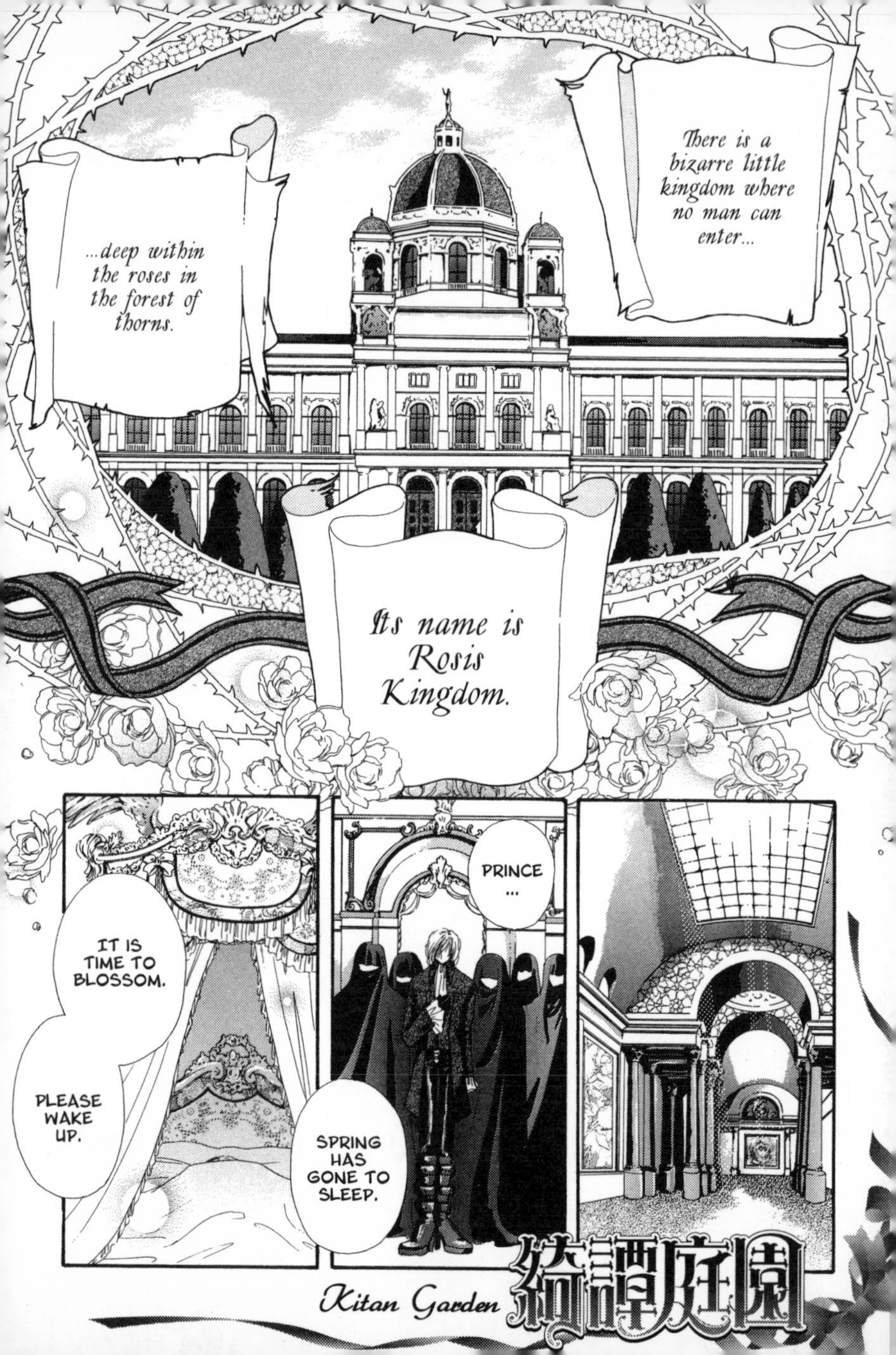
There is a bizarre little kingdom where no man can enter...
...deep within the roses in the forest of thorns.
Its name is Rosis Kingdom.
PRINCE ...
SPRING HAS GONE TO SLEEP.
IT IS TIME TO BLOSSOM.
PLEASE WAKE UP.
綺譚庭園
Kitan Garden

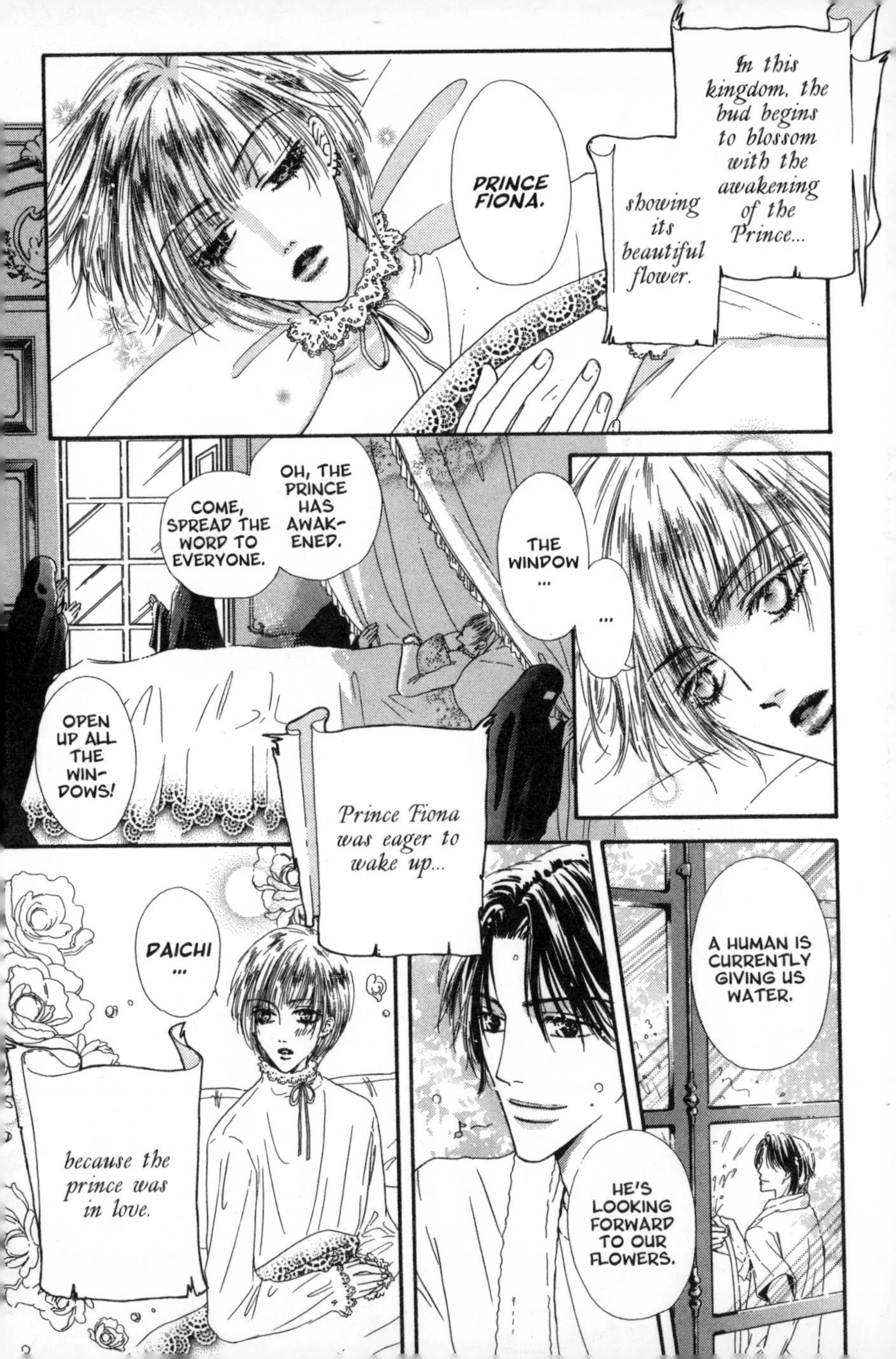
In this kingdom, the bud begins to blossom with the awakening of the Prince...
showing its beautiful flower.
PRINCE FIONA.
THE WINDOW ...
...
OH, THE PRINCE HAS AWAKENED.
COME, SPREAD THE WORD TO EVERYONE.
OPEN UP ALL THE WINDOWS!
Prince Fiona was eager to wake up...
A HUMAN IS CURRENTLY GIVING US WATER.
HE'S LOOKING FORWARD TO OUR FLOWERS.
DAICHI ...
because the prince was in love.

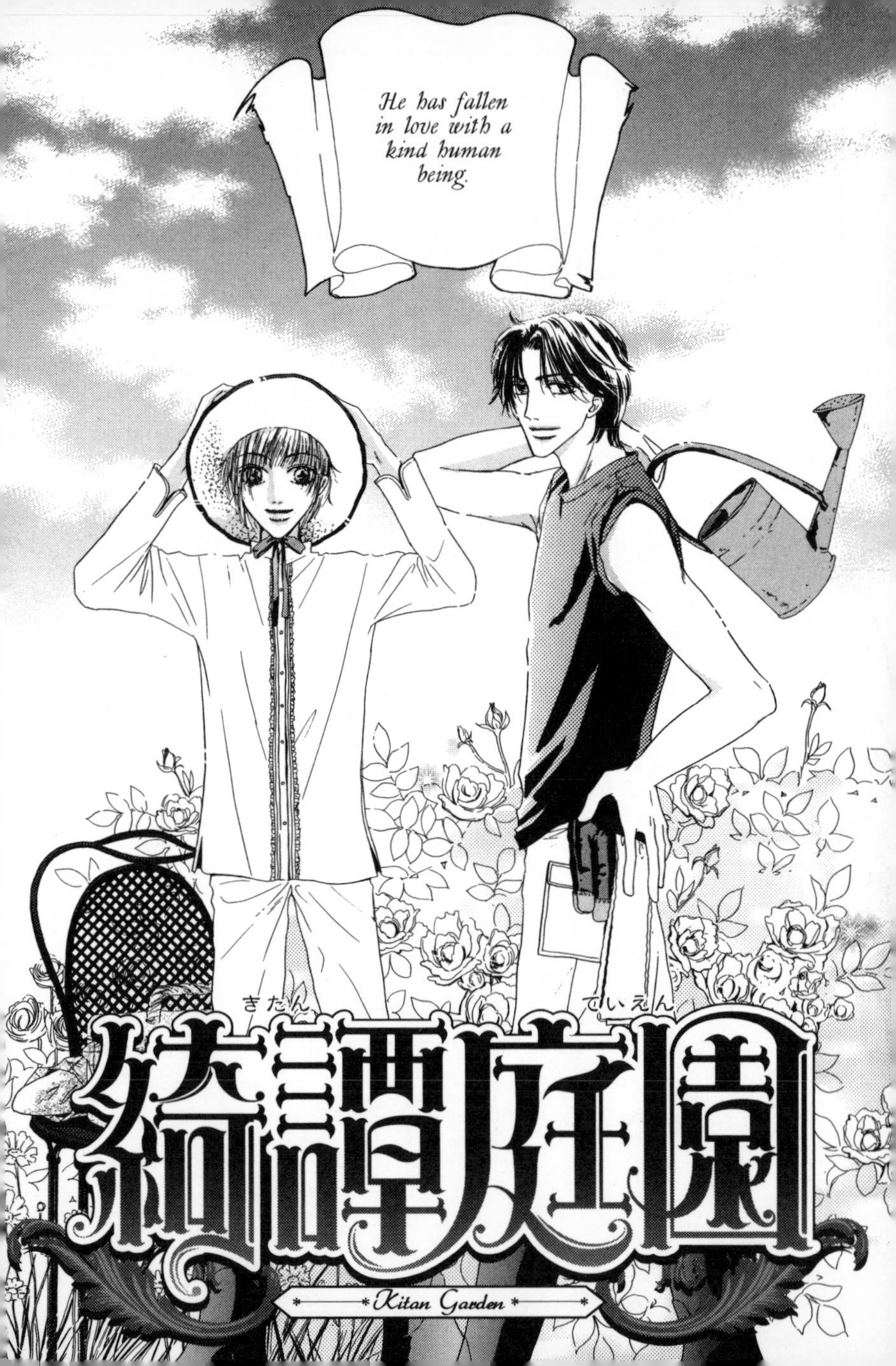
He has fallen in love with a kind human being.
きたん ていえん
綺譚庭園
Kitan Garden

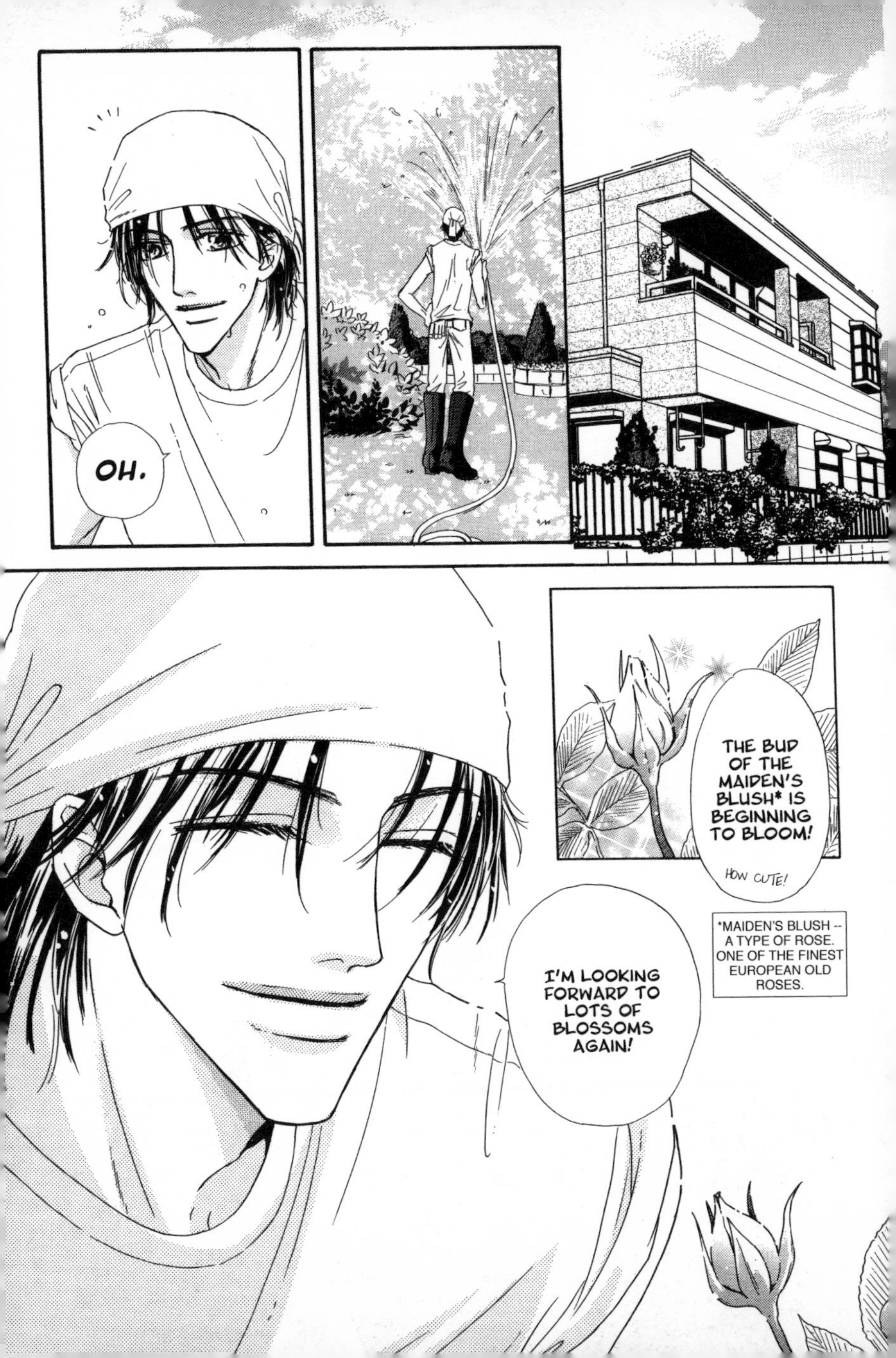
OH.
THE BUD OF THE MAIDEN'S BLUSH* IS BEGINNING TO BLOOM!
HOW CUTE!
I'M LOOKING FORWARD TO LOTS OF BLOSSOMS AGAIN!
*MAIDEN'S BLUSH -- A TYPE OF ROSE. ONE OF THE FINEST EUROPEAN OLD ROSES.

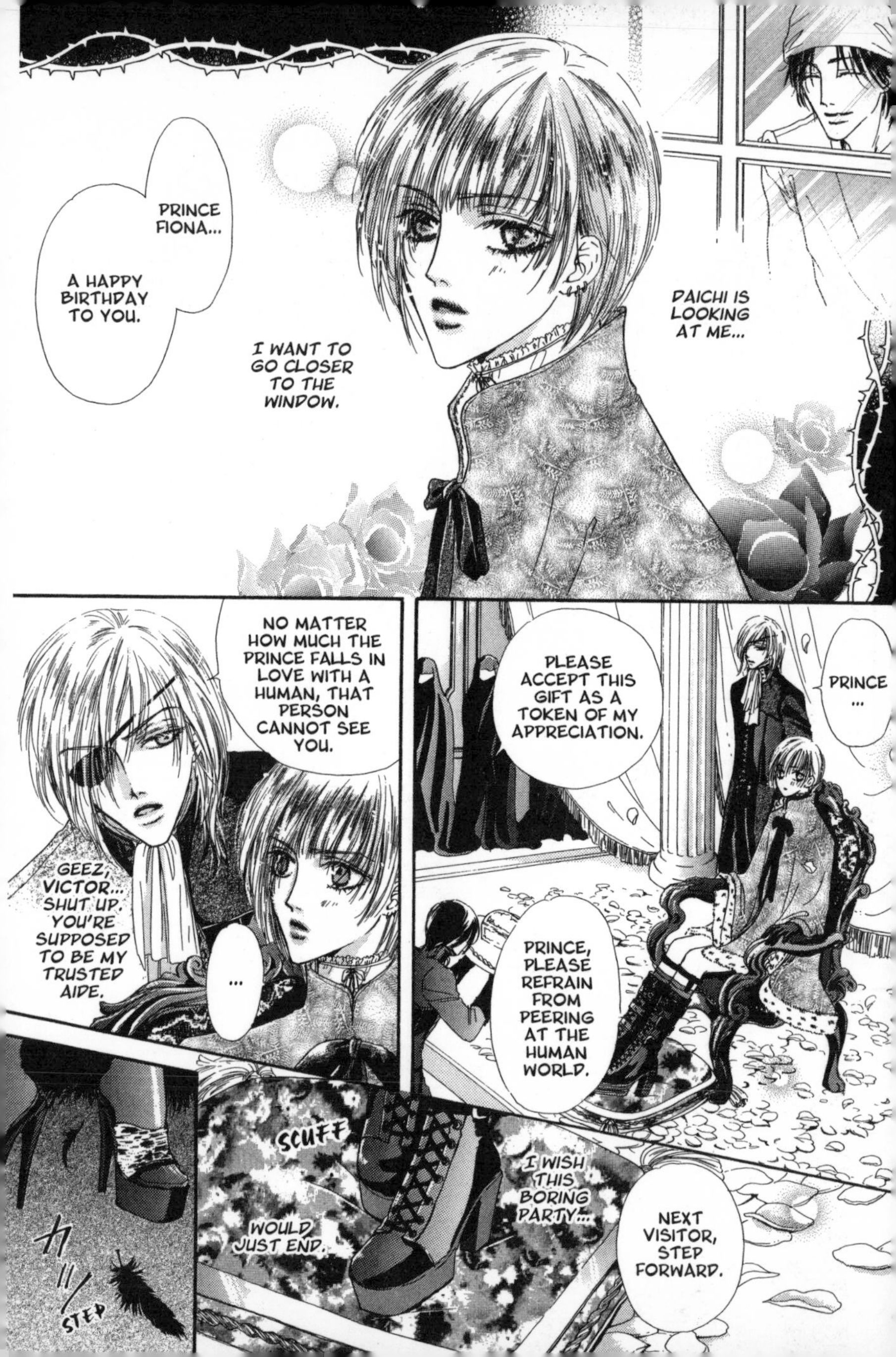
DAICHI IS LOOKING AT ME...
I WANT TO GO CLOSER TO THE WINDOW.
PRINCE FIONA...
A HAPPY BIRTHDAY TO YOU.
PRINCE ...
PLEASE ACCEPT THIS GIFT AS A TOKEN OF MY APPRECIATION.
PRINCE, PLEASE REFRAIN FROM PEERING AT THE HUMAN WORLD.
NO MATTER HOW MUCH THE PRINCE FALLS IN LOVE WITH A HUMAN, THAT PERSON CANNOT SEE YOU.
...
GEEZ, VICTOR... SHUT UP. YOU'RE SUPPOSED TO BE MY TRUSTED AIDE.
NEXT VISITOR, STEP FORWARD.
I WISH THIS BORING PARTY...
SCUFF
WOULD JUST END.
STEP

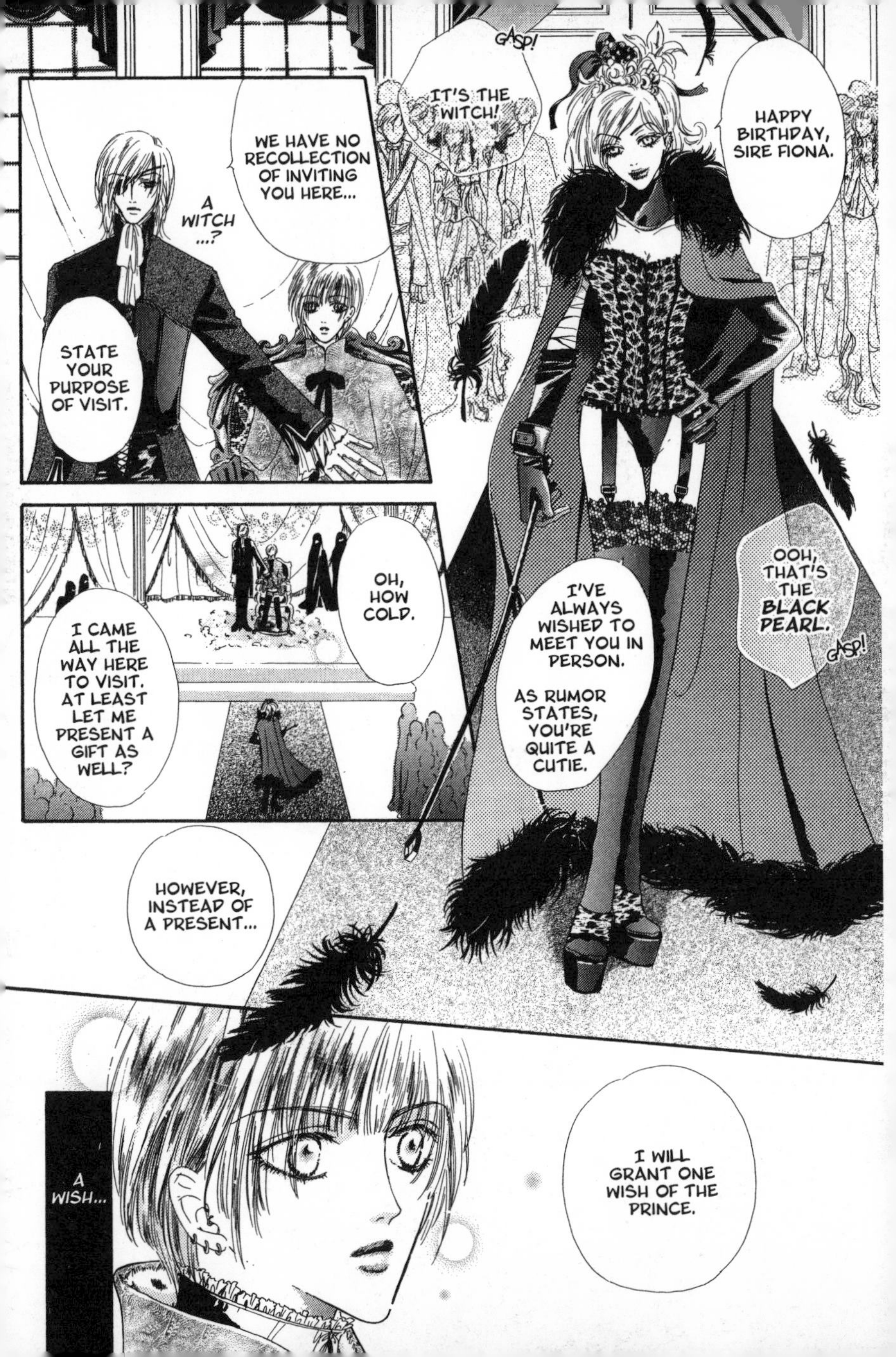
GASP!
IT'S THE WITCH!
HAPPY BIRTHDAY, SIRE FIONA.
OOH, THAT'S THE **BLACK PEARL.**
GASP!
I'VE ALWAYS WISHED TO MEET YOU IN PERSON.
AS RUMOR STATES, YOU'RE QUITE A CUTIE.
WE HAVE NO RECOLLECTION OF INVITING YOU HERE...
A WITCH ...?
STATE YOUR PURPOSE OF VISIT.
OH, HOW COLD.
I CAME ALL THE WAY HERE TO VISIT. AT LEAST LET ME PRESENT A GIFT AS WELL?
HOWEVER, INSTEAD OF A PRESENT...
I WILL GRANT ONE WISH OF THE PRINCE.
A WISH...

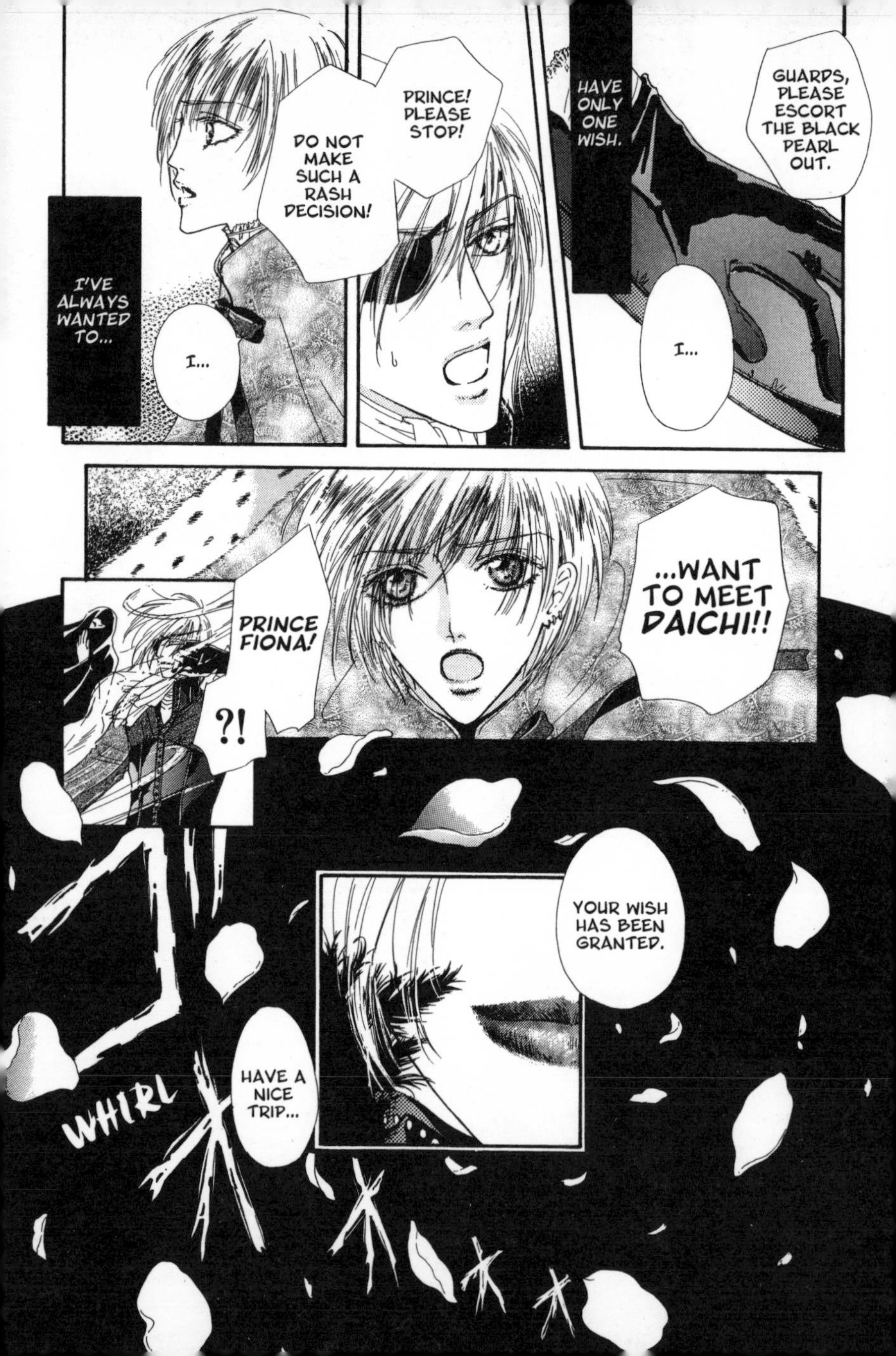
GUARDS, PLEASE ESCORT THE BLACK PEARL OUT.
HAVE ONLY ONE WISH.
I...
PRINCE! PLEASE STOP!
DO NOT MAKE SUCH A RASH DECISION!
I'VE ALWAYS WANTED TO...
I...
...WANT TO MEET DAICHI!!
PRINCE FIONA!
?!
YOUR WISH HAS BEEN GRANTED.
HAVE A NICE TRIP...
WHIRL

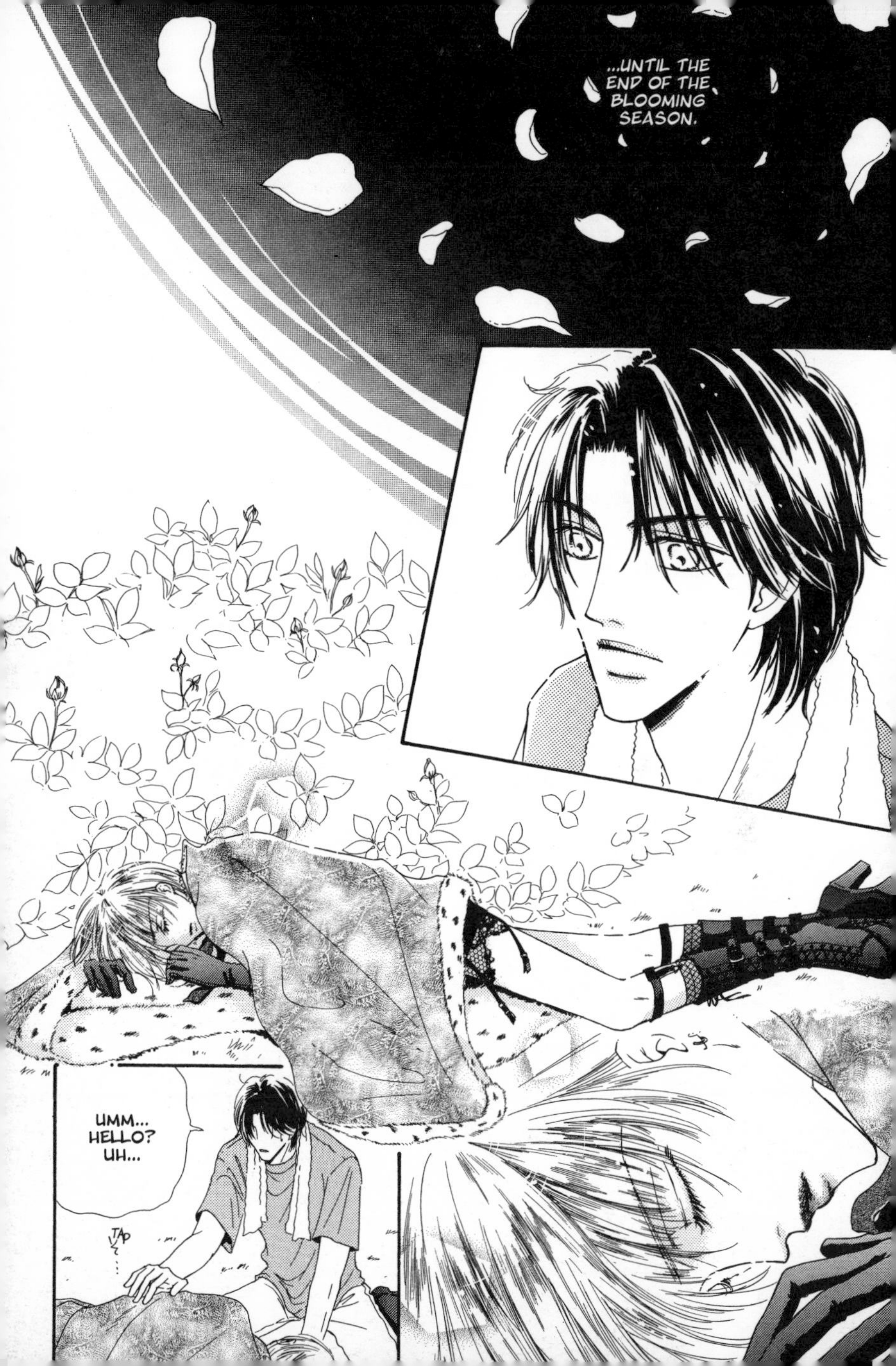
...UNTIL THE END OF THE BLOOMING SEASON.
UMM... HELLO? UH...
TAP

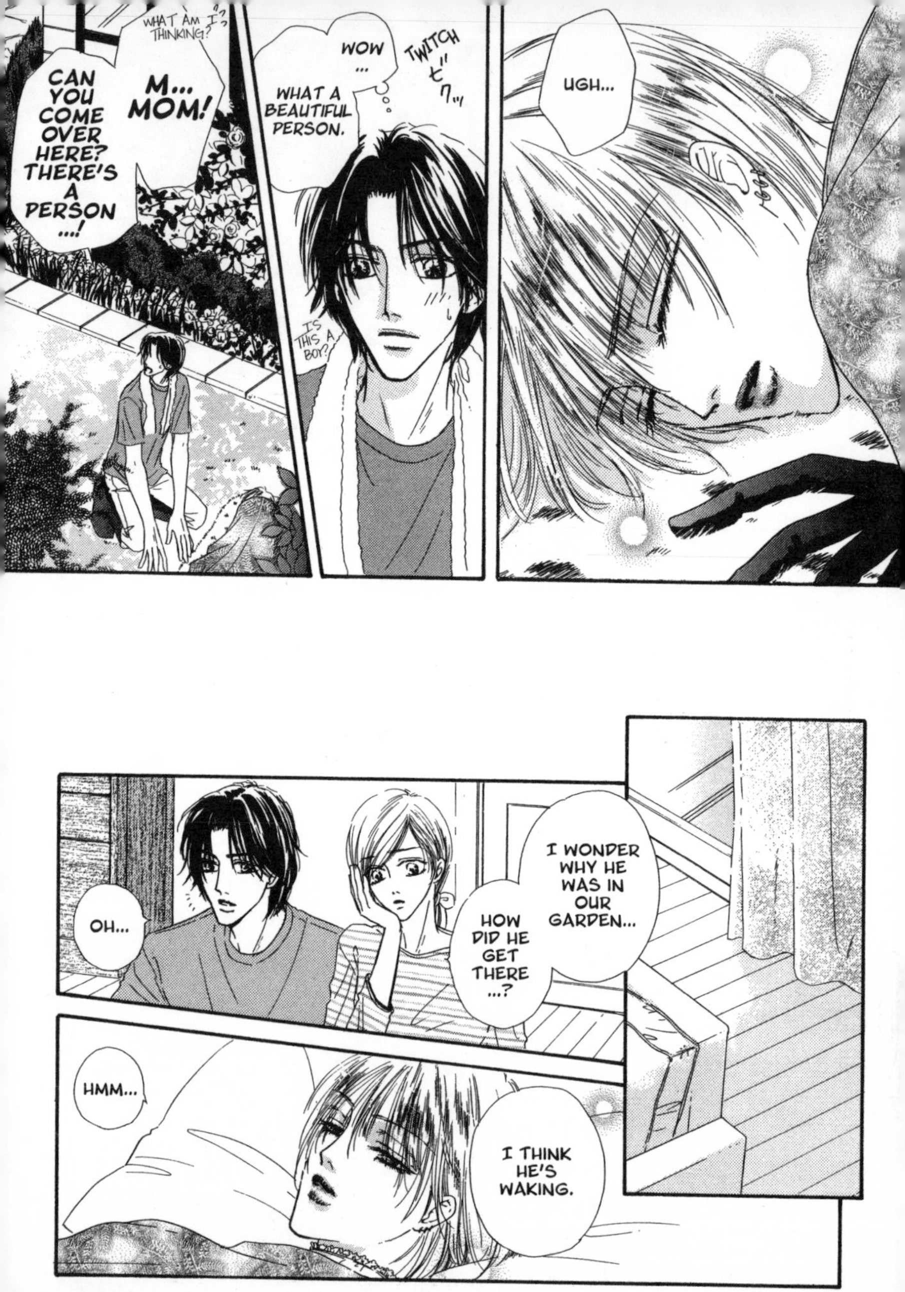
UGH...
WOW...
TWITCH
WHAT A BEAUTIFUL PERSON.
IS THIS A BOY?
WHAT AM I THINKING?
M... MOM!
CAN YOU COME OVER HERE? THERE'S A PERSON ...!
I WONDER WHY HE WAS IN OUR GARDEN...
HOW DID HE GET THERE ...?
OH...
I THINK HE'S WAKING.
HMM...

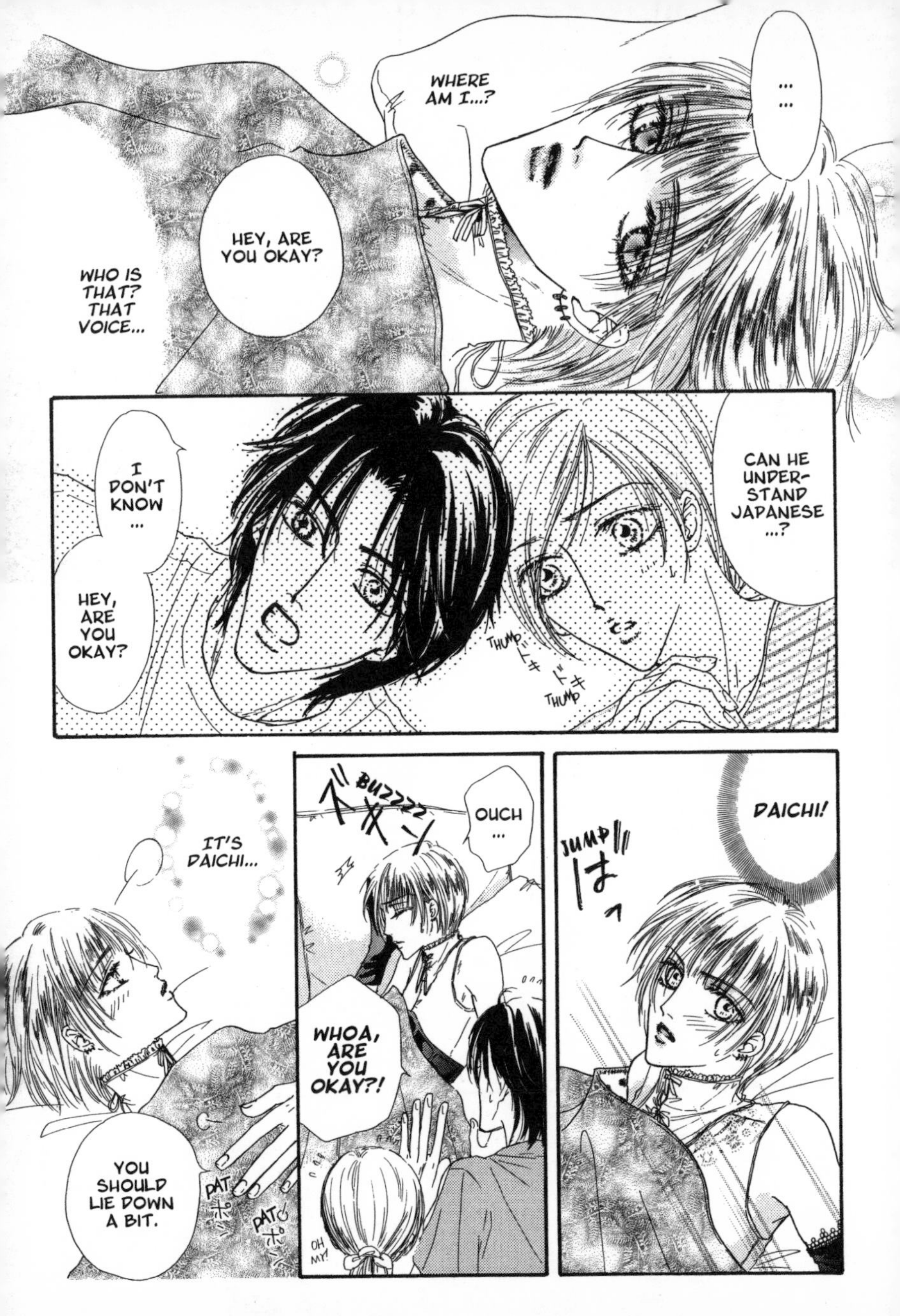
... ...
WHERE AM I...?
HEY, ARE YOU OKAY?
WHO IS THAT? THAT VOICE...
CAN HE UNDER-STAND JAPANESE ...?
I DON'T KNOW ...
HEY, ARE YOU OKAY?
THUMP
THUMP
DAICHI!
JUMP
BUZZZZZ
OUCH ...
WHOA, ARE YOU OKAY?!
OH MY!
IT'S DAICHI...
YOU SHOULD LIE DOWN A BIT.
PAT
PAT

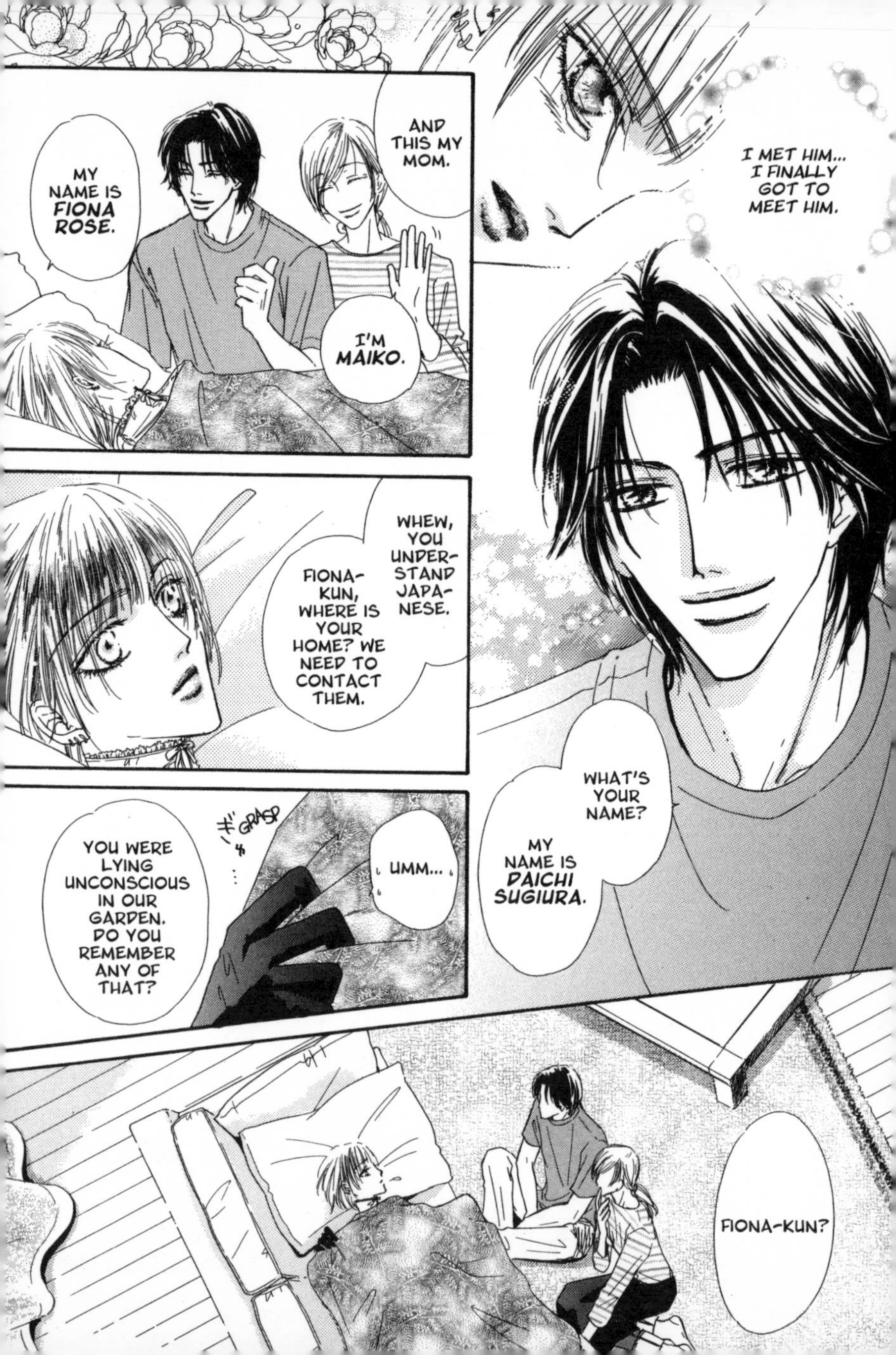
I MET HIM... I FINALLY GOT TO MEET HIM.
WHAT'S YOUR NAME?
MY NAME IS DAICHI SUGIURA.
AND THIS MY MOM.
MY NAME IS FIONA ROSE.
I'M MAIKO.
WHEW, YOU UNDER-STAND JAPA-NESE.
FIONA-KUN, WHERE IS YOUR HOME? WE NEED TO CONTACT THEM.
GRASP
UMM...
YOU WERE LYING UNCONSCIOUS IN OUR GARDEN. DO YOU REMEMBER ANY OF THAT?
FIONA-KUN?

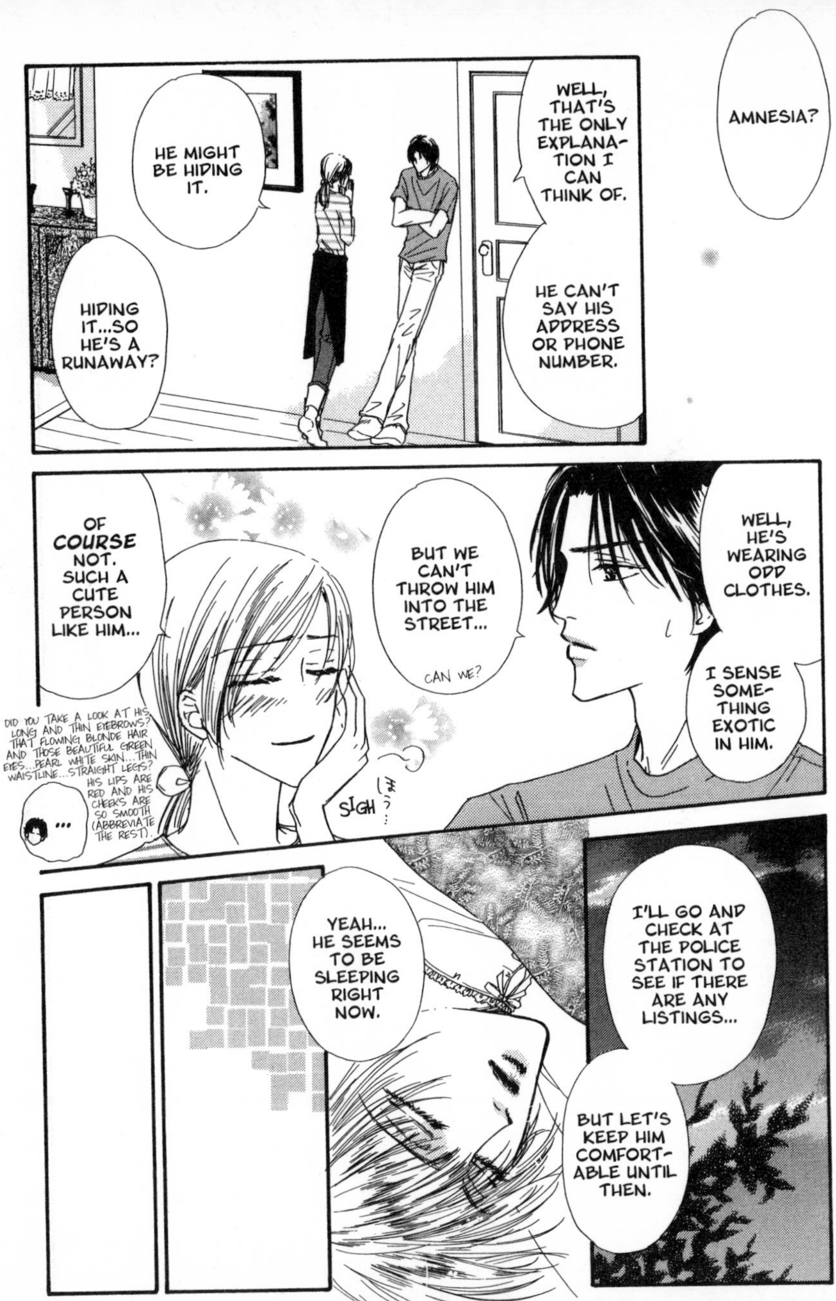
AMNESIA?
WELL, THAT'S THE ONLY EXPLANATION I CAN THINK OF.
HE CAN'T SAY HIS ADDRESS OR PHONE NUMBER.
HE MIGHT BE HIDING IT.
HIDING IT...SO HE'S A RUNAWAY?
WELL, HE'S WEARING ODD CLOTHES.
I SENSE SOMETHING EXOTIC IN HIM.
BUT WE CAN'T THROW HIM INTO THE STREET...
CAN WE?
SIGH
ほぅ…
OF COURSE NOT. SUCH A CUTE PERSON LIKE HIM...
DID YOU TAKE A LOOK AT HIS LONG AND THIN EYEBROWS? THAT FLOWING BLONDE HAIR AND THOSE BEAUTIFUL GREEN EYES...PEARL WHITE SKIN...THIN WAISTLINE...STRAIGHT LEGS? HIS LIPS ARE RED AND HIS CHEEKS ARE SO SMOOTH (ABBREVIATE THE REST).
...
I'LL GO AND CHECK AT THE POLICE STATION TO SEE IF THERE ARE ANY LISTINGS...
BUT LET'S KEEP HIM COMFORTABLE UNTIL THEN.
YEAH... HE SEEMS TO BE SLEEPING RIGHT NOW.

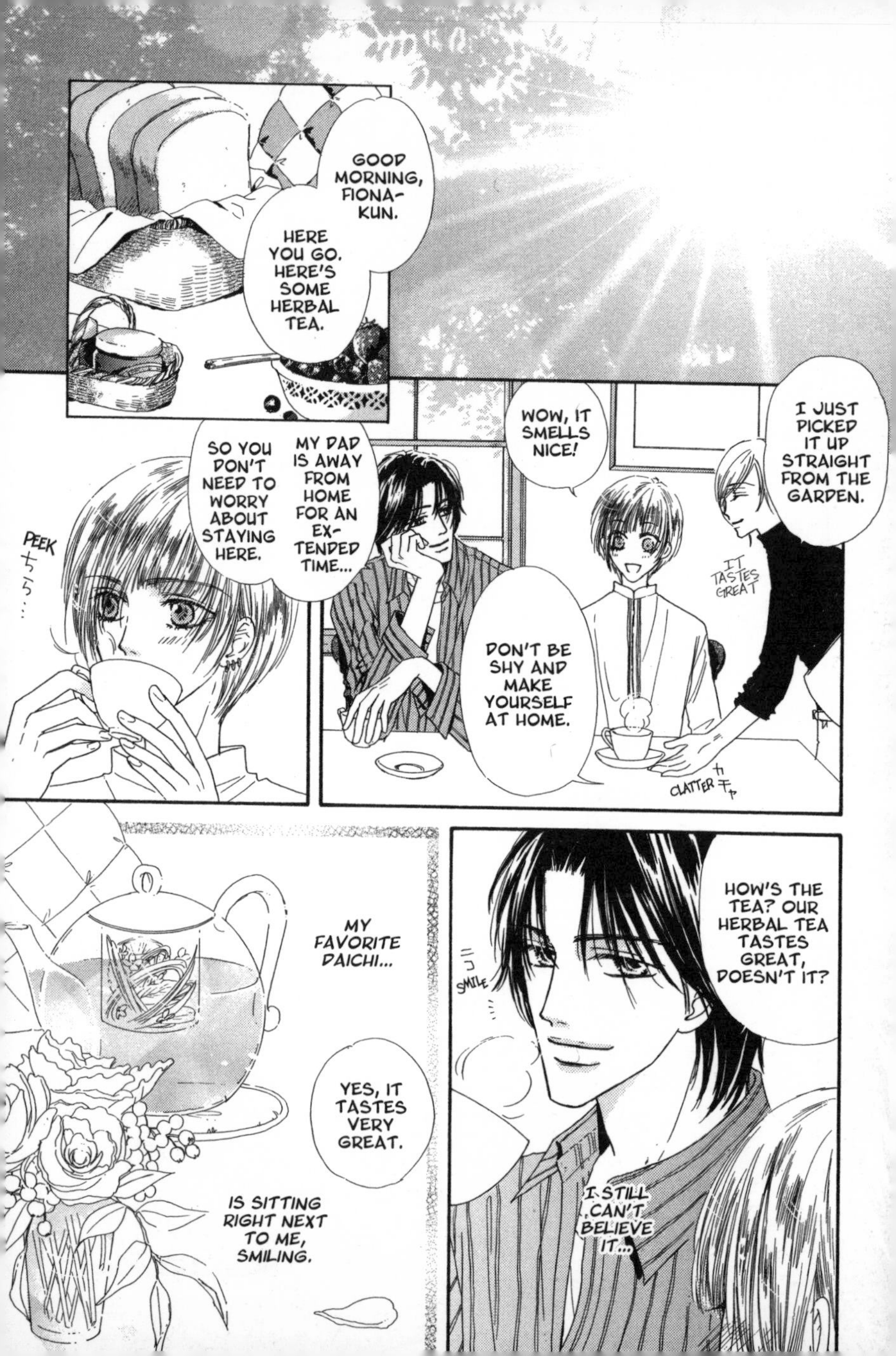
GOOD MORNING, FIONA-KUN.
HERE YOU GO. HERE'S SOME HERBAL TEA.
I JUST PICKED IT UP STRAIGHT FROM THE GARDEN.
WOW, IT SMELLS NICE!
IT TASTES GREAT
MY DAD IS AWAY FROM HOME FOR AN EXTENDED TIME...
SO YOU DON'T NEED TO WORRY ABOUT STAYING HERE.
DON'T BE SHY AND MAKE YOURSELF AT HOME.
CLATTER
PEEK
ちら…
HOW'S THE TEA? OUR HERBAL TEA TASTES GREAT, DOESN'T IT?
SMILE
I STILL CAN'T BELIEVE IT...
MY FAVORITE DAICHI...
YES, IT TASTES VERY GREAT.
IS SITTING RIGHT NEXT TO ME, SMILING.

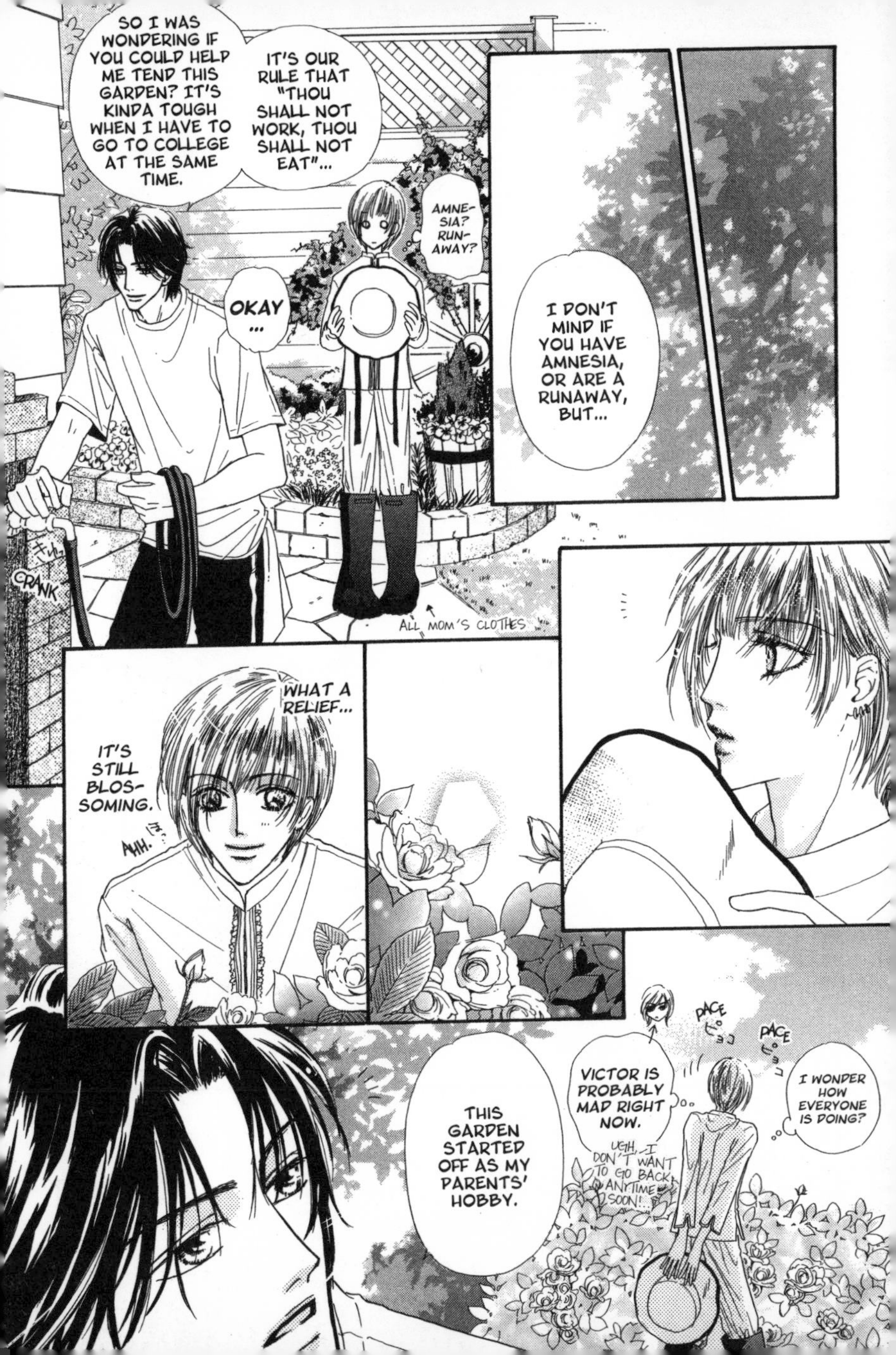

I DON'T MIND IF YOU HAVE AMNESIA, OR ARE A RUNAWAY, BUT...
AMNESIA? RUNAWAY?
IT'S OUR RULE THAT "THOU SHALL NOT WORK, THOU SHALL NOT EAT"...
SO I WAS WONDERING IF YOU COULD HELP ME TEND THIS GARDEN? IT'S KINDA TOUGH WHEN I HAVE TO GO TO COLLEGE AT THE SAME TIME.
OKAY ...
CRANK
ALL MOM'S CLOTHES
WHAT A RELIEF...
IT'S STILL BLOSSOMING.
AHH.
I WONDER HOW EVERYONE IS DOING?
PACE
PACE
VICTOR IS PROBABLY MAD RIGHT NOW.
UGH, I DON'T WANT TO GO BACK ANYTIME SOON!
THIS GARDEN STARTED OFF AS MY PARENTS' HOBBY.

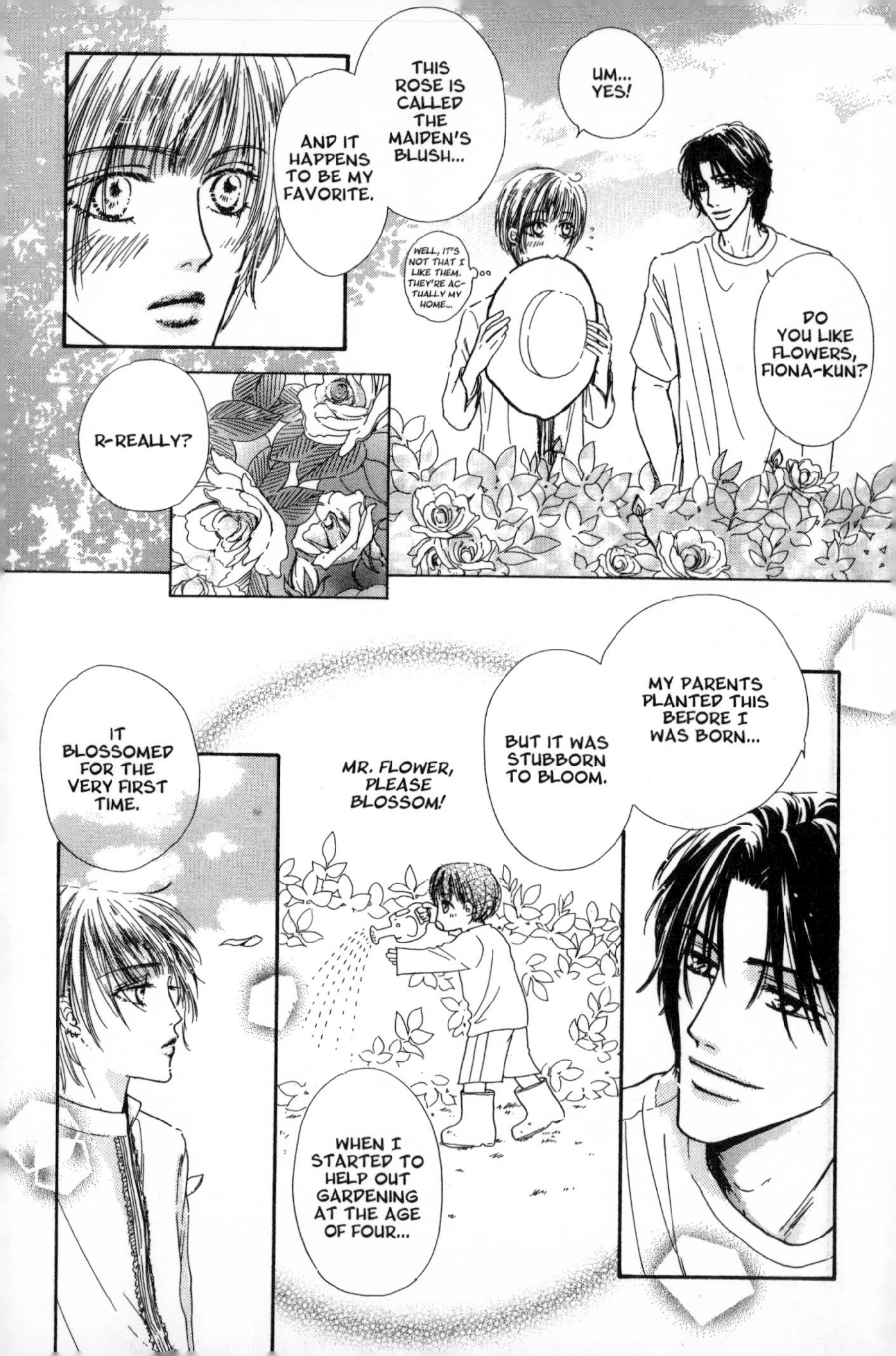
DO YOU LIKE FLOWERS, FIONA-KUN?
UM... YES!
WELL, IT'S NOT THAT I LIKE THEM. THEY'RE ACTUALLY MY HOME...
THIS ROSE IS CALLED THE MAIDEN'S BLUSH...
AND IT HAPPENS TO BE MY FAVORITE.
R-REALLY?
MY PARENTS PLANTED THIS BEFORE I WAS BORN...
BUT IT WAS STUBBORN TO BLOOM.
MR. FLOWER, PLEASE BLOSSOM!
WHEN I STARTED TO HELP OUT GARDENING AT THE AGE OF FOUR...
IT BLOSSOMED FOR THE VERY FIRST TIME.

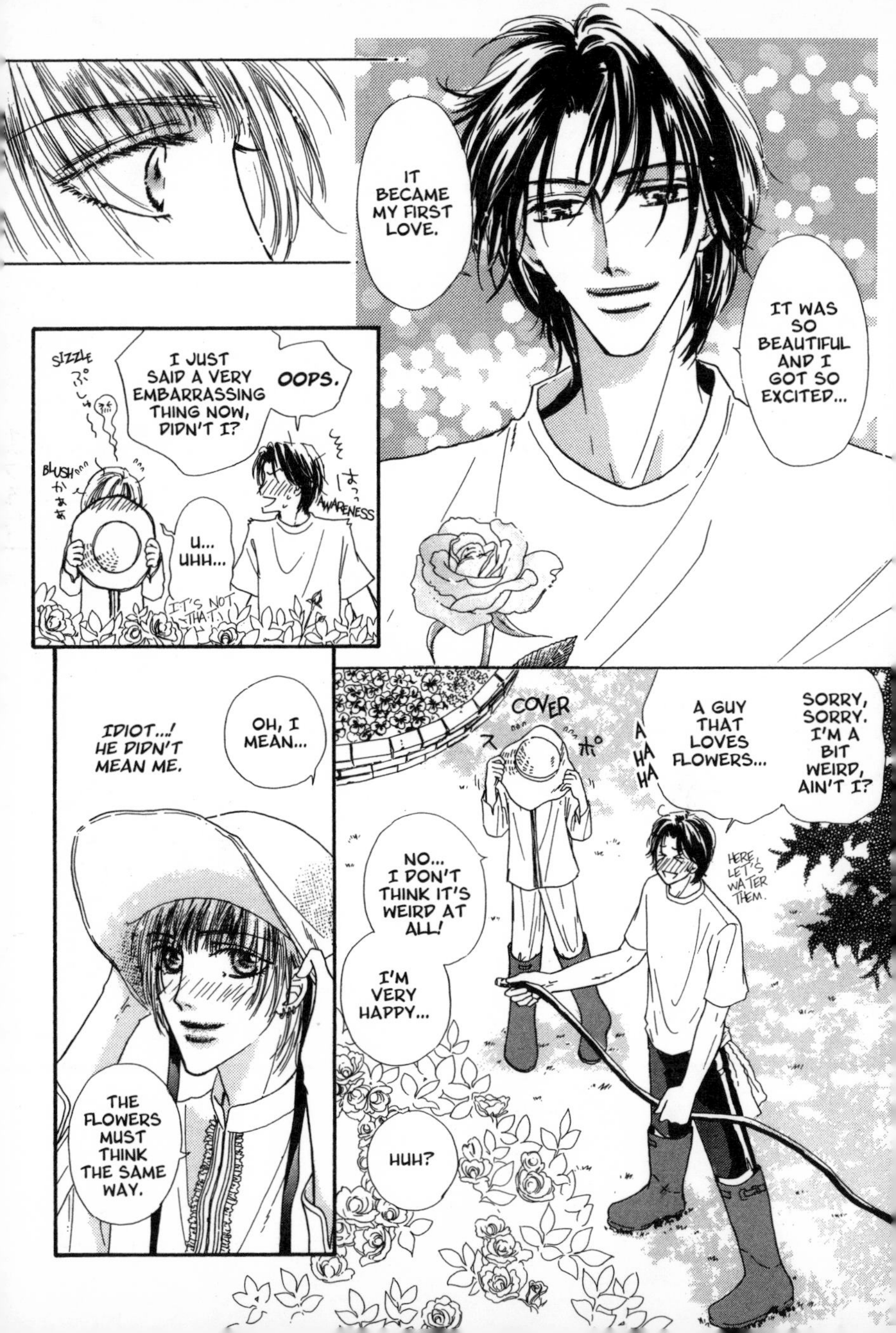
IT BECAME MY FIRST LOVE.
IT WAS SO BEAUTIFUL AND I GOT SO EXCITED...
OOPS.
I JUST SAID A VERY EMBARRASSING THING NOW, DIDN'T I?
はっ AWARENESS
SIZZLE ぷしゅ
BLUSH かぁぁ
U... UHH...
IT'S NOT THAT.
SORRY, SORRY. I'M A BIT WEIRD, AIN'T I?
A GUY THAT LOVES FLOWERS...
A HA HA
COVER スポ
HERE, LET'S WATER THEM.
NO... I DON'T THINK IT'S WEIRD AT ALL!
I'M VERY HAPPY...
HUH?
OH, I MEAN...
IDIOT...! HE DIDN'T MEAN ME.
THE FLOWERS MUST THINK THE SAME WAY.

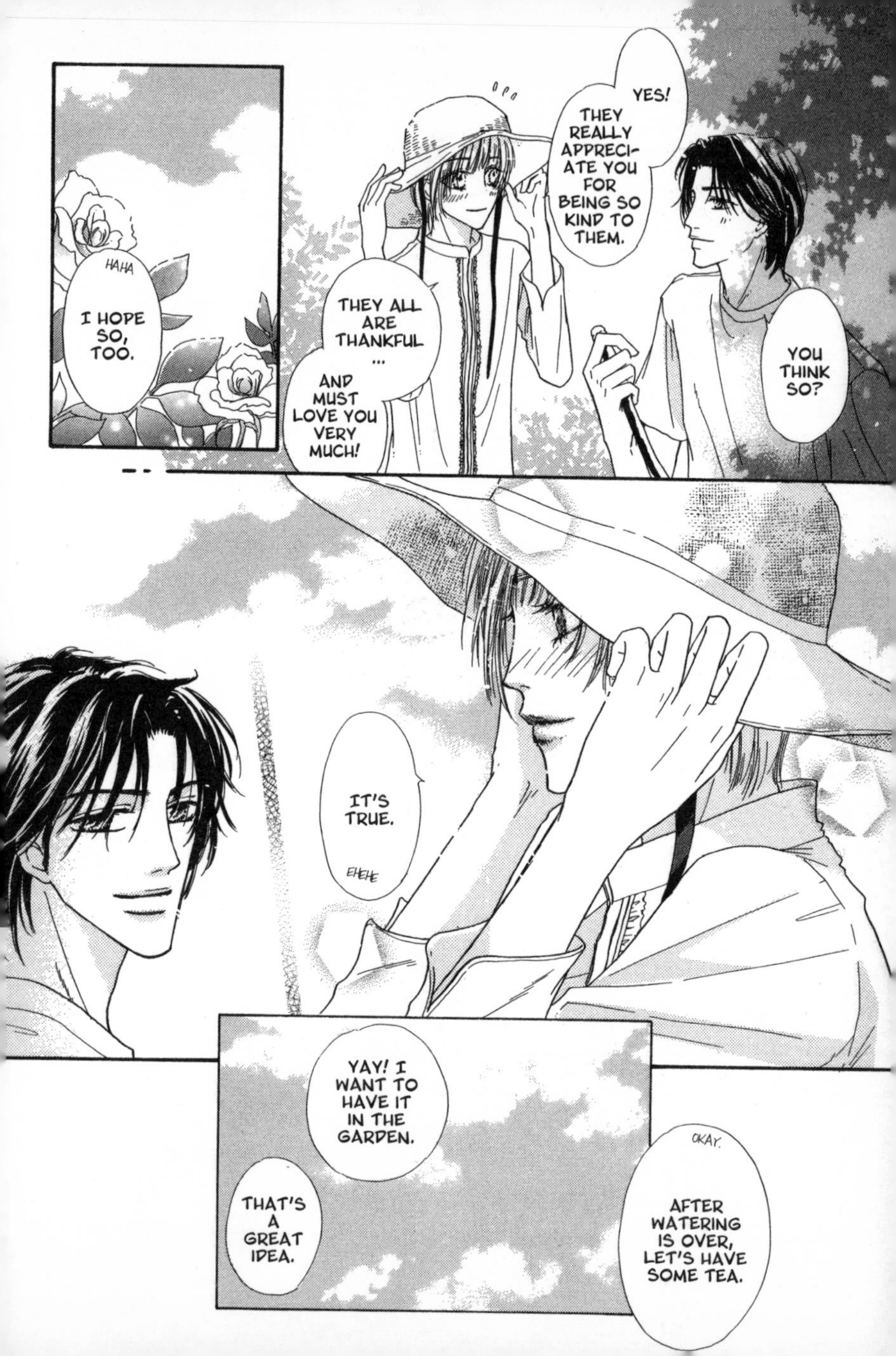
YES!
THEY REALLY APPRECIATE YOU FOR BEING SO KIND TO THEM.
YOU THINK SO?
THEY ALL ARE THANKFUL...
AND MUST LOVE YOU VERY MUCH!
HAHA
I HOPE SO, TOO.
IT'S TRUE.
EHEHE
OKAY.
AFTER WATERING IS OVER, LET'S HAVE SOME TEA.
YAY! I WANT TO HAVE IT IN THE GARDEN.
THAT'S A GREAT IDEA.

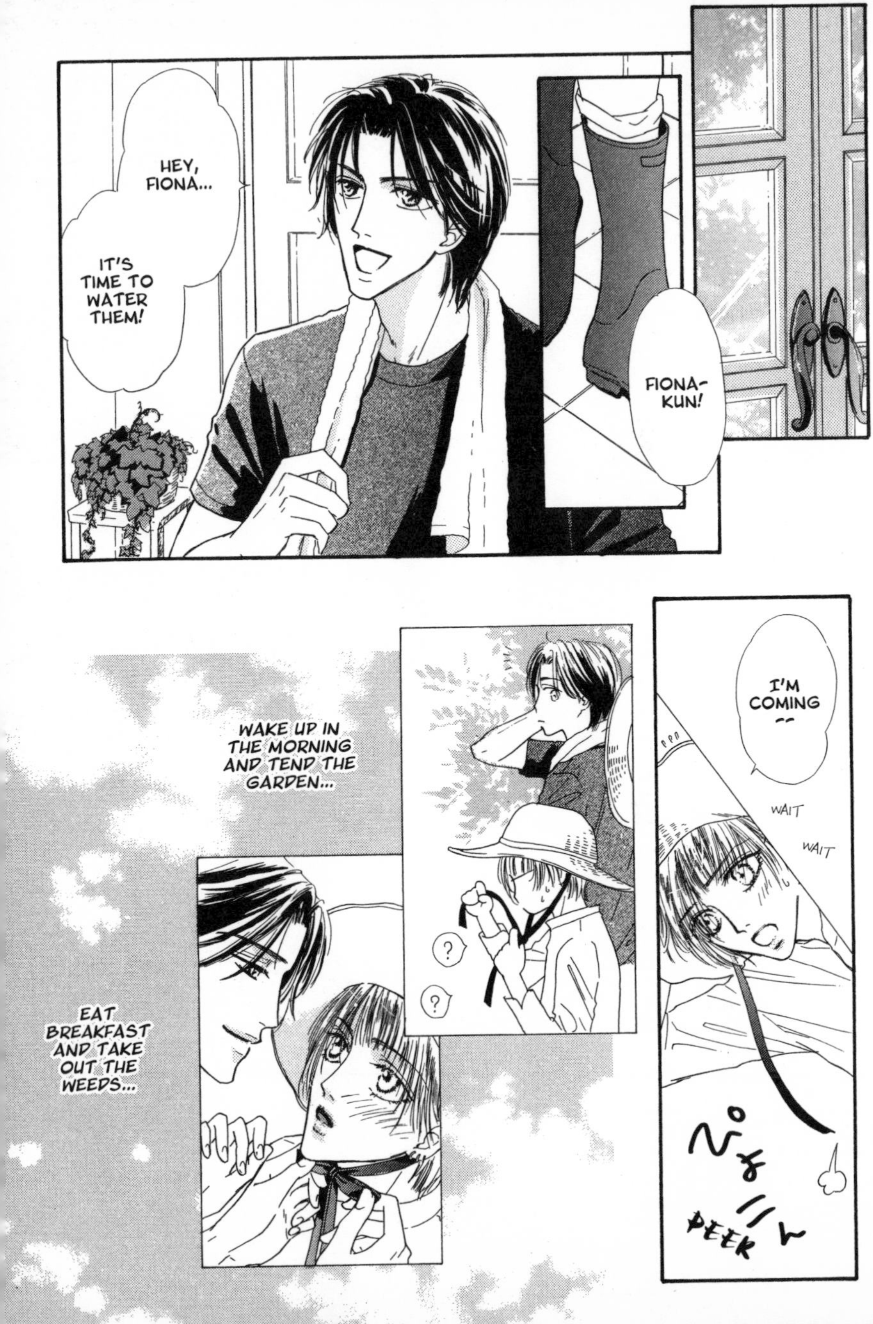
FIONA-KUN!
HEY, FIONA...
IT'S TIME TO WATER THEM!
I'M COMING --
WAIT
WAIT
PEEK
WAKE UP IN THE MORNING AND TEND THE GARDEN...
?
?
EAT BREAKFAST AND TAKE OUT THE WEEDS...

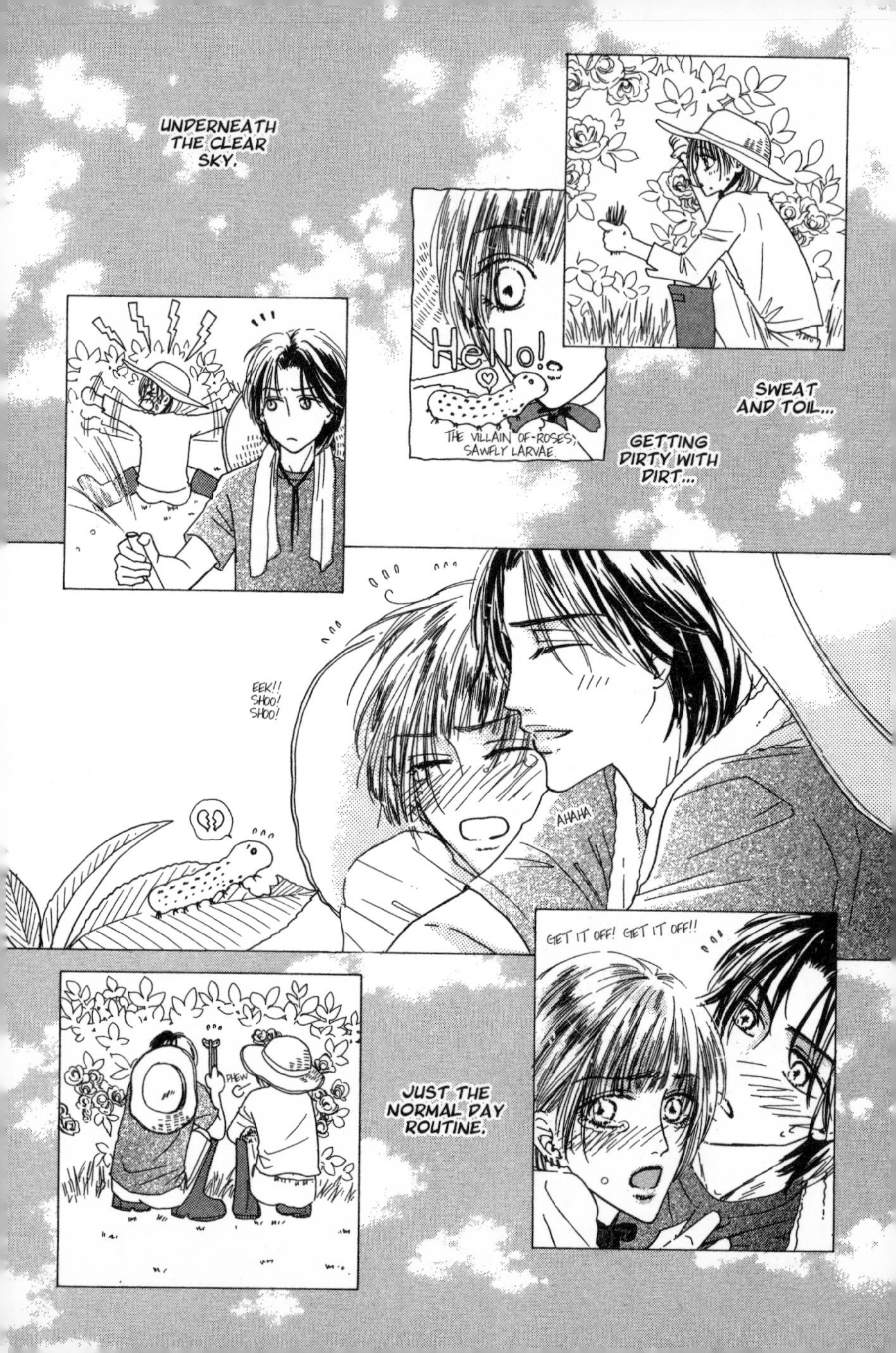
Hello!
THE VILLAIN OF-ROSES; SAWFLY LARVAE.
UNDERNEATH THE CLEAR SKY.
SWEAT AND TOIL...
GETTING DIRTY WITH DIRT...
AHAHA
EEK!! SHOO! SHOO!
GET IT OFF! GET IT OFF!!
JUST THE NORMAL DAY ROUTINE.
PHEW

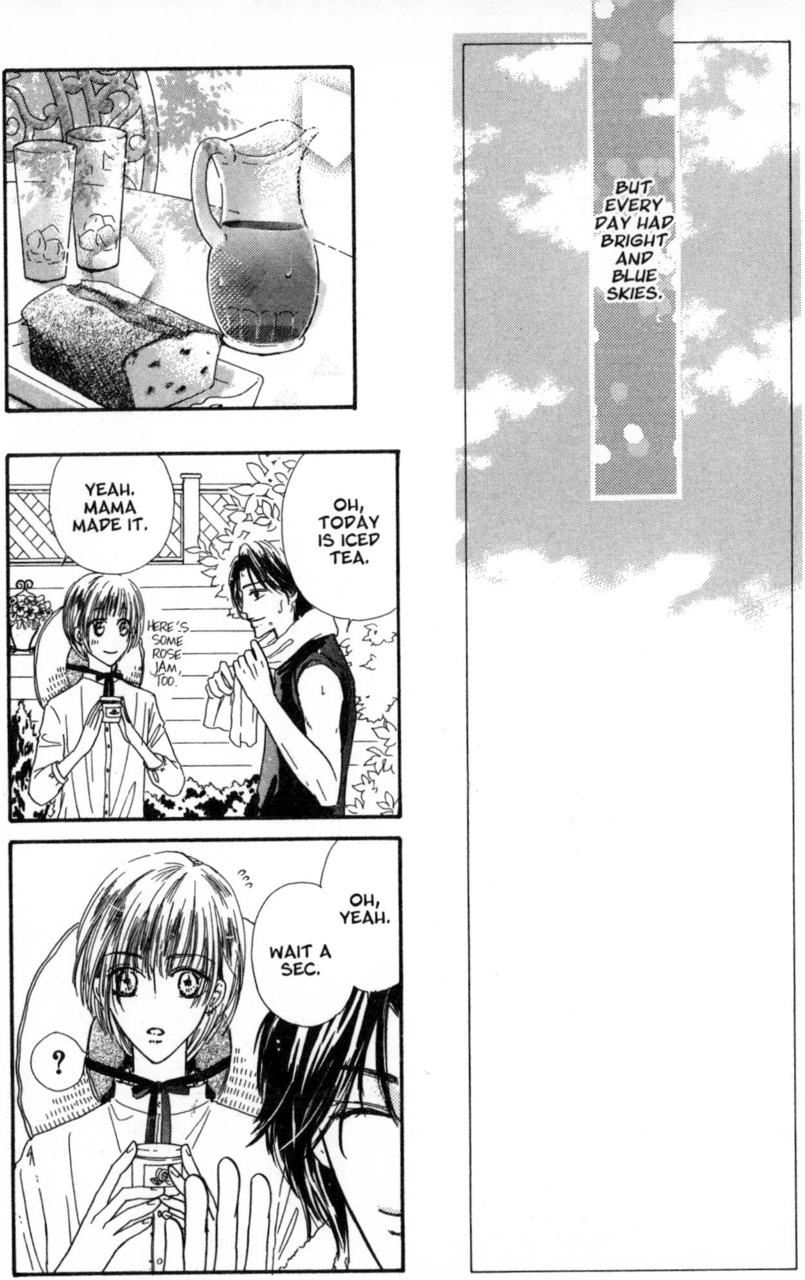
BUT EVERY DAY HAD BRIGHT AND BLUE SKIES.
OH, TODAY IS ICED TEA.
YEAH. MAMA MADE IT.
HERE'S SOME ROSE JAM, TOO.
OH, YEAH.
WAIT A SEC.
?

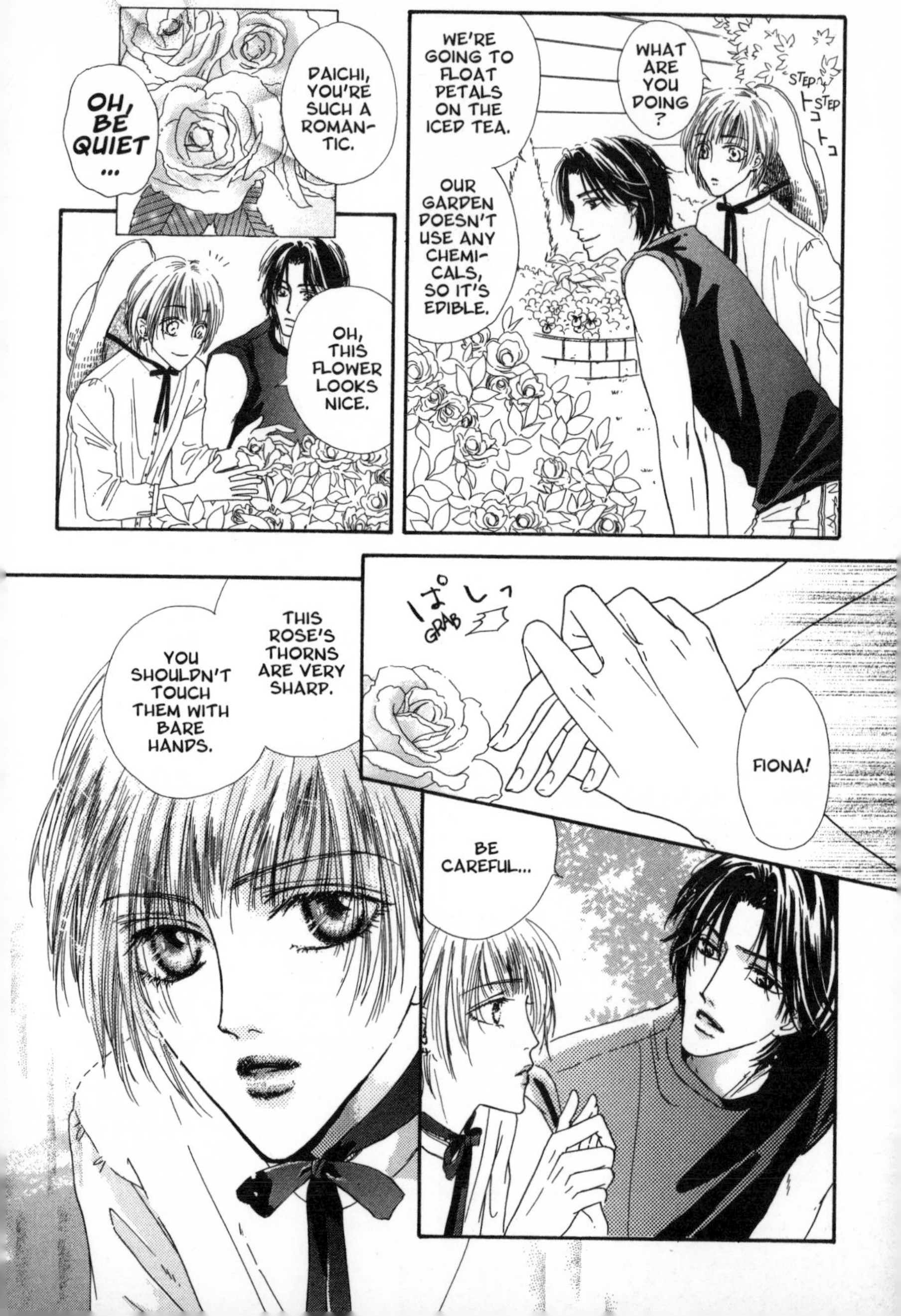
WHAT ARE YOU DOING?
STEP STEP
トコトコ
WE'RE GOING TO FLOAT PETALS ON THE ICED TEA.
OUR GARDEN DOESN'T USE ANY CHEMICALS, SO IT'S EDIBLE.
DAICHI, YOU'RE SUCH A ROMANTIC.
OH, BE QUIET...
OH, THIS FLOWER LOOKS NICE.
ぱしっ
GRAB
FIONA!
BE CAREFUL...
THIS ROSE'S THORNS ARE VERY SHARP.
YOU SHOULDN'T TOUCH THEM WITH BARE HANDS.

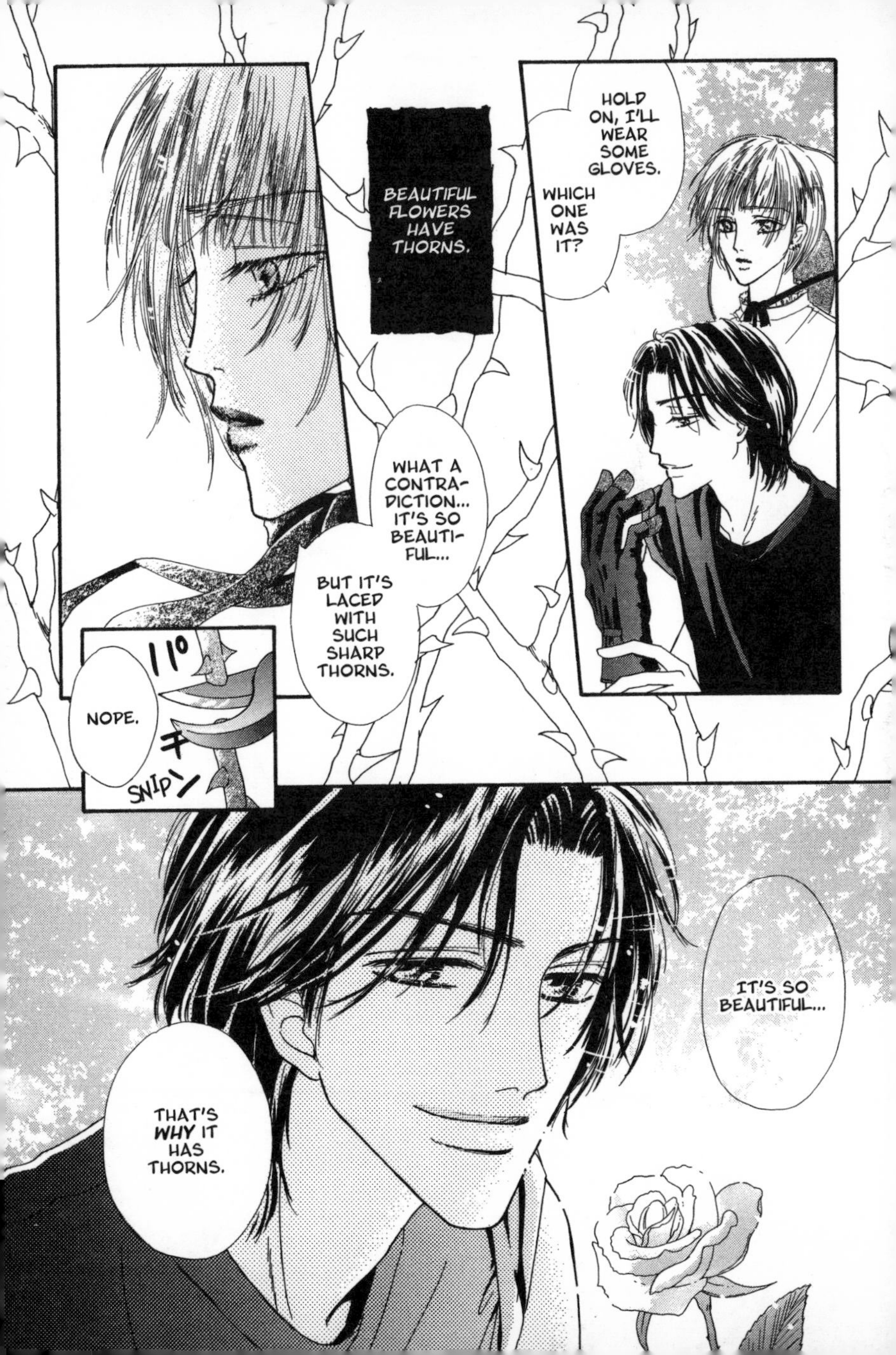

HOLD ON, I'LL WEAR SOME GLOVES.
WHICH ONE WAS IT?
BEAUTIFUL FLOWERS HAVE THORNS.
WHAT A CONTRADICTION... IT'S SO BEAUTIFUL...
BUT IT'S LACED WITH SUCH SHARP THORNS.
NOPE.
SNIP
IT'S SO BEAUTIFUL...
THAT'S **WHY** IT HAS THORNS.

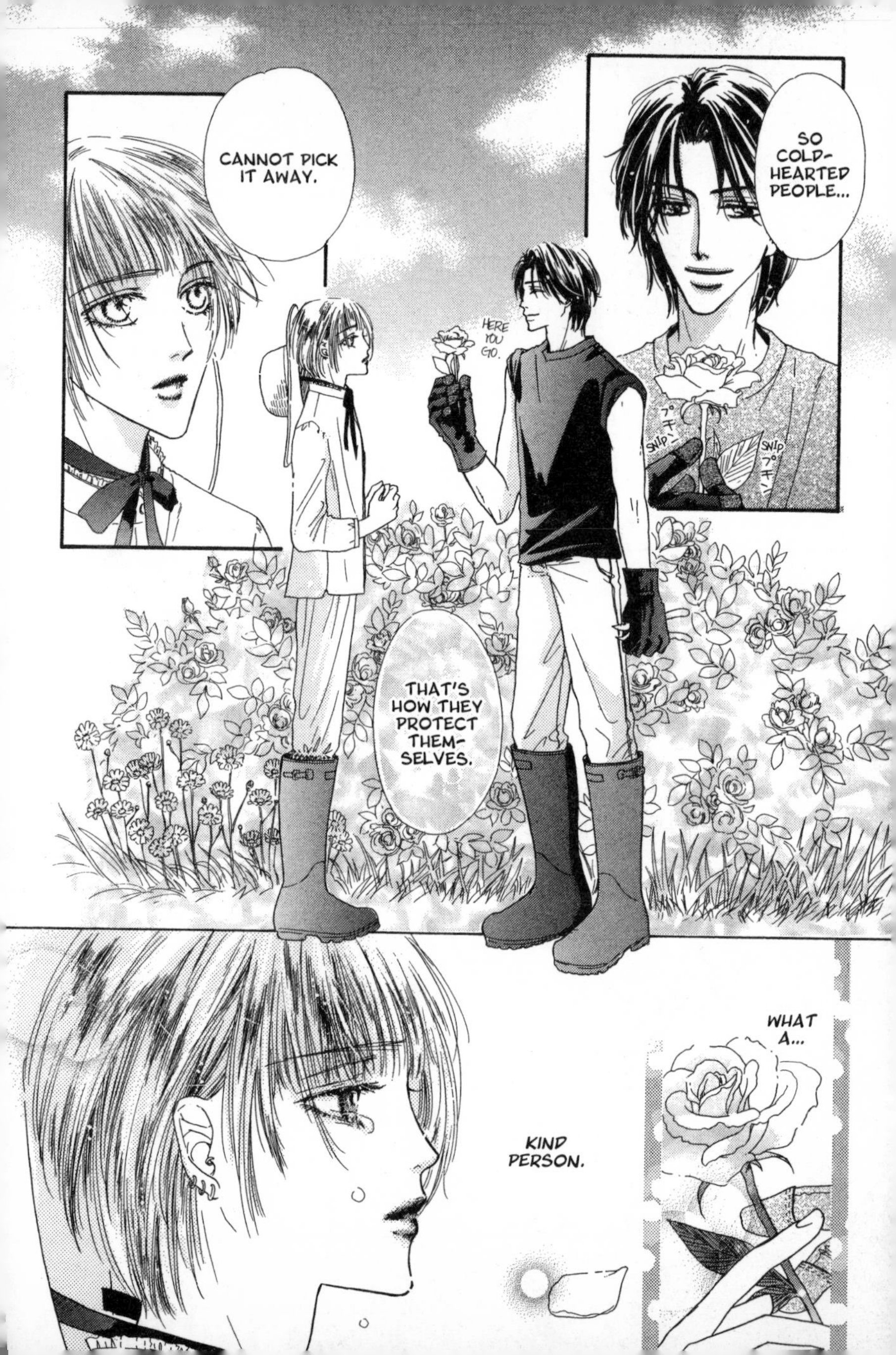
SO COLD-HEARTED PEOPLE...
SNIP
プチン
SNIP
プチン
CANNOT PICK IT AWAY.
HERE YOU GO.
THAT'S HOW THEY PROTECT THEM-SELVES.
WHAT A...
KIND PERSON.

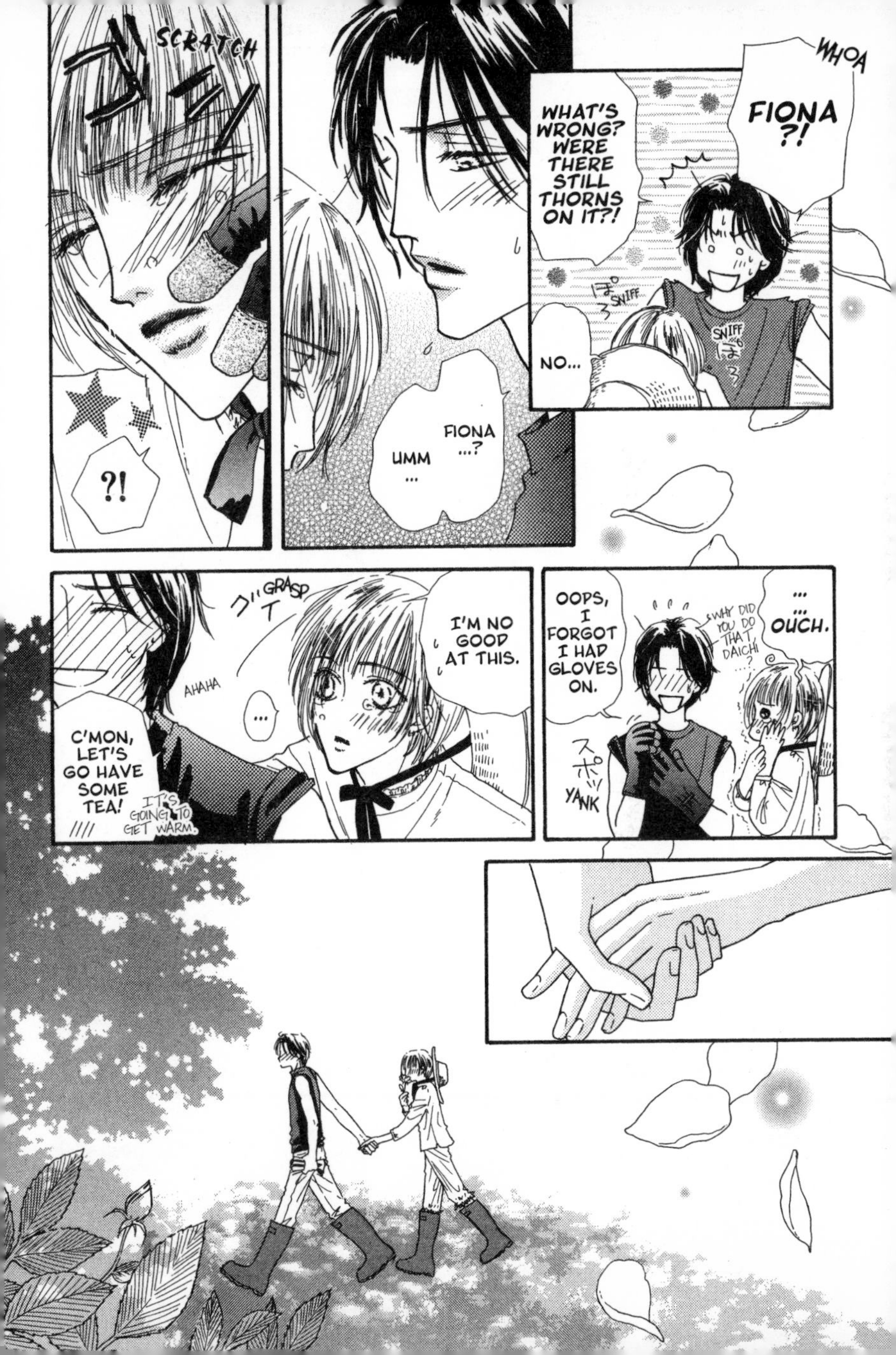
WHOA
FIONA ?!
WHAT'S WRONG? WERE THERE STILL THORNS ON IT?!
SNIFF
NO...
SNIFF
FIONA ...?
UMM ...
SCRATCH
?!
... ... OUCH.
WHY DID YOU DO THAT, DAICHI ...?
OOPS, I FORGOT I HAD GLOVES ON.
YANK
GRASP
I'M NO GOOD AT THIS.
...
AHAHA
C'MON, LET'S GO HAVE SOME TEA!
IT'S GOING TO GET WARM.

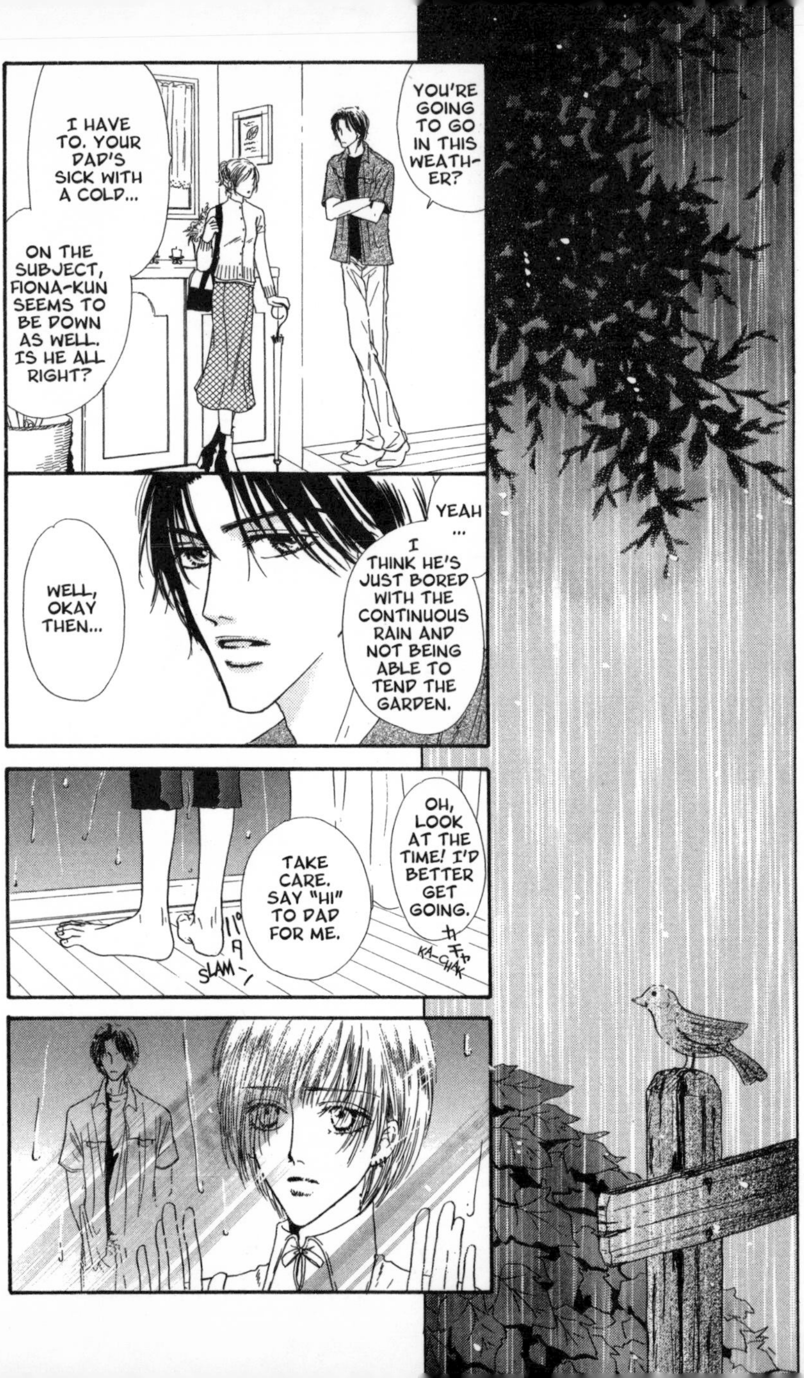
YOU'RE GOING TO GO IN THIS WEATHER?
I HAVE TO. YOUR DAD'S SICK WITH A COLD...
ON THE SUBJECT, FIONA-KUN SEEMS TO BE DOWN AS WELL. IS HE ALL RIGHT?
YEAH... I THINK HE'S JUST BORED WITH THE CONTINUOUS RAIN AND NOT BEING ABLE TO TEND THE GARDEN.
WELL, OKAY THEN...
OH, LOOK AT THE TIME! I'D BETTER GET GOING.
TAKE CARE. SAY "HI" TO DAD FOR ME.
KA-CHAK
SLAM

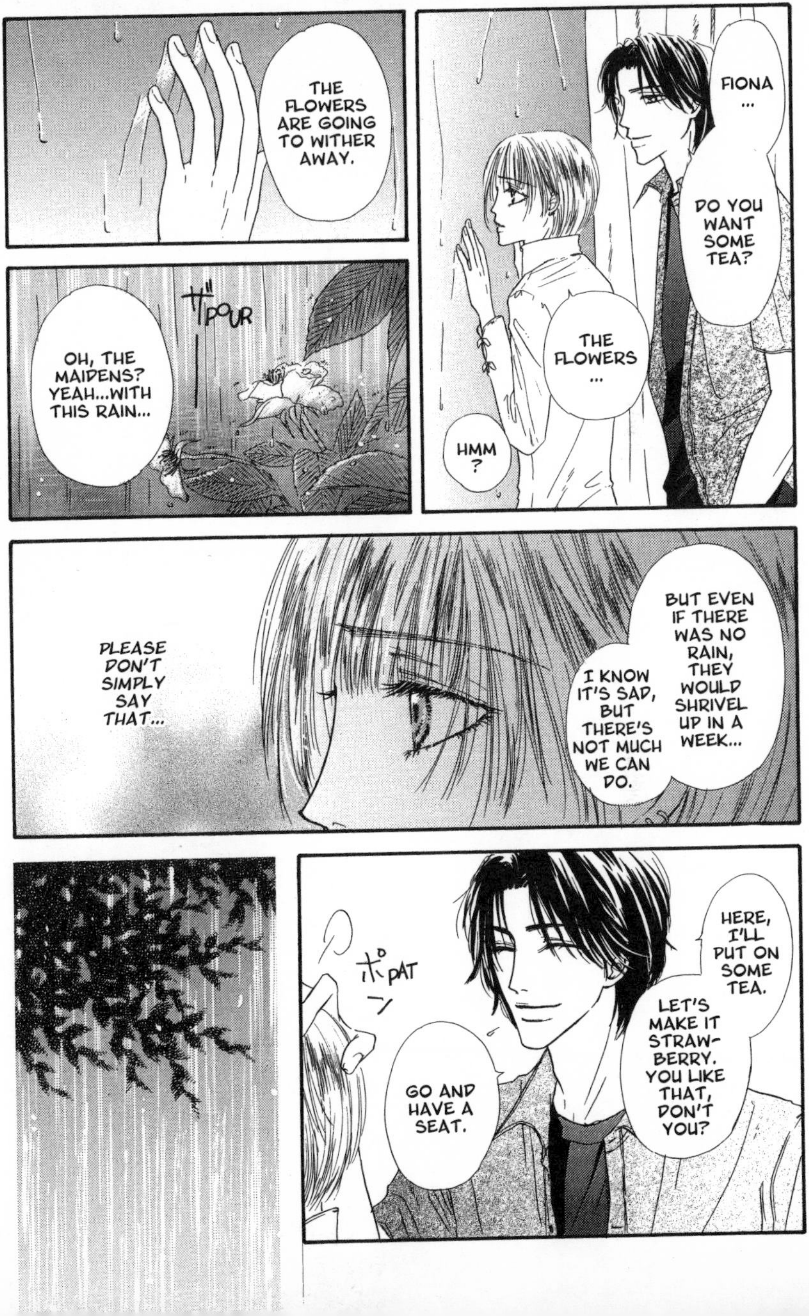
FIONA ...
DO YOU WANT SOME TEA?
THE FLOWERS ...
HMM ?
THE FLOWERS ARE GOING TO WITHER AWAY.
POUR
OH, THE MAIDENS? YEAH...WITH THIS RAIN...
BUT EVEN IF THERE WAS NO RAIN, THEY WOULD SHRIVEL UP IN A WEEK...
I KNOW IT'S SAD, BUT THERE'S NOT MUCH WE CAN DO.
PLEASE DON'T SIMPLY SAY THAT...
HERE, I'LL PUT ON SOME TEA.
LET'S MAKE IT STRAWBERRY. YOU LIKE THAT, DON'T YOU?
PAT
GO AND HAVE A SEAT.

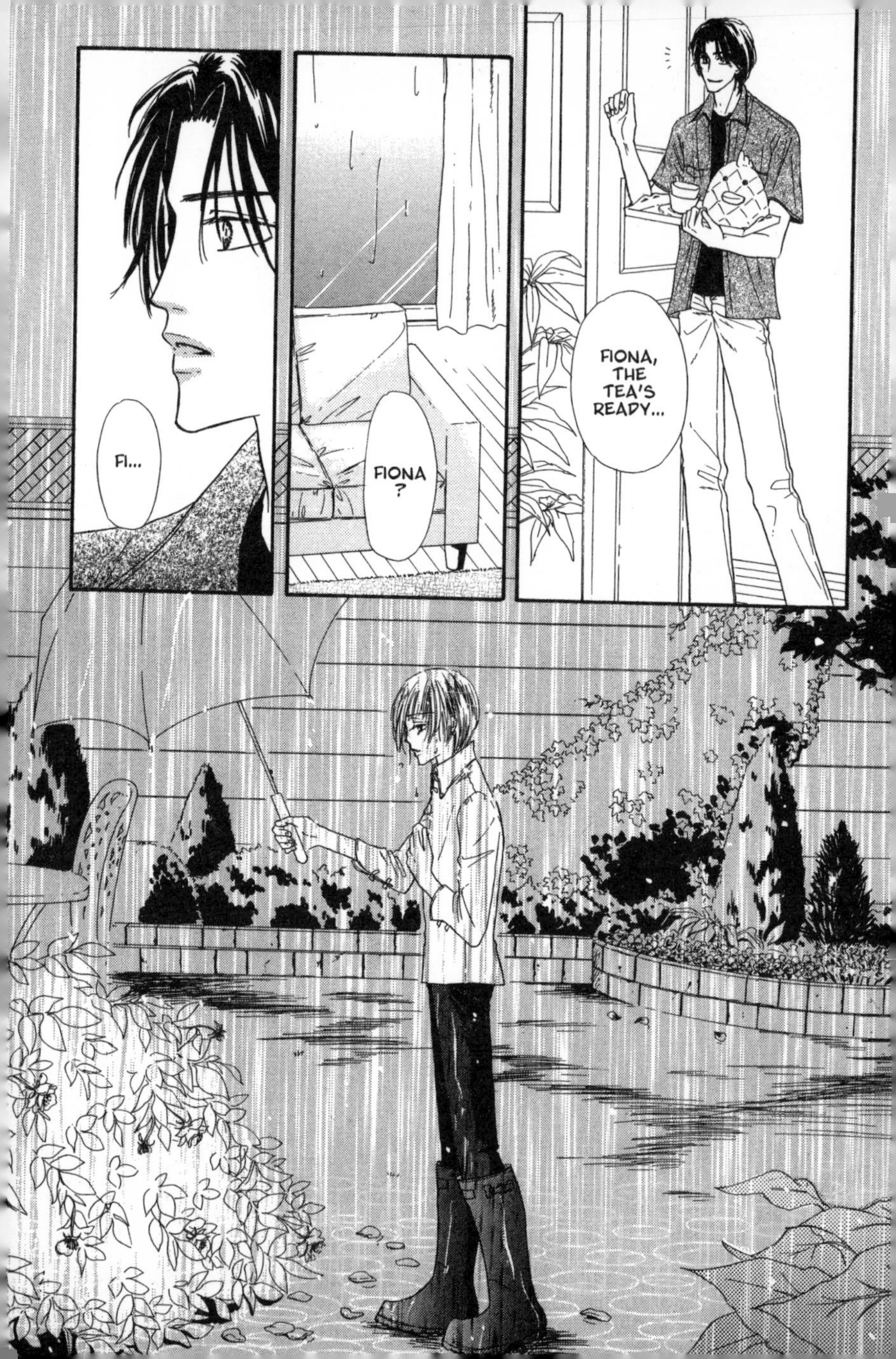
FIONA, THE TEA'S READY...
FIONA ?
FI...

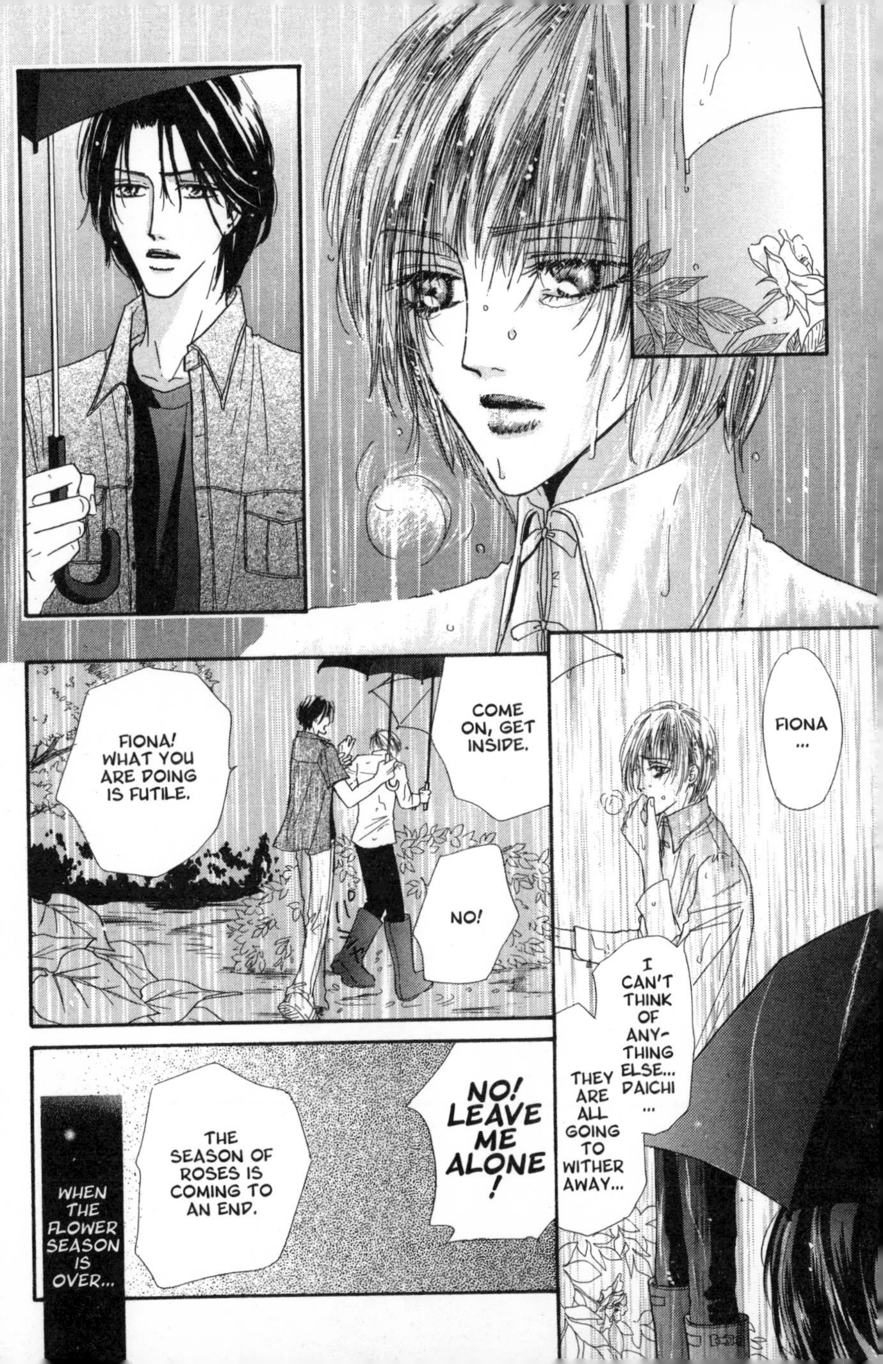
FIONA ...
I CAN'T THINK OF ANYTHING ELSE... DAICHI ...
THEY ARE ALL GOING TO WITHER AWAY...
COME ON, GET INSIDE.
FIONA! WHAT YOU ARE DOING IS FUTILE.
NO!
NO! LEAVE ME ALONE!
THE SEASON OF ROSES IS COMING TO AN END.
WHEN THE FLOWER SEASON IS OVER...

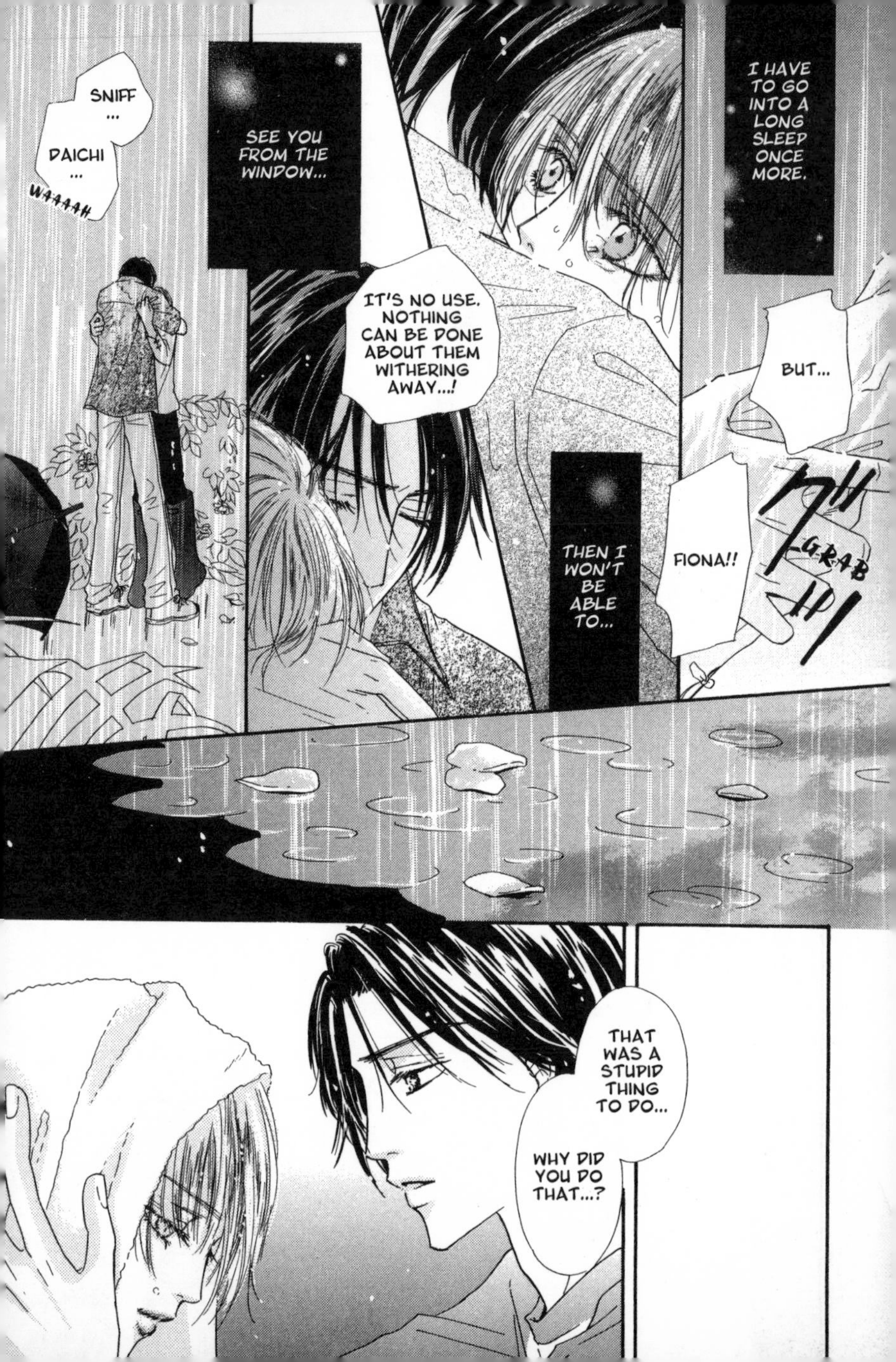
I HAVE TO GO INTO A LONG SLEEP ONCE MORE.
BUT...
FIONA!!
GRAB
THEN I WON'T BE ABLE TO...
SEE YOU FROM THE WINDOW...
IT'S NO USE. NOTHING CAN BE DONE ABOUT THEM WITHERING AWAY...!
SNIFF ... DAICHI ...
WAAAAH
THAT WAS A STUPID THING TO DO...
WHY DID YOU DO THAT...?

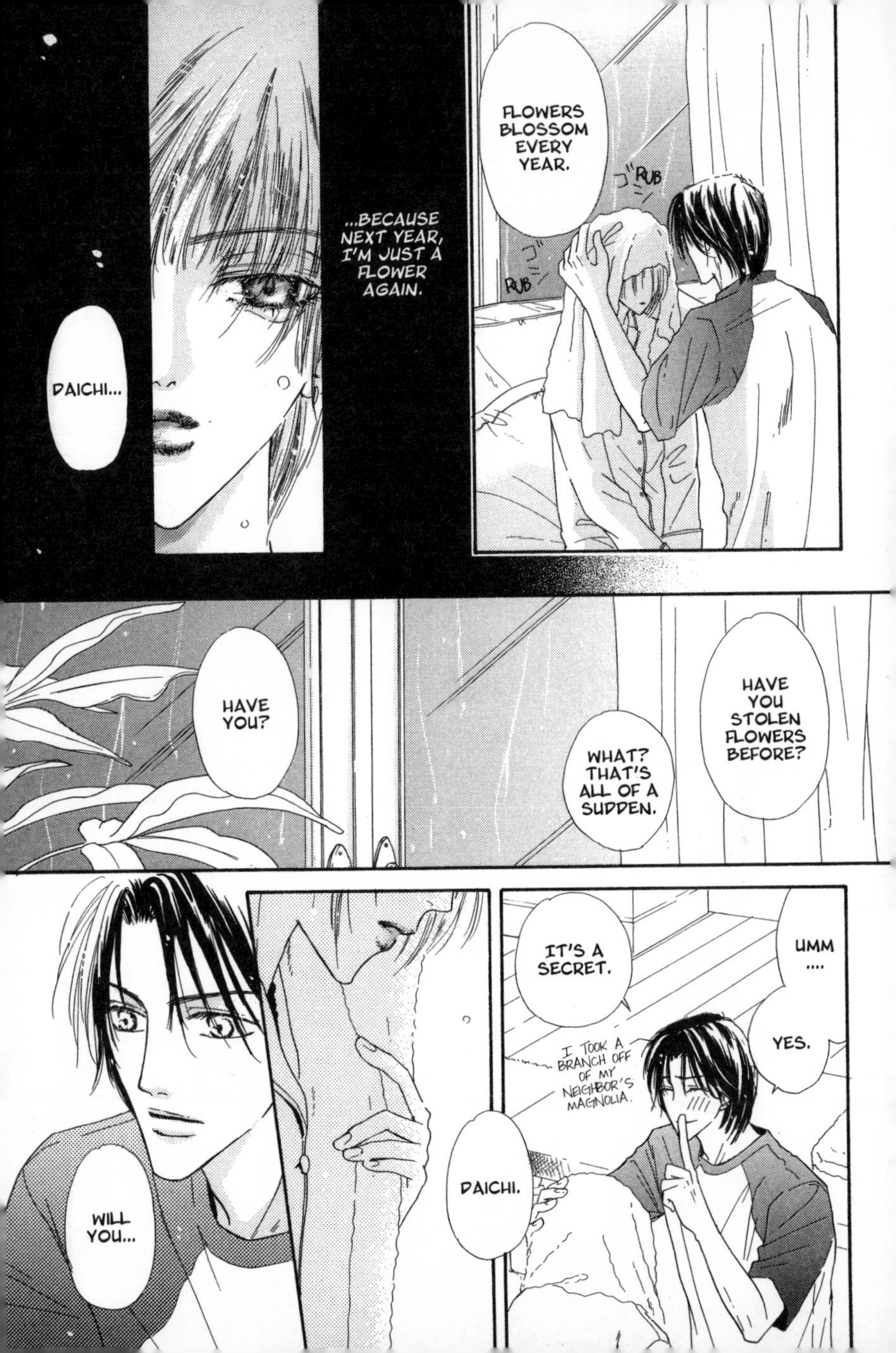
FLOWERS BLOSSOM EVERY YEAR.
RUB
RUB
...BECAUSE NEXT YEAR, I'M JUST A FLOWER AGAIN.
DAICHI...
HAVE YOU STOLEN FLOWERS BEFORE?
WHAT? THAT'S ALL OF A SUDDEN.
HAVE YOU?
UMM ....
IT'S A SECRET.
YES.
I TOOK A BRANCH OFF OF MY NEIGHBOR'S MAGNOLIA.
DAICHI.
WILL YOU...

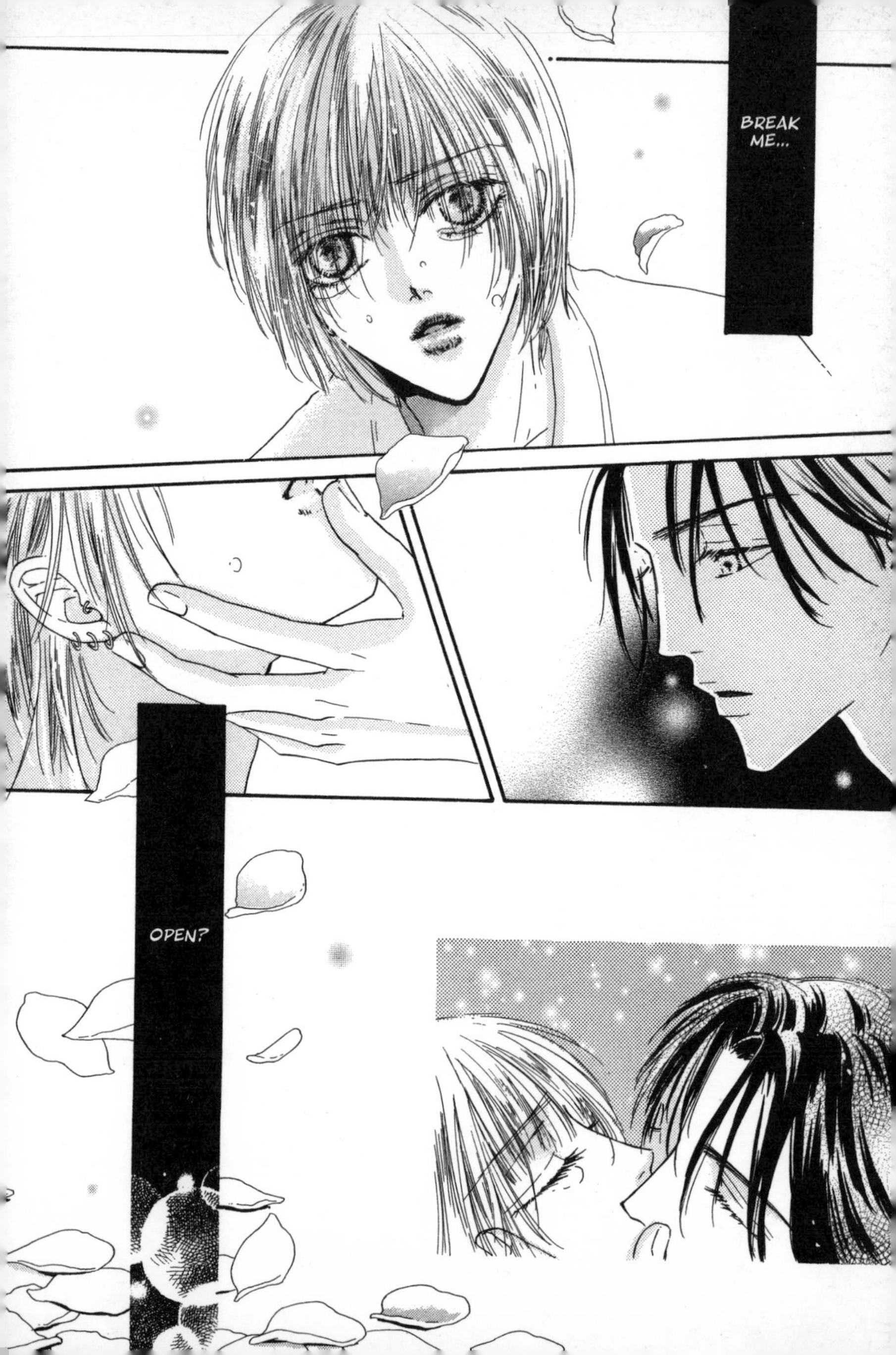
BREAK ME...
OPEN?

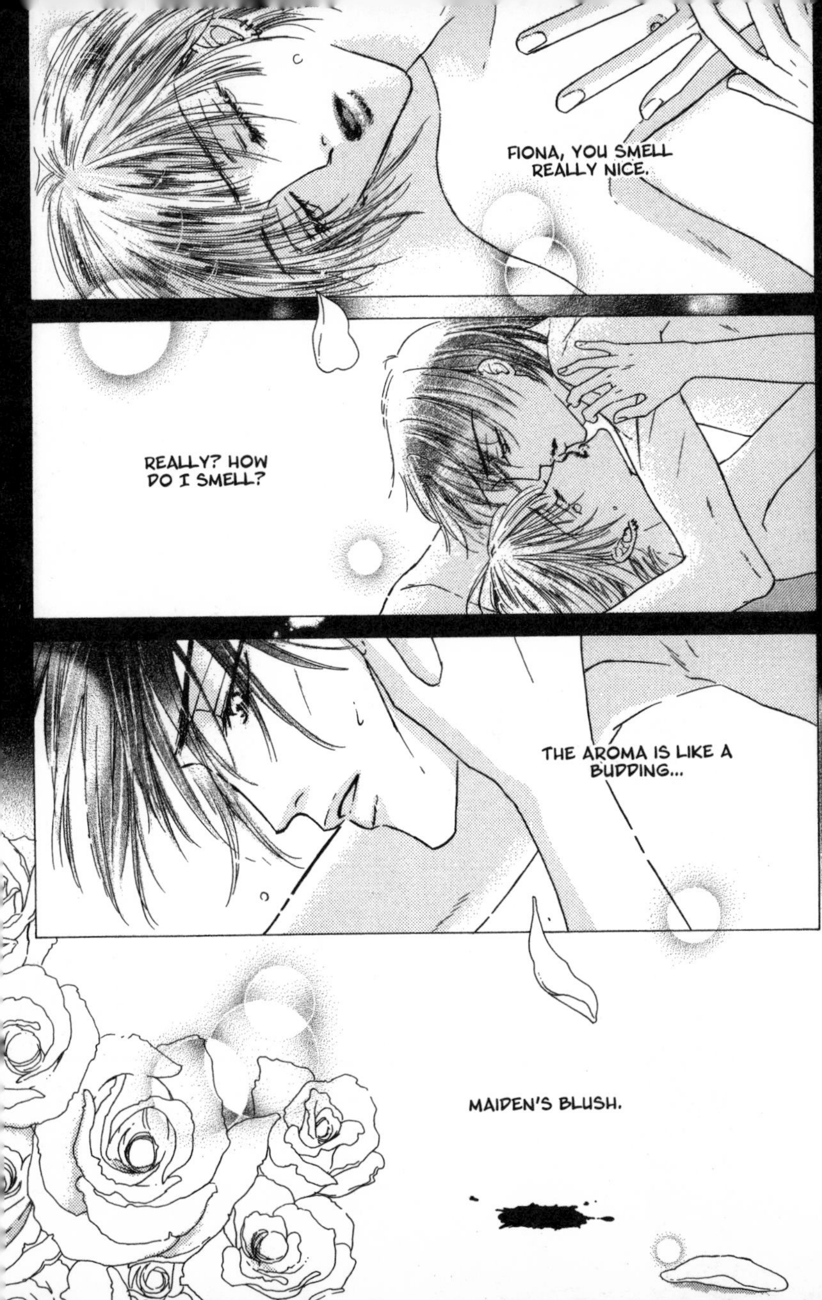
FIONA, YOU SMELL REALLY NICE.
REALLY? HOW DO I SMELL?
THE AROMA IS LIKE A BUDDING...
MAIDEN'S BLUSH.

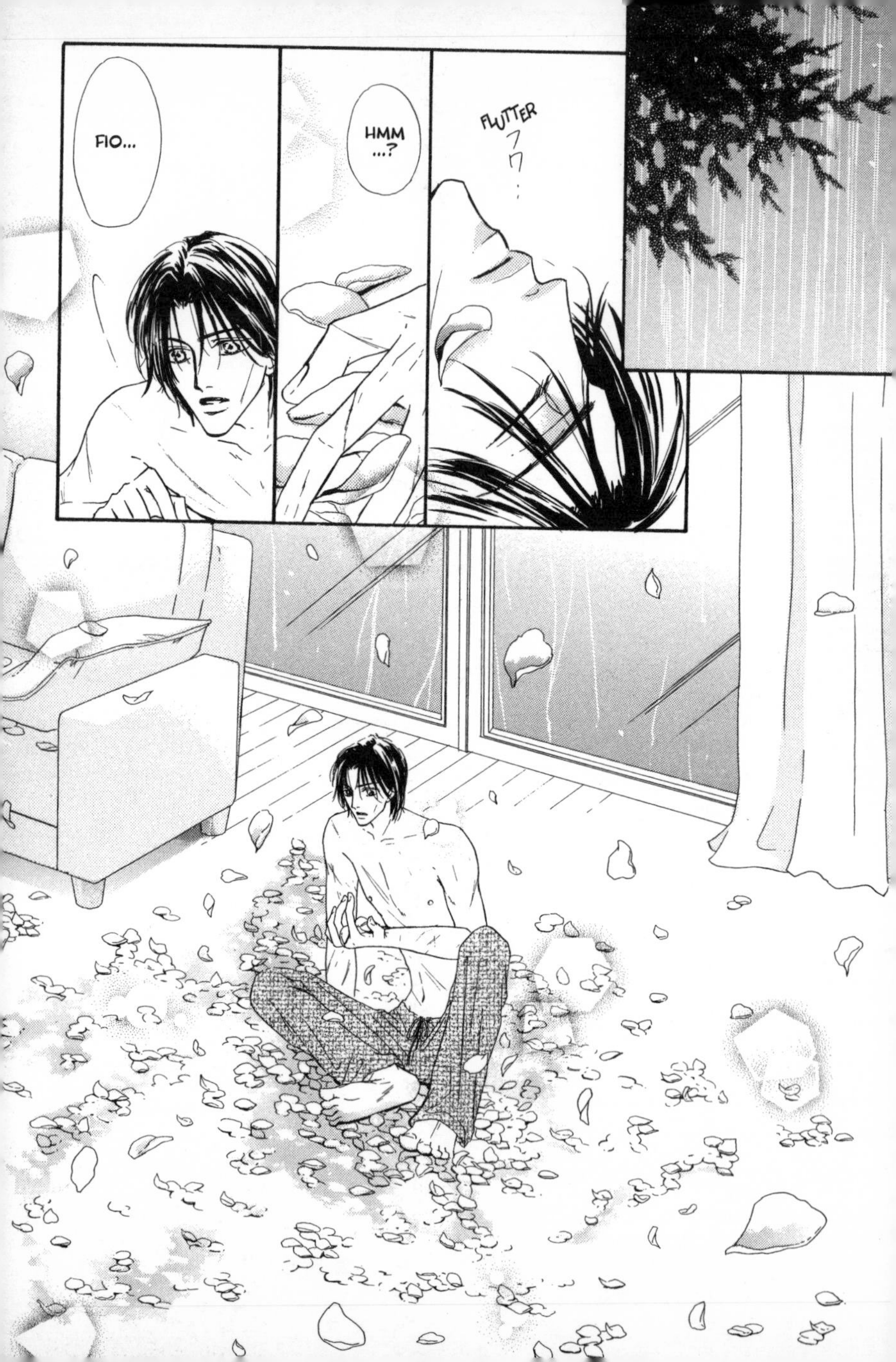
FLUTTER
フワ・・
HMM ...?
FIO...

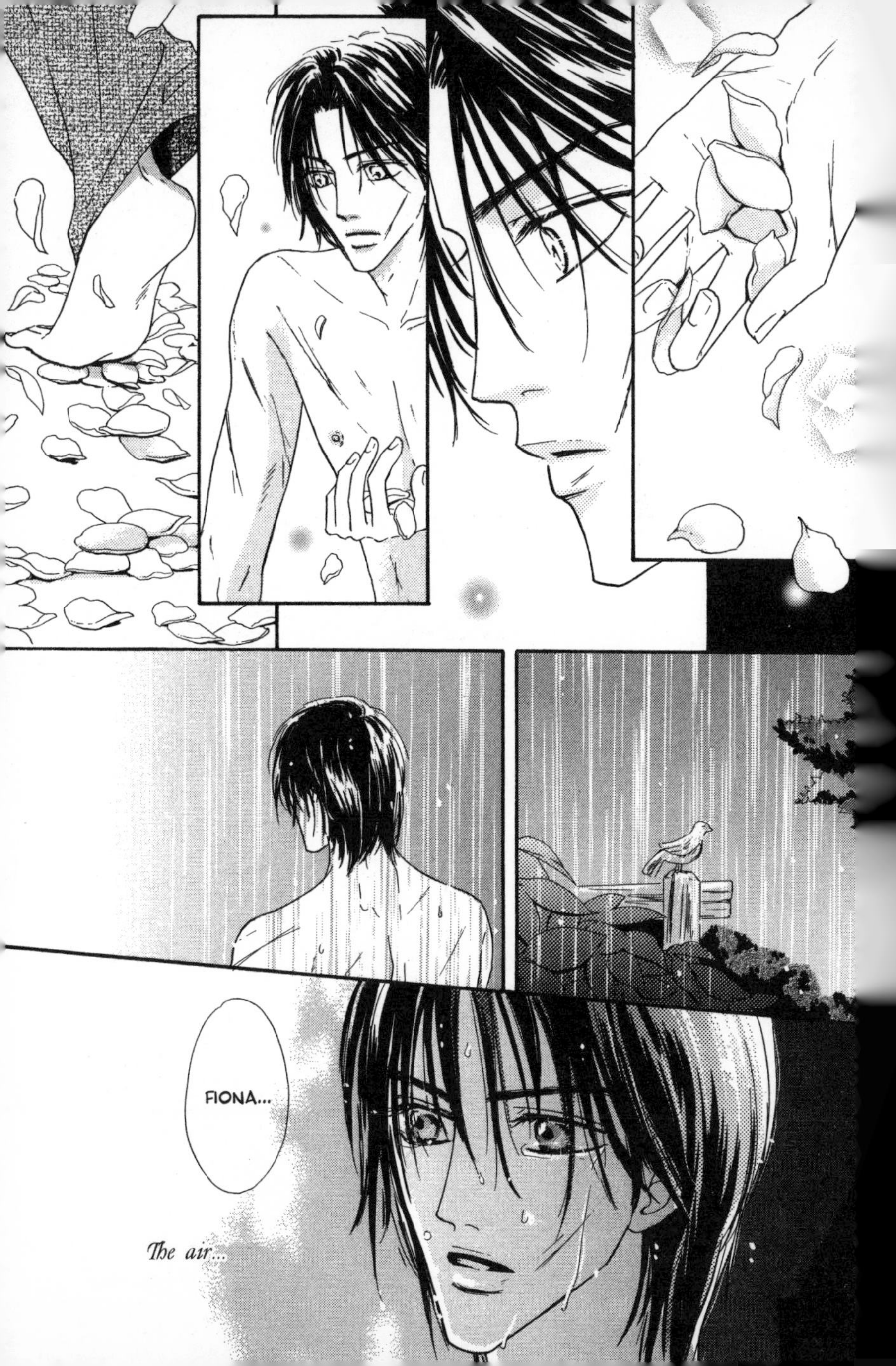
FIONA...
The air...

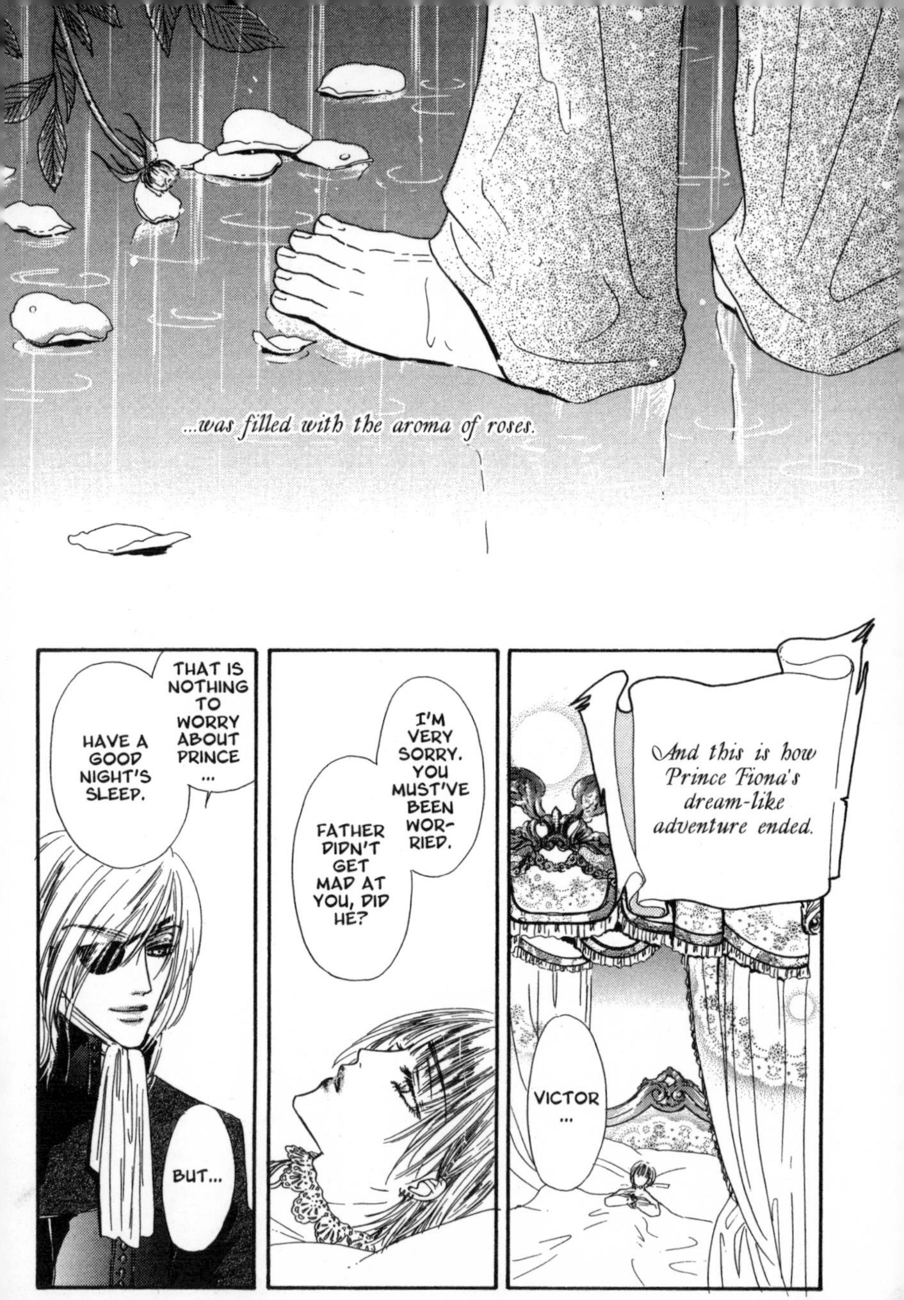
...was filled with the aroma of roses.
And this is how Prince Fiona's dream-like adventure ended.
VICTOR ...
I'M VERY SORRY. YOU MUST'VE BEEN WOR-RIED.
FATHER DIDN'T GET MAD AT YOU, DID HE?
THAT IS NOTHING TO WORRY ABOUT PRINCE ...
HAVE A GOOD NIGHT'S SLEEP.
BUT...

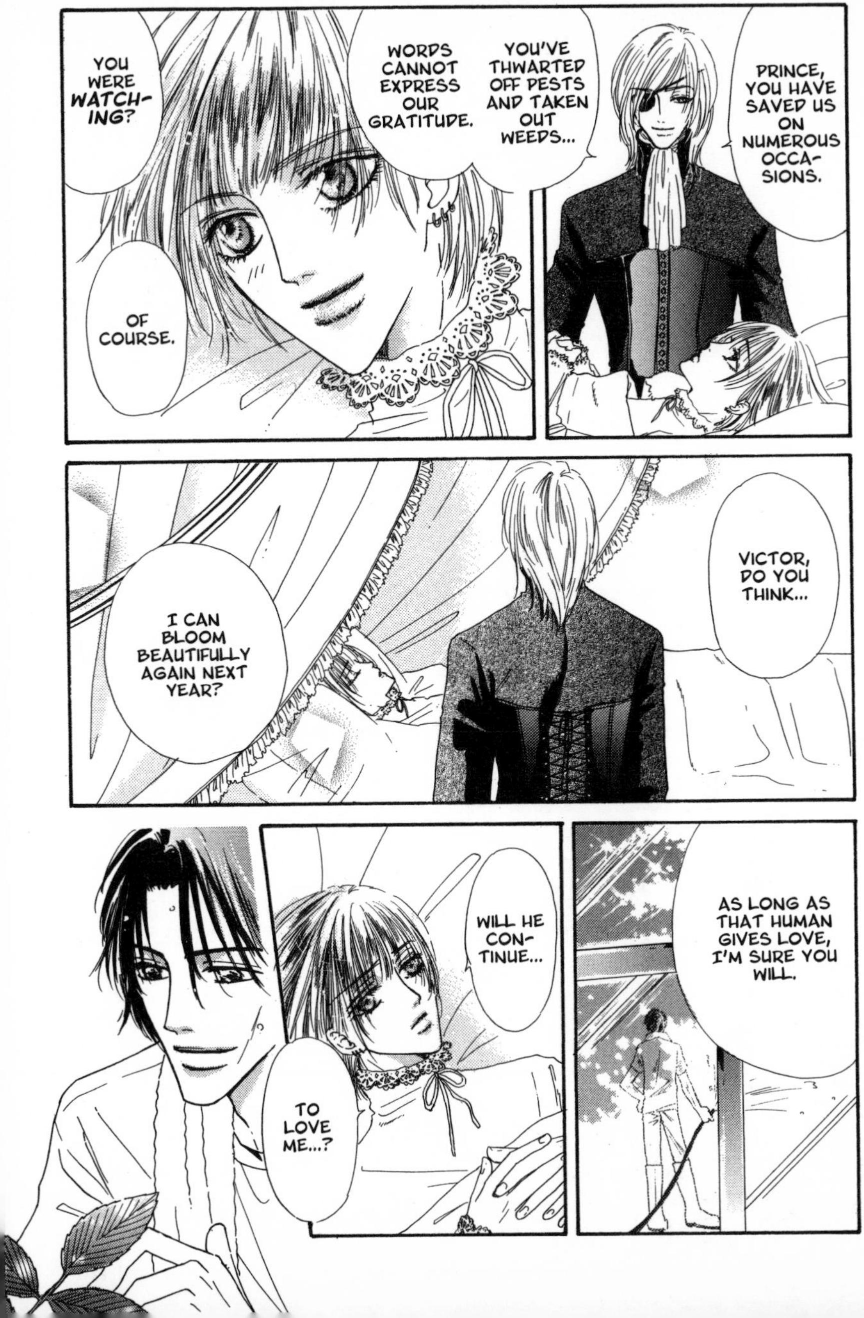
PRINCE, YOU HAVE SAVED US ON NUMEROUS OCCASIONS.
YOU'VE THWARTED OFF PESTS AND TAKEN OUT WEEDS...
WORDS CANNOT EXPRESS OUR GRATITUDE.
YOU WERE WATCHING?
OF COURSE.
VICTOR, DO YOU THINK...
I CAN BLOOM BEAUTIFULLY AGAIN NEXT YEAR?
AS LONG AS THAT HUMAN GIVES LOVE, I'M SURE YOU WILL.
WILL HE CONTINUE...
TO LOVE ME...?

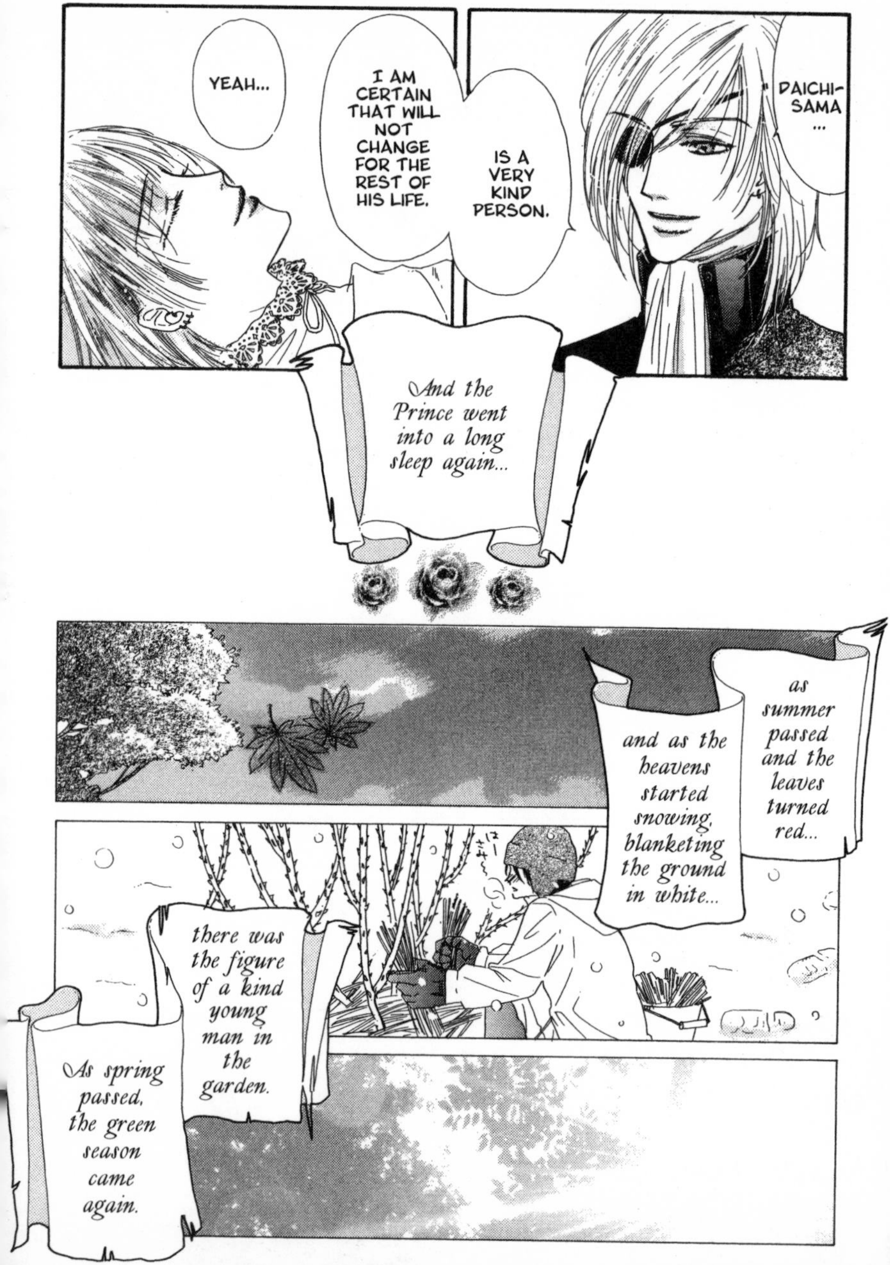
DAICHI-SAMA ...
IS A VERY KIND PERSON.
I AM CERTAIN THAT WILL NOT CHANGE FOR THE REST OF HIS LIFE.
YEAH...
And the Prince went into a long sleep again...
as summer passed and the leaves turned red...
and as the heavens started snowing, blanketing the ground in white...
there was the figure of a kind young man in the garden.
As spring passed, the green season came again.

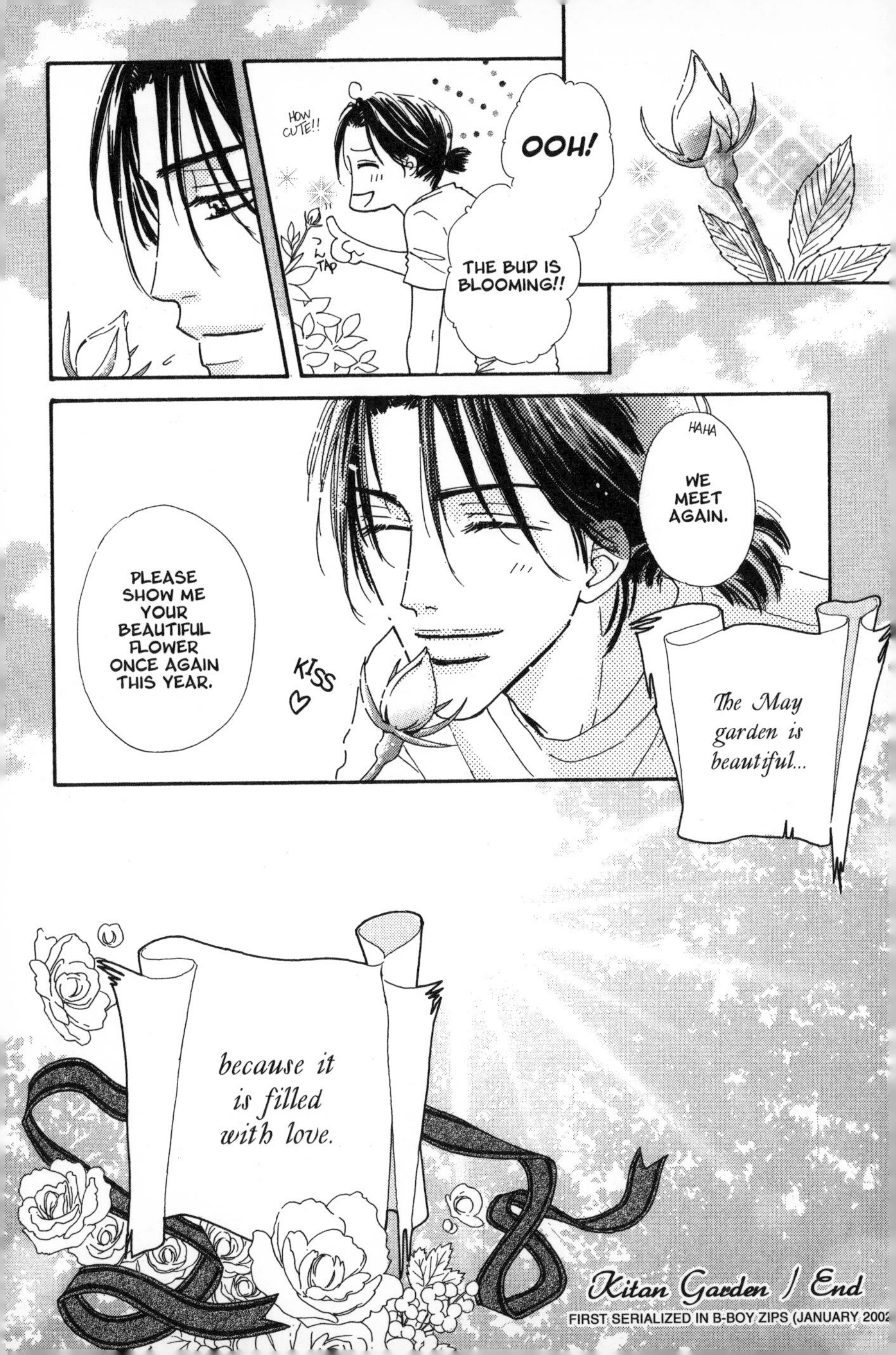
OOH!
HOW CUTE!!
THE BUD IS BLOOMING!!
TAP
HAHA
WE MEET AGAIN.
PLEASE SHOW ME YOUR BEAUTIFUL FLOWER ONCE AGAIN THIS YEAR.
KISS
The May garden is beautiful...
because it is filled with love.
Kitan Garden / End
FIRST SERIALIZED IN B-BOY ZIPS (JANUARY 2002

bonds

...

situation

...

KITAN garden

...

sakura

Presented by Tōko Kawai

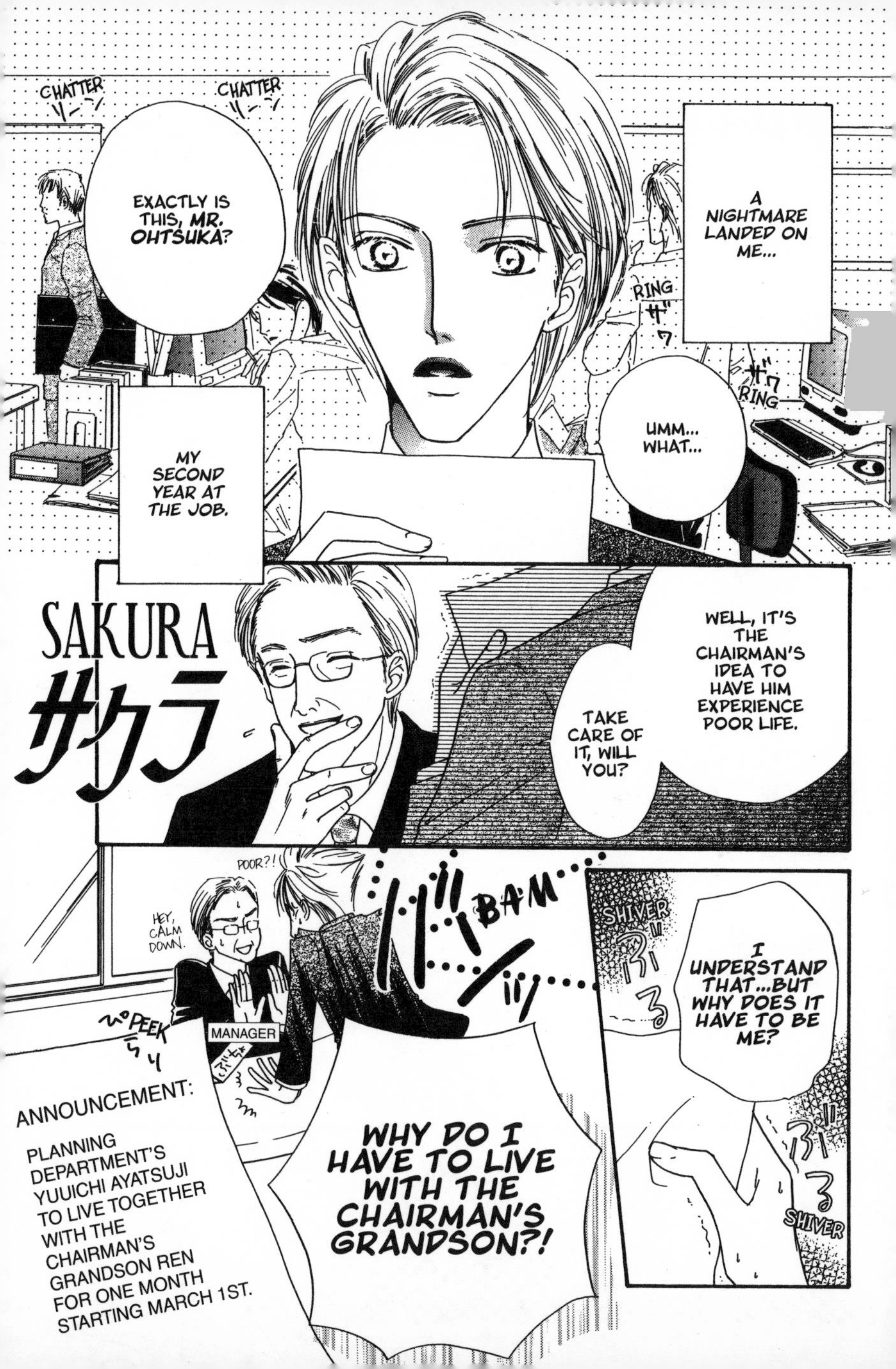
A NIGHTMARE LANDED ON ME...
RING
RING
UMM... WHAT...
CHATTER
CHATTER
EXACTLY IS THIS, MR. OHTSUKA?
MY SECOND YEAR AT THE JOB.
SAKURA
サクラ
WELL, IT'S THE CHAIRMAN'S IDEA TO HAVE HIM EXPERIENCE POOR LIFE.
TAKE CARE OF IT, WILL YOU?
SHIVER
I UNDERSTAND THAT...BUT WHY DOES IT HAVE TO BE ME?
SHIVER
BAM
WHY DO I HAVE TO LIVE WITH THE CHAIRMAN'S GRANDSON?!
POOR?!
HEY, CALM DOWN.
MANAGER
PEEK
ANNOUNCEMENT:
PLANNING DEPARTMENT'S YUUICHI AYATSUJI TO LIVE TOGETHER WITH THE CHAIRMAN'S GRANDSON REN FOR ONE MONTH STARTING MARCH 1ST.

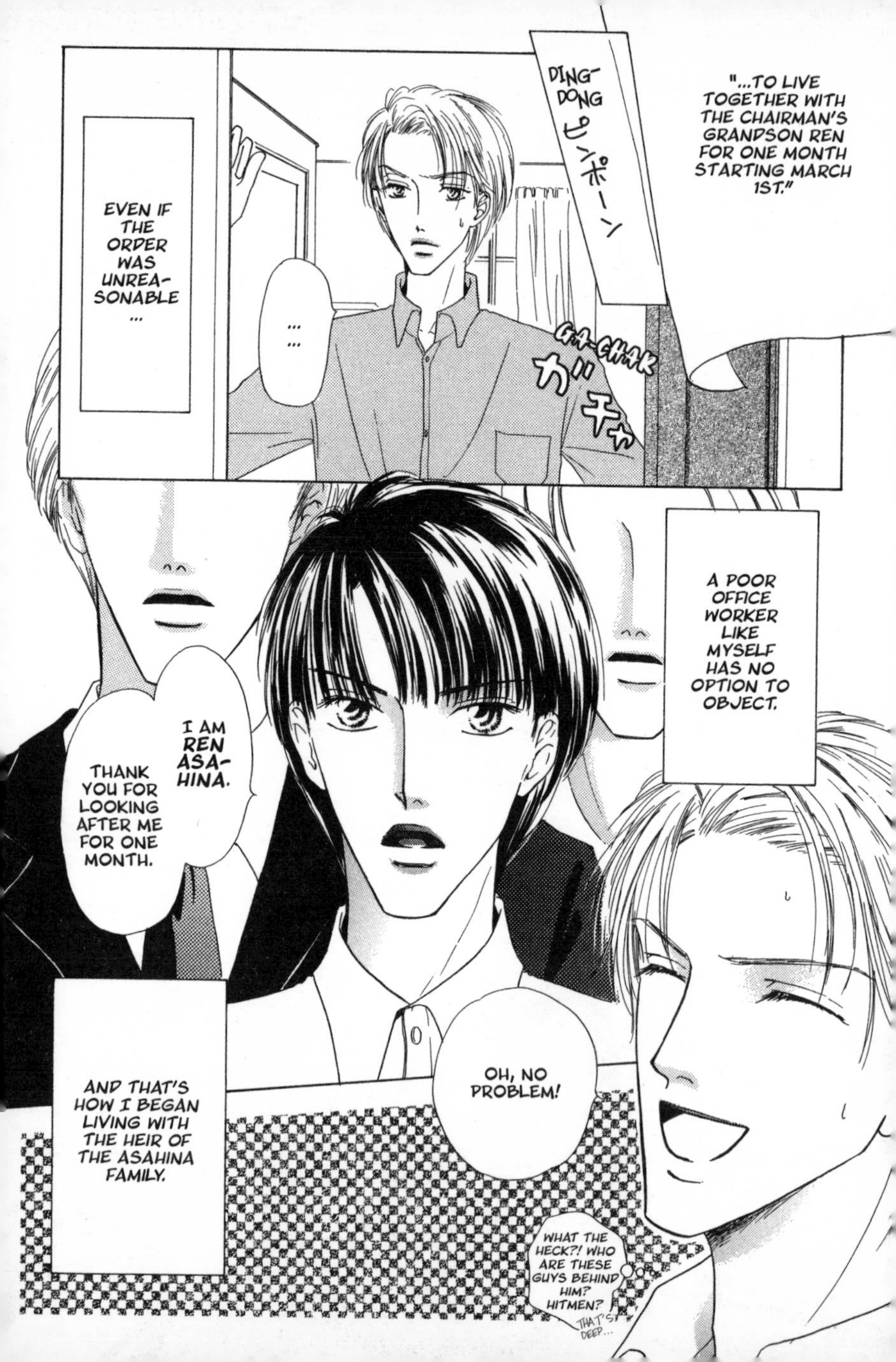
"...TO LIVE TOGETHER WITH THE CHAIRMAN'S GRANDSON REN FOR ONE MONTH STARTING MARCH 1ST."
DING-DONG
ピンポーン
GA-CHAK
ガチャ
......
EVEN IF THE ORDER WAS UNREASONABLE...
A POOR OFFICE WORKER LIKE MYSELF HAS NO OPTION TO OBJECT.
I AM REN ASAHINA.
THANK YOU FOR LOOKING AFTER ME FOR ONE MONTH.
OH, NO PROBLEM!
WHAT THE HECK?! WHO ARE THESE GUYS BEHIND HIM? HITMEN?
THAT'S DEEP...
AND THAT'S HOW I BEGAN LIVING WITH THE HEIR OF THE ASAHINA FAMILY.

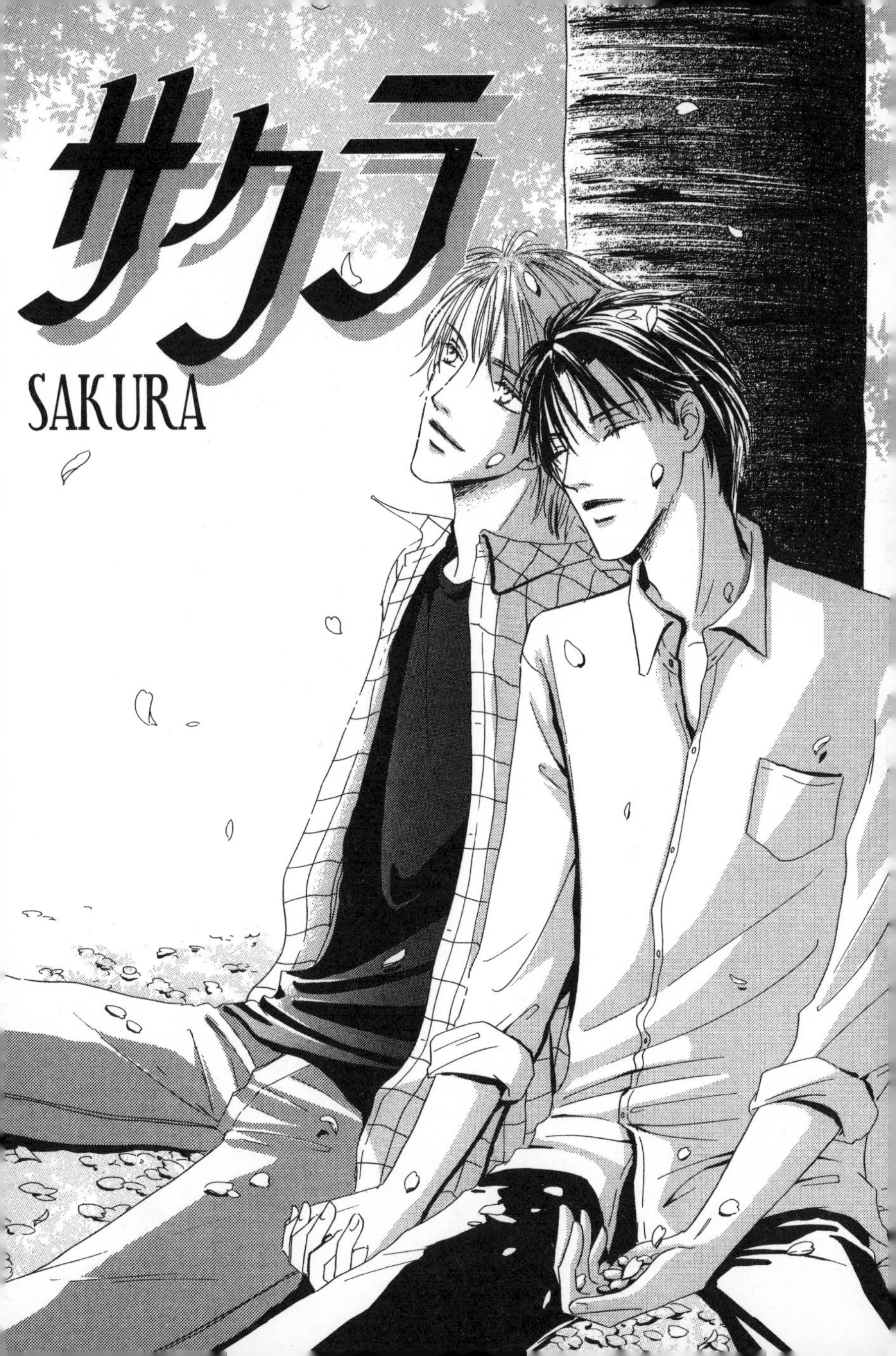
サクラ
SAKURA

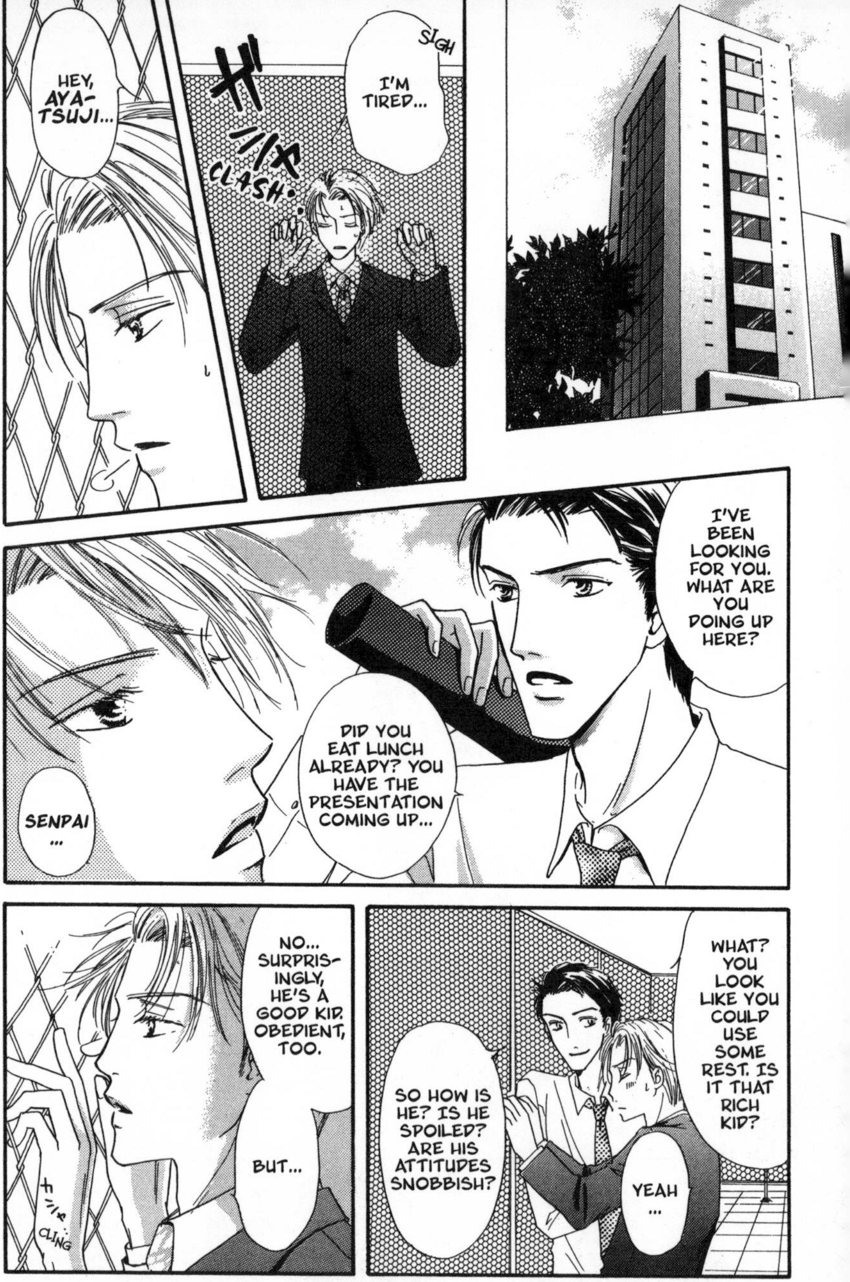
SIGH
I'M TIRED...
CLASH
HEY, AYA-TSUJI...
I'VE BEEN LOOKING FOR YOU. WHAT ARE YOU DOING UP HERE?
DID YOU EAT LUNCH ALREADY? YOU HAVE THE PRESENTATION COMING UP...
SENPAI...
WHAT? YOU LOOK LIKE YOU COULD USE SOME REST. IS IT THAT RICH KID?
YEAH...
SO HOW IS HE? IS HE SPOILED? ARE HIS ATTITUDES SNOBBISH?
NO... SURPRIS-INGLY, HE'S A GOOD KID. OBEDIENT, TOO.
BUT...
CLING

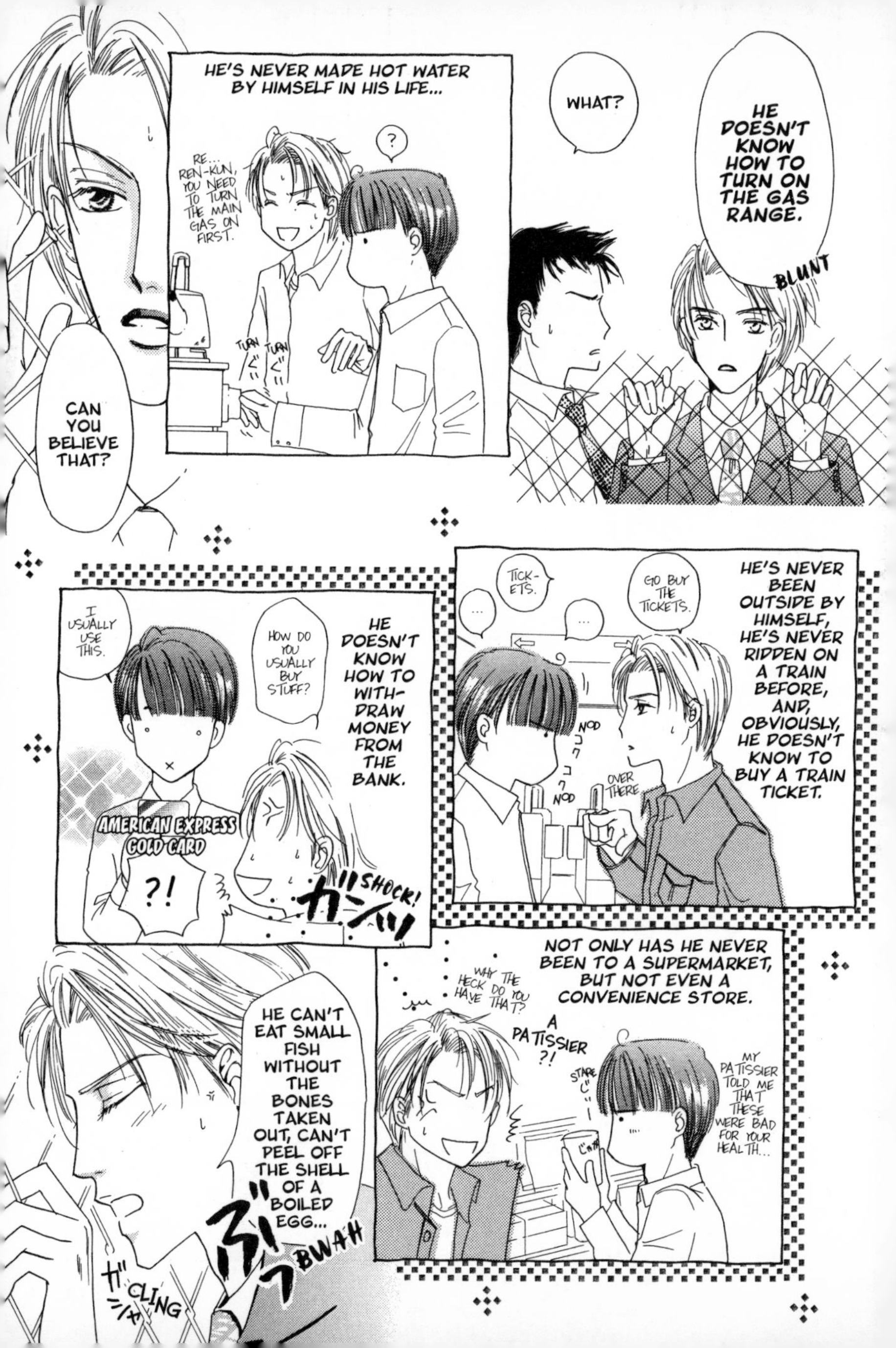

HE DOESN'T KNOW HOW TO TURN ON THE GAS RANGE.
BLUNT
WHAT?
HE'S NEVER MADE HOT WATER BY HIMSELF IN HIS LIFE...
?
RE... REN-KUN, YOU NEED TO TURN THE MAIN GAS ON FIRST.
TURN TURN
CAN YOU BELIEVE THAT?
HE'S NEVER BEEN OUTSIDE BY HIMSELF, HE'S NEVER RIDDEN ON A TRAIN BEFORE, AND, OBVIOUSLY, HE DOESN'T KNOW TO BUY A TRAIN TICKET.
GO BUY THE TICKETS.
TICK-ETS.
...
...
NOD NOD
OVER THERE
HE DOESN'T KNOW HOW TO WITH-DRAW MONEY FROM THE BANK.
HOW DO YOU USUALLY BUY STUFF?
I USUALLY USE THIS.
AMERICAN EXPRESS GOLD CARD
?!
SHOCK!
NOT ONLY HAS HE NEVER BEEN TO A SUPERMARKET, BUT NOT EVEN A CONVENIENCE STORE.
MY PATISSIER TOLD ME THAT THESE WERE BAD FOR YOUR HEALTH...
STARE
A PATISSIER?!
WHY THE HECK DO YOU HAVE THAT?
HE CAN'T EAT SMALL FISH WITHOUT THE BONES TAKEN OUT, CAN'T PEEL OFF THE SHELL OF A BOILED EGG...
BWAH
CLING

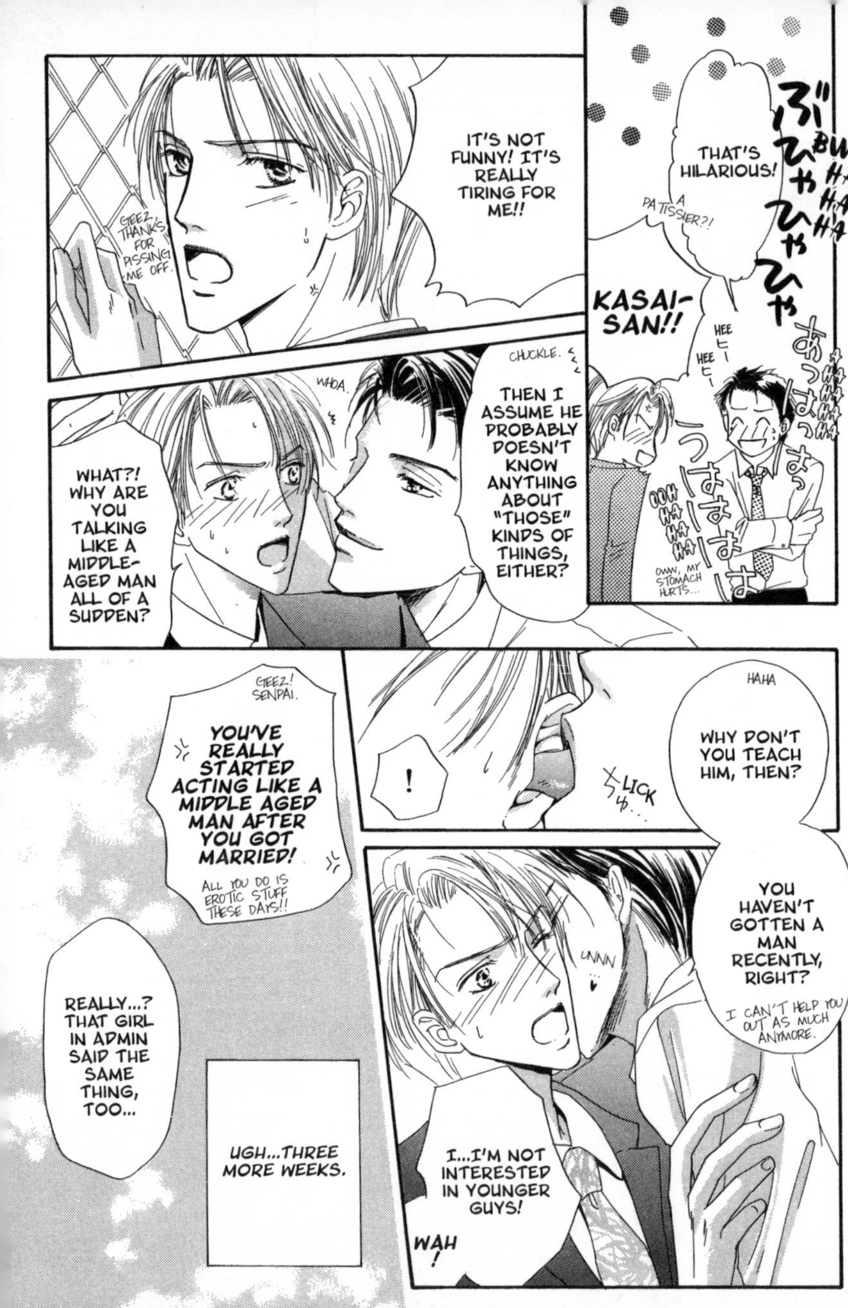

ぶひゃひゃひゃ
BWAH HA HA HA
THAT'S HILARIOUS!
A PATISSIER?!
KASAI-SAN!!
HEE ヒー
HEE ヒー
あっはっはっ
AHAHAHAHA
うはははは
OOH HA HA HA
OWW, MY STOMACH HURTS...
IT'S NOT FUNNY! IT'S REALLY TIRING FOR ME!!
GEEZ THANKS FOR PISSING ME OFF.
CHUCKLE. くっく
THEN I ASSUME HE PROBABLY DOESN'T KNOW ANYTHING ABOUT "THOSE" KINDS OF THINGS, EITHER?
WHOA.
WHAT?! WHY ARE YOU TALKING LIKE A MIDDLE-AGED MAN ALL OF A SUDDEN?
HAHA
WHY DON'T YOU TEACH HIM, THEN?
LICK ちゅ...
!
YOU HAVEN'T GOTTEN A MAN RECENTLY, RIGHT?
I CAN'T HELP YOU OUT AS MUCH ANYMORE.
UNNN
I...I'M NOT INTERESTED IN YOUNGER GUYS!
WAH!
GEEZ! SENPAI.
YOU'VE REALLY STARTED ACTING LIKE A MIDDLE AGED MAN AFTER YOU GOT MARRIED!
ALL YOU DO IS EROTIC STUFF THESE DAYS!!
REALLY...? THAT GIRL IN ADMIN SAID THE SAME THING, TOO...
UGH...THREE MORE WEEKS.

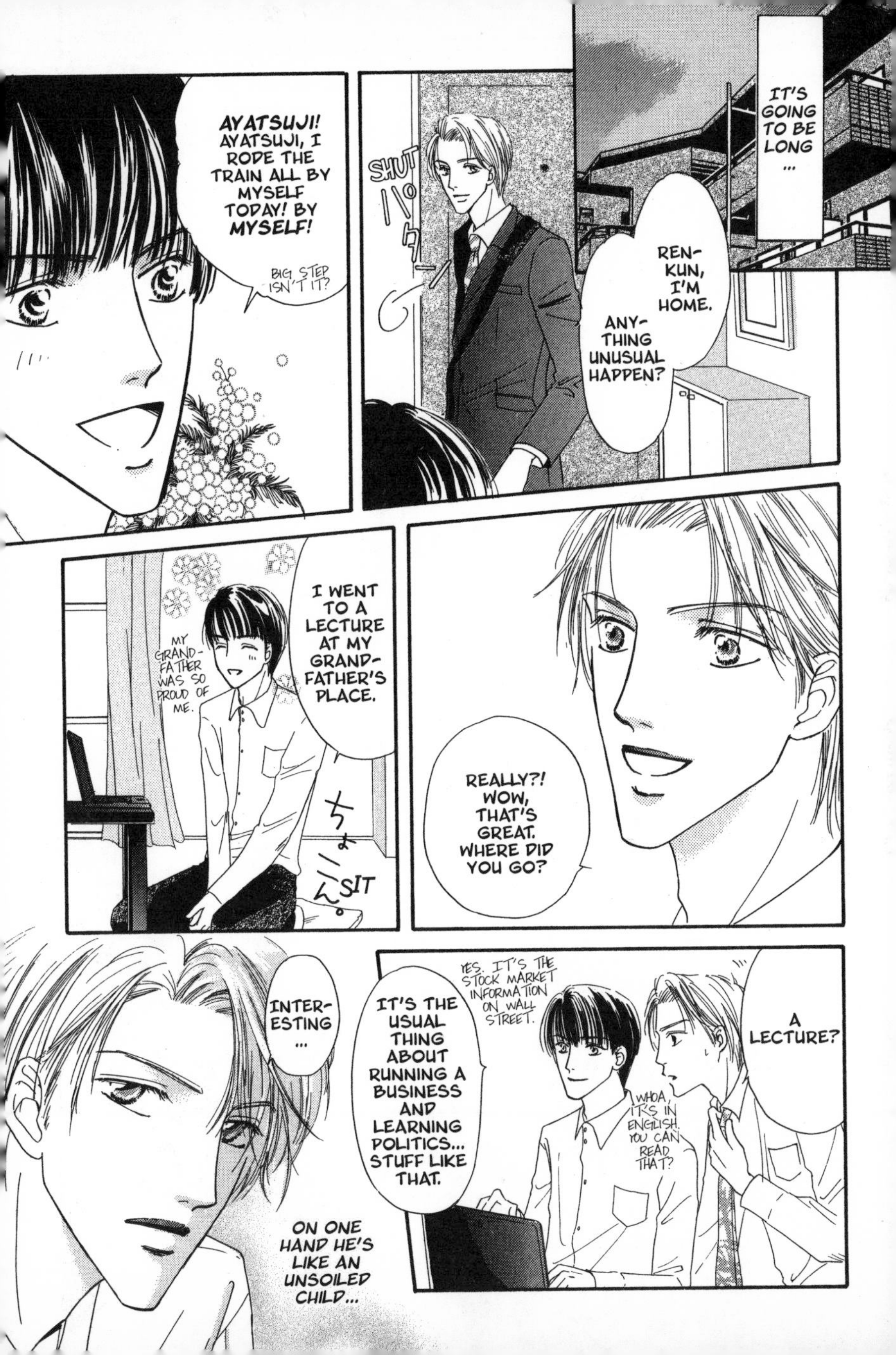
IT'S GOING TO BE LONG ...
REN-KUN, I'M HOME.
ANYTHING UNUSUAL HAPPEN?
SHUT
AYATSUJI! AYATSUJI, I RODE THE TRAIN ALL BY MYSELF TODAY! BY MYSELF!
BIG STEP ISN'T IT?
REALLY?! WOW, THAT'S GREAT. WHERE DID YOU GO?
I WENT TO A LECTURE AT MY GRANDFATHER'S PLACE.
MY GRANDFATHER WAS SO PROUD OF ME.
SIT
A LECTURE?
YES. IT'S THE STOCK MARKET INFORMATION ON WALL STREET.
WHOA, IT'S IN ENGLISH. YOU CAN READ THAT?
IT'S THE USUAL THING ABOUT RUNNING A BUSINESS AND LEARNING POLITICS... STUFF LIKE THAT.
INTERESTING ...
ON ONE HAND HE'S LIKE AN UNSOILED CHILD...

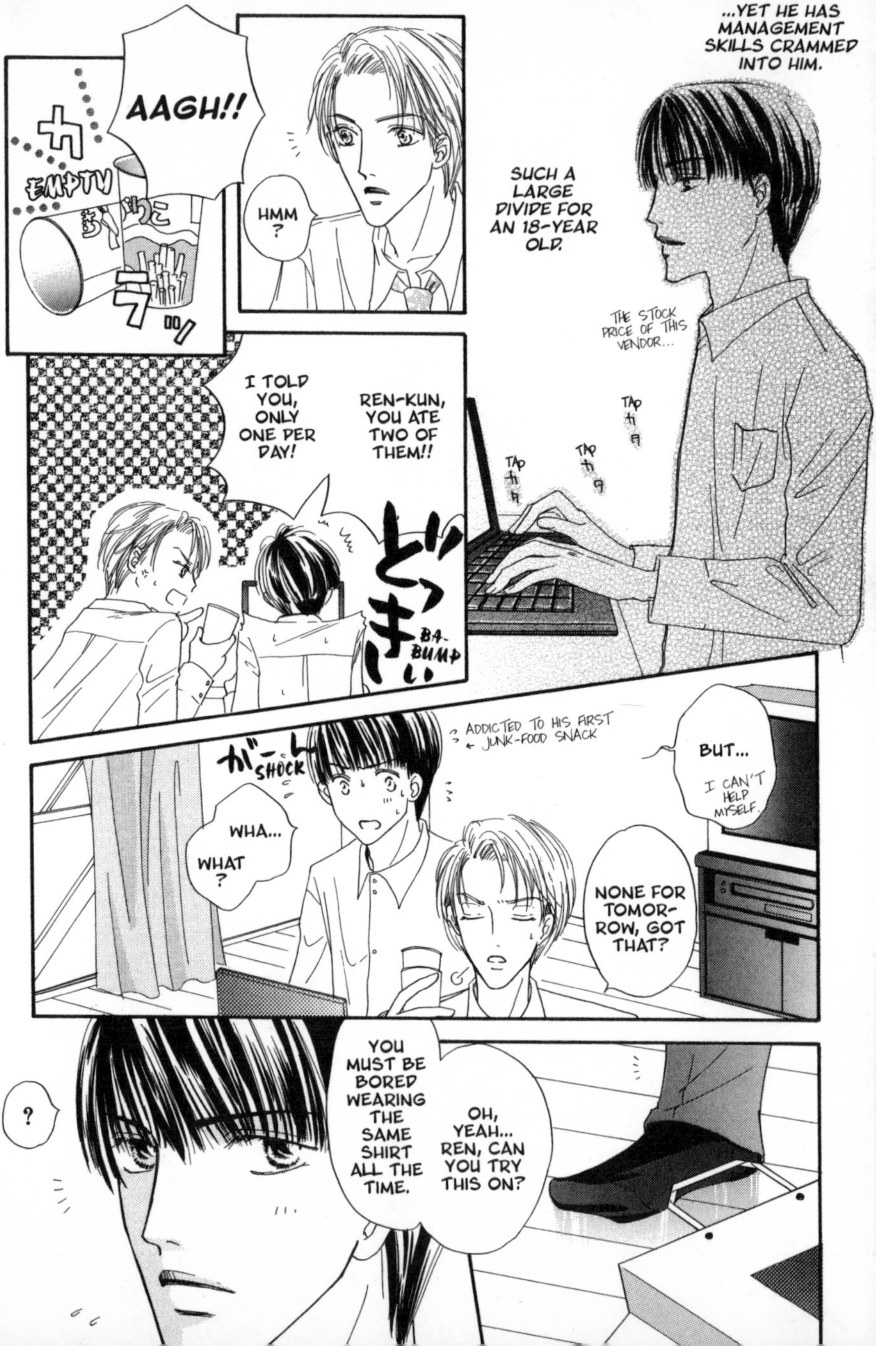

...YET HE HAS MANAGEMENT SKILLS CRAMMED INTO HIM.
SUCH A LARGE DIVIDE FOR AN 18-YEAR OLD.
THE STOCK PRICE OF THIS VENDOR...
TAP
TAP
TAP
HMM?
AAGH!!
EMPTY
REN-KUN, YOU ATE TWO OF THEM!!
I TOLD YOU, ONLY ONE PER DAY!
BA-BUMP
BUT... I CAN'T HELP MYSELF.
NONE FOR TOMORROW, GOT THAT?
ADDICTED TO HIS FIRST JUNK-FOOD SNACK
SHOCK
WHA... WHAT?
OH, YEAH... REN, CAN YOU TRY THIS ON?
YOU MUST BE BORED WEARING THE SAME SHIRT ALL THE TIME.
?

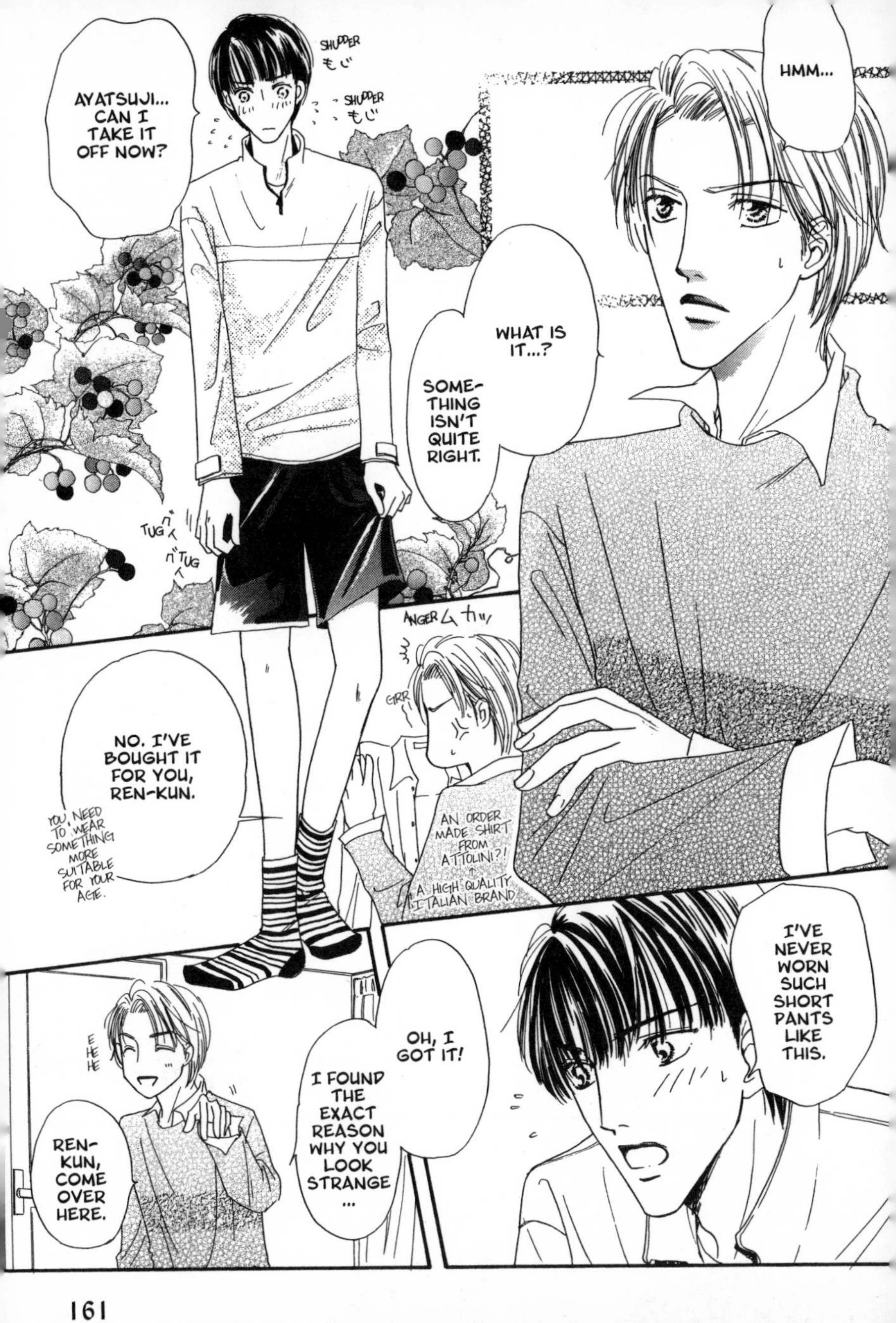
HMM...
WHAT IS IT...?
SOMETHING ISN'T QUITE RIGHT.
AYATSUJI... CAN I TAKE IT OFF NOW?
SHUDDER もじ
SHUDDER もじ
TUG グイ
グイ TUG
ANGER ムカッ
GRR
AN ORDER MADE SHIRT FROM ATTOLINI?!
↑ A HIGH QUALITY ITALIAN BRAND
NO. I'VE BOUGHT IT FOR YOU, REN-KUN.
YOU NEED TO WEAR SOMETHING MORE SUITABLE FOR YOUR AGE.
I'VE NEVER WORN SUCH SHORT PANTS LIKE THIS.
OH, I GOT IT!
I FOUND THE EXACT REASON WHY YOU LOOK STRANGE...
EHEHE
REN-KUN, COME OVER HERE.

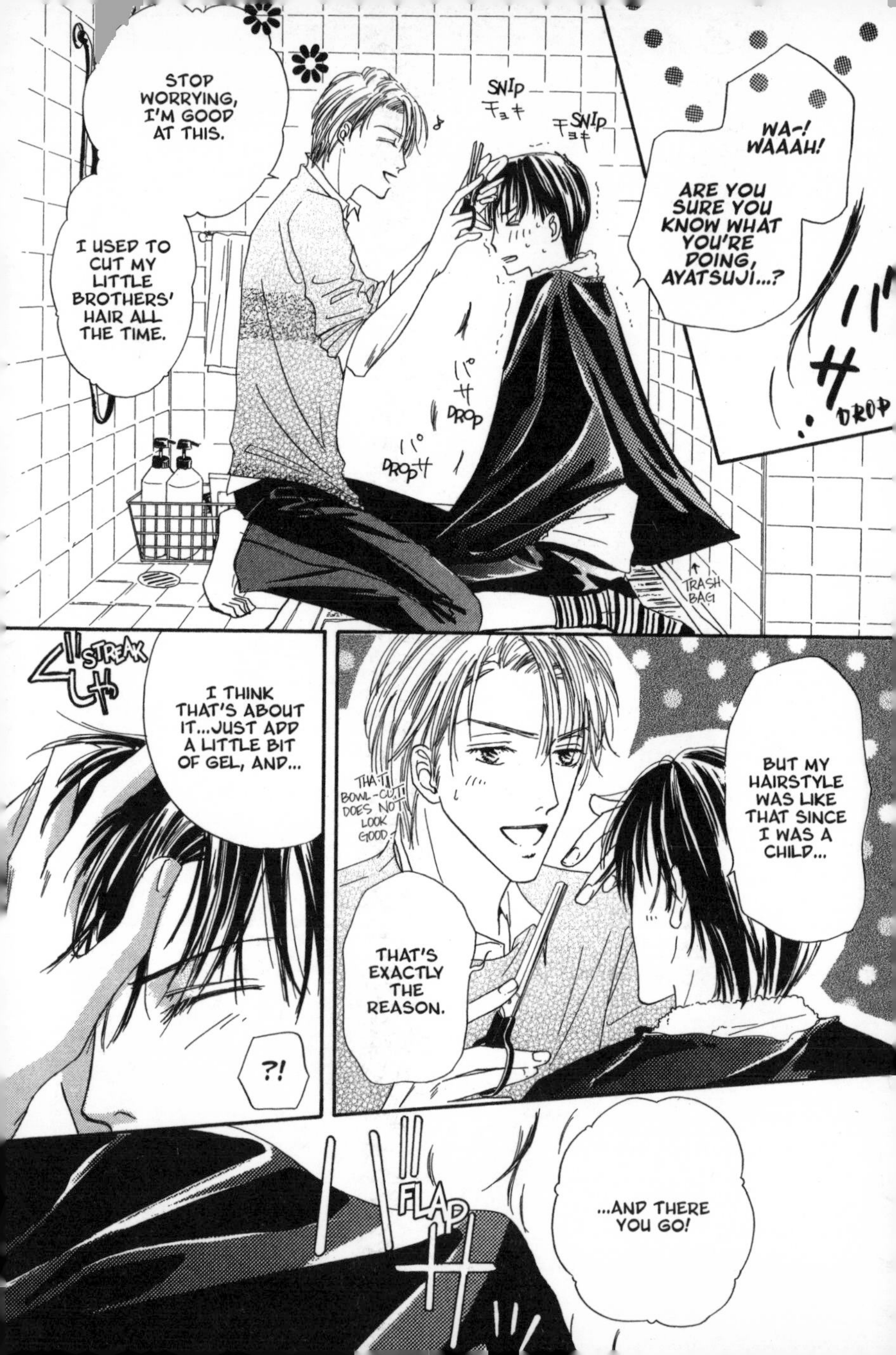
WA-! WAAAH!
ARE YOU SURE YOU KNOW WHAT YOU'RE DOING, AYATSUJI...?
DROP
SNIP
SNIP
STOP WORRYING, I'M GOOD AT THIS.
I USED TO CUT MY LITTLE BROTHERS' HAIR ALL THE TIME.
DROP
DROP
TRASH BAG
BUT MY HAIRSTYLE WAS LIKE THAT SINCE I WAS A CHILD...
THAT BOWL-CUT DOES NOT LOOK GOOD
THAT'S EXACTLY THE REASON.
STREAK
I THINK THAT'S ABOUT IT...JUST ADD A LITTLE BIT OF GEL, AND...
?!
...AND THERE YOU GO!
FLAP

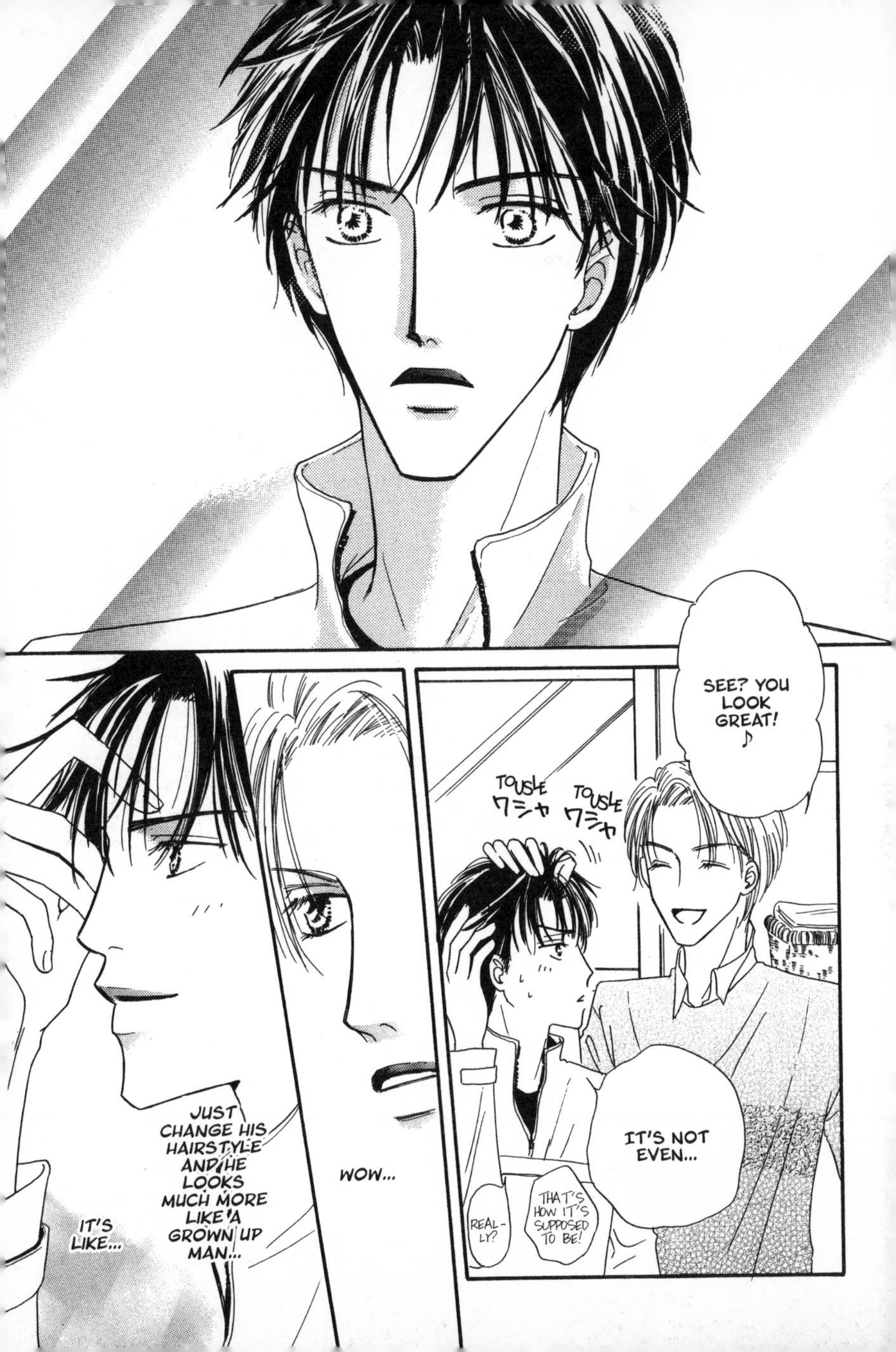
SEE? YOU LOOK GREAT! ♪
TOUSLE ワシャ
TOUSLE ワシャ
IT'S NOT EVEN...
THAT'S HOW IT'S SUPPOSED TO BE!
REAL-LY?
WOW...
JUST CHANGE HIS HAIRSTYLE AND HE LOOKS MUCH MORE LIKE A GROWN UP MAN...
IT'S LIKE...

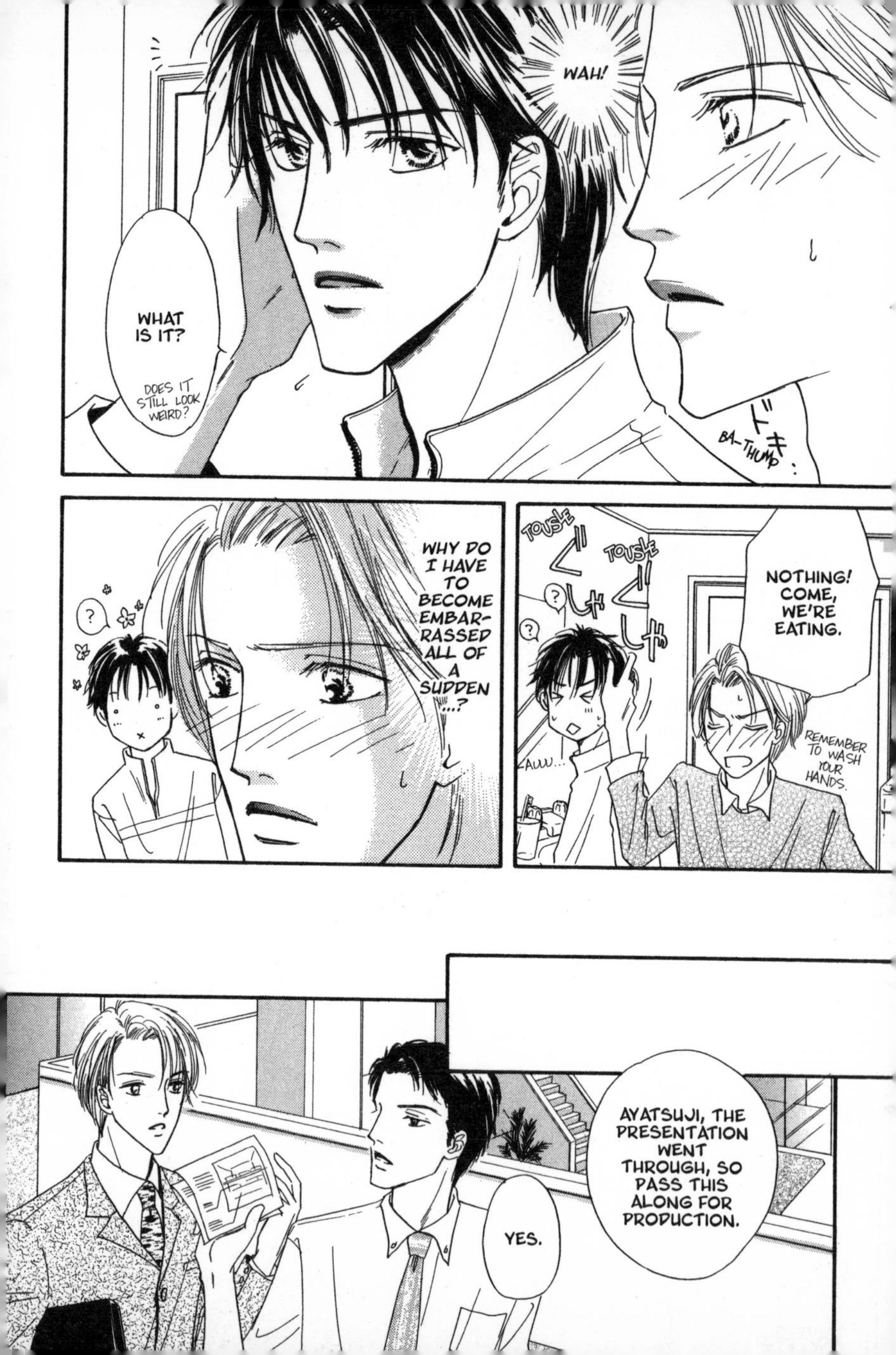
WAH!
WHAT IS IT?
DOES IT STILL LOOK WEIRD?
BA-THUMP
NOTHING! COME, WE'RE EATING.
REMEMBER TO WASH YOUR HANDS.
TOUSLE
TOUSLE
AWW...
WHY DO I HAVE TO BECOME EMBARRASSED ALL OF A SUDDEN ...?
AYATSUJI, THE PRESENTATION WENT THROUGH, SO PASS THIS ALONG FOR PRODUCTION.
YES.

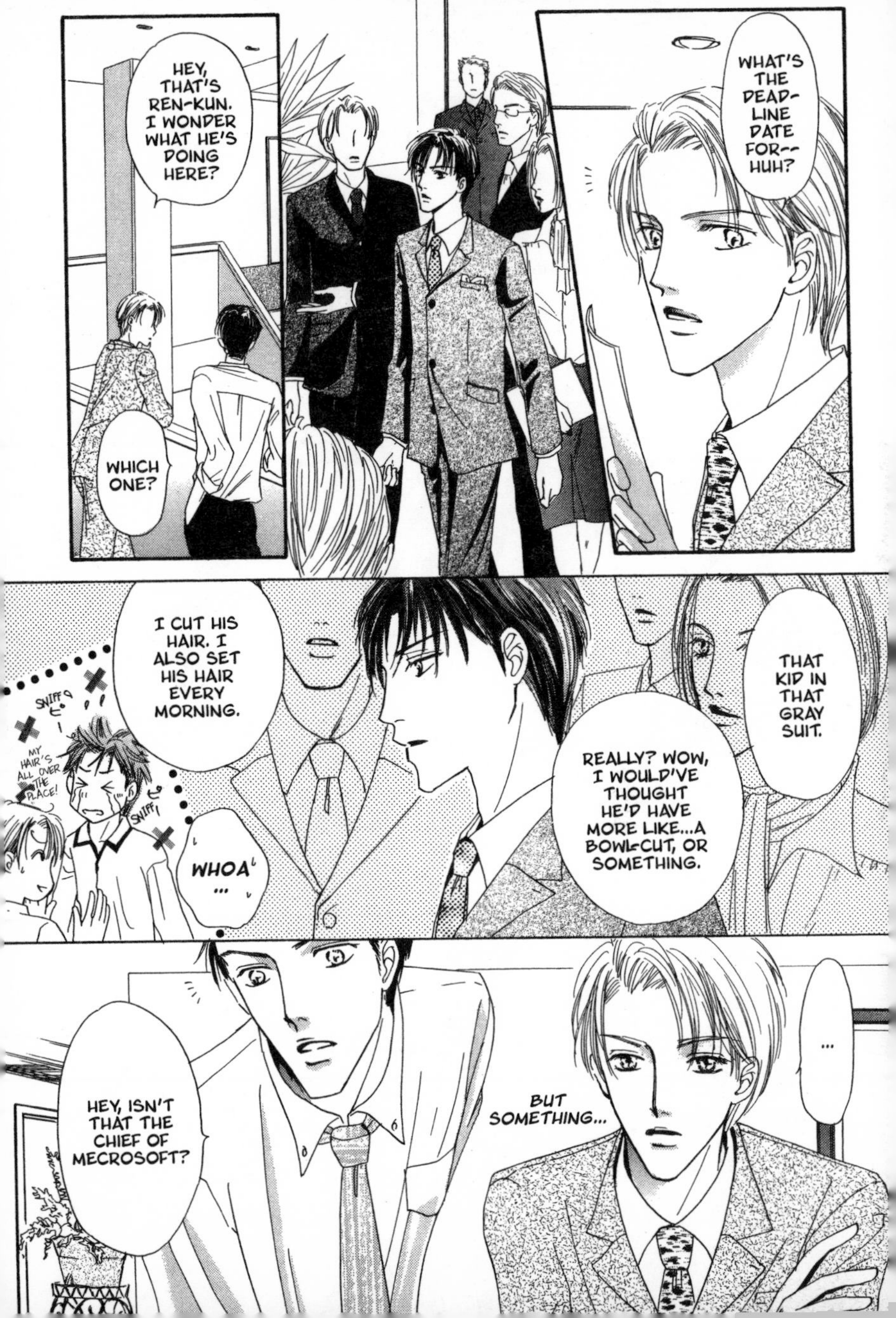
WHAT'S THE DEAD-LINE DATE FOR-- HUH?
HEY, THAT'S REN-KUN. I WONDER WHAT HE'S DOING HERE?
WHICH ONE?
THAT KID IN THAT GRAY SUIT.
REALLY? WOW, I WOULD'VE THOUGHT HE'D HAVE MORE LIKE...A BOWL-CUT, OR SOMETHING.
I CUT HIS HAIR. I ALSO SET HIS HAIR EVERY MORNING.
WHOA...
SNIFF
MY HAIR'S ALL OVER THE PLACE!
SNIFF
...
BUT SOMETHING...
HEY, ISN'T THAT THE CHIEF OF MECROSOFT?

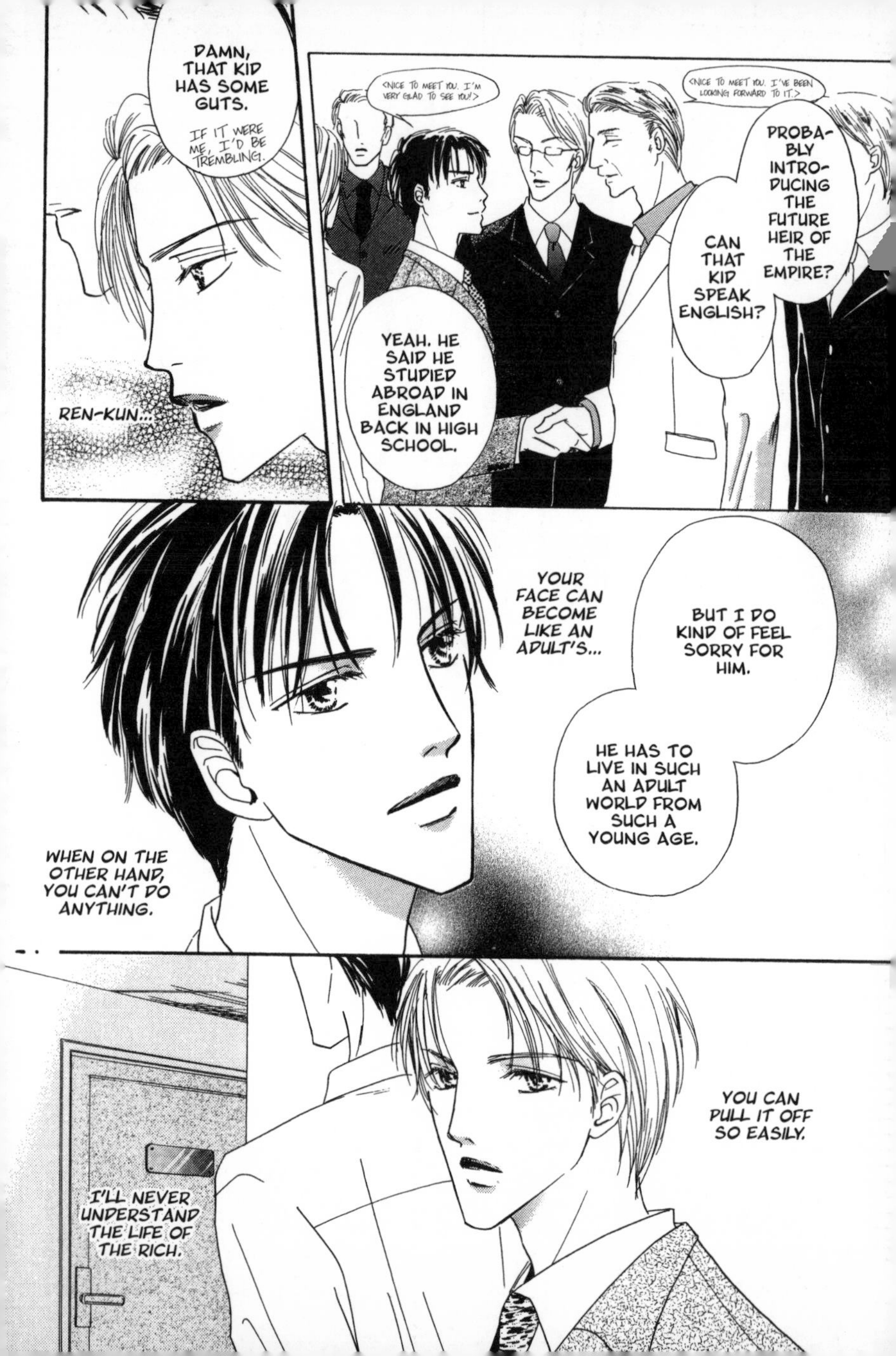
<NICE TO MEET YOU. I'VE BEEN LOOKING FORWARD TO IT.>
<NICE TO MEET YOU. I'M VERY GLAD TO SEE YOU!>
PROBABLY INTRODUCING THE FUTURE HEIR OF THE EMPIRE?
CAN THAT KID SPEAK ENGLISH?
YEAH. HE SAID HE STUDIED ABROAD IN ENGLAND BACK IN HIGH SCHOOL.
DAMN, THAT KID HAS SOME GUTS.
IF IT WERE ME, I'D BE TREMBLING.
REN-KUN...
BUT I DO KIND OF FEEL SORRY FOR HIM.
HE HAS TO LIVE IN SUCH AN ADULT WORLD FROM SUCH A YOUNG AGE.
YOUR FACE CAN BECOME LIKE AN ADULT'S...
WHEN ON THE OTHER HAND, YOU CAN'T DO ANYTHING.
YOU CAN PULL IT OFF SO EASILY.
I'LL NEVER UNDERSTAND THE LIFE OF THE RICH.

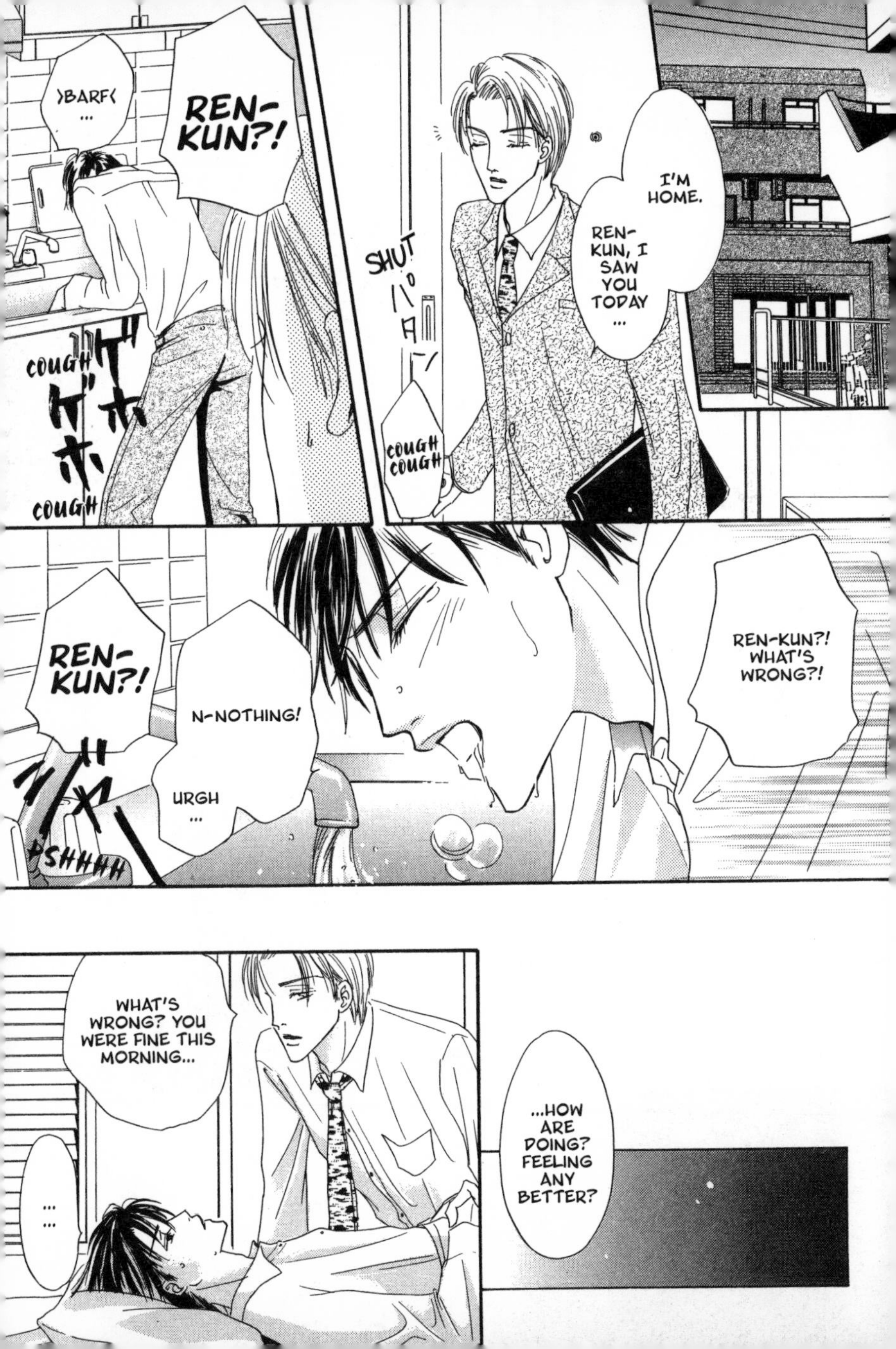
I'M HOME.
REN-KUN, I SAW YOU TODAY ...
SHUT
COUGH COUGH
REN-KUN?!
›BARF‹ ...
COUGH
COUGH
REN-KUN?! WHAT'S WRONG?!
N-NOTHING!
URGH ...
REN-KUN?!
PSHHHH
...HOW ARE DOING? FEELING ANY BETTER?
WHAT'S WRONG? YOU WERE FINE THIS MORNING...
... ...

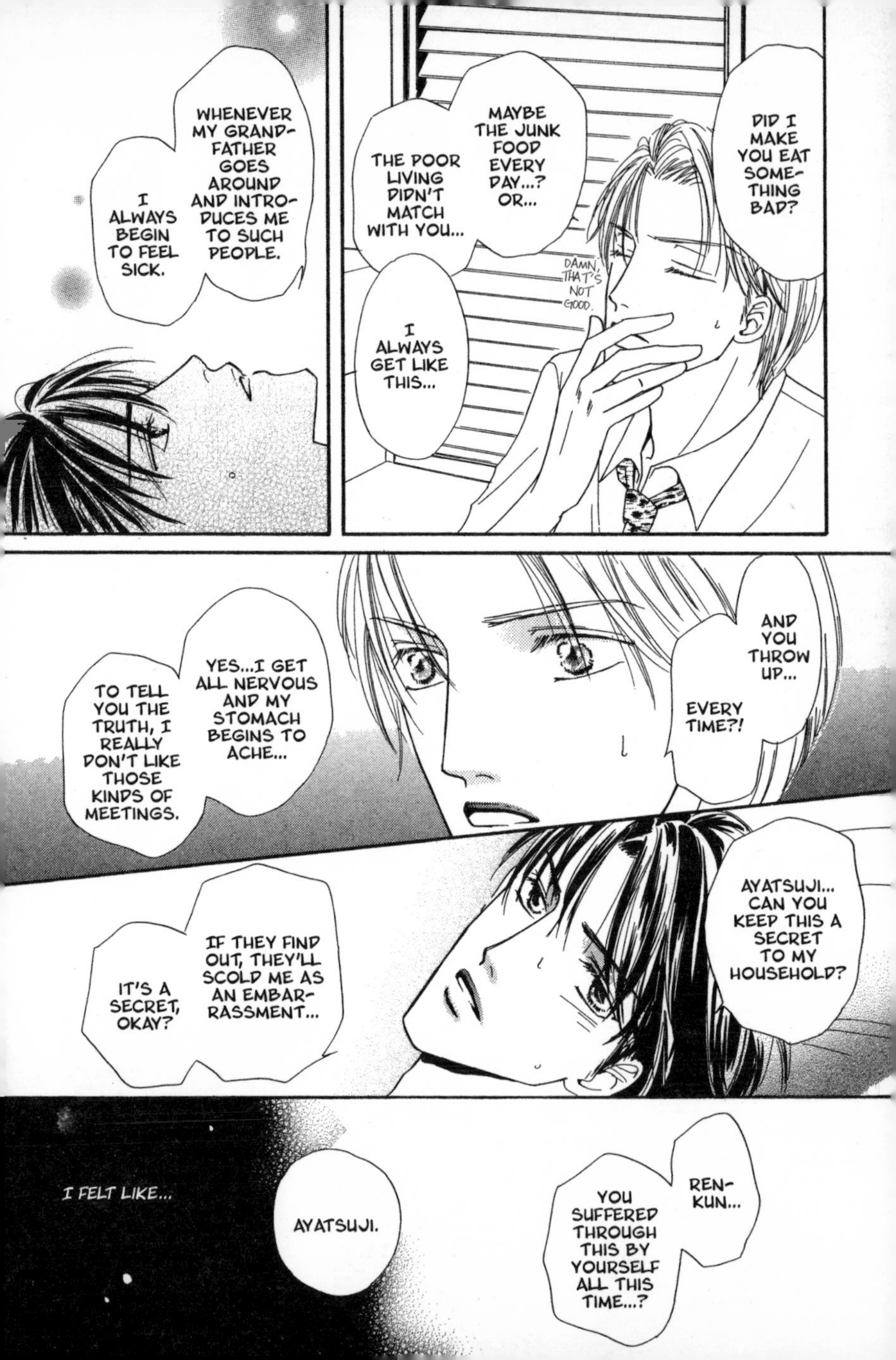
DID I MAKE YOU EAT SOMETHING BAD?
MAYBE THE JUNK FOOD EVERY DAY...? OR...
THE POOR LIVING DIDN'T MATCH WITH YOU...
DAMN, THAT'S NOT GOOD.
I ALWAYS GET LIKE THIS...
WHENEVER MY GRANDFATHER GOES AROUND AND INTRODUCES ME TO SUCH PEOPLE.
I ALWAYS BEGIN TO FEEL SICK.
AND YOU THROW UP...
EVERY TIME?!
YES...I GET ALL NERVOUS AND MY STOMACH BEGINS TO ACHE...
TO TELL YOU THE TRUTH, I REALLY DON'T LIKE THOSE KINDS OF MEETINGS.
AYATSUJI... CAN YOU KEEP THIS A SECRET TO MY HOUSEHOLD?
IF THEY FIND OUT, THEY'LL SCOLD ME AS AN EMBARRASSMENT...
IT'S A SECRET, OKAY?
REN-KUN...
YOU SUFFERED THROUGH THIS BY YOURSELF ALL THIS TIME...?
AYATSUJI.
I FELT LIKE...

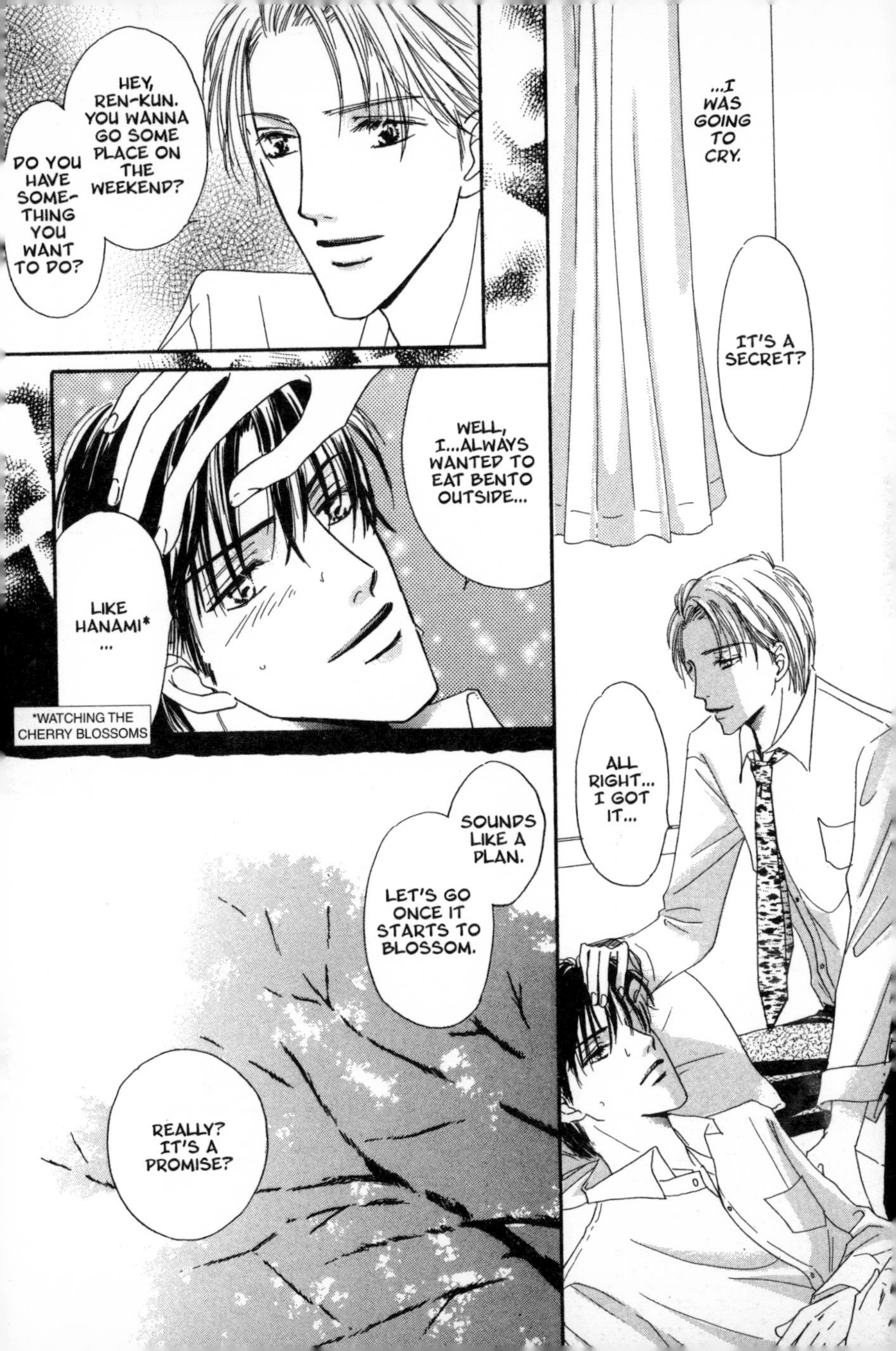
...I WAS GOING TO CRY.
IT'S A SECRET?
ALL RIGHT... I GOT IT...
HEY, REN-KUN. YOU WANNA GO SOME PLACE ON THE WEEKEND?
DO YOU HAVE SOMETHING YOU WANT TO DO?
WELL, I...ALWAYS WANTED TO EAT BENTO OUTSIDE...
LIKE HANAMI* ...
*WATCHING THE CHERRY BLOSSOMS
SOUNDS LIKE A PLAN.
LET'S GO ONCE IT STARTS TO BLOSSOM.
REALLY? IT'S A PROMISE?

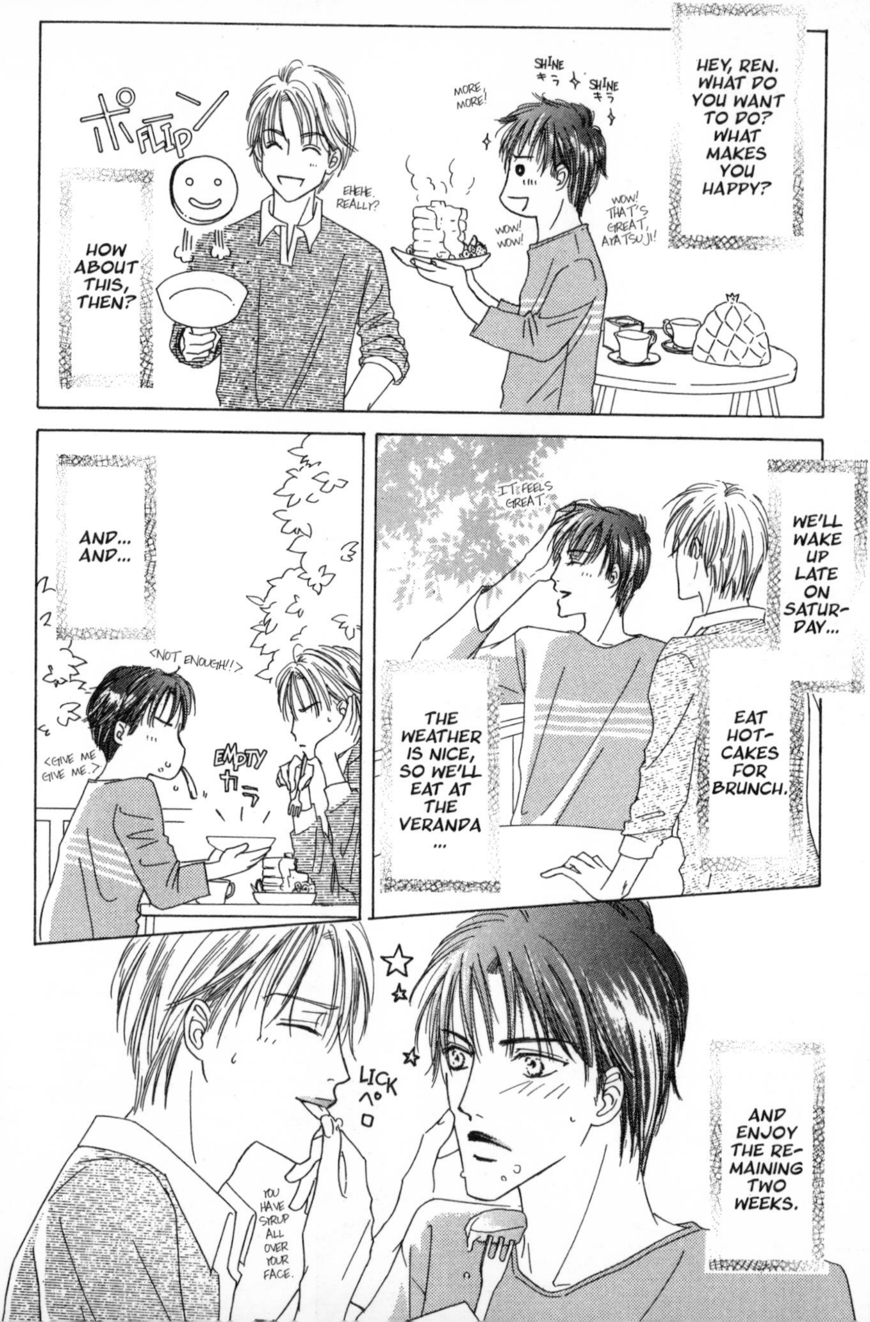
HEY, REN. WHAT DO YOU WANT TO DO? WHAT MAKES YOU HAPPY?
SHINE
SHINE
MORE, MORE!
WOW! THAT'S GREAT, AYATSUJI!
WOW! WOW!
EHEHE. REALLY?
FLIP
HOW ABOUT THIS, THEN?
WE'LL WAKE UP LATE ON SATURDAY...
IT FEELS GREAT.
EAT HOT-CAKES FOR BRUNCH.
THE WEATHER IS NICE, SO WE'LL EAT AT THE VERANDA ...
AND... AND...
<NOT ENOUGH!!>
EMPTY
<GIVE ME GIVE ME.>
AND ENJOY THE RE-MAINING TWO WEEKS.
LICK
YOU HAVE SYRUP ALL OVER YOUR FACE.

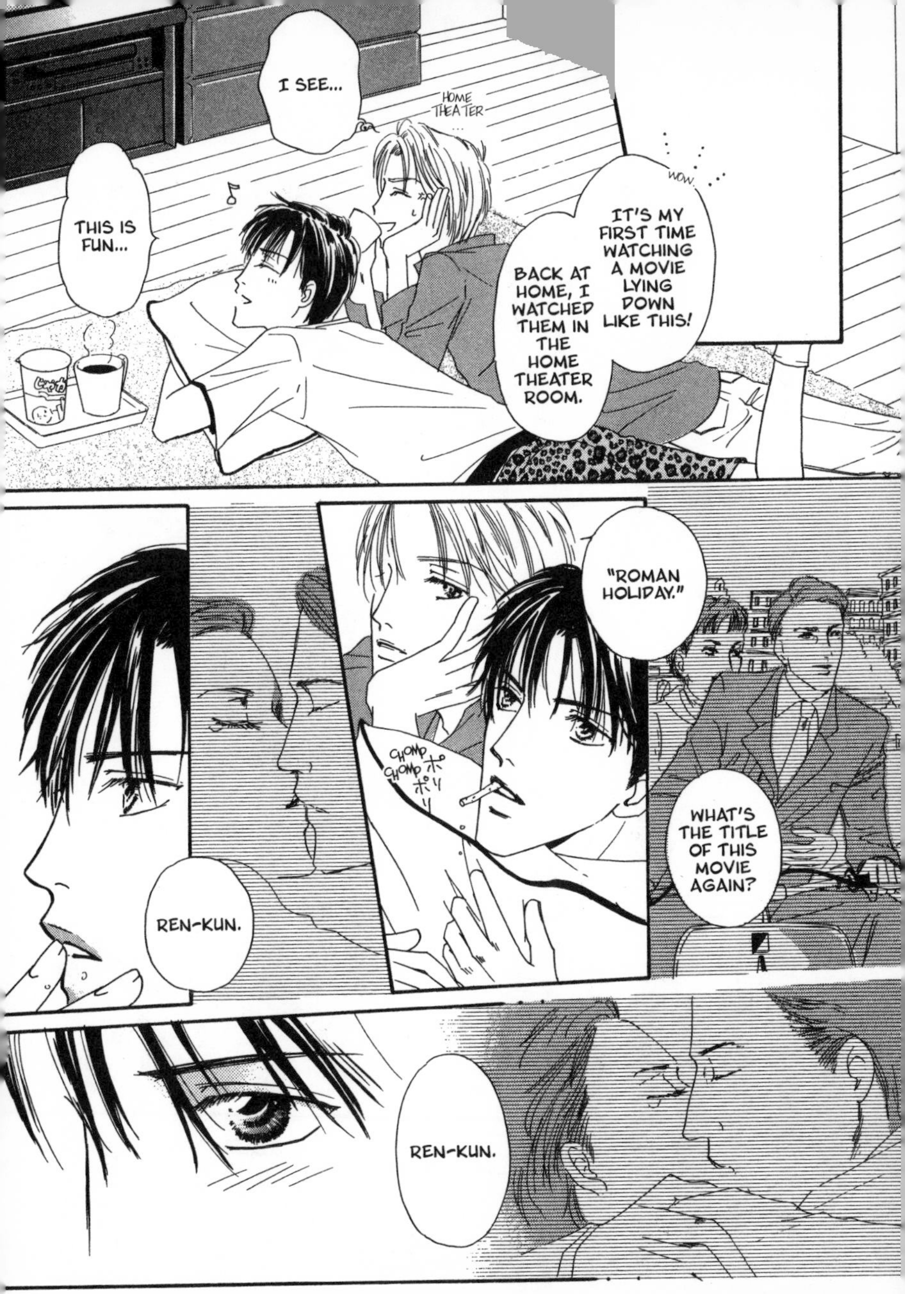
WOW...
IT'S MY FIRST TIME WATCHING A MOVIE LYING DOWN LIKE THIS!
BACK AT HOME, I WATCHED THEM IN THE HOME THEATER ROOM.
HOME THEATER...
I SEE...
THIS IS FUN...
WHAT'S THE TITLE OF THIS MOVIE AGAIN?
"ROMAN HOLIDAY."
CHOMP CHOMP ポリポリ
REN-KUN.
REN-KUN.

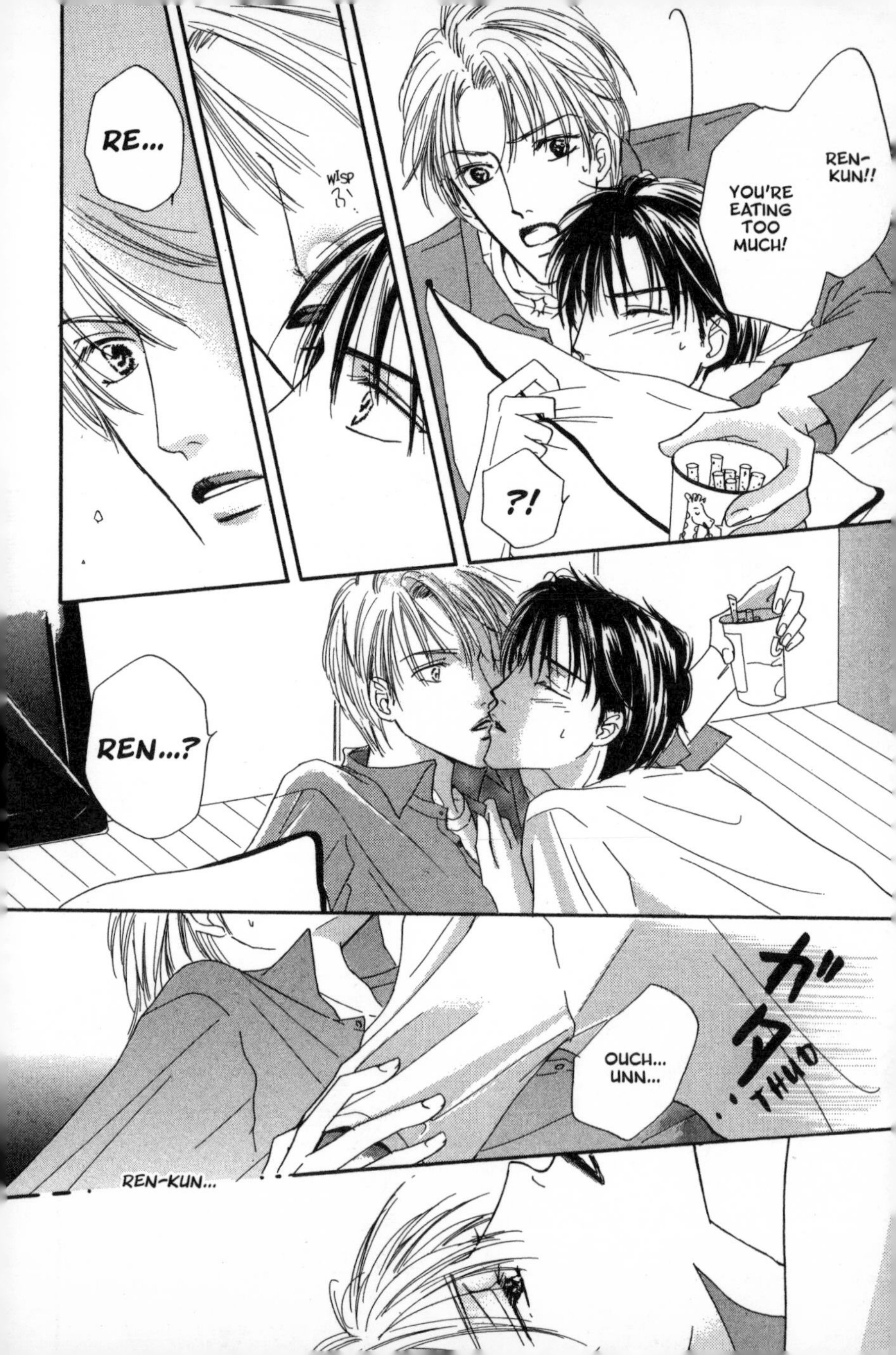
REN-KUN!!
YOU'RE EATING TOO MUCH!
?!
WISP
RE...
REN...?
ガタ
THUD
OUCH... UNN...
REN-KUN...

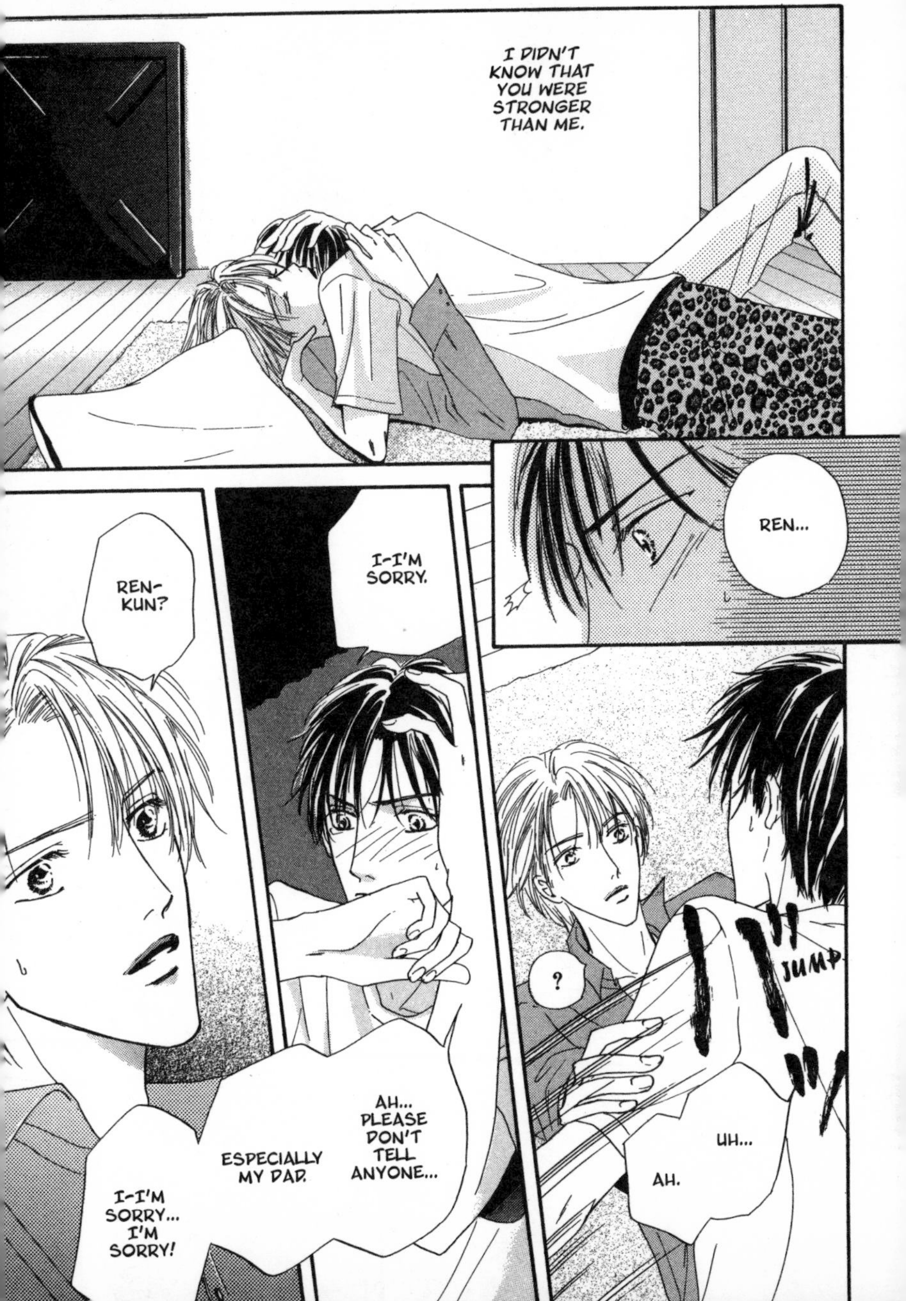
I DIDN'T KNOW THAT YOU WERE STRONGER THAN ME.
REN...
?
JUMP
UH...
AH.
I-I'M SORRY.
AH... PLEASE DON'T TELL ANYONE...
ESPECIALLY MY DAD.
REN-KUN?
I-I'M SORRY... I'M SORRY!

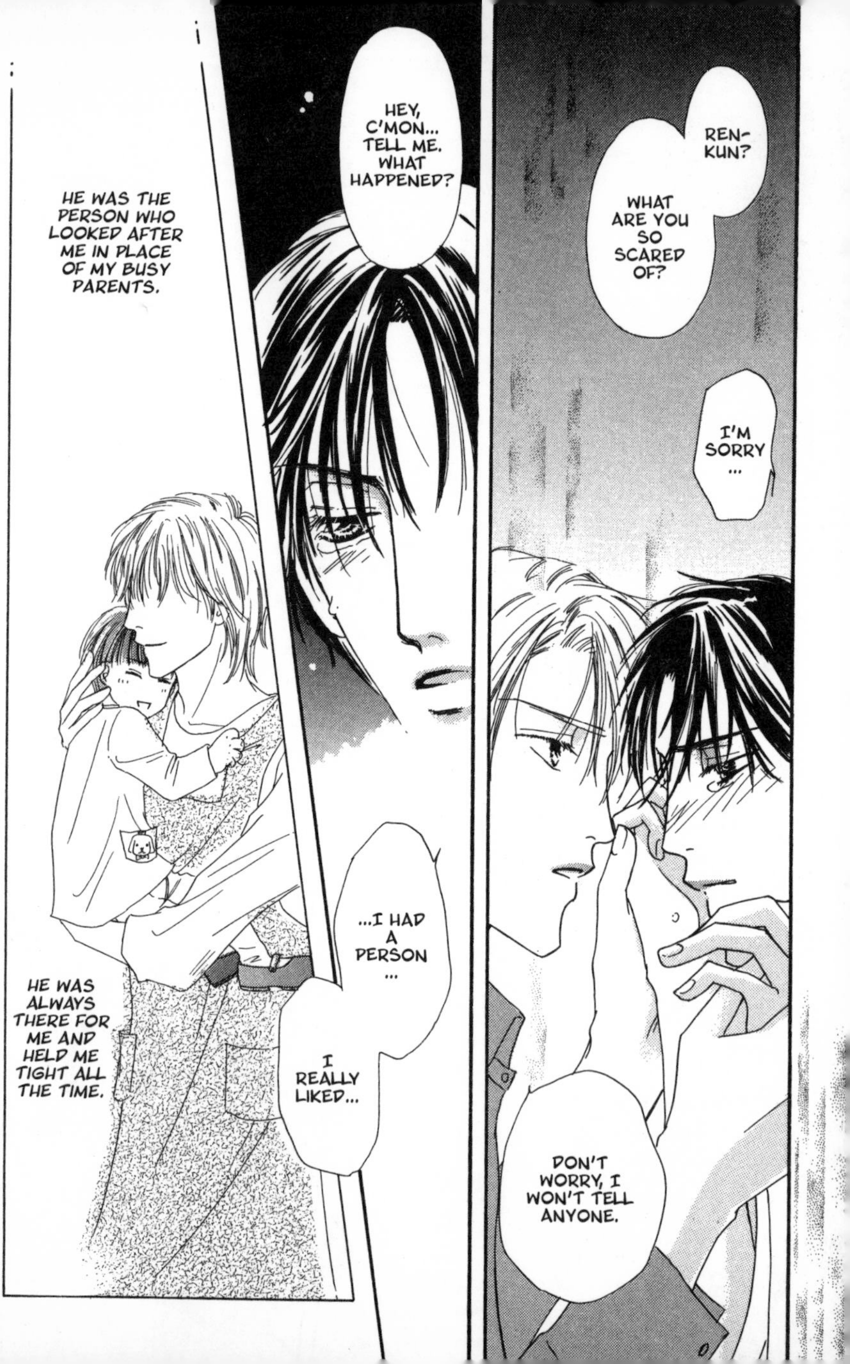
REN-KUN?
WHAT ARE YOU SO SCARED OF?
I'M SORRY...
DON'T WORRY, I WON'T TELL ANYONE.
HEY, C'MON... TELL ME. WHAT HAPPENED?
...I HAD A PERSON...
I REALLY LIKED...
HE WAS THE PERSON WHO LOOKED AFTER ME IN PLACE OF MY BUSY PARENTS.
HE WAS ALWAYS THERE FOR ME AND HELD ME TIGHT ALL THE TIME.

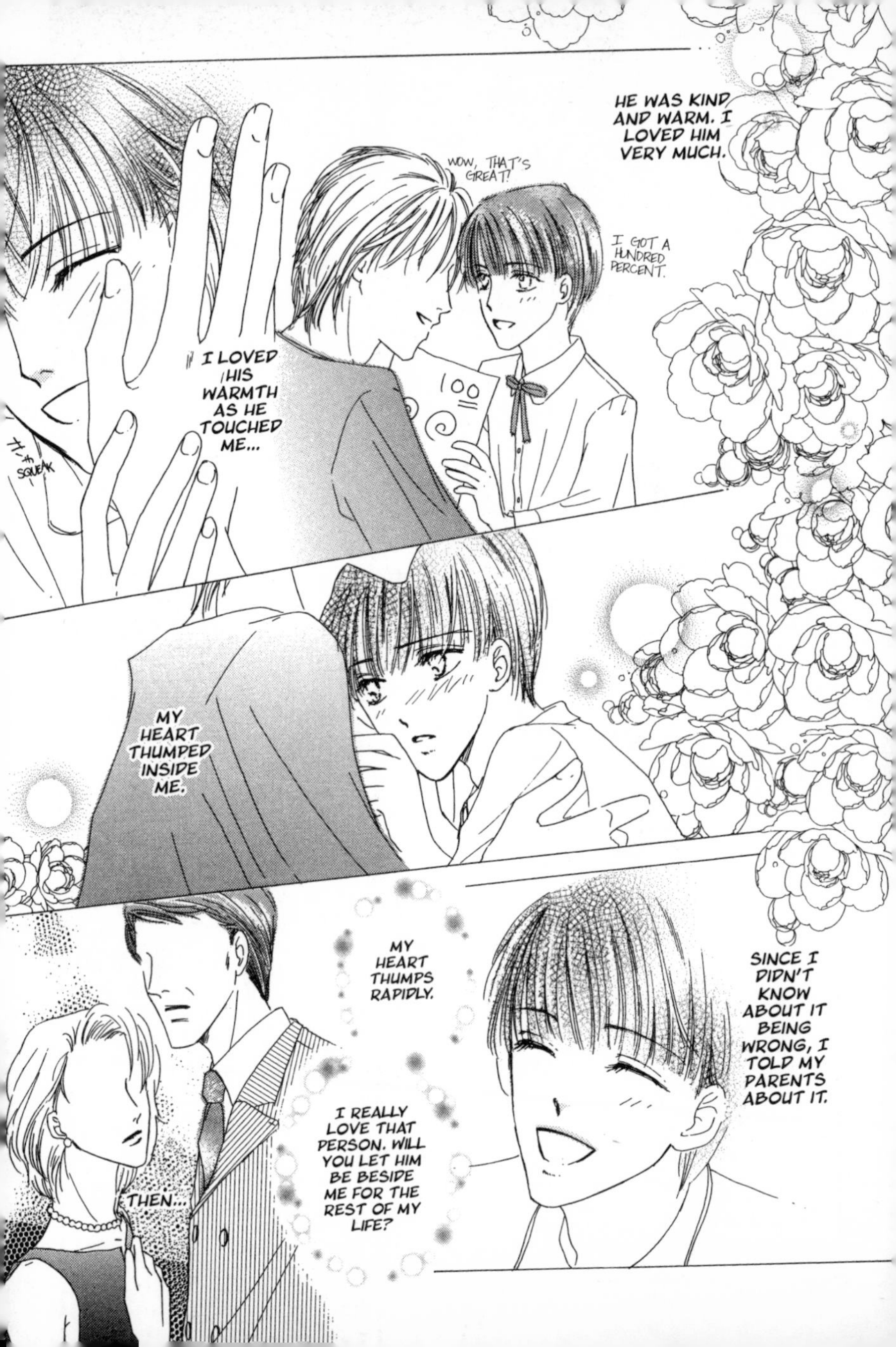
HE WAS KIND AND WARM. I LOVED HIM VERY MUCH.
I GOT A HUNDRED PERCENT.
WOW, THAT'S GREAT!
100
I LOVED HIS WARMTH AS HE TOUCHED ME...
SQUEAK
MY HEART THUMPED INSIDE ME.
SINCE I DIDN'T KNOW ABOUT IT BEING WRONG, I TOLD MY PARENTS ABOUT IT.
MY HEART THUMPS RAPIDLY.
I REALLY LOVE THAT PERSON. WILL YOU LET HIM BE BESIDE ME FOR THE REST OF MY LIFE?
THEN...

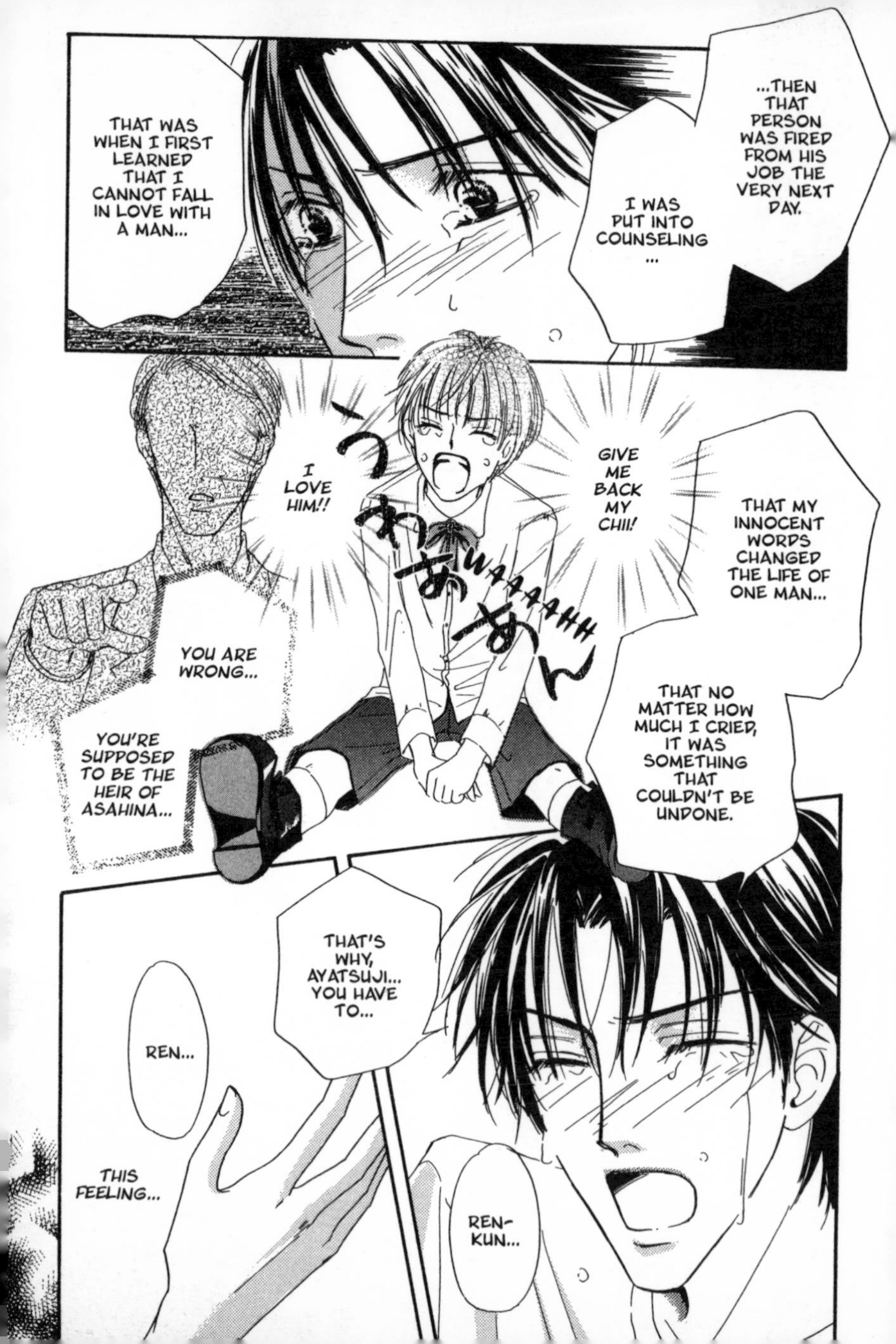
...THEN THAT PERSON WAS FIRED FROM HIS JOB THE VERY NEXT DAY.
I WAS PUT INTO COUNSELING ...
THAT WAS WHEN I FIRST LEARNED THAT I CANNOT FALL IN LOVE WITH A MAN...
THAT MY INNOCENT WORDS CHANGED THE LIFE OF ONE MAN...
GIVE ME BACK MY CHII!
I LOVE HIM!!
WAAAAAAAHHH
YOU ARE WRONG...
YOU'RE SUPPOSED TO BE THE HEIR OF ASAHINA...
THAT NO MATTER HOW MUCH I CRIED, IT WAS SOMETHING THAT COULDN'T BE UNDONE.
THAT'S WHY, AYATSUJI... YOU HAVE TO...
REN-KUN...
REN...
THIS FEELING...

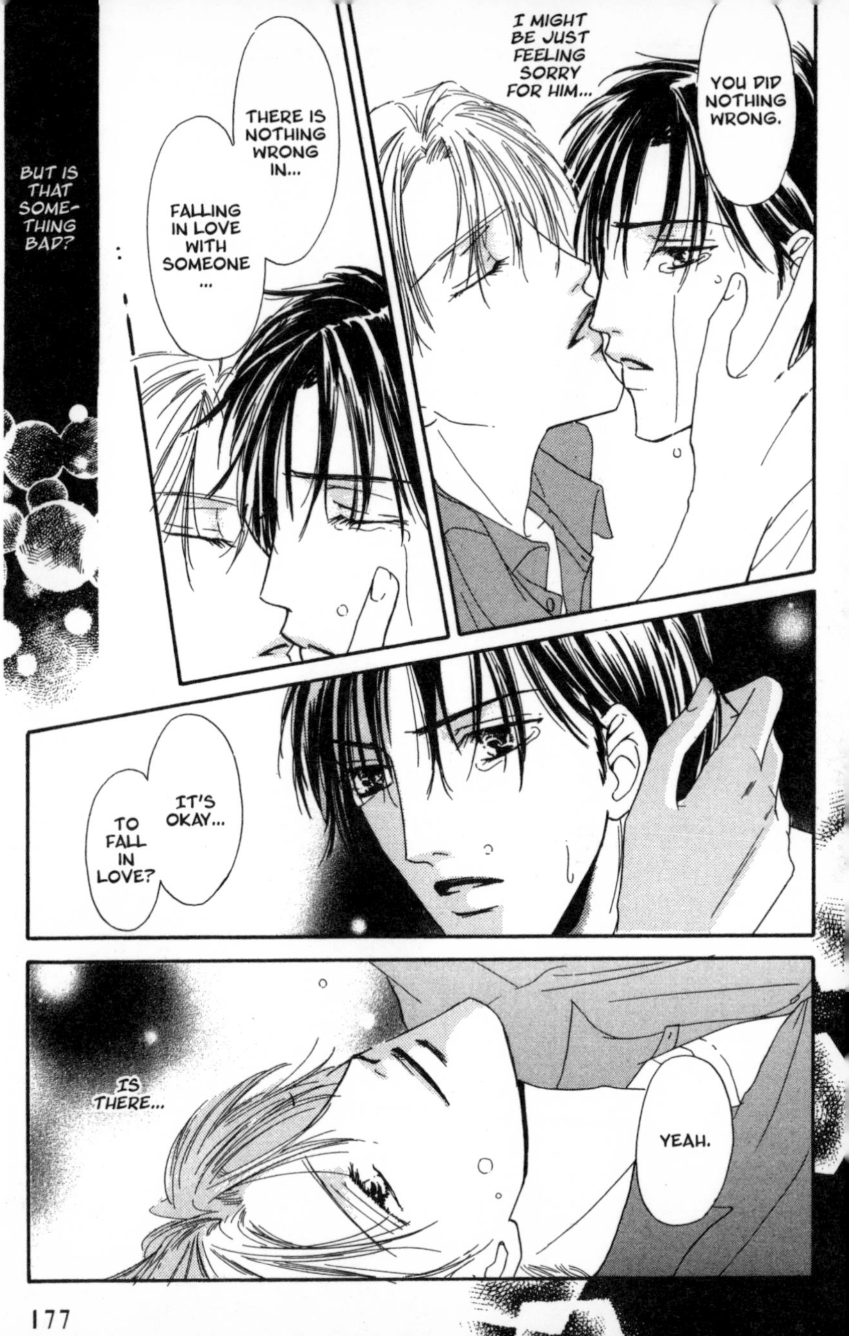
YOU DID NOTHING WRONG.
I MIGHT BE JUST FEELING SORRY FOR HIM...
THERE IS NOTHING WRONG IN...
FALLING IN LOVE WITH SOMEONE ...
BUT IS THAT SOME-THING BAD?
IT'S OKAY...
TO FALL IN LOVE?
YEAH.
IS THERE...

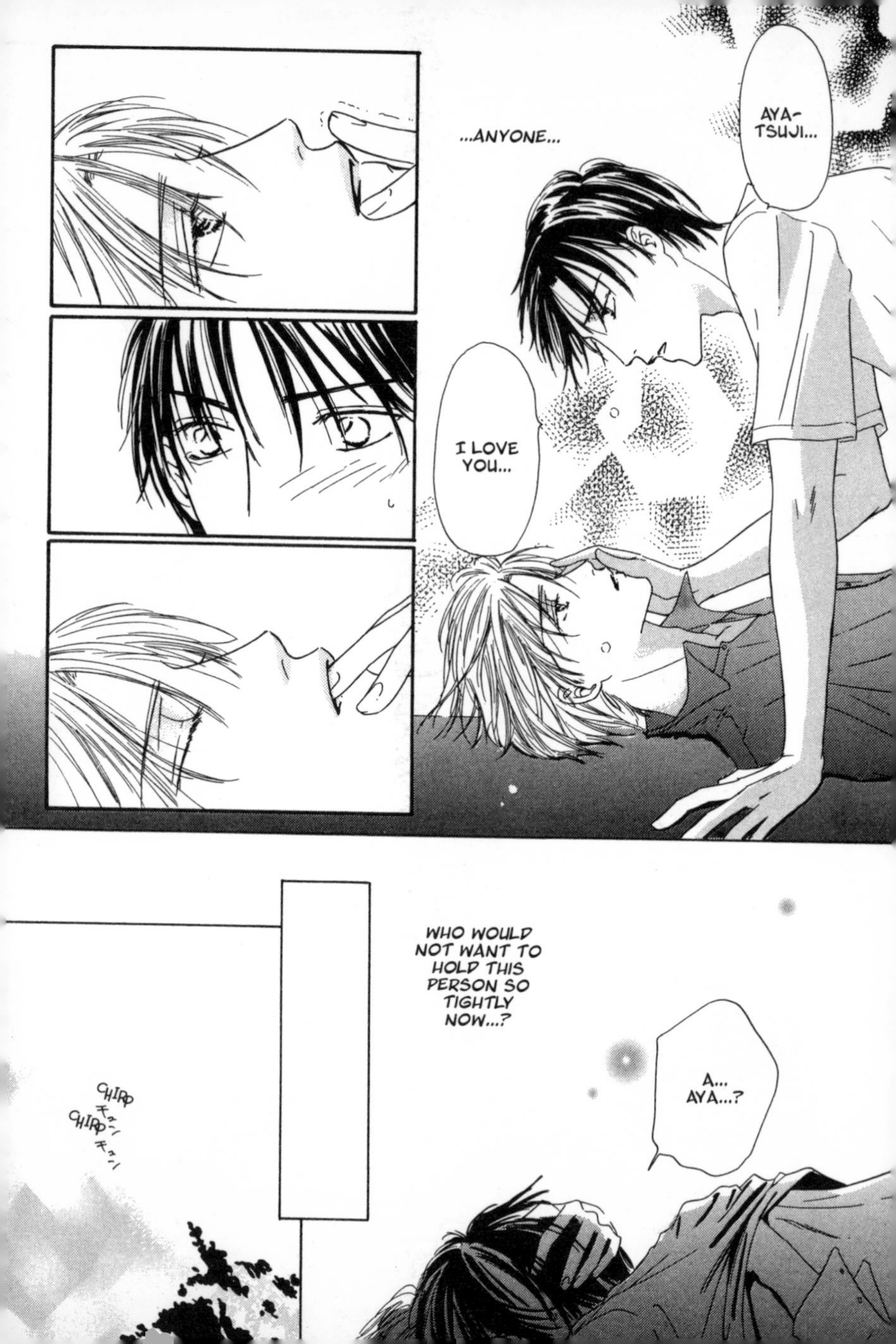
AYA-TSUJI...
...ANYONE...
I LOVE YOU...
WHO WOULD NOT WANT TO HOLD THIS PERSON SO TIGHTLY NOW...?
A... AYA...?
CHIRP
CHIRP

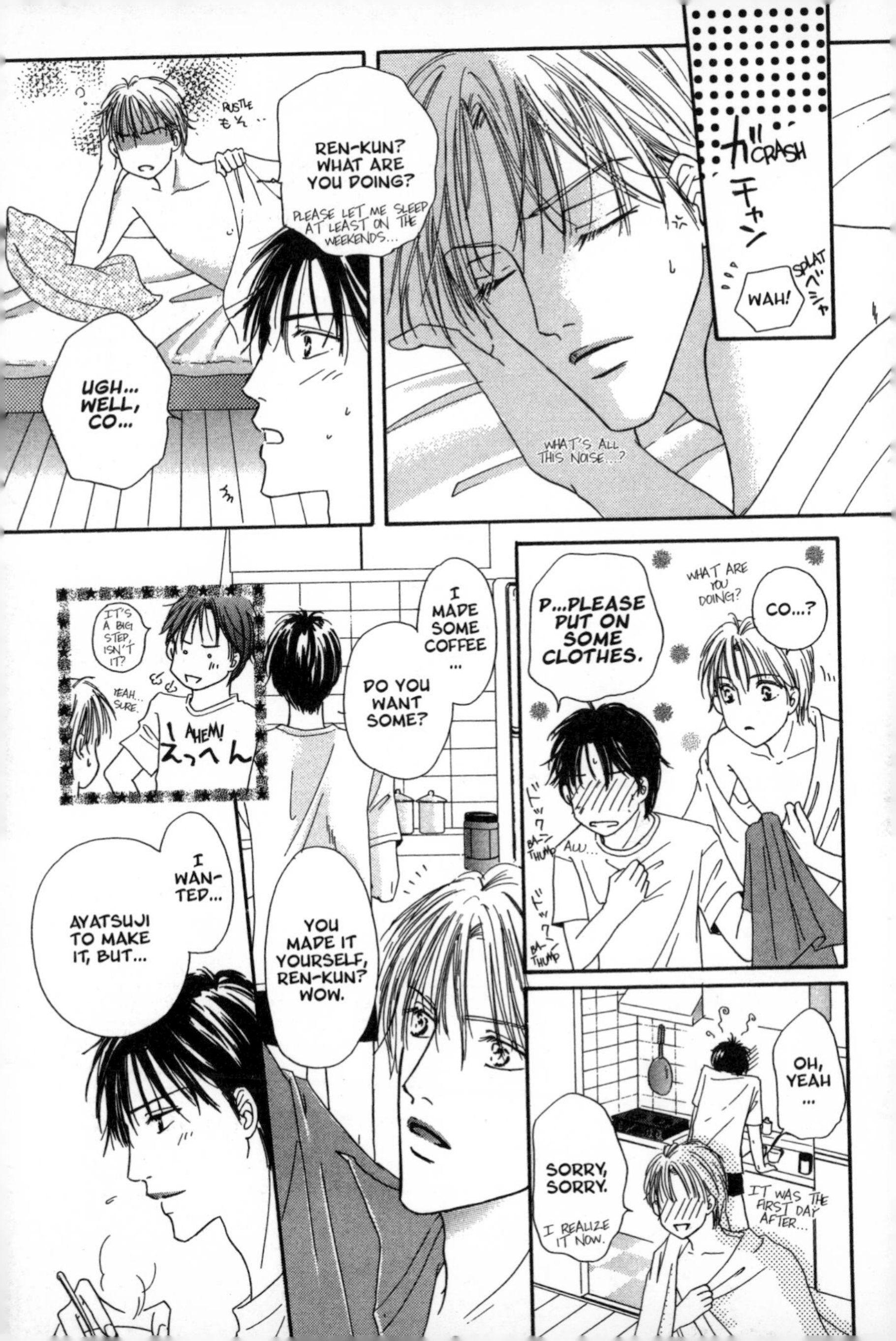
ガチャン CRASH
WAH!
SPLAT べシャ
WHAT'S ALL THIS NOISE...?
RUSTLE もそ...
REN-KUN? WHAT ARE YOU DOING?
PLEASE LET ME SLEEP AT LEAST ON THE WEEKENDS...
UGH... WELL, CO...
CO...?
WHAT ARE YOU DOING?
P...PLEASE PUT ON SOME CLOTHES.
BA-THUMP
AWW...
BA-THUMP
OH, YEAH...
SORRY, SORRY.
I REALIZE IT NOW.
IT WAS THE FIRST DAY AFTER...
I MADE SOME COFFEE...
DO YOU WANT SOME?
IT'S A BIG STEP, ISN'T IT?
YEAH... SURE.
I AHEM! えっへん
YOU MADE IT YOURSELF, REN-KUN? WOW.
I WANTED...
AYATSUJI TO MAKE IT, BUT...

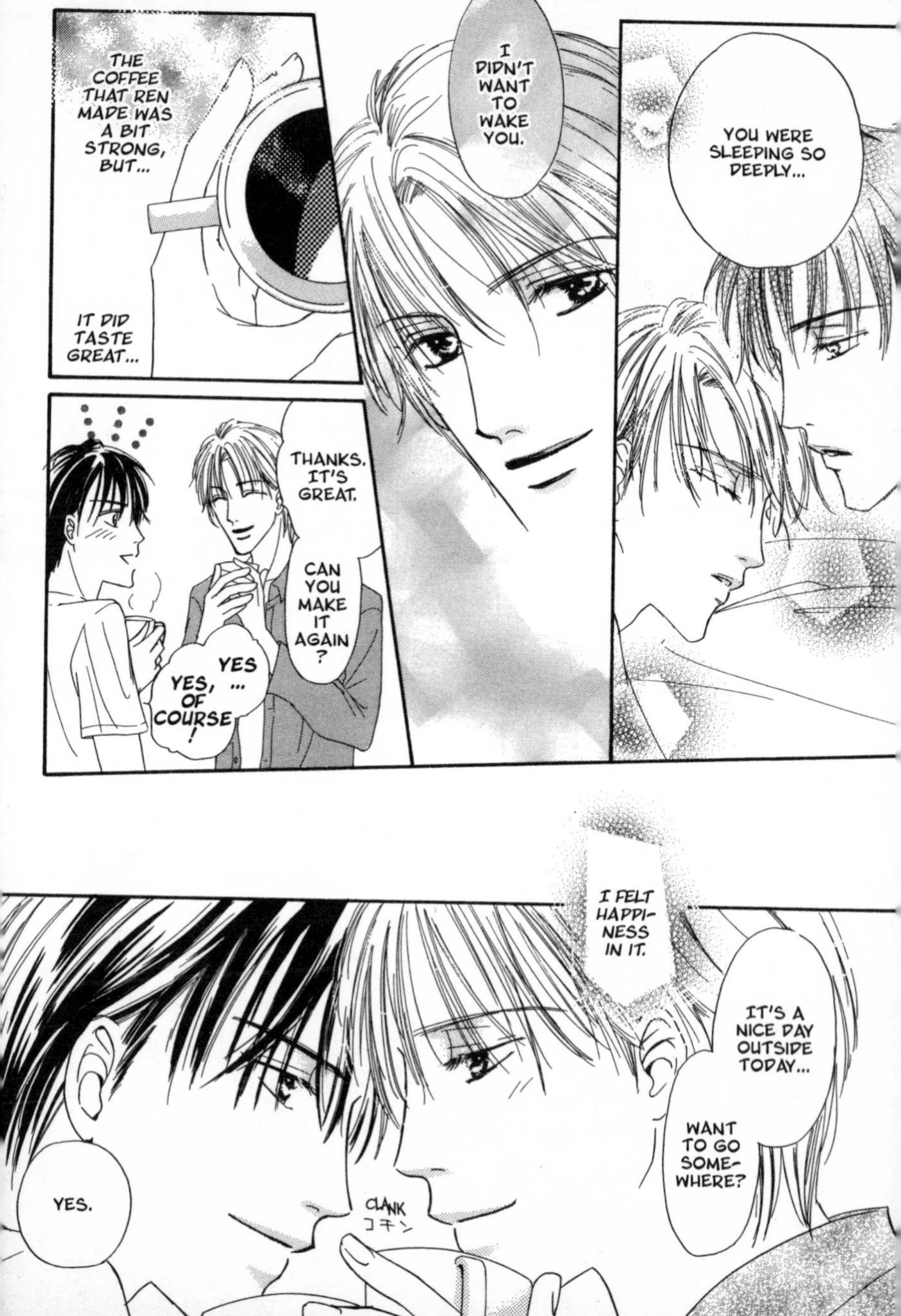
YOU WERE SLEEPING SO DEEPLY...
I DIDN'T WANT TO WAKE YOU.
THE COFFEE THAT REN MADE WAS A BIT STRONG, BUT...
IT DID TASTE GREAT...
THANKS. IT'S GREAT.
CAN YOU MAKE IT AGAIN?
YES...
YES, OF COURSE!
I FELT HAPPINESS IN IT.
IT'S A NICE DAY OUTSIDE TODAY...
WANT TO GO SOMEWHERE?
CLANK
コキン
YES.

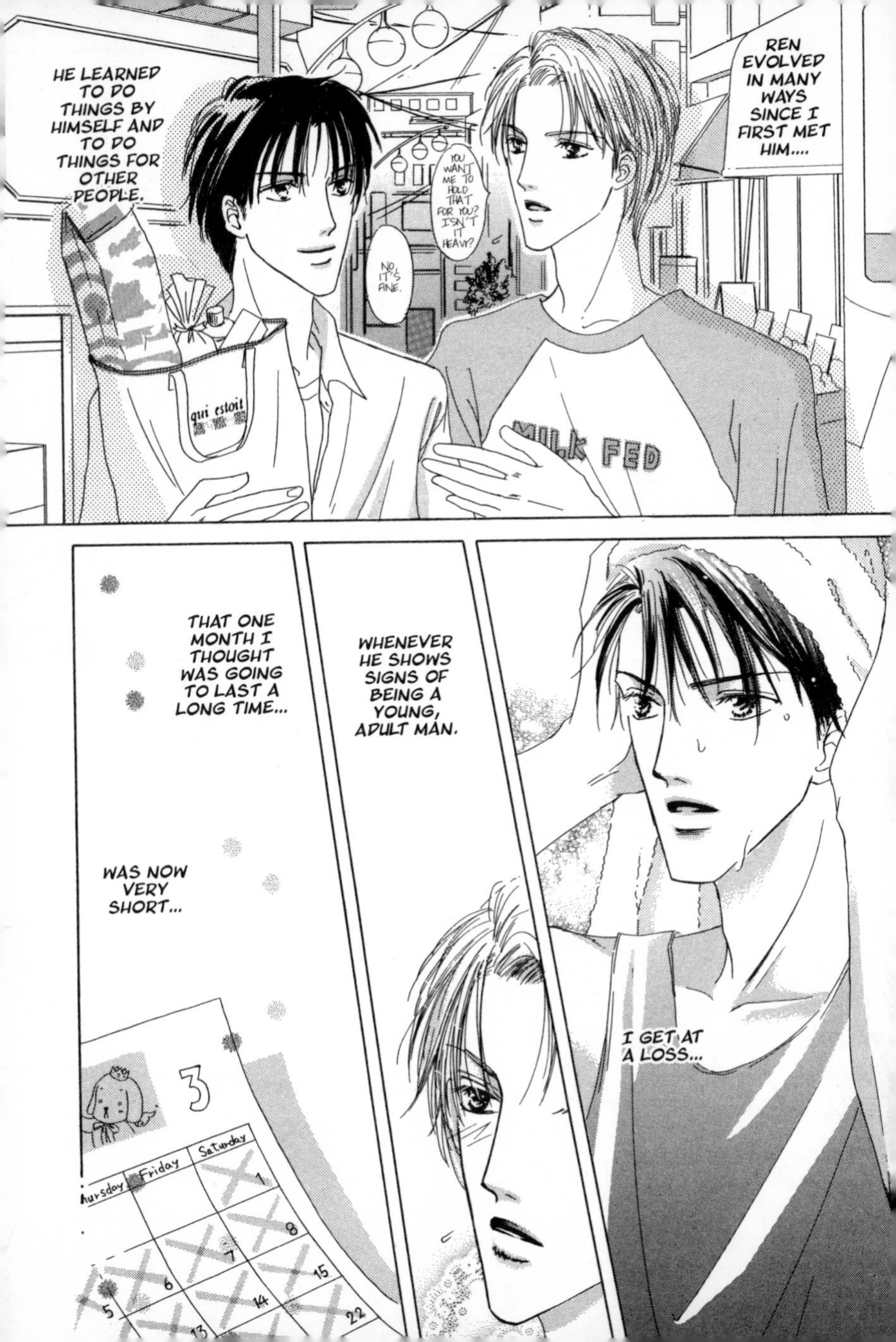
REN EVOLVED IN MANY WAYS SINCE I FIRST MET HIM....
YOU WANT ME TO HOLD THAT FOR YOU? ISN'T IT HEAVY?
NO, IT'S FINE.
HE LEARNED TO DO THINGS BY HIMSELF AND TO DO THINGS FOR OTHER PEOPLE.
MILK FED
qui estoit
I GET AT A LOSS...
WHENEVER HE SHOWS SIGNS OF BEING A YOUNG, ADULT MAN.
THAT ONE MONTH I THOUGHT WAS GOING TO LAST A LONG TIME...
WAS NOW VERY SHORT...
3
Saturday
Friday
hursday
1
8
7
6
5
15
14
13
22

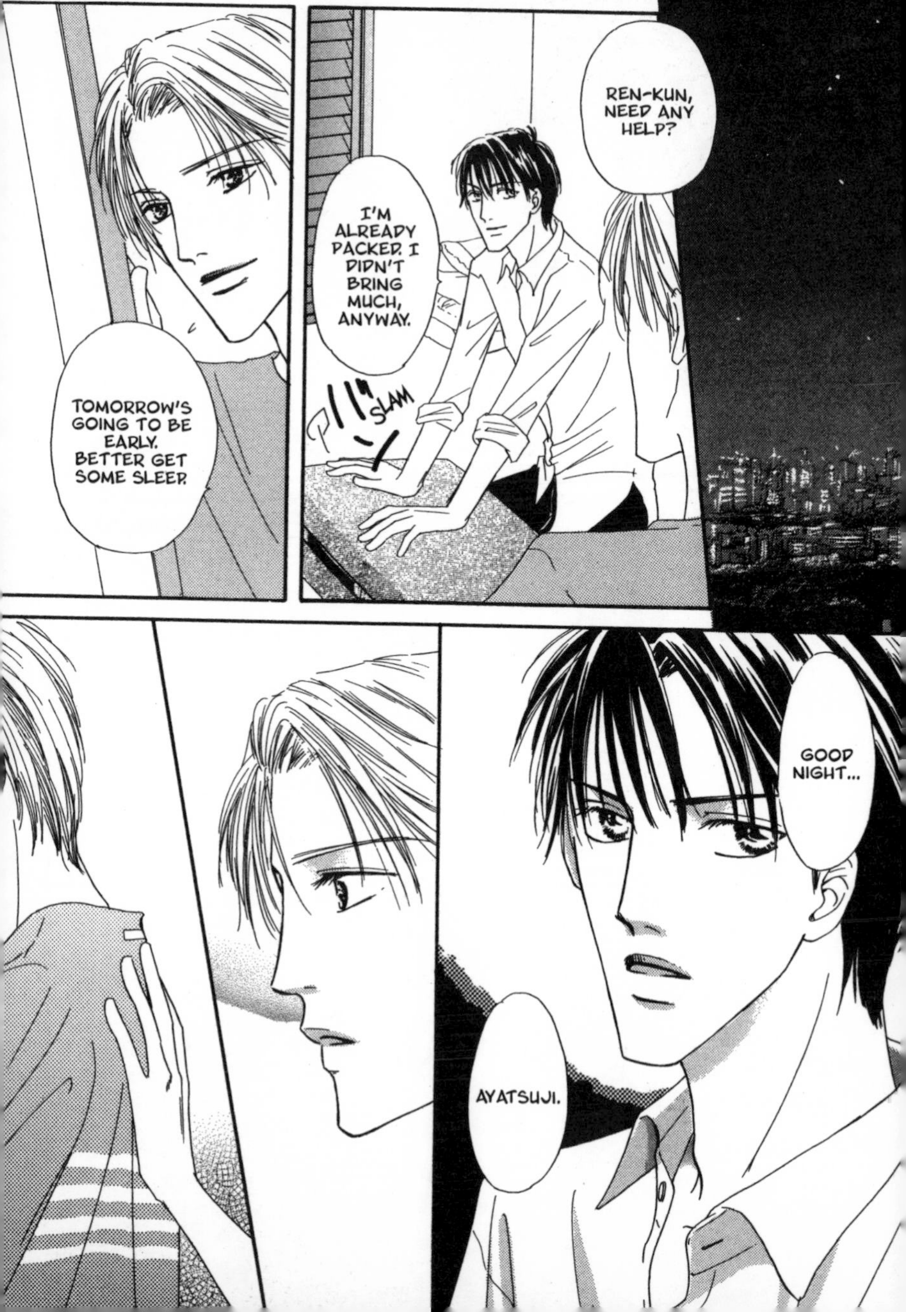
REN-KUN, NEED ANY HELP?
I'M ALREADY PACKED. I DIDN'T BRING MUCH, ANYWAY.
SLAM
TOMORROW'S GOING TO BE EARLY. BETTER GET SOME SLEEP.
GOOD NIGHT...
AYATSUJI.

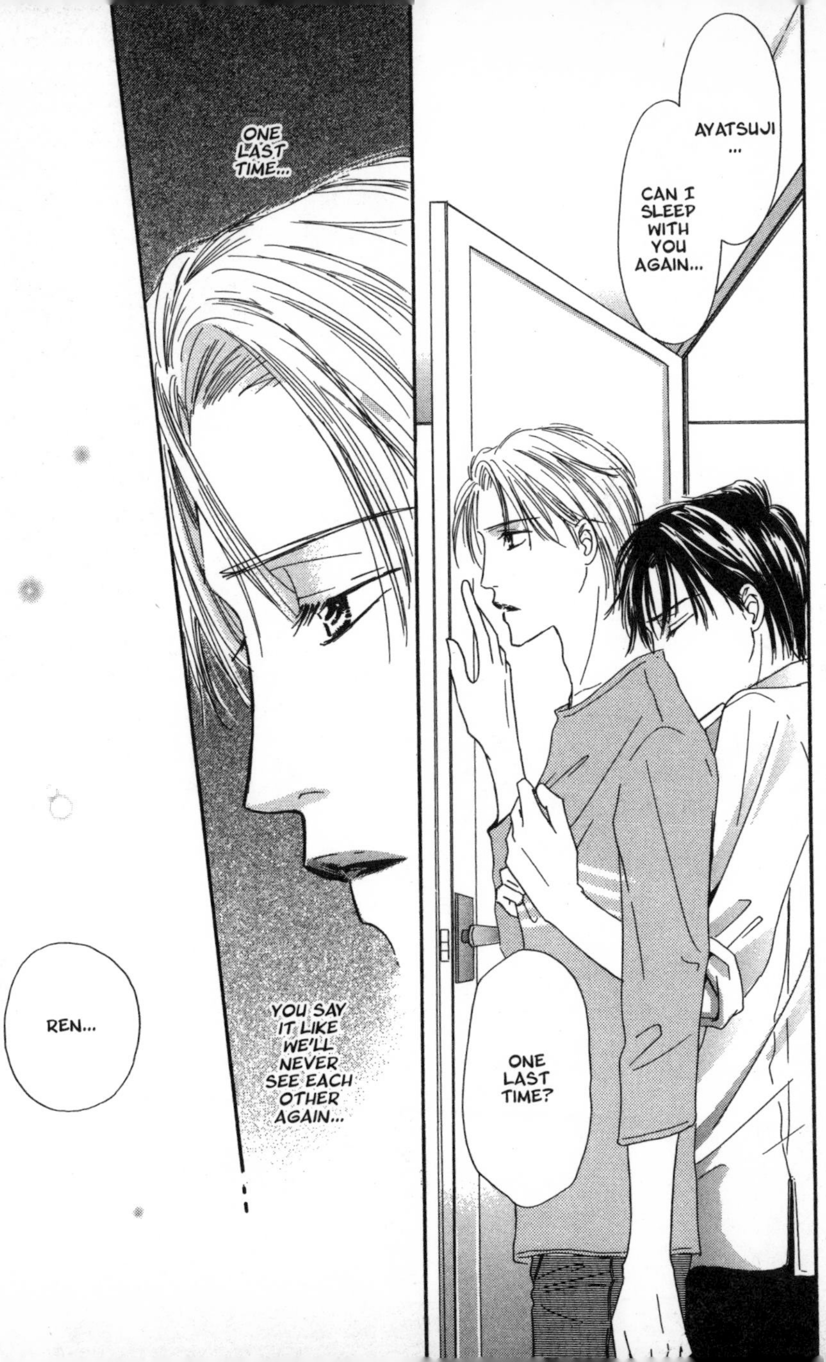
AYATSUJI ...
CAN I SLEEP WITH YOU AGAIN...
ONE LAST TIME?
ONE LAST TIME...
YOU SAY IT LIKE WE'LL NEVER SEE EACH OTHER AGAIN...
REN...

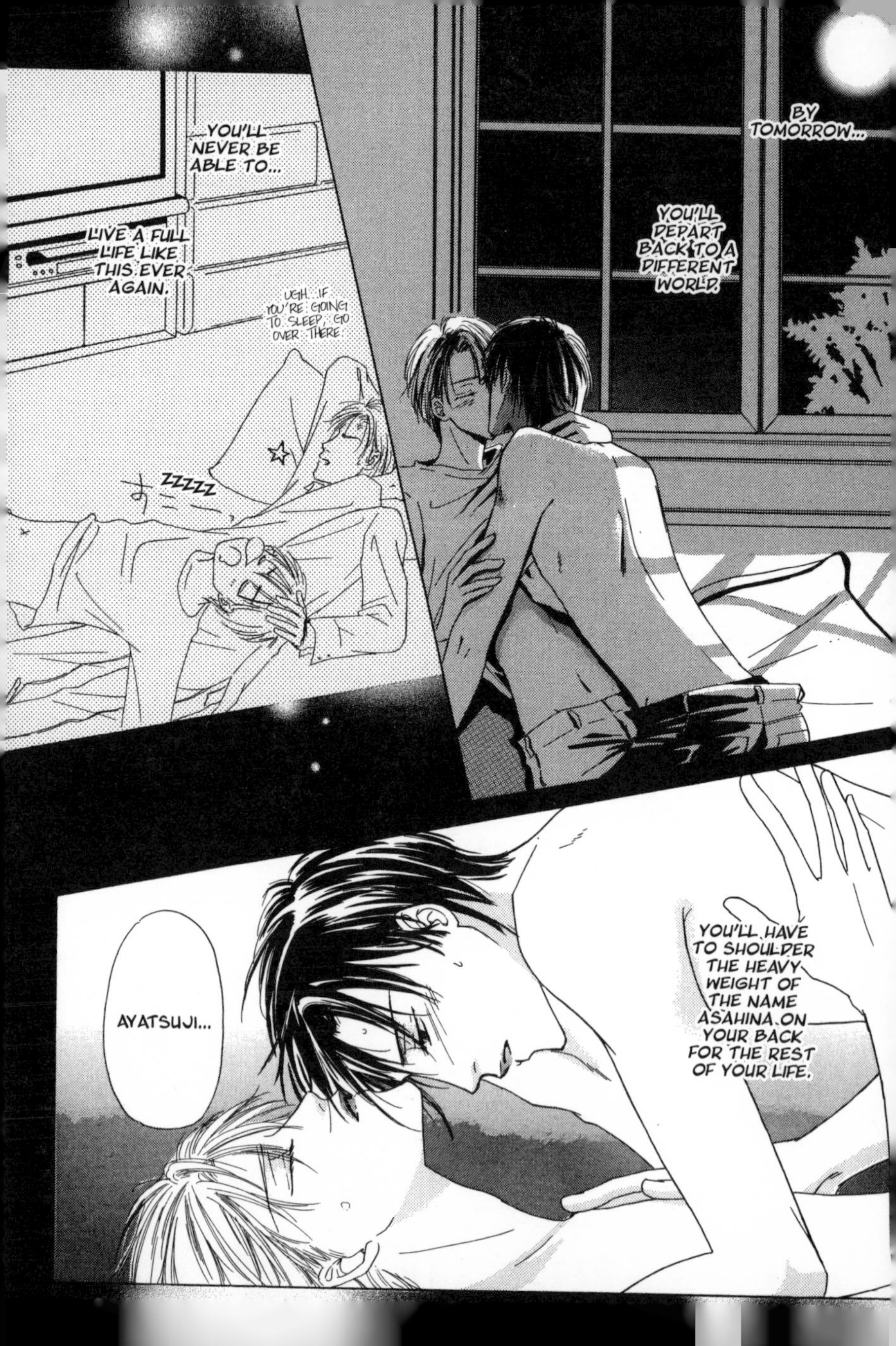
BY TOMORROW...
YOU'LL DEPART BACK TO A DIFFERENT WORLD.
YOU'LL NEVER BE ABLE TO...
LIVE A FULL LIFE LIKE THIS EVER AGAIN.
UGH. IF YOU'RE GOING TO SLEEP, GO OVER THERE.
ZZZZZ
YOU'LL HAVE TO SHOULDER THE HEAVY WEIGHT OF THE NAME ASAHINA ON YOUR BACK FOR THE REST OF YOUR LIFE.
AYATSUJI...

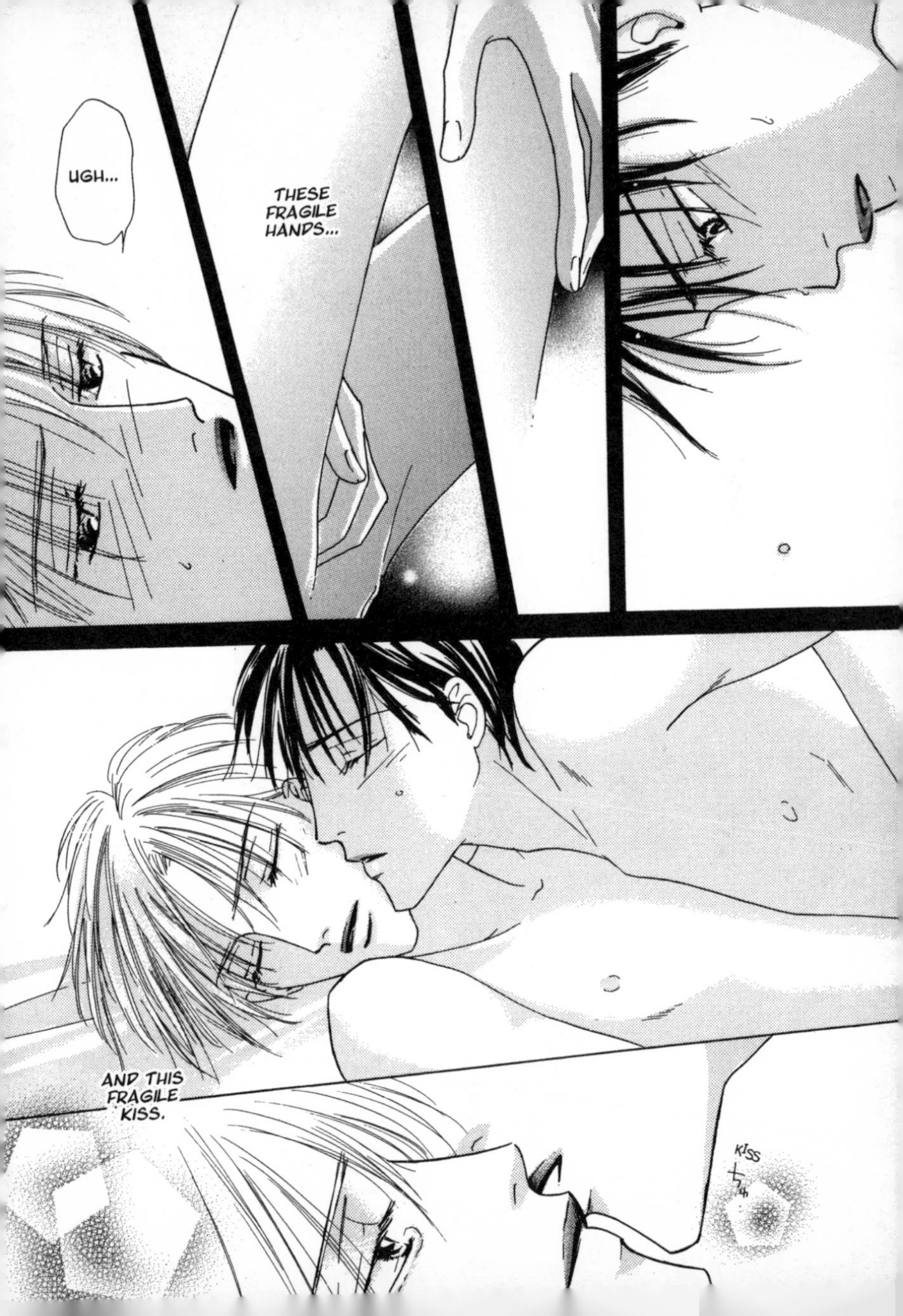
THESE FRAGILE HANDS...
UGH...
AND THIS FRAGILE KISS.
KISS

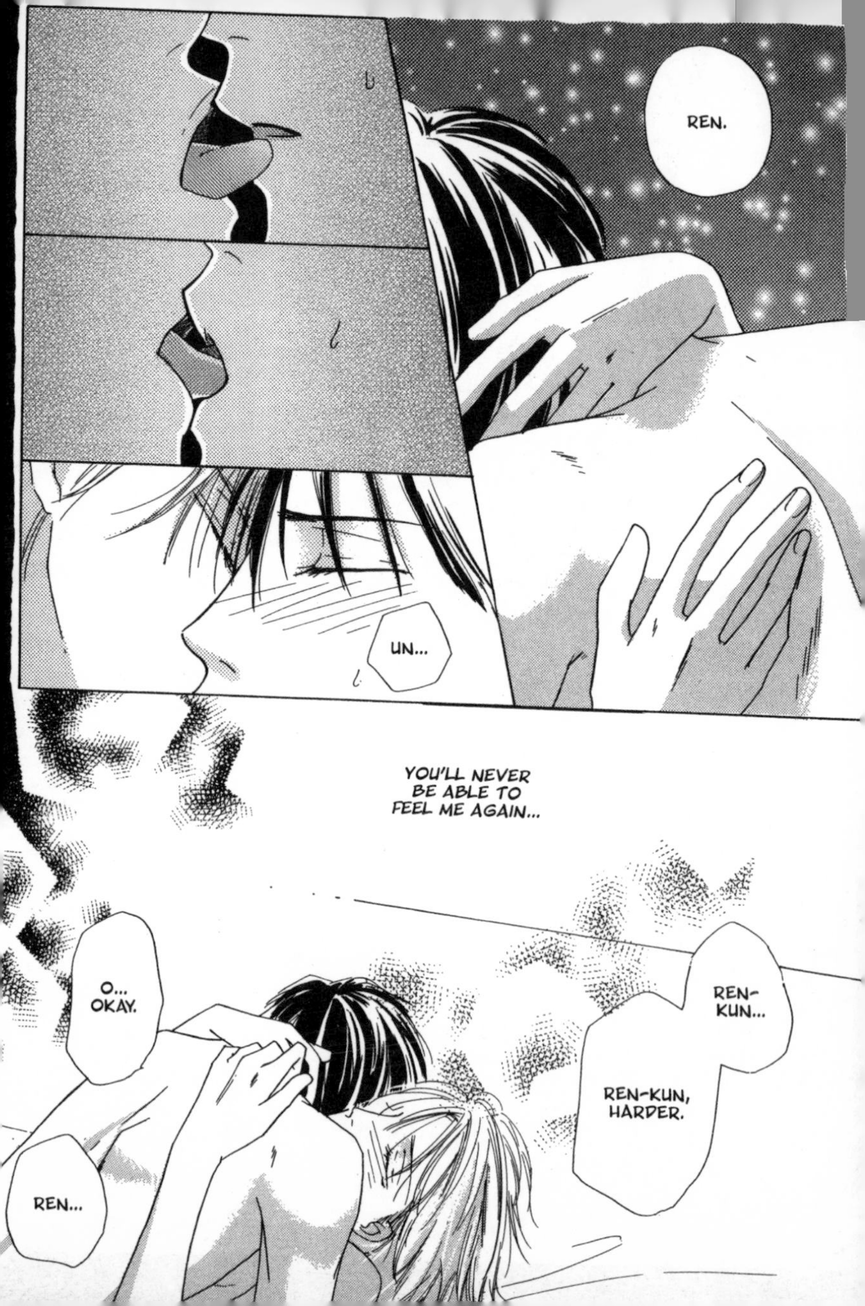
REN.
UN...
YOU'LL NEVER BE ABLE TO FEEL ME AGAIN...
REN-KUN...
REN-KUN, HARDER.
O... OKAY.
REN...

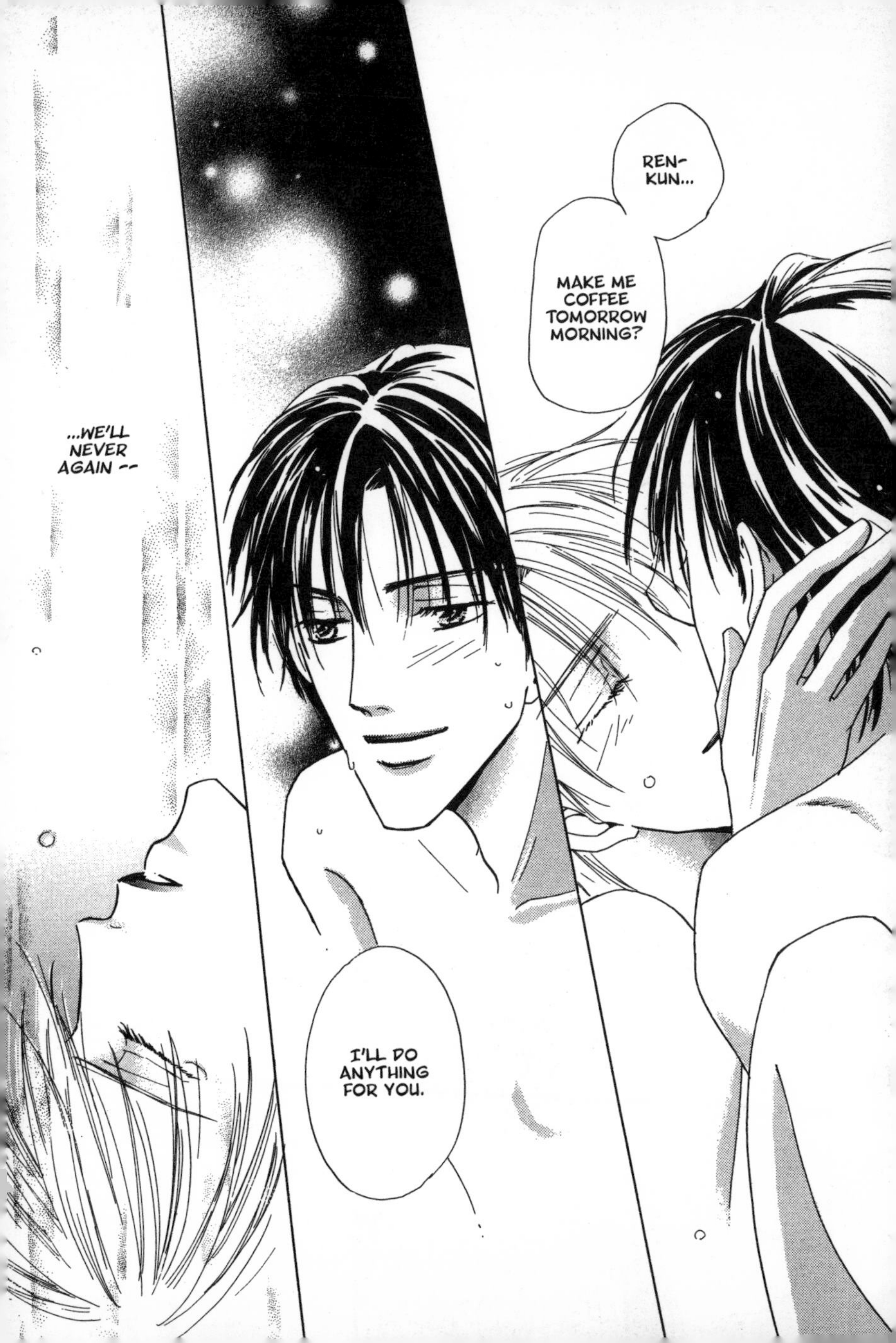
REN-KUN...
MAKE ME COFFEE TOMORROW MORNING?
I'LL DO ANYTHING FOR YOU.
...WE'LL NEVER AGAIN --

I WISH MORNING WOULD NEVER COME...

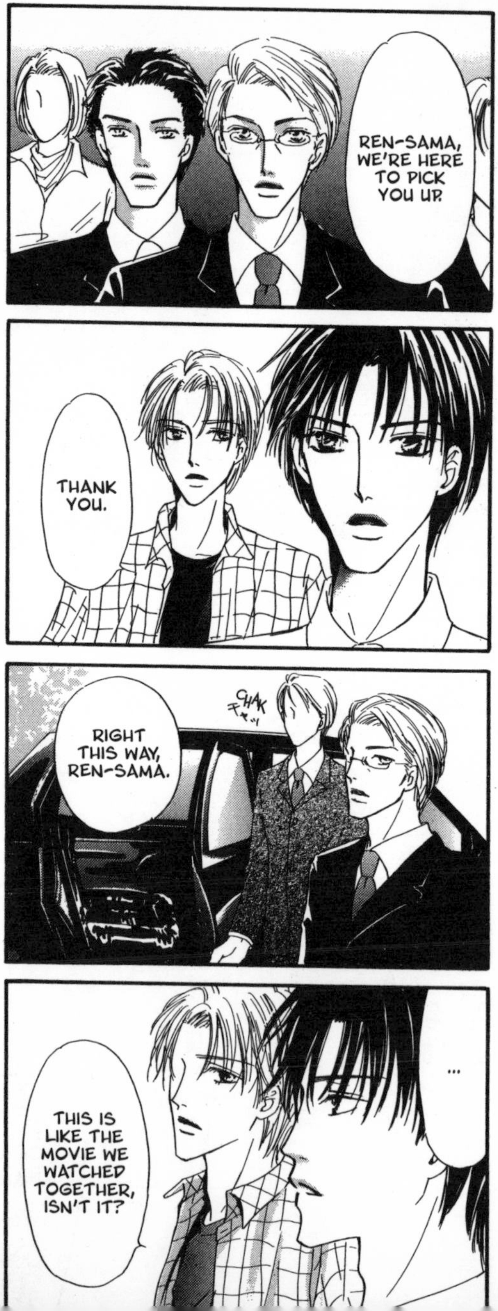
REN-SAMA, WE'RE HERE TO PICK YOU UP.
THANK YOU.
CHAK
RIGHT THIS WAY, REN-SAMA.
...
THIS IS LIKE THE MOVIE WE WATCHED TOGETHER, ISN'T IT?

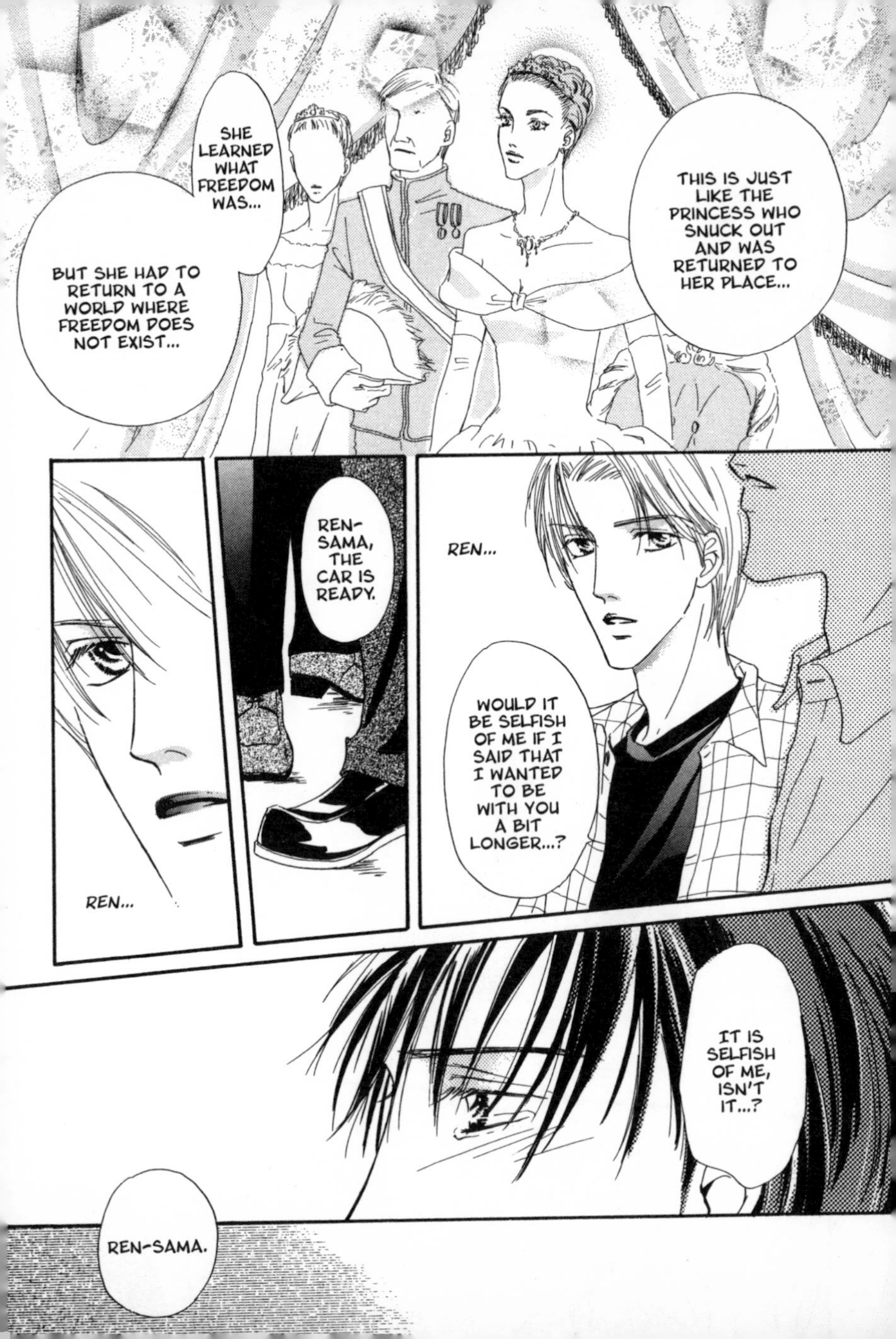
THIS IS JUST LIKE THE PRINCESS WHO SNUCK OUT AND WAS RETURNED TO HER PLACE...
SHE LEARNED WHAT FREEDOM WAS...
BUT SHE HAD TO RETURN TO A WORLD WHERE FREEDOM DOES NOT EXIST...
REN...
WOULD IT BE SELFISH OF ME IF I SAID THAT I WANTED TO BE WITH YOU A BIT LONGER...?
REN-SAMA, THE CAR IS READY.
REN...
IT IS SELFISH OF ME, ISN'T IT...?
REN-SAMA.

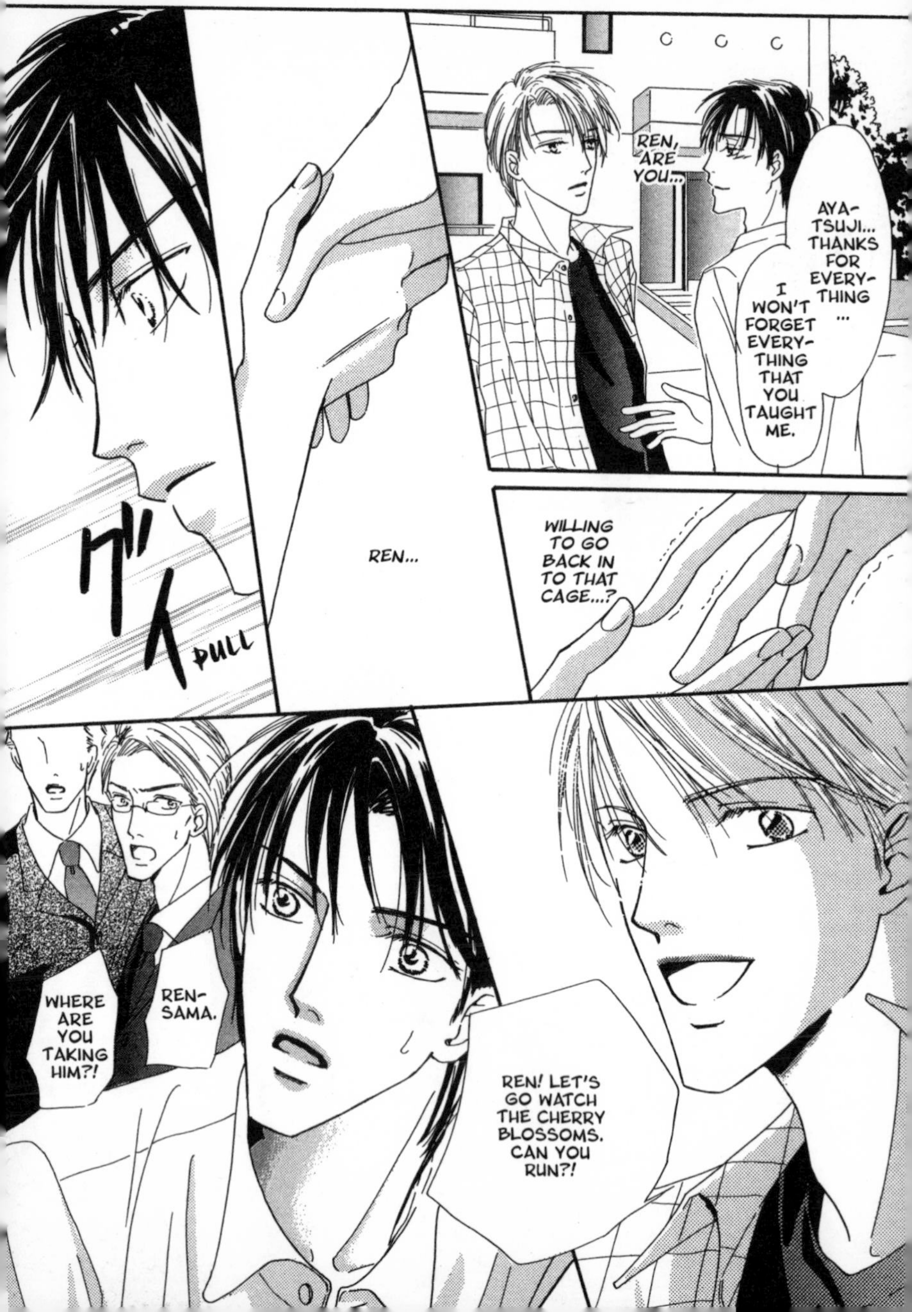

AYA-TSUJI... THANKS FOR EVERY-THING...
I WON'T FORGET EVERY-THING THAT YOU TAUGHT ME.
REN, ARE YOU...
WILLING TO GO BACK IN TO THAT CAGE...?
REN...
グイ
PULL
REN! LET'S GO WATCH THE CHERRY BLOSSOMS. CAN YOU RUN?!
REN-SAMA.
WHERE ARE YOU TAKING HIM?!

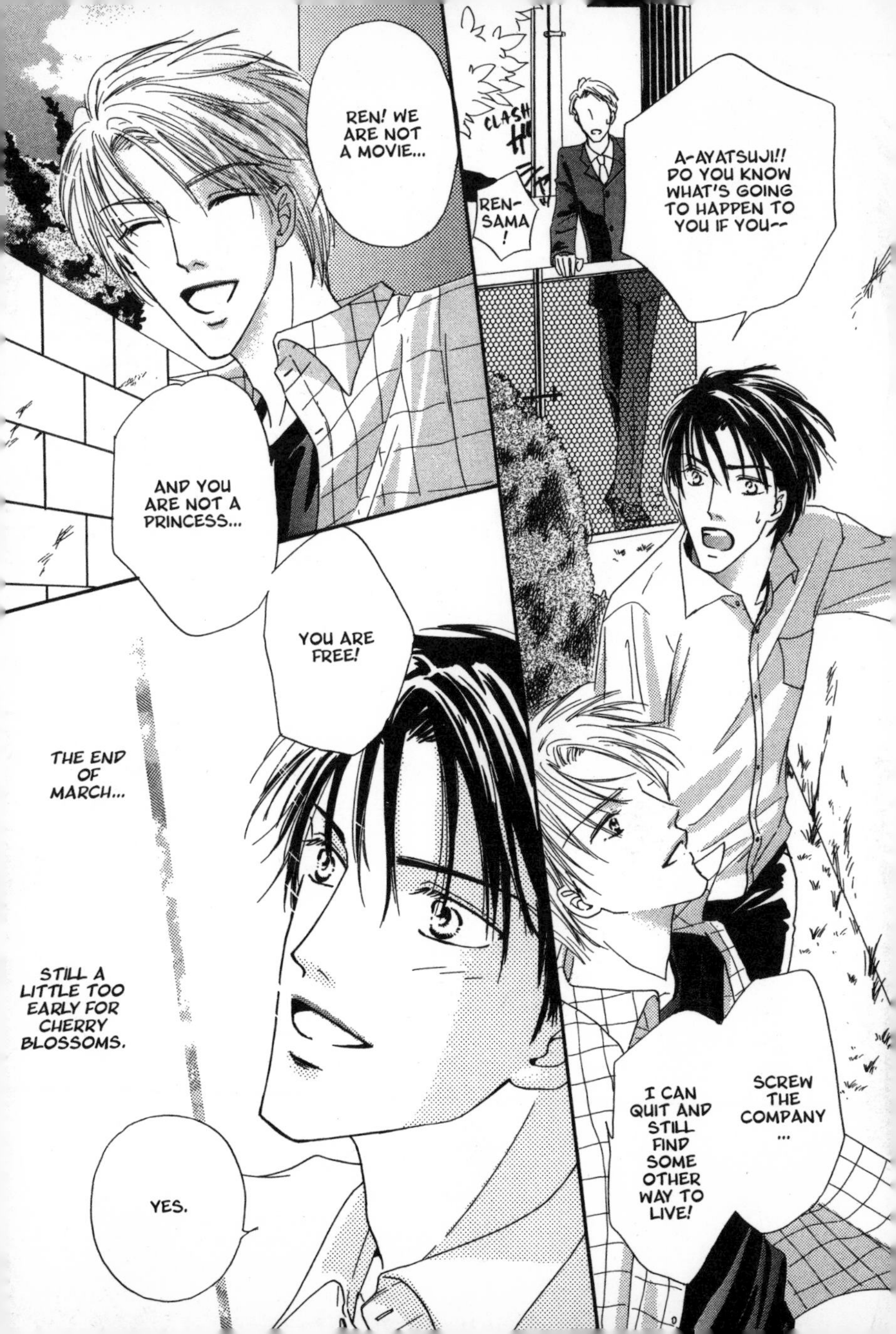
CLASH
REN-SAMA!
A-AYATSUJI!! DO YOU KNOW WHAT'S GOING TO HAPPEN TO YOU IF YOU--
SCREW THE COMPANY...
I CAN QUIT AND STILL FIND SOME OTHER WAY TO LIVE!
REN! WE ARE NOT A MOVIE...
AND YOU ARE NOT A PRINCESS...
YOU ARE FREE!
THE END OF MARCH...
STILL A LITTLE TOO EARLY FOR CHERRY BLOSSOMS.
YES.

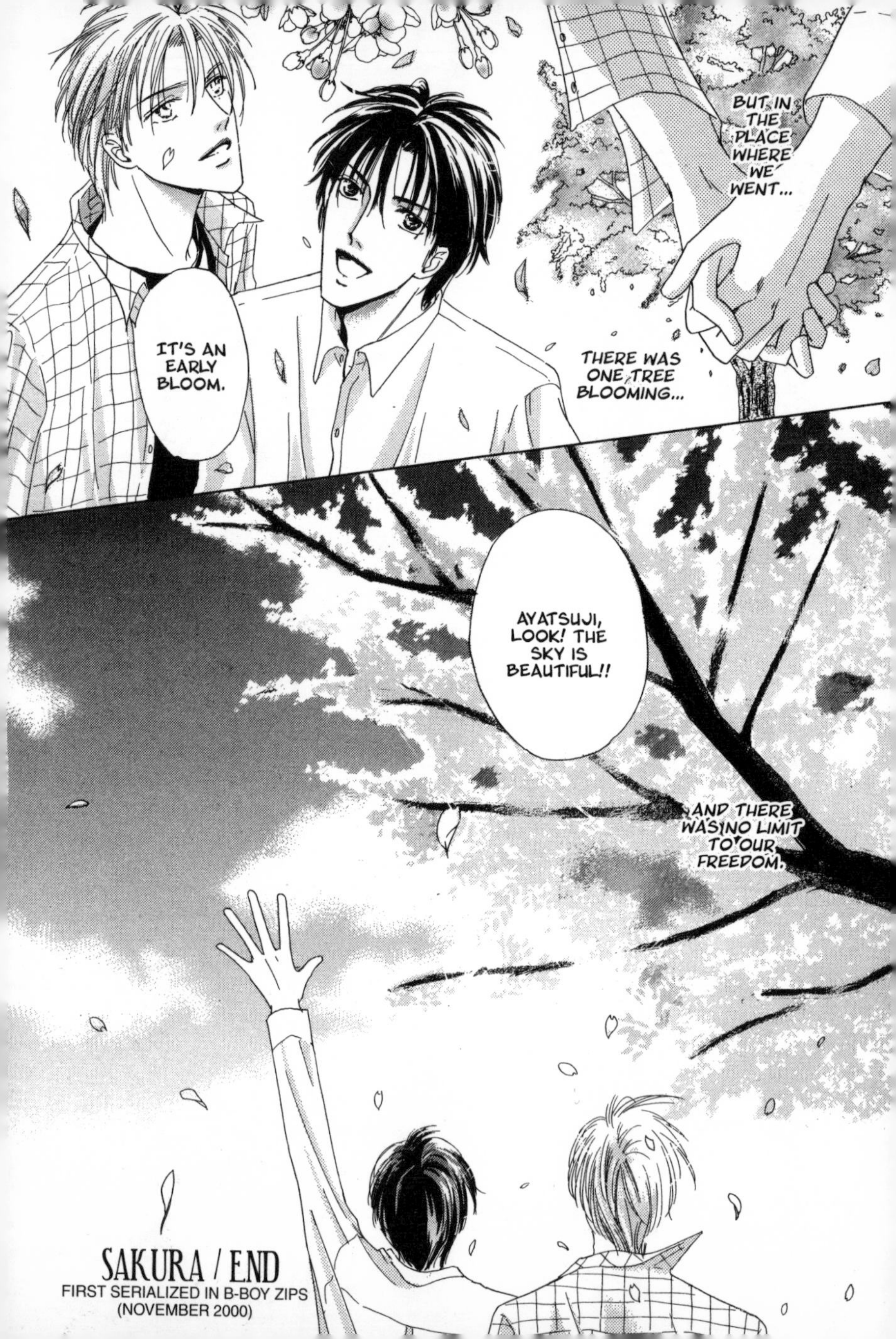
BUT IN THE PLACE WHERE WE WENT...
THERE WAS ONE TREE BLOOMING...
IT'S AN EARLY BLOOM.
AYATSUJI, LOOK! THE SKY IS BEAUTIFUL!!
AND THERE WAS NO LIMIT TO OUR FREEDOM.

SAKURA / END

FIRST SERIALIZED IN B-BOY ZIPS
(NOVEMBER 2000)

■ HELLO EVERYONE. THIS IS TOKO KAWAI. THIS BOOK IS A COMPILATION OF MY COMIC SHORTS. I'LL GO AHEAD AND WRITE COMMENTS ON EACH OF THESE STORIES. (I APOLOGIZE IN ADVANCE FOR CONTAINING TOO MANY WORDS.)

【bónd(z)】 "BONDS"

I ALWAYS WANTED TO WRITE SOMETHING THAT INVOLVED PIERCING. YES, PIERCING. WHAT IS EVERYONE'S THOUGHT ABOUT THIS? I LOVE IT. I LOVED THE SELF-IMPALEMENT CONDUCT WITH NEEDLES AS CHILD. I HAPPILY HELD OUT MY ARM WHENEVER I GOT VACCINATION AND FLU SHOTS, DONATED BLOOD, AND RECEIVED PROTEIN (I STILL LOVE IT TO THIS DAY). ALSO, I WOULD LIKE TO ADD THAT THE VERSION IN THIS BOOK HAS ADDITIONAL PAGES FROM WHEN IT WAS FIRST PUBLISHED IN THE MAGAZINE. DUE TO PAGE RESTRICTIONS, SEVERAL PAGES HAD TO BE TAKEN OUT AT THAT TIME, BUT THESE WERE ADDED BACK IN FOR THIS BOOK. IF YOU LIKED IT WITHOUT THE ADDITIONAL PAGES, I APOLOGIZE. BY THE WAY, THE ACCENTUATION OF "BOND(Z)" HAS BEEN CUSTOMIZED A LITTLE BIT BY MYSELF -- IT IS NOT A TYPO.

SITUATION

I WONDER WHAT WAS THIS? I WANTED TO MAKE YOH-KUN GO THROUGH THE TORTURE. HOWEVER, I DON'T THINK I PULLED THIS OFF AS I HOPED FOR. OH, WELL.

KITAN GARDEN

TOKO KAWAI'S FIRST AND ONLY FANTASY MANGA. ROSES -- I LOVE THEM. I WANT TO DROWN IN ROSE PETALS. BETWEEN YOU AND ME, I ACTUALLY LOVED THE EYE-MASK WEARING VICTOR BETTER THAN THE MAIN CHARACTERS. THAT EYE-PATCH THAT I PUT JUST FOR THE SAKE OF IT HIT IT DEEP WITHIN ME. I HAD ALL THESE THOUGHTS COME UP, LIKE THE PRINCE HIT HIM IN THE EYE WITH A THORNY WHIP, OR ROSE PETALS STARTED TO FLOW FROM THAT ONE EYE SOCKET, AND THAT SHOVES THE PRINCE OFF, ETC. ETC. IT'S THE TRUTH.

SAKURA

...CAN I PASS ON THE COMMENT FOR THIS...? I'M SORRY. YOU MUST BE POKING AT YOUR EYES AFTER READING THIS. IT WAS ONLY THREE YEARS AGO! OH, HOW EMBARRASSING...!! I WOULD LIKE TO THINK THAT I'VE EVOLVED QUITE A BIT SINCE THEN...

THERE WAS A ROMAN EMPEROR WHO KILLED HIS MINIONS BY DROWNING THEM IN ROSE PETALS AND SUFFOCATING THE CONDEMNED WITH THEIR AROMA. THAT EMPEROR'S NAME WAS HELIOGABALUS (AKA: ELAGABALUS). IT WILL NEVER SHOW UP IN HISTORY TESTS, THOUGH. VIVA, DEKADAN!*

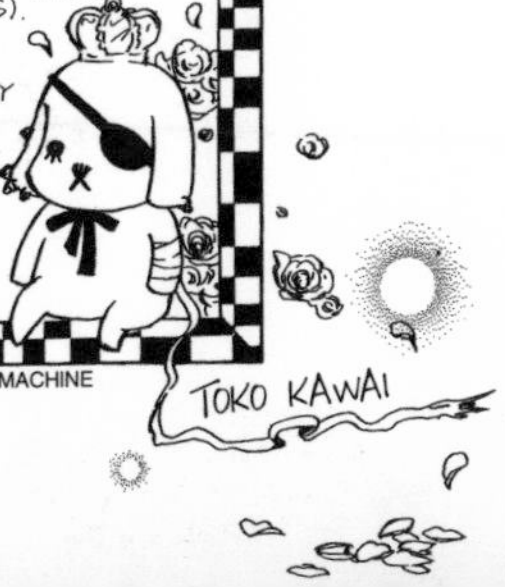
TOKO KAWAI

*A PACHISLOT MACHINE

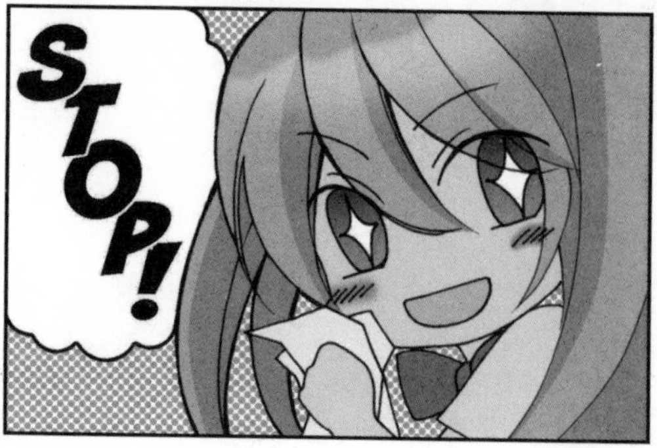
STOP!

801-chan Says!

"Manga reads from right to left, not the usual left to right you may be familar with.

So unless you want to spoil the ending, flip me over and start from the other side!"

TRANSLATION AND EDITOR'S NOTES

COVER FLAP

THE AUTHOR'S EXCLAMATION OF "*GO! GO! GO!*" REFERS TO THE HANSHIN TIGERS, WHO WON THE PENNANT IN 2003 -- WHEN THIS MANGA WAS FIRST RELEASED.

SAKURA (P.169)

REN MENTIONS HANAMI, A JAPANESE TRADITION OF VIEWING FLOWERS -- USUALLY CHERRY BLOSSOMS. THE TITLE "SAKURA" IS THE KANJI FOR ORNAMENTAL CHERRY TREES AND THEIR BLOSSOMS.

AFTERWORD (P.193)

DEKA DAN IS A WESTERN OUTLAW-THEMED PACHISLOT (PACHINKO + SLOT) GAME.

Thanks for reading with us!

• 801-chan